ABC's of Selling

The Irwin Series in Marketing

Consulting Editor   Gilbert A. Churchill, Jr.
University of Wisconsin, Madison

ABC'S OF SELLING

Charles Futrell
Texas A&M University

Second Edition 1989

Homewood, Illinois 60430

© RICHARD D. IRWIN, INC., 1985 and 1989

Acquisitions editor: Jeanne M. Teutsch
Project editor: Margaret Haywood
Production manager: Irene H. Sotiroff
Designer: Hunter Graphics
Artist: Precision Graphics
Compositor: Better Graphics, Inc.
Typeface: 10/12 Palatino
Printer: R. R. Donnelley & Sons Company

Library of Congress Cataloging-in-Publication Data

Futrell, Charles.
    ABC's of selling / Charles Futrell.—2nd ed.
       p.   cm.
    Bibliography: p.
    Includes index.
    ISBN 0-256-06867-4 (pbk.) : $24.95
    1. Selling.   I. Title.
HF5438.25.F868 1989
658.8'5—dc 19   88–6905

Printed in the United States of America
2 3 4 5 6 7 8 9 0 DO 5 4 3 2 1 0 9

To my children Amy and Gregory, two of the best salespeople I know

About the Author

Charles Futrell

Charles Futrell is professor of marketing at Texas A&M University. Charles is a salesperson turned professor.

Before beginning his academic career Professor Futrell worked in sales and marketing capacities for eight years with the Colgate-Palmolive Company, Upjohn Company, and Ayerst Laboratories. An excellent classroom teacher, he has written or cowritten seven successful texts for the college and professional audience, and his work in sales and marketing management has appeared in numerous national and international journals.

Dr. Futrell also serves as a frequent reviewer for several academic journals including the Journal of Marketing, *the* Journal of Marketing Research, *and the* Journal of Personal Selling and Sales Management. *In his fifteen years as a university instructor and teacher for various executive development programs and industrial groups, such as the Bank Marketing Association's banking schools, he has developed numerous innovative instructional materials including computer simulations, computerized classroom materials, and video exercises. This background has resulted in his being used as a frequent speaker, researcher, and consultant to industry.*

Professor Futrell enjoys coaching Little League baseball, jogging, photography, and fishing.

Preface

ABC's of Selling presents the *essential* material for the course on personal selling. It can also be used as a supplement in the sales management course should the instructor wish to thoroughly cover personal selling.

ABC's of Selling is written by a salesperson turned professor. For eight years I worked in sales with Colgate, Upjohn, and Ayerst. As a professor, I have taught selling to thousands of college students, business people, and industry sales personnel, developing and using the strategies, practices, and techniques presented in this text. Further, each year I spend time in fieldwork with sales personnel. In my classes and programs, I stress learning-by-doing examples and exercises, and videotape role-playing of selling situations. This text is the result of these experiences.

ABC's of Selling was conceived as a method of providing ample materials for readers to construct their own sales presentations after studying the text. This allows the instructor the flexibility of focusing on the how-to-sell approach within the classroom. Covering the basic foundations for understanding the concepts and practices of selling in a practical, straightforward, and readable manner, it provides students with a textbook for use in preparing sales presentations and role-playing exercises.

Teacher and student response to the material has been fantastic. This edition has added current examples as well as new selling ideas and techniques, and it introduces you to many new profiled successful salespeople. Those familiar with the earlier edition will still find the features, advantages, and benefits that made the book an effective teaching and learning resource.

Several of our friends profiled in the previous edition have updated their materials for you. As we look back on these people, it is great to see how successful they have been. In a few short years, for example:

- Matt Suffoletto moved from a marketing staff position to manager of U.S. channel operations.
- Sandra Snow was promoted several times and is now in the home office involved in training.

- Bruce Scagel was promoted to manager of sales training for Scott Paper. He is now manager of sales training for M & M—Mars.

These are a few examples. Several people moved to opportunities outside of the job they had when previously profiled. Gary Grant, for example, was promoted to marketing director of NCR's U.S. operations and is now in business for himself. Successful salespeople seem to be always on the move, seeking new challenges. It will be interesting to see where our salespeople profiled in this edition will be by our third

As you read the profiles, think about what these people have accomplished in sales—people like the Fingerhuts who left teaching in public schools to create a multimillion dollar company and Jack Pruett who previously drove a Pepsi-Cola delivery truck and now sells $1 million of jewelry out of a retail store. The people profiled in your book are incredible individuals—individuals who have mixed hard work with sales talent to become successful.

Many features have been included to stimulate interest. Each chapter contains numerous buyer-seller dialogues, actual industry examples, comments from successful salespeople and sales managers, as well as interesting profiles of sales personnel from Fortune 500 companies and smaller businesses. Each company represented by a salesperson profiled in the book selected one of their outstanding salespeople to contribute to the learning of selling practices that can make a successful salesperson. Additionally, selling materials and photographs were provided by numerous companies whose contributions have greatly increased the educational quality of this text.

Further, each chapter provides chapter objectives, key terms, a chapter summary, and review and discussion questions to facilitate understanding. Projects and case problems presented at the end of each chapter have been carefully selected. The text, exercises, projects, and cases have all been classroom tested.

The 14 chapters contained in the text are divided into four parts:

1. *Selling as a Profession* emphasizes the career, rewards, and duties of the professional salesperson and illustrates the importance of the sales function to the organization's success.

2. *Preparation for Successful Selling* presents the background information salespeople use to develop their sales presentations.

3. *The Dynamics of Selling* covers the entire selling process from prospecting to follow-up and is the heart of the text. State-of-the-art selling strategies, practices, and techniques are presented in a how-to fashion.

4. *Special Selling Topics* discusses the importance of the proper use of

managing one's time and sales territory. For this edition, a new chapter was added on the social, ethical, and legal issues in selling.

For the instructor, a large, comprehensive manual accompanies the text to aid in class preparation. Please examine it for additional selling and teaching tips and examples. Also, check with your Irwin sales rep for other possible supplements.

I have had the good fortune to receive excellent assistance in preparing this text from the following outstanding sales instructors: Ames Barber, Adirondack Community College; Milton J. Bergstein, Pennsylvania State University; Norman Cohn, Milwaukee Tech; William H. Crookston, California State University, Northridge; Gary Donnelly, Casper College; Earl Emery, Baker Junior College of Business; Ric Gorno, Cypress College; Deborah Lawe, San Francisco State University; Ken Miller, Kilgore College; Harry Moak, Macomb Community College; Roy Payne, Purdue University; Camille P. Schuster, Virginia Tech; Robert Smith, Illinois State University; Ed Snider, Mesa Community College; William A. Stull, Utah State University; and John Todd, University of Tampa.

A very special thanks goes to the professional sales force who has done so much for the success of this text. Additionally, many of the profiled salespeople made content suggestions which were incorporated throughout the text. They also answered many of the end-of-the-chapter exercises and cases.

For the use of their selling exercises and cases, I am especially grateful to Professors Dick Nordstrom, California State University-Fresno and George Wynn, James Madison University. Additionally, a special thanks goes to Amy Futrell for her excellent editorial work.

Finally, I wish to thank the sales trainers, salespeople, and sales managers who helped teach me the art of selling when I carried the sales bag full time. I hope I have done justice to their great profession of selling.

I hope you learn from and enjoy the text. I enjoyed preparing it for you. Readers are urged to forward their comments on this text to me. I wish you great success in your selling efforts. Remember, it's the salesperson who gets the customer's orders that keeps the wheels of industry turning. America cannot do without you.

Charles Futrell

Profiles

Successful salespeople and sales managers profiled throughout this text greatly added to the educational value of the text and its lively, real-life examples. To these people—thanks!

Michael Bevan—Parbron International of Canada

Terry and Paul Fingerhut—Steamboat Party Sales, Inc., Tupperware

Bill Frost—AT&T Communications

Morgan Jennings—Richard D. Irwin, Inc.

Jim Mobley—General Mills, Inc.

George Morris—The Prudential Insurance Company of America

Vikki Morrison—First Team Walk-In Realty, California

Jack Pruett—Bailey Banks and Biddle

Emmett Reagan—Xerox Corporation

Bruce Scagel—Scott Paper Company

Linda Slaby-Baker—The Quaker Oats Company

Sandra Snow—The Upjohn Company

Matt Suffoletto—International Business Machines IBM

Ed Tucker—Cannon Financial Group, Georgia

Contents

I SELLING AS A PROFESSION   2

1 THE LIFE AND TIMES OF THE PROFESSIONAL SALESPERSON   4

Matt Suffoletto   *IBM*

Why Choose a Sales Career?: *A Variety of Sales Jobs Are Available. Freedom of Action: You're on Your Own. Job Challenge Is Always There. Opportunities for Advancement Are Great. You Can Move Quickly into Management. Rewards: The Sky's the Limit.* The Salesperson's Activities as a Territorial Manager. Is a Sales Career Right for you?: *A Sales Manager's View of the Recruit.* Success in Selling—What Does It Take?: *Love of Selling. Willingness to Work Hard. Need to Achieve. Have an Optimistic Outlook. Be Knowledgeable. Value Time. Ask Questions and Then Listen to Uncover Customer Needs. Serve Your Customer.* The Sales Process Used by Successful Salespeople. Summary of Major Selling Issues.

Case

1-1 Linda Baker of Quaker Oats Moves Quickly up the Corporate Sales Ladder, 32

II PREPARATION FOR SUCCESSFUL SELLING   38

2 THE PSYCHOLOGY OF SELLING: WHY PEOPLE BUY   40

Jim Mobley   *General Mills*

Why People Buy—The Black Box Approach. Psychological Influences on Buying: *Motivation to Buy Must Be There. Maslow's Need Hierarchy Provides Clues. Economic Needs: The Most Bang for the Buck. Awareness of Needs: Some Are Unsure.* A *FAB*ulous Approach to Buyer Need Satisfaction: *The Product's Features: So What? The Product's Advantages: Prove It? The Product's Benefits: Sell It. Order Can Be Important.*

Why Do Producers Buy?: *Value Analysis: A Powerful Selling Tool*. How to Determine Important Buying Needs—A Key of Success. Your Buyer's Perception. Buyer Perceptions, Attitudes, and Beliefs Are Learned: *Example of a Buyer's Misperceptions*. The Buyer's Personality Should Be Considered: *Self-Concept. Selling Based on Personality. Adapt Your Presentation to the Buyer's Style*. You Can Classify Buying Situations: *Some Decisions Are Routine. Some Decisions Are Limited. Some Decisions Are Extensive*. View Buyers as Decision Makers: *Need Arousal. Collectiion of Information. Information Evaluation. Purchase Decision. Postpurchase*. To Buy or Not to Buy—A Choice Decision. Summary of Major Selling Issues.

Cases
2-1 Economy Ceiling Fans, Inc., 83
2-2 McDonald's Ford Dealership, 84
2-3 Frank's Drilling Service, 85

3 **COMMUNICATION AND PERSUASION:
IT'S NOT ALL TALK**   86

C. Edward Tucker   *Cannon Financial Institute*

Communication: It Takes Two: *Salesperson-Buyer Communication Process Requires Feedback*. Nonverbal Communication: Watch for It: *Concept of Space. Communication through Appearance and the Handshake. Body Language Gives You Clues*. Barriers to Communication. Master Persuasive Communication and You Maintain Control: *Feedback Guides Your Presentation. Empathy Puts You in Your Customer's Shoes. Keep It Simple, You Silver-Tongued Devil. Creating Mutual Trust Develops Friendship. Listening Clues You In. Your Attitude Makes the Difference. Proof Statements Make You Believable*. Summary of Major Selling Issues.

Cases
3-1 Skaggs Manufacturing, 112
3-2 Lanier Dictaphone (A), 113

4 **SO, WHAT DO I NEED TO KNOW?**   114

Michael Bevan   *Parbron International*

Where'd You Learn That? Sources of Sales Knowledge. Why Salespeople Require Knowledg: *Knowledge Increases Confidence in Salespeople. . . . And in Buyers. Know Your Firm. General Company Information*. Know Your Product. A

Little Knowledge of Distribution Can Go a Long Way: *Conflict and Cooperation in Distribution Channels.* Advertising Aids Salespeople: *Types of Advertising Differ. Why Spend Money on Advertising?* Sales Promotion Generates Sales for You: *Point-of-Purchase Displays: Get 'em Out There. Shelf Positioning Is Important to Your Success. Premiums.* What's It Worth? Pricing Your Product: *Types of Prices. Discounts Lower the Price.* Markup Represents Gross Profit: *Be Creative in Your Pricing Techniques. Customer Credit: Get 'em to Pay on Time.* Know Your Competition, Industry, and Economy. Summary of Major Selling Issues.

Cases
4-1 Claire Cosmetics, 149
4-2 McBath Feminine Apparel, 150

III THE DYNAMICS OF SELLING 152

5 PROSPECTING—THE LIFEBLOOD OF SELLING 154

Vikki Morrison   *FirstTeam Walk-In Realty*

The Sales Process Has 10 Steps. Steps before the Sales Presentation. Prospecting—Lifeblood of Selling: *Where to Find Prospects.* Who Makes the Industrial Buying Decision? Who Should I Talk To?: *Planning a Prospective Strategy. Prospecting Methods.* What Is the Best Prospecting Method? Obtaining the Sales Interview: *The Benefits of Appointment Making.* Summary of Major Selling Issues.

Cases
5-1 Lanier Dictaphone (B), 180
5-2 Micro-Office Electronics System, 180

6 PLANNING THE SALES CALL IS A MUST! 182

Bill Frost   *AT&T*

Customer Sales Planning—The Preapproach: *Reasons for Planning the Sales Call. Elements of Sales Call Planning.* The Prospect's Mental Steps: *Attention. Interest. Desire. Conviction. Purchase or Action.* Overview of the Sales Process. Summary of Major Selling Issues.

Cases
6-1 Ms. Hansen's Mental Steps in Buying Your
    Product, 197
6-2 Machinery Lubricants, Inc., 198

xviii

7 CAREFULLY SELECT WHICH SALES PRESENTATION METHOD TO USE　　　200

Emmett Reagan, Senior Training　*Analyst, Xerox Corporation*

The Right to Approach. Sales Presentation Methods—Select One Carefully: *Memorized Sales Presentation. The Formula Presentation. The Need-Satisfaction Presentation. The Problem-Solution Presentation. Which Is the Best Presentation Method? Select the Presentation Method, Then the Approach.* Summary of Major Selling Issues.

Cases
7-1 Cascade Soap Company, 219
7-2 A Retail Sales Presentation, 219

8 BEGIN YOUR PRESENTATION STRATEGICALLY　　　222

Jack Pruett　*Bailey Banks & Biddle*

The Approach—Opening the Sales Presentation: *Your Attitude during the Approach. The First Impression of You Is Critical to Success. The Situational Approach. Openings with Statements. Demonstration Openings. Opening with Questions.* The Use of Questions Results in Sales Success: *The Direct Question. The Nondirective Question. The Rephrasing Question. The Redirect Question. Three Rules for Using Questions.* He Is Still Not Listening? You Need to Be Flexible in Your Approach. Summary of Major Selling Issues.

Cases
8-1 The Thompson Company, 251
8-2 The Copy Corporation, 252
8-3 Electronic Office Security Corporation, 253

9 ELEMENTS OF MAKING A GREAT PRESENTATION　　　256

Linda M. Slaby-Baker　*Quaker Oats*

The Purpose of the Presentation. Three Essential Steps within the Presentation. The Sales Presentation Mix: *Persuasive Communications. Participation Is Essential to Success. Proof Statements Build Believability. The Visual Presentation—Show and Tell. Visual Aids Help Tell the Story.* Dramatization Improves Your Chances. Demonstrations Prove It!: *Reasons for Using Visual Aids, Dramatics, and Demonstrations.*

Guidelines for Using Visual Aids, Dramatics, and Demonstrations. The Trial Close—A Major Step in the Sales Presentation: *Sell Sequence.* The Ideal Presentation. Be Prepared for Presentation Difficulties: *How to Handle Interruptions. Should You Discuss Your Competition? Be Professional. When the Presentation Takes Place. Diagnose the Prospect to Determine Your Sales Presentation.* Summary of Major Selling Issues.

Cases
9-1 Dyno Electro Cart Company, 295
9-2 Fresh Mouth: Selling a New Mouthwash, 296
9-3 Major Oil, Inc., 300

10 WELCOME YOUR PROSPECT'S OBJECTIONS   304

Bruce Scagel   *M&M—Mars*

Welcome Objections! When Do Prospects Object? Who Is the Toughest Prospect? What Are Objections? Objections and the Sales Process. Four Major Categories of Objections: *The Hidden Objection. The Stalling Objection. The No-Need Objection. The Money Objection.* Handle Objections as They Arise. Techniques for Meeting Objections: *Don't Be Afraid to Pass Up an Objection. Rephrase an Objection as a Question. Forestalling Objections Is Sometimes Necessary. Send It Back with the Boomerang Method. Ask Questions to Smoke Out Objections. Direct Denial Should Be Used Tactfully. Anticipating Objections Comes with Experience. Compensation or Counterbalance Method. Let a Third Party Answer.* Basic Points to Consider in Meeting Objections: *Anticipate Objections. Consider Objections as Opportunities. Be Positive. Understand Objections.* After Meeting the Objection—What to Do?: *First, Use a Trial Close. Move Back into Your Presentation. Move to Close Your Sale. If You Cannot Overcome the Objection.* Summary of Major Selling Issues.

Cases
10-1 Handy Dan, 343
10-2 Ace Building Supplies, 343
10-3 Your Price Is Too High, 344
10-4 Electric Generator Corporation (B), 344
10-5 Vacuum Cleaner Inc., 345

11 CLOSE, CLOSE, CLOSE   348

George W. Morris   *Prudential Life Insurance*

When Should I Pop the Question? Reading Buying Signals. What Makes a Good Closer?: *Ask for the Order and Shut Up! Get the Order and Get Out!* How Many Times Should You Close? Closing under Fire. Difficulties with Closing. Essentials of Closing Sales. Twelve Steps to a Successful Closing. Prepare Several Closing Techniques: *The Alternnative Choice Close Is an Old Favorite. The Assumptive Close. The Compliment Close Inflates the Ego. The Summary of Benefits Close Is Most Popular. The Continuous-Yes Close Generates Positive Responses. The Minor-Points Close Is Not Threatening. The T-Account or Balance Sheet Close Was Ben Franklin's Favorite. The Standing-Room-Only Close Gets Action. The Probability Close.* Prepare a Multiple Close Sequence. Close Based on the Situation. Research Reinforces Book's Sales Success Strategies: *Keys to Improved Selling.* Summary of Major Selling Issues.

Cases

11-1 Skaggs Omega, 379
11-2 Central Hardware Supply, 380

12 WINNING IN THE LONG RUN: BUILDING A RELATIONSHIP THROUGH SERVICE

382

Morgan Jennings   *Richard D. Irwin, Inc.*

Super Salespeople Discuss Service: *Turn Follow-Up and Service into a Sale.* Account Penetration Is a Secret to Success. Service Can Keep Your Customers. You Lose a Customer—Keep on Trucking! Increasing Your Customer's Sales. When You Do Not Make the Sale. Return Goods Make You a Hero. Handle Complaints Fairly. Build a Professional Reputation. Do's and Don'ts for Industrial Salespeople. Summary of Major Selling Issues.

Cases

12-1 California Adhesives Corporation, 404
12-2 Sport Shoe Corporation, 404

IV SPECIAL SELLING TOPICS

406

13 TIME AND TERRITORY MANAGEMENT IS A KEY TO SUCCESS

408

Terry and Paul Fingerhut   *Steamboat Party Sales, Inc. (Tupperware)*

What Is a Sales Territory?: *Why Establish Sales Territories? Why Sales Territories May Not Be Developed* Elements of Time in Territory Management: *Salesperson's Sales Quota. Account Analysis. Develop Account Objectives and Sales Quotas. Territory-Time Allocation. Customer Sales Planning. Scheduling and Routing. Using the Telephone for Territorial Coverage. Territory and Customer Evaluation.* Summary of Major Selling Issues.

Case
13-1 Your Selling Day: A Time and Territory Game, 433

14 SOCIAL, ETHICAL, AND LEGAL ISSUES IN SELLING

436

Sandra Snow   *The Upjohn Company*

The Social Responsibility of Business: *Why Assume Social Responsibilities? How Managers View Ethics.* Ethics in Dealing with Salespeople: *Level of Sales Pressure. Decisions Affecting Territory. To Tell the Truth? Employee Rights.* Are These Socially Responsible Actions? Salespeople's Ethics in Dealing with Their Employers: *Misusing Company Assets. Moonlighting. Cheating. Affecting Fellow Salespeople.* Ethics in Dealing with Customers: *Bribes. Misrepresentation. Price Discrimination. Tie-In Sales. Exclusive Dealership. Sales Restrictions.* What to Do? Summary of Major Selling Issues.

Cases
14-1 Fancy Frozen Foods, 458
14-2 Sports Togs, Inc., 459

NOTES   463

INDEX   467

ABC's of Selling

I SELLING AS A PROFESSION

Selling Your Best Product . . . Yourself

Customer satisfaction means more than just satisfaction with your product or service.

The first time, perhaps, you sell the product by satisfying a need. But after that, you're selling *yourself*—your knowledge and effort. Because along with the product the customer buys you! Your success in selling yourself—in making the buyer identify *you* with the product and company, look forward to seeing *you*, ask for *you* when he calls, be grateful to *you* when a delivery is speeded up or a snarl untangled—determines when the buyer stops being a customer and becomes an account!

1 THE LIFE AND TIMES OF THE PROFESSIONAL SALESPERSON

Learning Objectives

1. To discuss why people choose a sales career.
2. To examine the types of sales jobs and selling situations.
3. To better understand the salesperson's job activities.
4. To present the characteristics salespeople profiled in this book believe are needed for success.
5. To introduce the 10 steps in the sales process.

Key Terms for Selling

Order-taker
Delivery salesperson
Order-getter
Sales engineer
Tangible products
Intangible services
Service sales representative

Detail salesperson
Career path
Key account
Nonfinancial rewards
Financial rewards
Territory manager

Profile

Matt Suffoletto
IBM

My name is Matt Suffoletto. I joined IBM as a marketing representative in 1969, after earning a bachelor's degree in management science from Rensselaer Polytechnic Institute in Troy, N.Y. Since then I have held a number of marketing line and staff positions. I am currently manager of U.S. channel operations, responsible for the selection for all remarketers of IBM products.

While in college, I decided that I wanted to pursue a sales career. My technical background led me to seek employment in a company with a high technology product line. In addition, I was looking for a growing company in a growth industry.

IBM was one of the companies that fit my criteria. They have a strong emphasis on marketing and customer service and offer a clear opportunity for advancement. I still believe that the first successful sales call of my professional career was selling myself to IBM.

Career opportunities for salespeople are unlimited. That statement is evidenced by the vast number of former salespeople who are in key executive positions with Fortune 500 companies. What young salesperson doesn't dream of becoming a corporate vice president of sales?

Within IBM, the first step in launching yourself into a sales management career is to establish a consistent sales performance and maintain it for several years. However, you must keep in mind that you will be competing with other outstanding salespeople for job promotion, so sales performance just gets you into the running. Qualities such as leadership, creativity, adaptability, intelligence, and dedication are the real difference makers.

When I started in sales I had a very narrow view of my possible career opportunities. Through exposure to positions other than direct sales, I learned of a multitude of attractive alternatives. Though career alternatives are numerous, several areas that are closely related to sales are product development, marketing research, advertising, administration, personnel, business planning, and marketing support.

The rewards of a successful sales career are unparalleled by those of any other business career that comes to mind. First and foremost is the personal satisfaction derived from the culmination of a sale. Personal recognition is high on the salesperson's list of motivational needs, and sales management responds to those needs with a wealth of recognition programs. Second, the financial rewards for a successful salesperson are outstanding. It is not uncommon for the best salespeople to earn incomes equivalent to those of top corporate managers. Finally, there is a wealth of personal gain to be realized through a commitment to excellence, for no career has a better yardstick of excellence than sales. Sales, more than any other vocation, offers a close relationship between effort and reward.

He came on muleback, dodging Indians as he went, with a pack full of better living and a tongue full of charms. For he was the great American salesman, and no man ever had a better thing to sell.

He came by rickety wagon, one jump behind the pioneers, carrying axes for the farmer, fancy dress goods for his wife, and encyclopedias for the farmer's ambitious boy. For he was the great practical democrat, spreader of good things among more and more people.

He came by upper berth and dusty black coupe, selling tractors and radios, iceboxes and movies, health and leisure, ambition and fulfillment. For he was America's emissary of abundance, Mr. High-Standard-of-Living in person.

He rang a billion doorbells and enriched a billion lives. Without him there'd be no American ships at sea, no busy factories, no 60 million jobs. For the great American salesman is the great American civilizer, and everywhere he goes he leaves people better off.[1]

The salesperson makes valuable contributions to our way of life by selling goods and services that benefit individuals and industry. Red Motley, who was a sales training consultant, once said, "Nothing happens until somebody sells something." Selling brings in the money and causes cash registers across the country to ring. For centuries the salespeople of the world have been causing goods and services to change hands.

More than ever, today's salespeople are a dynamic power in the business world. They are responsible for generating more revenue in our economy than workers in any other single profession. The efforts of salespeople have a direct impact on such diverse areas as:

- The success of new products.
- Keeping existing products on the retailer's shelf.
- Construction of manufacturing facilities.
- Opening businesses and keeping them open.

- Generating sales orders that result in the loading of trucks, trains, ships, airplanes, and pipelines that carry goods to customers all over the world.

The salesperson is engaged in a highly honorable, challenging, rewarding, and professional career. In this chapter you are introduced to the career, rewards, and duties of the salesperson. The chapter begins by examining why people choose sales careers.

Why Choose a Sales Career?

Five major reasons for choosing a sales career are (1) the wide variety of sales jobs available, (2) the freedom of being on your own, (3) the challenge of selling, (4) the opportunity for advancement in your company, and (5) the rewards offered by a career in sales.

A Variety of Sales Jobs Are Available

As members of a firm's sales force, salespeople are a vital element in the firm's effort to market their goods and services profitably. Personal selling accounts for major expenditures by most companies, and presents a large number of career opportunities. It has been estimated that American firms spend over $100 billion on their salespeople, which equals the amount spent on sales promotion and advertising. There are some 10 million people employed in selling jobs, and some 180,000 new college and university graduates will become salespeople every year. It is further estimated that from one-half million to one million new or experienced salespeople will be needed annually by industry for the remainder of the decade.[2] Table 1–1 presents several examples of the outlook for sales occupations.[3]

Figure 1–1 provides a glimpse of the American salesperson.[4] The data shown represent estimates of these particular characteristics and are not meant to be totally accurate but to provide general information. For example, the 1980 Census of Population reports 68,694 women in product sales, other than retail sales, out of a total of 433,496 salespeople, or slightly less than 16 percent of the total. However, the services sector of the economy and other nonmanufacturing industries have high percentages of females. For example, financial, publishing, and cosmetic industries traditionally contain 40 to 50 percent females.

The profile indicates that the sales position is professional in nature. Salespeople are well-educated, young, loyal, and well-trained and receive above-average pay. We also see that it is costly to operate a sales force. Salespeople work long hours and must be persistent in closing sales with their customers.

Table 1–1
Sample Employment Opportunities in Sales Occupations

Marketing and Sales Occupations (Subgroup Occupation)	Estimated Employment, 1984	Percent Change in Employment, 1985–1995	Numerical Increase in Employment, 1984–1995	Employment Prospects
Insurance sales workers	371,000	9	34,000	Employment expected to grow more slowly than average due to increasing productivity and changing business practices. Opportunities will be best for ambitious people who enjoy selling and develop expertise in many different types of insurance and investments.
Manufacturers' sales workers	547,000	9	51,000	Employment expected to grow more than the average as some manufacturers switch to wholesalers to market and distribute their products.
Real estate agents and brokers	363,000	14	52,000	Employment expected to rise as fast as average in response to growing demand for housing and other properties. However, the field is highly competitive, and well-trained, ambitious people who enjoy selling should have the best chance for success.
Retail sales workers	4,001,000	15	583,000	Employment expected to grow about as fast as average. High turnover should create many openings for full-time, part-time, and temporary workers.
Securities and financial brokers	81,000	39	32,000	Employment expected to grow much faster than average as economic growth and rising personal incomes increase the funds available for investment. However, the field will continue to be competitive; many beginners drop out because they are unable to establish a suitable clientele. Many jobs will be created as banks expand into nontraditional financial services.
Travel agents	72,000	44	32,000	Employment expected to grow much faster than average. Economic growth is expected to result in rapid increase in both vacation and business-related travel.
Wholesale trade sales workers	1,248,000	30	369,000	Employment expected to grow faster than average as wholesalers sell a wider variety of products and improve customer service. Many job openings will be created as wholesalers enlarge their sales territory by establishing regional sales offices.

The Sales Force of the Future. Marketers mapping long-range sales strategies through the mid-1990s will have to deal with a sales force whose complexion will change markedly.[5] Mostly, marketers can expect to have more women calling on prospects and accounts. They will also benefit from healthy productivity gains by their salespeople and experience considerable difficulty in hiring younger trainees.

Figure 1–1
Profile of the American Salesperson

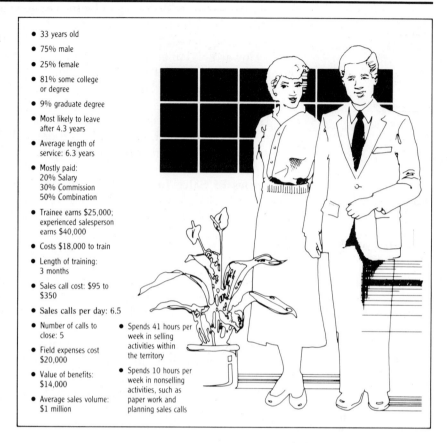

- 33 years old
- 75% male
- 25% female
- 81% some college or degree
- 9% graduate degree
- Most likely to leave after 4.3 years
- Average length of service: 6.3 years
- Mostly paid:
  20% Salary
  30% Commission
  50% Combination
- Trainee earns $25,000; experienced salesperson earns $40,000
- Costs $18,000 to train
- Length of training: 3 months
- Sales call cost: $95 to $350
- Sales calls per day: 6.5
- Number of calls to close: 5
- Field expenses cost $20,000
- Value of benefits: $14,000
- Average sales volume: $1 million
- Spends 41 hours per week in selling activities within the territory
- Spends 10 hours per week in nonselling activities, such as paper work and planning sales calls

These trends will be triggered by the aging of the baby boom generation and the baby bust group that followed it. The effects of this maturation process are at the core of the federal government's new long-range projections developed by the Bureau of Labor Statistics' Office of Economic Growth and Employment Projections (OEGEP) that cover the economy, labor force, industry, and occupations.

While the total labor force (people with jobs plus those looking for work) will increase 15.6 million (13.8 percent) between 1984 and 1995, two thirds of the newcomers will be women. Considering that "the total number of salesworkers is projected to increase at a faster-than-average 20 percent," says John Lukasiewicz, OEGEP economist, the more rapid growth rate implies that marketers will have to hire women to a greater degree to keep their sales forces expanding.

Marketers can be encouraged by the changed age mix of tomorrow's work force. "Nearly three fourths of the 1995 labor force will be in the prime working ages (25 to 54 years) compared with *two* thirds in 1984," notes Howard N. Fullerton, demographic statistician in OEGEP. In fact, prime-age workers will swell 21 million, while younger (16–24) and older (55 and up) workers will decline 3.7 million and 1.6 million, respectively.

Thus, the sales force of the 1990s will be older, decidedly more female, and more productive. Plus, there will be an above-average growth rate in the number of needed salespeople.

Categories of Sales Jobs. Sales activities are of infinite variety and diversity. A useful way to classify the many types of sales jobs is to place a job in one of nine major categories. These categories can then be arrayed on the basis of their complexity and difficulty, as seen in Figure 1–2.

Category 1. Position where the salesperson is predominantly an inside **order-taker,** like the McDonald hamburger salesperson standing behind the counter. Since most customers have already made up their minds to buy, all the seller does is serve them. The salesperson may use suggestion selling by asking if they want a large order of french fries rather than a small order, but opportunities for creative sales are few.

Category 2. Activities where the salesperson's job is predominantly to deliver the product, such as milk, bread, fuel, oil, etc. The outside

Figure 1–2
The Complexity and Difficulty of These Nine Sales Job Categories Increase as They Move from Order-Taker to Order-Getter

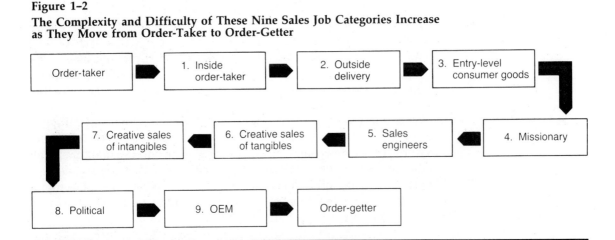

delivery salesperson's selling responsibilities are secondary. Obviously, good service and a pleasant manner will enhance customer acceptance and hence lead to more sales. However, few do any truly creative selling.

Category 3. Positions where the person is also predominantly an order-taker but works in the field, such as selling soap, food, and health and beauty aids to retailers. In their contacts with chain store personnel, they may even be discouraged from applying the hard sell.

As with the delivery salesperson, good service and a pleasant personality may enhance personal acceptance, but they too do little creative selling. This description relates primarily to the **order-getter,** an entry-level job. Key account salespeople for these same companies often use creative selling techniques with their large customers.

Category 4. Positions where the person is not expected or permitted to take an order but is called on to do "missionary" work and only to build goodwill or to educate the actual or potential user—the distiller's missionary man, the textbook publisher's salesperson, or the medical detailer representing an ethical pharmaceutical house. Some pharmaceutical manufacturers, however, do have their salespeople selling directly to the physician.

Category 5. Positions where the major emphasis is placed on technical knowledge such as the **sales engineer** who is primarily a consultant. This person may become so preoccupied with the technical aspects of a project that the individual forgets to close a sale.

Category 6. Positions that demand the sale of **tangible products** such as vacuum cleaners, refrigerators, house siding, encyclopedias. Here the salesperson often has a double task: to make the prospect dissatisfied with his or her present appliance or situation and then begin to sell the product. It is here that the salesperson needs to be persistent and must possess a high need to achieve success.

Category 7. Positions that require the creative sales of intangibles such as insurance, financial services, or advertising services. This sale of **intangible services** is ordinarily more difficult than that of tangibles. The salesperson can show, demonstrate, and dramatize tangible products.

Intangibles are often difficult for the prospect to comprehend. People cannot feel, smell, see, hear, or taste intangible products. This makes them more challenging to sell.

Category 8. Positions that require the political, indirect, or back-door sale of big-ticket items that have no truly competitive features. Here it is not the product primarily that is sold; it is the salesperson who sells her- or himself, hence the political connotation. Typical is the sale of flour to a bakery or cement to a builder.

The product is made to precise specifications. Quality and service offered by all the suppliers are essentially uniform. The price is standard everywhere. The salesperson has no price advantage nor special feature to offer. The only thing being sold is oneself, as one who can offer something to the buyer which is needed. If the salesperson can satisfy this need, the order for the product follows almost automatically.

Category 9. Positions that require presentations to several people, most of whom cannot say yes but all of whom can say no. Typical is the sale of components to an original equipment manufacturer (OEM) account where the presentation may need to be made to engineering, research, production, and purchasing personnel as well as to the decision maker. Even after the business has been obtained initially, it must be retained, often against competent and ruthless competition.[6]

Applications of the Sales Job Classifications. Rarely are these categories encountered exactly as described. Most sales positions are combinations or permutations of one or more of these categories. Thus it is obvious that sales positions vary widely in their nature and requirements.

The people in the first five classifications are salespeople often described as **service sales representatives.** While they must be employed to bring in additional business, which the employer would probably not obtain without their efforts, few create business in any sense. Many never attempt to close the sale. They perform useful services, but someone else—usually a sales manager, key account salesperson, or someone from the home office—must make the initial sale or make the final close if needed. In medical detailing, for example, other physicians often have greater influence on their colleagues than does the **detail salesperson.** In other instances, as with name brands (Swift, Colgate, Cheer, etc.), the demand that advertising and product acceptance has created is such that the merchant must stock the product, and the prime functions of the salespeople are to remind the dealers to reorder, set up displays, and check prices and distribution. Their biggest challenge is selling new products to retailers already overcrowded with products.

The salesperson who calls on a purchasing agent is seeking business from an individual whose business it is to buy. The salesperson's functions here are to convince the prospect that quality, price, terms, and service are better than those offered by competitors, and (even if those factors are equal) that the salesperson and his or her firm are nicer people to deal with. The clerk behind a store counter deals with customers who have already decided to buy something, or at least they are interested in looking at it and are ready to be convinced that they should buy it.

On the other hand, the creative or specialty salesperson or the individual working in highly competitive lines or working with a product that has no special advantages moves merchandise that cannot be sold in equal volume without the person. The salesperson has an infinitely more difficult selling task than does the representative in the first five categories mentioned above. In this sense, the individual is the only true salesperson, and, as a result, usually earns much more than the mere order-taker.

The specialty salesperson has a double selling problem: first, creating discontent with what the prospect already has before beginning to sell constructively; and second, overcoming the most powerful and obstinate resistance. For example, the prospect may never have heard of the product and at the outset has no desire whatever to purchase it. The prospect may even be prejudiced against it and may resent the intrusion of this stranger. In other instances, the prospect may want it, but wants or needs competing products more. Frequently, the prospect cannot afford it. To meet such sales situations successfully requires creative selling of the highest order.

Indirect or political (multiple) selling is qualitatively different from all other types of selling. It is completely unstructured, and usually takes place at a high level in the client organization. However, some political and most multiple selling require the maintenance of contacts at very low levels as well. Skill as a salesperson in the conventional sense is of secondary importance. Although dealing almost entirely in intangibles, if one (as a salesperson) can sell one's self and make one's self indispensable to the prospect, the sale of the product or service should result without any difficulty. Skills of this type are difficult to teach, and there are very few in the business world who possess them naturally. For this reason, these people are usually very highly paid. However, they are indispensable in obtaining and retaining large competitive accounts. They constitute a special elite in sales circles.

Multiple selling is without doubt the most difficult of categories of selling because it combines all the problems of political or indirect sales with a further complication: the representative may have to win over not only the decision maker, the one who can say yes, but also from 10 to 30 other people who cannot approve the order, but each of whom has the power to veto. An example is the original equipment manufacturer (OEM) components salesperson who must often convince not only the purchasing agent and the president, but also the factory superintendent, the shop foreman, and the people who are to operate the machines. This requires a salesperson who possesses great worldliness and sophistication, along with considerable manipulative skill. Above all, the salesperson must know and understand people, and have a very sharp eye for their weaknesses.

Freedom of Action: You're on Your Own

A second reason why people choose a sales career is the freedom it offers. A sales job provides possibly the greatest relative freedom of any career. Experienced employees in outside sales usually receive very little direct supervision and may go for days, even weeks, without seeing their bosses.*

Job duties and sales goals are explained by a boss. Then salespeople are expected to carry out these job duties and achieve their goals with minimum guidance. They usually leave home to contact customers. These customers may be around the corner or around the world.

Job Challenge Is Always There

Working alone with the responsibility of a territory capable of generating thousands (sometimes millions) of dollars in revenue for your company is a great personal challenge. This environment adds great variety to a sales job. Salespeople often deal with hundreds of different people and business firms over a period of time. It is much like operating your own business, without the burdens of true ownership.

Because of the unique challenges and duties of a sales career, the type of person who succeeds in sales might conceivably be the subject of the following quote from Tex Schramm, president of the Dallas Cowboys professional football team:

You attract a unique kind of person; competitive by nature, he has to feed his ego with success and public recognition. He is judged by the public. His incentive comes on Sunday before the crowd . . . and at the end of the season when the playoff money is won.[7]

Sales personnel are much like Schramm's football players. They are competitive, need success, thrive on recognition, and want high financial rewards when they are successful.

Opportunities for Advancement Are Great

Successful salespeople have many opportunities to move into top management positions. In many instances this advancement comes very

---

* Outside sales usually are made off the employer's premises and involve person-to-person contact. Inside sales occur on the premises, as in retail and telephone contact sales.

quickly. Companies like General Mills, Inc., Quaker Oats, and Xerox Corporation may promote successful salespeople to managerial positions such as district sales managers after they have been with the company for only two years.

A sales personnel **career path,** as Figure 1–3 depicts, is the upward sequence of job movements during a sales career. Occasionally people without previous sales experience are promoted into sales management positions. However, 99 percent of the time a career in sales management begins with an entry-level sales position. Firms believe that an experienced sales professional has the credibility, knowledge, and background to assume a higher position in the company.

Most companies have two or three successive levels of sales positions, beginning at the junior or trainee level. Beginning as a salesperson allows a person to:

Learn about the attitudes and activities of the company's salespeople.

Become familiar with customer attitudes toward the company, its products, and its salespeople.

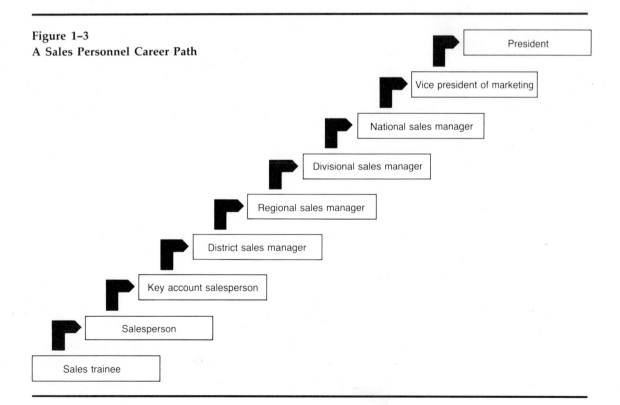

Figure 1–3
A Sales Personnel Career Path

President

Vice president of marketing

National sales manager

Divisional sales manager

Regional sales manager

District sales manager

Key account salesperson

Salesperson

Sales trainee

> Gain first-hand knowledge of products and their application, which is most important in technical sales.
>
> Become seasoned in the world of business.

After training, a salesperson is given responsibility for a sales territory. The person now moves into a regular sales position. In a relatively short time, the salesperson can earn the status and financial rewards of a senior sales position, contacting the larger, more important customers. Some companies refer to this function as a **key account** sales position. A person may choose to stop here or may opt to move into sales management. Keep in mind that while most recruiters today want to hire a person who can sell, they also look for management potential in their salespeople.

You Can Move Quickly into Management

The first managerial level is usually the district sales manager's position. It is not uncommon for people to be promoted to this position within two to three years after joining the company. From district sales manager a person may move into higher levels of sales management.

When asked why they like their jobs, first-line sales managers will say it is because of the rewards. By rewards they mean both financial rewards and nonfinancial rewards (such as the great challenge and the feeling of making a valuable contribution to their salespeople and the company). Managers also frequently mention that this position represents their first major step up toward the top. They have made the "cut" and are a member of the management team. Instead of having responsibility for $1 million in sales, as a salesperson does, the manager is responsible for $10 million.

With success, many jobs throughout the sales force and in the corporate marketing department open up. This can include sales training, sales analysis, advertising, and product management. Frequently, traveling the upward career path involves numerous moves from field sales to corporate, back to the field, then to corporate, back to the field, and so forth. However, the sales experience prepares people for the more responsible jobs in the company.

Success also brings financial rewards. As shown in Table 1–2, the route to the top is typically through sales and marketing.[8] Thus, a beginning sales job is often a stepping stone to these higher positions. The larger a company's revenues, the heavier the responsibility of the chief executive, and thus the larger the compensation. Today, it's common for a CEO's total compensation to be over $1 million annually.

Leaving aside compensation at the top echelons, both corporate and field sales managers typically receive higher salaries than others (such as production, advertising, product, or personnel managers) at the same

Table 1–2 **Profile of a CEO**	A composite of the chief executive officer (CEO) of a large U.S. corporation. Note the "route to the top" section in the career path below.

The position:
Title: Chairman and chief executive officer.
Compensation: $473,500 salary and bonus plus several benefits.
Workload: 60 or more hours in an average week.
Drawbacks: Insufficient time for family and outside interests.

Career path:
Route to the top: Sales/marketing.
Number of employers: 2.4.
Years with present company: 23.
Number of locations with present company: No more than 2.

The person:
Age: 56.6 years.
Marital status: In first marriage.
Religion: Protestant.
Education: Advanced degree.
Ranking of priorities: Family first, then work, country, and community.

organizational level. Salary is just one part of compensation. Many firms offer elaborate packages that include extended vacation and holiday periods; pension programs; health, accident, and legal insurance programs; automobiles and auto expenses; payment of professional association dues; educational assistance for themselves and sometimes for their families; financial planning assistance; company airplanes; home and entertainment expenses; and free country club membership. The higher the sales position, the greater the benefits offered. Salary is also typically related to:

- Annual sales volume of units managed.
- Number of salespeople managed.
- Length of experience in sales.
- Annual sales volume of the firm.

Rewards: The Sky's the Limit

As a salesperson you can look forward to two types of rewards—nonfinancial and financial.

Nonfinancial Rewards.   Sometimes called *psychological income* or *intrinsic rewards*, **nonfinancial rewards** are generated by the individual, not given by the company. You know the job has been done well, for instance, when you have skillfully delivered a sales presentation.

Examples of Many Sales
Career Opportunities and Rewards

Today's top sales people are well-trained professionals. As the major factors contributing to their success, they list honesty, sincerity, service to customers (both before and after a sale), and long hours of research. Most of the compensation of the top income earners comes from commissions. Let's meet a few of these super salesmen and saleswomen.

Jim Hansberger, 39, has come a long way from his student days at the University of Georgia where he formed a club to invest in the stock market. As a financial consultant at Shearson Lehman/American Express in 1984 (not a good year on Wall Street), he earned in excess of $650,000. He was involved in handling many financial services, mainly for individual customers, including real estate management and retirement plans.

Helen McVoy was a 65-year-old grandmother and plant collector. She also was a national sales director for Mary Kay Cosmetics, earning $375,000 in 1984, largely on commissions from sales made by sales representatives that she supervised.

Don Wilson, 43, was the top sales representative for New York Life Insurance Company in 1984, earning about $470,000 in commissions. Based in Anchorage, Alaska, Don's major clients were privately held companies that bought everything from employee benefit programs to estate-planning programs from him.

Dorothy Cole, 33, was a district sales representative manager for Compaq Computer. Based in Los Angeles in 1984, she had an income in the "high five figures." She sold Compaq personal computers (which are IBM-compatible models) to computer chains such as Computerland and Inacomp.

Greg Finneran, 58, was one of 3M's (Scotch Tape, etc.) most highly paid sales reps in 1984. He was based in New Jersey and sold a line of sandpaper, tape, and window insulation to home-center stores.

Nancy Reck, 30, was a successful sales representative for Xerox Corp., selling Xerox copiers and electronic typewriters door to door to small companies while her husband was in graduate school. Her income in 1984 was estimated at about $50,000, even though she had a low-volume territory of 17 counties in her home state of North Carolina. Since then she was promoted to a new job that was a stepping-stone to management.[9]

When you successfully meet the challenges of your job, it produces a feeling of self-worth, and you realize that your job is important. Everyone wants to feel good about a job, and a selling career allows you to experience these good feelings, these intrinsic rewards, daily. Salespeople often report that the nonfinancial rewards of their jobs are just as important to them as financial rewards.

Financial Rewards.   Many are attracted to selling because in a sales career **financial rewards** are usually based solely on performance. Many professional salespeople have opportunities to earn large salaries. These salaries average even higher than salaries for other types of workers at the same organizational level. People with no experience can find sales jobs paying $18,000 to $35,000. With several years' experience, their earnings can rise to $45,000 or even more. In addition, their employers furnish them with cars and allowances for travel, customer entertainment, and meals.

Such practices indicate that employers recognize the importance of their salespeople and are willing to pay them an above-average salary year after year. This leads to an important question: What are the main job activities salespeople perform to receive such high salaries? Before answering this question, let's examine examples of salespeople earning above-average salaries.

The Salesperson's Activities as a Territorial Manager

The salesperson's roles or activities can vary from company to company, depending on whether sales involve goods or services, the firm's market characteristics, and the location of customers. For example, a salesperson selling *Encyclopaedia Britannica* or Avon products performs similar, but somewhat different, job activities than the industrial salesperson making sales calls for General Electric or RCA.

Most people believe that a salesperson only makes sales presentations, but there is much more to the job than person-to-person selling. The salesperson functions as a **territory manager**—planning, organizing, and executing activities that increase sales and profits in a given territory. A sales territory is comprised of a group of customers assigned within a geographical area. Figure 1–4 indicates just a few of the typical activities of a salesperson working for General Mills, Inc. As manager of a territory, the salesperson performs the following seven functions.

1. Provides Solutions to Customer's Problems.   Customers have needs that can be met and problems that can be solved by purchasing

Figure 1–4
Examples of a Consumer Goods Salesperson's Activities

General Mills' Becky Roy (1) reviews her customer sales call plan, (2) checks her shelf stock, (3) counts the merchandise in the back stockroom, (4) makes her sales presentation and plans an in-store promotion with the store manager, and (5) finally moves on to her next sales call.

goods or services. Salespeople seek to uncover potential or existing needs or problems and show how the use of their products or services can satisfy those needs or solve those problems.

2. Provides Service to Customers. Salespeople provide a wide range of services, including handling of complaints, returning damaged merchandise, providing samples, suggesting business opportunities, and developing recommendations on how the customer can promote products purchased from the salesperson.

If necessary, salespeople may even occasionally work at the customer's business. For example, a salesperson selling fishing tackle may arrange an in-store demonstration of a manufacturer's products and offer to repair fishing reels as a service to the retailer's customers. Furthermore, a manufacturer may have its salespeople sell to distributors or wholesalers. Then the manufacturer's representative may make sales calls with the distributor's salespeople to aid them in selling and servicing the distributor's customers.

3. Sells to Current and New Customers. The acquisition of new accounts is the lifeblood of a business; it brings new revenues into the company. This important job must be done if a salesperson's territory is to grow.

While new accounts are crucial, salespeople also strive to increase the sales volume of their present customers by encouraging them to purchase additional items within the same product line along with any new product offerings.

4. Helps Customers Resell Products to Their Customers.   A major part of many sales jobs is for the salesperson to help wholesalers and retailers resell the products that they have purchased. The salesperson helps wholesale customers sell products to retail customers and helps retail customers sell products to consumers.

Consider the Quaker Oats salesperson selling a product to grocery wholesalers. Not only must the wholesaler be contacted, but also grocery retailers must be called on, sales made, and orders written up and

A Typical Day for a Xerox Salesperson

You are responsible for your sales coverage, time, and budget. Help is available and you'll have plenty of marketing and service support; but you're expected to work independently, without constant direction.

Your day is devoted primarily to customer contact. Potential customers may phone the branch and ask to see a Xerox representative. More likely, however, you will acquire customers by making appointments or by visiting businesses to meet the decision makers, discuss their needs, and offer solutions to their problems. As part of your position, you'll make product presentations, either at the Xerox branch office or at the customer's office. You will also spend a fair amount of time on the telephone, following up leads, arranging appointments, and speaking with managers in a variety of businesses and organizations.

In working with customers, you'll need to solve a number of problems. What Xerox product best fits the customer's needs? How do Xerox products compare with the competition? Should the machine be purchased or leased? What's the total cash outlay—and per copy cost—for the machine and its service? How should the product be financed? Where should the machine be placed for maximum efficiency? What training is needed for employees? How can Xerox products meet future office needs?

You'll also be engaged in a number of customer support activities, such as expediting product deliveries, checking credit, writing proposals, and training customer employees in the use of the product. You might also refer customers to other Xerox sales organizations and make joint calls with representatives from these organizations.

Each day will bring you new challenges to face and problems to solve. Your days will be busy and interesting.[10]

sent to the wholesaler. In turn, the wholesaler sells and delivers the products to the retailers. The Quaker Oats salesperson also develops promotional programs to help the retailer sell the firm's products. These programs involve supplying advertising materials, putting on store demonstrations, and setting up product displays.

5. Helps Customers Use Products after Purchase. The salesperson's job is not over after the sale is made. Often customers must be shown how to obtain the full benefit from the product. For example, after a customer buys an IBM computer system, technical specialists help the buyer learn how to operate the equipment.

6. Builds Goodwill with Customers. A selling job is people-oriented, entailing face-to-face contact with the customer. Many sales are based, to some extent, on friendship and trust. The salesperson needs to develop a personal, friendly, businesslike relationship with everyone who may influence a buying decision. This is an ongoing part of the salesperson's job, and it requires integrity, high ethical standards, and a sincere interest in satisfying customers' needs.

7. Provides Company with Market Information. Salespeople provide information to their companies on such topics as competitors' activities, customers' reactions to new products, complaints about products or policies, market opportunities, and their own job activities. This information is so important for many companies that their salespeople are required to send in weekly or monthly reports on the activities of the firm's competition in their territory. Salespeople are a vital part of their employers' information retrieval system.

When combined, and properly carried out, these seven sales job activities produce a successful sales performance. An example of how a salesperson integrates these activities helps to better understand the sales job. See the insert, "A Typical Day for a Xerox Salesperson," on page 21.

Is a Sales Career Right for You? _____

It may be too early in your life to determine if you really want to be a salesperson. The balance of this book will aid you in investigating sales as a career. Your search for a career, any career, begins with *you*. In considering a sales career, be honest and realistic with yourself. Ask yourself questions such as these:

- What are my past accomplishments?
- What are my future goals?

- Do I want to have the responsibility of a sales job?
- Do I mind travel? How much travel is acceptable?
- How much freedom do I want in the job?
- Do I have the personality characteristics for the job?

Your answers to these questions can help you analyze the various types of sales jobs and establish criteria for evaluating job openings. You should determine the industries, types of products or services, and specific companies in which you have an interest.

College placement offices, libraries, and business periodicals offer a wealth of information on companies as well as sales positions in them. Conversations with friends and acquaintances who are involved in selling, or have been in sales, can give you realistic insight into what challenges, rewards, and disadvantages the sales vocation offers. To better prepare yourself to obtain a sales job, you must understand what companies look for in their salespeople.

A Sales Manager's View of the Recruit

The following discussion of what sales managers consider when hiring a salesperson is based on a summary of a talk given by a sales manager to a sales class. It is reasonably representative of what companies look for when hiring salespeople.

We look for outstanding applicants who are mature and intelligent. They should be able to handle themselves well in the interview, demonstrating good interpersonal skills. They should have a well-thought-out career plan and be able to discuss it rationally. They should have a friendly, pleasing personality. A clean, neat appearance is a must. They should have a positive attitude, be willing to work hard, be ambitious, and demonstrate a good degree of interest in the employer's business field. They should have good grades and other personal, school, and business accomplishments. Finally, they should have clear goals and objectives in life. The more common characteristics on which applicants for our company are judged are (1) appearance, (2) self-expression, (3) maturity, (4) personality, (5) experience, (6) enthusiasm, and (7) interest in the job.

People often consider a sales career because they have heard that a person can earn a good salary selling. They think anyone can sell. These people have really not considered all of the facts. As you are beginning to see, a sales job has high rewards because it also has many important responsibilities. Companies do not pay high salaries for nothing. As you will see in this book, a sales career involves great challenges that require hard work by qualified individuals. Let us review the characteristics of a successful salesperson.

Success in Selling—What Does It Take? _____

Throughout this book you will read comments from salespeople about their jobs. In order to answer the question, "What makes a salesperson successful?" I asked them what they felt was required of them to be successful salespeople. The eight most frequently mentioned characteristics were (1) love of their job, (2) willingness to work hard, (3) need to achieve success, (4) optimistic outlook, (5) knowledge of their job, (6) careful use of selling time, (7) ability to listen to customers, and (8) customer service. Each of these characteristics is described more fully below.

Love of Selling

The successful salesperson is an individual who loves selling, finds it exciting, and is strongly convinced that the product being sold offers something of great value. Prudential Life Insurance salesperson George Morris states it best by saying, "To be successful you need a very deep commitment to your product and what it will do."* In selling her Amway products, Bernice Hansen emphasizes that she "has wonderful products that everyone needs. . . . If you believe in what you are doing as strongly as I do, you have the self-confidence to be successful."[11]

To be sure, a love of selling itself is one characteristic of successful salespeople. Irving Rousso, who made a salary of $547,875 selling for the Russ Togs Corporation, says, "I'm still hungry and don't ask me why. I just know that it still gives me a thrill and a chill every time I get a reorder."[12] Other salespeople quoted throughout this book made similar comments about how their enthusiasm for their work helps them to be successful. This eagerness to do their job results in hard work.

Willingness to Work Hard

Successful salespeople will tell you that even though they enjoy it, selling requires long hours of hard work, day in and day out, to reach their personal goals. This usually means working at night to plan the next day's activities and working on many Saturdays and sometimes Sundays.

A ten- to twelve-hour work day is common. It is their love of work and their need for success that apparently motivates some salespeople to make this personal sacrifice. Matt Suffoletto of IBM says, "If you would make each sales call, presentation, or proposal as if it were the single event from which you will gain quota attainment, recognition, or promotion, you will always be miles in front of your competition."

---

* A profile of George Morris appears in Chapter 11.

Underlying a tolerance for hard work, there is often a desire for success in life.

Need to Achieve

Each of us has a desire to be successful; yet some individuals seem to have a much higher desire for success. Successful salespeople have, as part of their personality, a strong work ethic and a high need to strive for success. If people love their work, are willing to work hard, and have a strong desire to achieve success, do you think they will be successful? I believe you would say yes to that question.

Steve Gibson, a stockbroker for Smith Barney, finds "being second best is not good enough. I am personally challenged to be many customers' best broker. I want to excel. I've found that asking myself the simple question 'Did I do my best?' at the end of each business day is sufficient."[13] "Second is not good enough," "Go beyond the call of duty," and "Make that second effort," are frequent comments of successful salespeople.

Don't Quit

When things go wrong, as they sometimes will,
When the road you're trudging seems all uphill,
When the funds are low and the debts are high,
And you want to smile, but you have to sigh,
When care is pressing you down a bit—
Rest if you must, but don't you quit.
Life is queer with its twists and turns,
As every one of us sometimes learns,
And many a person turns about
When they might have won had they stuck it out.
Don't give up though the pace seems slow—
You may succeed with another blow.
Often the struggler has given up
When he might have captured the victor's cup;
And he learned too late
When the night came down,
How close he was to the golden crown.
Success is failure turned inside out—
So stick to the fight when you're hardest hit—
It's when things seem worst that you mustn't quit.

The need to achieve involves persistence. Consider former president Calvin Coolidge's following comments:

Nothing in this world can take the place of persistence. *Talent will not. Nothing is more common than unsuccessful men with talent. Genius will not. Unsuccessful genius is almost a proverb. Education will not. The world is full of educated derelicts. Persistence and determination alone are omnipotent. The slogan ''press on'' has solved and always will solve the problems of the human race.*

The enthusiastic person who is willing to work hard in pursuit of a goal must be optimistic!

Have an Optimistic Outlook

All of the salespeople I know credit a positive attitude toward their companies, products, customers, themselves, and life as major reasons for their success. Successful salespeople are enthusiastic and confident, and constantly think of themselves as successful. Sure, salespeople have times when things do not go as they wish. Yet their positive mental attitude helps them to overcome periodic problems. They continually look for methods to improve their attitude.

One method of maintaining a positive self-image is illustrated in the credo of Elbert Hubbard. At the age of 35, Hubbard retired as a highly successful soap salesman. He went on to become successful as a magazine publisher, a marketer of books and furniture, and a direct mail specialist. Elbert Hubbard's business credo was as follows:

I believe in myself.

I believe in the goods I sell.

I believe in the firm for whom I work.

I believe in my colleagues and helpers.

I believe in American business methods.

I believe in producers, creators, manufacturers, distributors, and in all industrial workers of the world who have a job and hold it down.

I believe that Truth is an asset.

I believe in good cheer and in good health, and I recognize the fact that the first requisite in success is not to achieve the dollar, but to confer a benefit, and that the reward will come automatically and usually as a matter of course.

I believe in sunshine, fresh air, spinach, applesauce, laughter, buttermilk, babies, bombazine, and chiffon, always remembering that the greatest word in the English language is *sufficiency*.

I believe that when I make a sale, I make a friend.

And I believe that when I part with a man, I must do it in such a way that when he sees me again, he will be glad and so will I.

I believe in the hands that work, and the brains that think, and in the hearts that love.

Amen, and Amen.

Although Mr. Hubbard's philosophy may sound a bit old-fashioned, it all boils down to:

- Believing in yourself.
- Thinking of yourself as a success.
- Being enthusiastic when helping buyers—being service-oriented.
- Being positive in your outlook on life and the job.

In no other career is the need to think positively more important than in sales. As a salesperson you should examine your inner self, commonly referred to as your self-concept, and make sure you have a positive, enthusiastic attitude toward yourself, your work, and your customers.

Optimism and hard work are building blocks for success. In addition, top salespeople believe job and product knowledge are also necessary if you wish to be successful in a sales career.

Be Knowledgeable

Successful salespeople place a great deal of emphasis on being thoroughly knowledgeable in all aspects of their business. This helps them to project a professional image and to build customer confidence. The comments later in the book from salespeople representing such companies as General Mills, AT&T, and The Upjohn Company discuss the need to be informed. Take, for example, Steve Gibson of Smith Barney who says:

Successful salespeople gain a broad knowledge of their business through reading and observation. Learning through study, such as reading, does not end after college—it begins! Many professionals have extensive personal libraries. In general, sales professionals often are not coached or motivated by their companies to read enough. You may have to do it on your own. Subscribe to such publications as your industry's trade magazines, The Wall Street Journal, *and* Business Week. *Routinely visit your local book stores and public and college libraries. Keep abreast of local, state, national, and international news. Take an evening course at a local college.*

As products and services become more complex, companies place even greater emphasis on training their salespeople, and salespeople on training themselves. It is no wonder that corporate recruiters seek above-average individuals to fill their entry-level sales positions.

This knowledge characteristic also includes awareness of the most up-to-date ideas concerning selling skills. Successful salespeople are experts at developing and presenting talks that sell their products. They are constantly educating themselves on methods of better determining customers' needs and of effectively communicating the benefits of their products in order to satisfy those needs.

Salespeople read books and magazine articles on selling, and they attend sales training courses to learn how to sell their products better. This knowledge is incorporated into their sales presentation, which is rehearsed until it sounds like a natural conversation between seller and buyer. Another characteristic that is found in good salespeople is the careful use of time.

Value Time

Since there is only so much time in the day for contacting customers and there are so many demands on their time, successful salespeople value time and use it wisely by carefully planning their day's activities. Effective time management is a must. What customer will be called on, what product is to be presented, and how to go about presenting it must be planned carefully.

Ask Questions and Then Listen to Uncover Customer Needs

Joe Gandolfo, who sold over *$1 billion* of life insurance in a single year, has a sign on his office wall that reads: "God gave you two ears and one mouth, and He meant for you to do twice as much listening as talking."[14]

Good salespeople are good listeners. They ask questions to uncover prospects' needs and then listen as prospects answer the questions and state their needs. Then they show how their products' benefits will fulfill these needs. The ability to identify and meet customer needs separates the successful salesperson from the average salesperson. To meet customers' needs successfully, you have to provide service.

Serve Your Customer

The most important of all these characteristics for establishing a lasting sales relationship with a customer is to be willing to provide service. Customers must believe that you care about them and their welfare. Successful salespeople respect their customers, treat them fairly, honestly like them, and develop a good working relationship with them much like a partnership. They provide outstanding service to each.

> ## What Is a Customer?
>
> - Customers are the most important people in any business.
> - Customers are not dependent on us. We are dependent on them.
> - Customers are not an interruption of our work. They are the purpose of it.
> - Customers do us a favor in doing business with us. We aren't doing customers a favor by waiting on them.
> - Customers are part of our business—not outsiders. Customers are not just money in the cash register. Customers are human beings with feelings, and they deserve to be treated with respect.
> - Customers are people who come to us with needs and wants. It is our job to fill them.
> - Customers deserve the most courteous attention we can give them.
> - Customers are the lifeblood of this and every business. Customers pay your salary. Without customers we would have to close our doors.
> - Don't ever forget it.

These factors help them to earn the respect of their customers and to be considered professional businesspeople with high ethics. Steve Gibson says, "I've found the Golden Rule of 'Do unto others . . .' always to be a basis of earning respect."

The Sales Process Used by Successful Salespeople

Much of your course will revolve around the sales process. The sales process refers to a sequential series of actions by the salesperson that leads toward the customer taking a desired action and ends with a follow-up to ensure purchase satisfaction. This desired action by a prospect is usually buying, and certainly that is the most important action. Such desired actions can also include advertising, displaying, or reducing the price of the product.

Although many factors may influence how a salesperson makes a presentation in any one situation, there does exist a logical, sequential

1. **Prospecting:** Locating and qualifying prospects.
2. **Preapproach:** Obtaining interview; determining sales call objective; developing customer profile, customer benefit program, and sales presentation strategies.
3. **Approach:** Meeting prospect and beginning customized sales presentation.
4. **Presentation:** Further uncovering needs; relating product benefits to needs using demonstration, dramatization, visuals, and proof statements.
5. **Trial close:** Asking prospect's *opinion* during and after presentation.
6. **Objections:** Uncovering objections.
7. **Meet objections:** Satisfactorily answering objections.
8. **Trial close:** Asking prospect's *opinion* after overcoming each objection and immediately before the close.
9. **Close:** Bringing prospect to the logical conclusion to buy.
10. **Follow-up and service:** Serving customer after the sale.

series of actions that, if followed, can greatly increase the chances of making a sale. This selling process involves 10 basic steps as briefly listed in Figure 1–5. Each of these steps will be discussed in greater detail in the following chapters.

Before a sales presentation can be attempted, several important preparatory activities should be carried out. This involves prospecting and planning the sales presentation. Steps 3 through 9 compose the sales presentation itself. Step 10 involves the important follow-up phase of the selling process to ensure customer satisfaction.

Before we discuss the sales process we will examine where personal selling fits into a firm's marketing effort. Then we will consider what a salesperson needs to know, such as why people buy.

Summary of Major Selling Issues

Personal selling is an old and honorable profession. It is responsible for helping to improve this country's standard of living and providing benefits to individual buyers through the purchase of products. Thousands of people have chosen a sales career because of the availability of sales jobs, the personal freedom it provides, its challenge, the multitude of opportunities for success, and its nonfinancial and financial rewards.

The salesperson's job requires the planning, organization, and execution of activities that increase sales and profits. These involve selling to new customers, obtaining reorders, selling new products, helping customers find new uses for present products, helping customers use products properly, and suggesting ways wholesalers and retailers can sell to their customers.

A person can become a successful salesperson through company and personal training and by the proper application of this knowledge in the development of skills and abilities for benefiting customers. It is also important to believe in the product or service being sold, work hard, want to succeed, and maintain a positive outlook toward both selling and oneself. In addition, a successful salesperson should be knowledgeable, should be able to plan, and should use selling time wisely. It is also important to be a good listener and to provide service to customers.

The remainder of the book will expand on these topics to provide you with the background either to improve your present selling ability or to help you decide if a sales career is the right one for you.

Review and Discussion Questions

1. Chapter 1 profiled Matt Suffoletto of IBM who commented on job rewards and opportunities of a sales career. Relate his comments to the book's description of job opportunities, a sales career path, and the rewards of the salesperson.

2. The term *salesperson* refers to many types of sales jobs. What are the major types of sales jobs available?

3. Chapter 1 described characteristics of several successful salespeople currently selling goods and services for national companies. Describe those characteristics and then discuss whether or not those same characteristics are also needed for success in other types of jobs.

4. People choose a particular career for many reasons. What are the five reasons someone might choose a sales career?

5. What is meant by the term *career path*? What are the various jobs to which a salesperson might be promoted in his company?

6. A salesperson manages a sales territory. A territory manager must perform numerous activities. What are seven important activities performed in the territory?

Projects

1. Interview one or more salespeople and write a brief report on what they like and dislike about their jobs, why they chose a sales career, what activities they perform, and what they believe it takes to succeed in selling their products.

2. Contact your college placement office and report on what they believe firms who are recruiting people for sales positions look for in applicants.

Case _____

1–1   Linda Baker of Quaker Oats Moves Quickly
up the Corporate Sales Ladder

Graduating with a degree in nutrition from the University of Houston
and working as a dietary supervisor for Hermann Hospital, as a food
intern for the catering department of the Braesword Marriott Hotel, and
as an order clerk for the produce department of the Fleming Foods
Supermarket chain while in college provided me with the academic and
practical background for my professional career in the food industry. I
began at Quaker Oats Company as a sales representative.

Promotions to account supervisor and later to account manager
came next. In 1983, after only three years with the company, I was
promoted into sales management. My first position was a zone sales
planning manager, then to a district manager, and finally to my current
position as region sales planning manager.

In all those positions, persuasive selling of my ideas and myself
were essential. Sales is a very competitive field. Good salespeople do not
necessarily make good sales managers. In sales management, I found
that I was no longer just selling Quaker products, but also the company
and my people!

In my first management position, zone sales planning manager, I
had no immediate people responsibility. The position was a staff position that reported to the zone sales manager. The position was twofold:
it involved the interviewing and training of new and experienced sales
representatives, and the preparation and analysis of trade deals and
sales information to the zone's field sales force.

In the grocery industry, field salespeople work out of their homes.
You are your own typist, secretary, and receptionist. Your experience of
an office environment is limited. In the field, you sometimes do not see
another team member or your boss for several weeks, whereas in the
office setting, you work and eat lunch with the same people everyday.
The change can be a difficult transition. You suddenly go from a varied
work environment to a structured office where you must learn to work
with secretaries, a zone manager, and zone development managers—all
who are accustomed to office procedures.

The position of zone sales planning manager was very challenging
because of the administrative responsibilities. I no longer impacted only
1 account, but now 45 to 50! It was extremely important that my correspondence be accurate—one misdirected letter or incorrect trade deal
affected the zone's total sales force and its direct accounts.

Preplanning was the best method in adapting to this position—
preplanning my time, letters, meetings, and phone conversations. I
tried to keep in mind their other responsibilities when delegating additional work to the secretarial staff. I strongly recommend a college

Exhibit 1

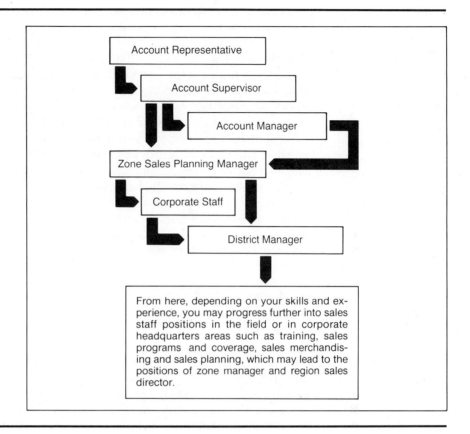

From here, depending on your skills and experience, you may progress further into sales staff positions in the field or in corporate headquarters areas such as training, sales programs and coverage, sales merchandising and sales planning, which may lead to the positions of zone manager and region sales director.

course in business writing to acquaint yourself with letter and proposal writing.

Other aspects of the position required analytical ability. I would discuss with marketing our needs for trade deal support in various marketing areas. I would then forecast what case volume and dollar volume we would sell on each packing.

To forecast the deal volume, I looked at the product's seasonality, market shares, and key account distribution levels. Typically, we would expect the account to purchase eight weeks of product in a four-week deal period.

Preparation of new item and special promotion sales aids also required extensive analyses. Whenever we would introduce a new item, I would analyze the market share of the product category, manufacturer, size, flavor, and packing growth. This information was compiled for the sales representatives' presentations. The sales aid was designed to present the information in bar graphs, pie charts, and line graphs. Obviously, computer training was essential.

Probably the most mentally and physically demanding job responsibility was the training of new sales representatives. In a period of two weeks, they were trained on the policies, the procedures, the products, and the art of selling some 150 Quaker products. Needless to say, this created an information overload, and the retention level of the new employee was at capacity. The initial training program acquaints the employee with the various job responsibilities of a Quaker representative. The refined details are then followed up by the district manager.

All in all, this position opened my eyes to corporate Quaker. Previously, I had dealt with only my market area and accounts. Now I had the knowledge to understand how marketing, sales, and distribution all work together to bring Quaker Oats products to the grocers' shelves.

My next position was district manager. My team was composed of seven full-time representatives and two part-timers. My district annual sales volume was 16MM, and I managed six direct accounts.

The first week I started in my new position, I had to do the following:

- Create a complete new district.
- Train four new employees.
- Set up my district office.

Needless to say, I was busy. Once again, I was working out of my home and acting as my own secretary, typist, and receptionist.

The greatest challenge to me as a district manager was motivating my team. First of all, I had never really managed people. During my first year, I read numerous books and attended seminars all in search of "How to Be a Good Manager." Unfortunately, all the books and seminars in the world cannot make you a good manager. You must just jump in feet first and get wet! I found the management of people to be a paradox: one day I was feeling the greatest sense of accomplishment and the next day—despair.

During my two-and-a-half years as a district manager, I managed at one time or another 17 different people, promoted 3 into management and 7 into progressive field sales positions, and trained 10 new employees. I was constantly out in the field training employees about how to effectively sell Quaker products. My job sometimes began at 5 A.M. and ended at 3 A.M.! Since my people and I were constantly out in the field, the majority of our communication was done at night over the telephone. I listened to everything from car problems to direct account new item acceptances.

Probably the best elements in making your team great are *your* attitude and *your* people's abilities. You are the first boss for the majority of your sales representatives. The way you manage and motivate them affects their outlook on their career. You must be able to understand how they think, act, and react.

Understandably, many young people have low confidence levels. You must show them how they can market their strengths to influence buyers and work effectively with fellow team members who are veterans in the business. I personally prefer a team of young, hungry, inexperienced employees to a group of veteran employees with experience but no drive. It is essential in sales to be persistent for success. Persistency is fueled by motivation.

You have to find each employee's hot button. Maybe he/she strives for perfection in a sales presentation or in his/her retail stores. It is *your* job to herald their achievements. Everyone loves to hear how great they are; compliments can go further than pay increases sometimes.

Finding the right people is truly an art. Some candidates can come across so polished and confident in an interview, but after two weeks on the job, you see a totally different person.

Sometimes an employee is certain about wanting a career in sales, but after six months on the job decides a career in an office job is more desirable. After a couple of bad experiences, you learn how to spot a rehearsed interview. I have found that several comprehensive interviews are essential to make a good hiring decision. The following are the types of interviews I recommend:

1. Screening interview (college campus—college recruiter).
2. Field interview (candidate works in the field with a sales representative).
3. Detailed interview/offer (district manager).

Hiring the right people is essential for ensuring a smooth sailing district. If you can hire the best, it frees you up for more pressing matters—such as sales volume.

The district manager's number one accountability is increasing sales volume. Each quarter the district was assigned a dollar volume quota for each product category. The quotas were then broken down at the territory level. The sales quotas plus additional merchandising and new item objectives were then written into a six-month sales incentive plan with assigned dollar amounts. An example of a sales dollar quota objective would be:

Sell the following quarterly dollar sales:

Division	Objectives 1st Quarter	Achieve Dollars	Objectives 2nd Quarter	Achieve Dollars
Human foods	$1,500,000	$1,400	$2,000,000	$1,400
Pet foods	1,000,000	1,200	1,300,000	1,200
Total	$2,500,000	$2,600	$3,300,000	$2,600

An example of a merchandising and new item objective would be:

New Item: Sell Account Z four sizes of Special Pet Dinners by July 1, 1986, and sell *2,500* cases on the introductory deal. If the person met this goal, they would earn a bonus of $450.

Merchandising: Sell Account Z a four-inch column ad, forced out displays (25 cases per store), and a temporary four-week price reduction on the Summer Vacation Sweepstakes Promotion. Here they would earn $400.

It was my job, as district manager, to oversee the development and execution of these objectives. These objectives were the key priority areas which would have the greatest impact on the next six-month volume. To keep abreast, I traveled extensively in the field checking retail store conditions and attended numerous direct account presentations.

My key role was to develop and guide the sales representatives in managing their territory or direct account. Areas of development were time management, presentation skills, and analysis of account trends. It was essential that I teach my employees how to assume control of their business. My directive was "Manage the account or territory as if it were your own business." Another thought-provoking question I asked was "If this were your own company, would you hire yourself?"

Sales, above all other careers, is driven by personal drive and success. I have seen a weak account turn around with new item acceptances and merchandising simply because of the salesperson calling on the account. Sales is a career for the high achiever, optimistic thinker, and professional administrator. Sales requires a personality that is self-motivated, independent, and energetic. Many job candidates cite "I like people" as a reason for getting into sales. Liking people helps, but *persuading* people who you like or dislike to buy your product or idea is the heart of selling!

I truly enjoyed my position as district manager. The people aspect of the job was the most challenging task I faced. The rewards were immeasurable. The position taught me how to become a leader, motivator, teacher, disciplinarian, administrator, and a fierce team competitor. If future sales management positions are as rewarding, I look forward to the opportunities.

My new position is region sales planning manager. I work with the three zones in the region in the collaboration of new item and merchandising objectives. I also assist the region director with special projects and region sales analyses. The position is a staff position with no people responsibility.

My future job possibilities will lead to our corporate office in Chicago. The next position would be a national sales planning position, then an assistant brand manager position. My long-term goal after these two positions is a zone manager position. Obviously, you can see, a career in sales requires moving for advancement.

Probably the best advice I can give about a career in sales management is to not be a carrot chaser. Set your goals based on your own personal needs and desires, not on what your co-worker is doing. The worst situation is to chase a position because of its title. Choose a career because it gives you a sense of fulfillment and purpose. Sales is a highly competitive, taxing career—it's not for everyone.

Questions:

1. What do you think of Linda Baker's career movements up the organizational ladder?
2. Be prepared to discuss the career of Linda Baker and her philosophy toward her sales career.

II PREPARATION FOR SUCCESSFUL SELLING

Why and How People Buy

Salespeople are trained to emphasize the benefits of their product or service. The idea is to "sell" the buyer with a positive approach. Often, however, sales are made by eliminating the negatives.

Most buyers operate out of three basic fears: The product won't do what the salesman says it will do; the product is not worth the price; others will think I used poor judgment.

How do you convert negatives to positives? First, you have to recognize these fears at work. Then administer the antidotes:

The product won't perform—demonstrate, show pictures or slides, provide case histories, leave samples if practical.

Not worth the price—reemphasize benefits and economies.

What others will think—this is the subtlest fear, but the most insidious. Offer support through testimonials and recommendations. If necessary, put words in the buyer's mouth—supply arguments that he can use to defend his position.

2 THE PSYCHOLOGY OF SELLING: WHY PEOPLE BUY

Learning Objectives

1. To emphasize the importance of relating a product's benefits to the customer's needs instead of only stressing features and advantages in the sales presentation. People buy benefits!
2. To illustrate techniques on how to determine a customer's needs.
3. To present factors that influence the consumer's buying decision.
4. To begin to stimulate ideas on methods for selling.

Key Terms for Selling

Black box
Stimulus-response
Needs
Wants
Maslow's need hierarchy
Economic needs
Conscious need level
Preconscious need level
Unconscious need level
Benefit selling
FAB selling technique
Feature
Advantage
Benefit
Industrial market
Value analysis
Unit cost
Return on investment
Perception
Selective exposure

Selective distortion
Selective retention
Learning
Attitudes
Belief
Personality
Self-concept
Real self
Self-image
Ideal self
Looking-glass self
Routine decision making
Limited decision making
Extensive decision making
Need arousal
Collection of information
Information evaluation
Purchase decision
Purchase satisfaction
Purchase dissonance

Profile

Jim Mobley
General Mills

After graduating from Southern Methodist University in Dallas, Jim Mobley began his sales career in 1968 as a Dallas area sales representative for General Mills, Inc., Grocery Products Sales Division. Over the years Jim has advanced through several different sales positions within General Mills to his present assignment of district sales manager. He is responsible for six account managers, two territory managers, two shelf management specialists, and for the sale of approximately 4,000,000 cases annually.

"General Mills salespeople," says Jim, "are involved in selling approximately 200 different consumer food products and sizes directly to grocery wholesalers, who in turn supply the retail grocery industry. These salespeople then contact individual food retailers to persuade them to purchase and promote General Mills products. To aid its salespeople in their selling effort, the company allows them to offer promotional price allowances and merchandising aids to their customer. Massive promotional campaigns involving advertising, couponing, and free samples are also directed towards the retailer's customers. Salespeople use these incentives and information in their sales presentation to help them make the sale.

"Why our customers buy is sometimes complicated by the fact that our customers normally stock a certain maximum number of products. The grocery industry operates on a very small per-unit net profit and is restricted by both warehouse and retail shelf space. In the majority of our sales of new items to accounts, we're not only selling the new product, but we must offer the account guidance in what similar product should be deleted. We also must show them where the new product fits into their product mix and where it is to be placed on the retail grocery shelf.

"It is important that we make our presentations in a professional manner with documentation on potential benefits such as sales and profits. We make it as easy as possible for an account to consider and purchase our products. For example, we may sell a product using test market results, volume potential for the account, and anticipated customer demand for the product. We then lay out a merchandising plan for the new product, which covers media support, coupon-

ing, consumer programs, and introductory price discounts. Market share information will show the account what products are weak, if a product must be eliminated from the retailer's shelf, and what products warrant deletion. Hopefully these products are not ours, but from time to time a weak product of ours sometimes falls into this group.

"Using good business rationale will add credibility to your sales presentations and build customer rapport and trust. Giving your buyer this type of credible information will build stronger presentations in the future as well as maintain the oh-so-valuable customer rapport. We deal with the same buyers day in and day out, and it is very important in our industry that we build the rapport and trust that is necessary for continually successful sales presentations.

"As you can see, a sales career offers an opportunity to be competitive and can be an exciting and challenging career. I personally have found sales to be rewarding, an excellent opportunity for growth within the company. Sales provides the opportunity to be challenged on a daily basis. These are things that are not found in all career avenues."

Joe Gandolfo has been reported to have sold more life insurance than any other person in the world. His sales average has been over $800 million each year. In 1975 he sold an incredible $1 billion worth of insurance policies.

Joe's philosophy of selling is that "selling is 98 percent understanding human beings and 2 percent product knowledge." Do not let that statement mislead you, for Joe holds the Charter Life Underwriter (CLU) designation as a member of the American College of Life Underwriters. He is extremely knowledgeable about insurance, tax shelters, and pension plans. In fact, he spends several hours a day studying recent changes on pensions and taxation. *"But,"* Joe says, *"I still maintain that it's not product knowledge but understanding of human beings that makes a salesman effective."*[1]

Joe Gandolfo's philosophy toward selling is shared by all successful salespeople, such as Jim Mobley. In order to sell, you need to understand people's needs and behavior. Corporations spend millions of dollars each year training their salespeople how to determine a prospect's buying needs, what factors influence these needs, and how to convert this information into the development of a sales presentation.

Part II of this book examines major areas of selling knowledge that salespeople should possess in order to develop a successful sales presentation. This chapter examines why and how an individual buys.

There are numerous influences on why people buy one product rather than another. We will discuss these reasons and apply them to the various steps in the customer's buying process. This chapter presents a number of selling techniques that will later aid you with your sales presentation.

Why People Buy—The Black Box Approach

The question of why people buy has interested salespeople for many years. Salespeople know that some customers buy their product after the presentation, yet wonder what thought process resulted in the decision to buy or not to buy. Prospective buyers are usually exposed to various types of sales presentations. In some manner a person internalizes or considers this information and then makes a buying decision. This process of internalization is referred to as a **black box** because we cannot see into the buyer's mind—meaning that the salesperson can apply the stimuli (a sales presentation) and observe the behavior of the prospect, but obviously cannot witness the prospect's actual decision-making process.

The classic model of buyer behavior shown in Figure 21 is called a **stimulus-response** model. A stimulus (sales presentation) is applied resulting in a response (purchase decision).[2] This model assumes that prospects will respond in some predictable manner to the sales presentation. Unfortunately, it does not tell us why they buy the product or not. This information is concealed in the black box.

Salespeople seek to understand as much as they can about the mental processes that yield the prospects' responses. We do know:

- That people buy for both practical (rational) and psychological (emotional) reasons.

- Methods salespeople can use to aid themselves in determining the prospects' thoughts during the sales presentations.

- Many of the factors buyers consider in making a purchase decision.

This chapter introduces you to these three important topics. Each topic emphasizes the salesperson's need to understand people's behavior.

Figure 2-1
Stimulus-Response Model of Buyer Behavior

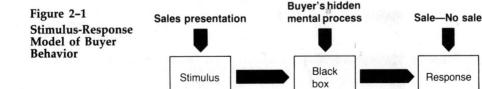

Sales presentation	Buyer's hidden mental process	Sale—No sale
Stimulus	Black box	Response

Psychological Influences on Buying _____

Since personal selling requires an understanding of human behavior, each salesperson must be concerned with a prospective customer's motivations, perceptions, learning, attitudes, and personality. Further, the salesperson should know how each type of behavior might influence a customer's purchase decision.

Motivation to Buy Must Be There

Human beings are motivated by needs and wants. These needs and wants build up inside, causing people to desire to buy a product—a new car or a new duplicating machine. People's **needs** result from a *lack of something desirable*. **Wants** are *needs learned by the person*. For example, people need transportation, but some want a Cadillac, while others prefer a Ford Mustang.

This example illustrates that both practical or rational reasons (the need for transportation) and emotional or psychological reasons (the desire for the prestige of owning a Cadillac) influence the buying decision. Different individuals have different reasons for wanting to buy. The salesperson must determine a prospect's needs and then match the product's benefits to the particular needs and wants of that prospect.

Maslow's Need Hierarchy Provides Clues

Years ago, psychologist Abraham H. Maslow developed a widely accepted categorization of human needs that he referred to as his **need hierarchy.** Maslow based his hierarchy of needs on several major assumptions. First, all individuals have in common certain basic needs that are the origins of their motivation. Second, these needs are hierarchical, in that one level of need satisfaction must be met before an individual progresses to the next level. Third, an unsatisfied need serves as a motivator. Fourth, once a need has been satisfied, it no longer acts as a motivator. Maslow proposed five basic levels of needs and defined them as:

Level 1 *Physiological needs* are necessary to maintain health and normal well-being, including food, drink, clothing, and shelter. Sales example: Newlyweds contact a realtor about buying their first home.

Level 2 *Safety needs* are desires for factors that give a safe and secure environment and freedom from danger, such as health and home insurance or deadbolt locks for the doors of one's house. Sales example: An elderly person enters a retail store asking about a security system for a house.

Level 3 *Social needs* include a feeling of belonging, friendship, love, and acceptance from others. Sales example: A person wants to join a tennis club.

Level 4 *Ego needs* are truly individual needs including self-esteem, personal reputation, and status. Fulfillment of esteem needs gives the individual a feeling of personal worth and self-confidence. Sales example: A new college graduate goes to buy a new sports car.

Level 5 *Self-actualization* needs relate to the desire to attain one's full potential in life and work.[3] Sales example: A person wanting to open a business goes to a bank to discuss a commercial loan.

Maslow's research examined an individual's personal needs. These needs can influence a person's buying decision and provide clues as to why someone would buy. As a salesperson, you should recognize that people have needs and that unmet needs will motivate them to buy your product. Certainly it is sometimes difficult to determine the particular type of need people expect to fulfill by purchasing a product. However, we do know that most individuals are concerned about their economic need.

Economic Needs: The Most Bang for the Buck

Economic needs are the buyer's need to purchase the most satisfying product for the money. Economic needs include not only price, but also quality (performance, dependability, durability), convenience of buying, and service. Some people's purchases are based primarily on economic need. However, most people consider the economic implications of all of their purchases along with other reasons for buying.

Many salespeople mistakenly assume that people base their buying decision solely on price. This is not always correct. A higher product price relative to competing goods can often be offset by such factors as service, quality, better performance, friendliness of the salesperson, or convenience of purchase.

Whatever a person's need might be, it is important for a salesperson to uncover it. Once you determine the individual's need, you are better prepared to develop your sales presentation in a manner relating your product's benefits to that particular need. This is not always easy to do, since people themselves may not be fully aware of their needs.

Awareness of Needs: Some Are Unsure

You have seen that people purchase products to satisfy various needs. Often, however, these needs are developed over such a long period of time that they may not be fully conscious of their reasons for buying or not buying a product. The buying decision can be complicated by their level of awareness of their needs. Three degrees or levels of need awareness have been identified—conscious, preconscious, and unconscious.[4]

At the first level, the **conscious level,** buyers are fully aware of their needs. These are the easiest people to sell to because they know what products they want and are willing to talk about their needs. A customer might say to the salesperson, "I'd like to buy a new car, and I want a Cadillac loaded with accessories. What can you show me?"

At the second level, the **preconscious level,** buyers may not be fully aware of their needs. Needs may not be fully developed in the conscious mind. They know what general type of product they want, but may not wish to discuss it with you fully. For example, a buyer may want to buy a certain product because of a strong ego need, yet be hesitant about telling you so. If you don't make a sale, and ask why, this buyer may present false reasons (such as saying your price is too high), rather than revealing the real motivation. Falsification is much easier than stating the true reasons for not buying your product, thus getting into a long conversation with you, arguing with you, or telling you that your product is unsatisfactory. You must avoid this brush-off and determine a buyer's real needs first and then relate your product's benefits to these needs.

At the third level, the **unconscious level,** people do not know why they buy a product, only that they do buy. When people say, "I really don't know what I want to buy," it may be true. Their buying motives might have been developed in early childhood and may have been repressed. In this case, the salesperson needs to determine which needs are influential. Often this can be accomplished by skillful questioning to draw out prospective buyers' unconscious needs. An awareness of the types of needs that buyers may have will allow you to present your product as a vehicle for the satisfaction of those needs. Several methods of presenting a product's benefits are available.

A *FAB*ulous Approach to Buyer Need Satisfaction

Possibly the most powerful selling technique used by successful sales-people today is **benefit selling.** In benefit selling the salesperson relates a product's benefits to the customer's needs, using the product's features and advantages as support. This technique is often referred to as the *FAB* **selling technique** (*F*eature, *A*dvantage, and *B*enefit). These key terms are defined as follows:

- A product **feature** is any *physical characteristic* of a product.

- A product **advantage** is the *performance characteristic* of a product that describes how it can be used or will help the buyer.

- A product **benefit** is a favorable *result* the buyer receives from the product because of a particular feature or advantage that has the ability to satisfy a buyer's need.

Selling Elephants And Ponies

Parable of the trip to the zoo: At the elephant cage, your daughter asks you about elephants. You tell her about their size, their tough hides, their strength, their appetites, their trunks and tusks, how they live for a hundred years, how they go away to die, how they never forget. She listens attentively and is very impressed.

At the pony pen, she asks about ponies. You're not as well-informed here, but you tell her what you know—how friendly they are, how they give rides and pull carts, how they eat sugar from your hand, how they make dandy pets.

The child now has a lot more information about elephants than she does about ponies, but **which one will she want to own?**

Moral: In selling, it's important to provide as much factual information as possible, but in the long run your job is to make the buyer want to own what you're selling.

The Product's Features: So What?

All products have features or characteristics. The following are examples:

size	terms	packaging
color	quantity	flavor
taste	price	service
quality	shape	uses
delivery	ingredients	technology

Descriptions of a product's features answer the question, "What is it?" Typically, when used by themselves in the sales presentation, features have little persuasive power since buyers are interested in specific benefits rather than features.

When discussing a product's features *alone*, imagine the customer is thinking, "So what? So your product has this shape or quality; how does it perform and how will it benefit me?" This situation warrants discussion of the product's advantages as they relate directly to the buyer's needs.

The Product's Advantages: Prove It!

Once a product feature is presented to the customer, the salesperson normally begins to discuss the advantages provided by that product's physical characteristics. This is much better than discussing only its features. Chances of making a sale are increased by describing the product's advantages, how a product can be used, or how it will help the buyer. Examples of product advantages follow:

> It is the fastest-selling soap on the market.
>
> You can store more information and retrieve it more rapidly with our computer.
>
> This machine will copy on both sides of the page instead of only one.

How does the prospective customer know that your claims for a product are true? Imagine a prospect thinking, "Prove it!" You have to be prepared to substantiate any claims you make.

Companies typically train their salespeople thoroughly on the product's physical and performance characteristics. A salesperson may have excellent knowledge of the product, yet be unable to describe it in terms that allow the prospect to visualize the benefits of purchasing it. This is because many salespeople present only a product's features and advantages, leaving the buyer to imagine its benefits.

While your chances of making a sale increase when you discuss both the features and the advantages of your product, you must learn how to stress product benefits that are important to the prospect in your presentation. Once you have mastered this selling technique, your sales will increase.

The Product's Benefits: Sell It

People are interested in what the product will do for them. Benefit selling appeals to the customer's personal motives by answering the question, "What's in it for me?" In your presentation you should stress how the prospect will benefit from the purchase rather than the features and advantages of your product.

To illustrate this idea of buying benefits instead of only features or advantages, consider four items: (1) a diamond ring, (2) camera film, (3) STP motor oil, and (4) movie tickets. Do people buy these products or services for their features or advantages? No, people buy the product's benefits such as:

Two-carat diamond ring—image of success, investment, or to please spouse.

Camera film—memories of places, friends, and family.

STP motor oil—engine protection, car investment, or peace of mind.

Movie tickets—entertainment, escape from reality, or relaxation.

As you can see, people are buying benefits, not a product's features or advantages. These benefits can be both practical, such as an investment, and psychological, such as an image of success. The salesperson needs to consider benefits to answer the prospect's question, "What's in it for me?"

Example: Vacuum cleaner salesperson to householder: "This vacuum cleaner's high speed motor (feature) works twice as fast (advantage) with less effort (advantage), saving you 15 to 30 minutes in cleaning time (benefit) and the aches and pains of pushing a heavy machine (benefit)."

Notice that the benefit specifically states favorable results of buying the vacuum cleaner, answering the buyer's question, "What's in it for *me*?" You can see the benefits are specific statements, not generalizations. Instead of just saying, "This vacuum cleaner will save you time," you also say, "You will save 15 to 30 minutes."

Notice that a benefit can result in a further benefit to the prospect. For example, by saving cleaning time (a benefit) you reduce the aches and pains of pushing a heavier machine (a benefit of a benefit). The following are examples of product benefits.

Time savings.

Increased sales.

Cost reductions.

More customers drawn into retail store.

Elimination of out-of-stock merchandise.

Greater profit.

Not only are benefits important, but it also is necessary to plan the order in which you introduce product benefits during your presentation, along with its features and advantages.

Order Can Be Important

Some salespeople prefer to state the benefit first and then state that the feature or advantage makes that benefit possible, such as, "The king-size Tide will bring you *additional profits* (benefits) because it is the *fastest selling size* (advantage)." In this example, the advantage supports the statement of derived customer benefits.

While stating the benefit first is the preferable method, you do not always have to discuss the three parts of the FAB formula in any particular order.

Example: Air conditioning salesperson to customer: "This air conditioner has a high energy efficiency rating (feature) *that will save you 10 percent on your energy costs* (benefit) because it uses less electricity (advantage)."

Example: Sporting goods salesperson to customer: "With this ball, you'll get an extra 10 to 20 yards on your drives (advantage) *helping to reduce your score* (benefit) because of its new solid core (feature)."

Example: Salesperson to buyer of grocery store health and beauty aids: "*You can increase your store traffic by 10 to 20 percent* (benefit) and *build your sales volume by at least 5 percent* (benefit) by advertising and reducing the price (feature) of Prell's economy size in your next Wednesday ad."

New salespeople are frequently not accustomed to using feature, advantage, and benefit phrases. To aid in making their use a regular part of your sales conversation, a standardized *FAB sequence* can be used as follows:

The product...

The . . (feature) . . . means you . . . (advantage) . . . the real benefit to you being . . . (benefit). . . .

This FAB sequence allows you to easily remember to state the product's benefit in a natural, conversational manner. For example, "*The* new solid core center of the Gunshot Golf Ball *means you* will have an extra 10 to 20 yards on your drives, *with the real benefit to you being* a lower score." You can substitute virtually any features, advantages, and benefits between these transition phrases to develop FAB sequences. Several sequences can be used one after another to emphasize your product's benefits.

Figure 2–2 presents five examples of features, advantages, and benefits of products. The first column lists features or product characteristics such as size, shape, performance and maintenance data. The second column shows advantages that arise from respective features. These are the performance characteristics, or what the product will do. The third column contains benefits to the customer of these features and advantages. For each major feature of your product you should develop the resulting advantage and benefit and incorporate these into your sales presentation, as will be discussed more fully in Chapter 9.

[Handwritten marginal notes:]

the product has

F - is
A - do
B - WIIFM

eg. this new receiver has a 1200 watt transformer (F) that gives excellent reproduction of sound (A) which will give you maximum enjoyment of your music.

what it is   *what it will do.*   *what are the benefits.*

	Features	Advantages	Benefits
Figure 2–2			
Examples of Features, Advantages, and Benefits	1. Nationally advertised consumer product	Will sell more product	Will make you high profit
	2. Air conditioner with high energy rating efficiency	Uses less electricity	Saves 10 percent energy costs
	3. Product made of stainless steel	Will not rust	Reduces your replacement costs
	4. Supermarket computer system with the IBM 3651 Store Controller	Can store more information and retrieve it rapidly by supervising up to 24 grocery check-out scanners and terminals and look up prices on up to 22,000 items	Provides greater accuracy, register balancing, store ordering, inventory management
	5. Five percent interest on money in bank checking NOW account	Earns interest that would not normally be received	Gives you one extra bag of groceries each month

Why should you emphasize benefits? There are two reasons. First, they fulfill a person's needs or solve a problem. That is what buyers want to know about. Second, your sales will increase. Stressing benefits in your presentation, rather than features or advantages, will bring you success. See Figure 2–3.

Why Do Producers Buy?

The **industrial market,** sometimes called the producer market, is composed of individuals and organizations that purchase products and services to be used in the production of other goods or services, which in turn are used in their own business. This includes manufacturers, government customers, and institutional customers. Government customers include city, county, state, and federal agencies. The United States federal government is the largest purchaser of products and services in the world. Institutional customers include public schools, universities, and hospitals.[5]

Buyers in the producer market seek to buy for many reasons. Some of the more common reasons usually evolve from some aspect of the cost and quality of the product. Specific primary buying needs or motives include the following:

- Increasing profits.
- Increasing sales.

Figure 2–3
Discuss Benefits to
Fulfill People's Needs
and to Increase Sales

Industrial salespeople, as this Wallace salesman, work closely with customers to design products and systems that fit their needs. In the health care industry, Wallace salespeople service several departments in a hospital, including selling to physicians in this clinical laboratory.

Consumer goods salespeople, like Todd Kephart and Becky Roy of General Mills, stress that a display of their nationally advertised product will result in increased sales and higher profits for this Kroger store.

- Producing a quality product.
- Improving the operation's efficiency (resulting in cost reductions).
- Helpfulness of the salesperson.
- Service.
- Payment.
- Trade-in allowances.
- Delivery.
- Buying a product at the lowest price.

As a salesperson, you should determine each buyer's important buying needs if you hope to be successful. You can then develop a sales presentation emphasizing your product's features, advantages, and benefits, and how they can fulfill those needs. One of the best and most often used methods of presenting your product's benefits to the buyer is value analysis.

Value Analysis: A Powerful Selling Tool

Industrial salespeople often include a value analysis in their sales presentation. A **value analysis** determines the best product for the money. It recognizes that a high-priced product may sometimes be a better value than a lower-priced product. Many firms routinely review a value analysis before they decide whether or not to purchase a product.

The value analysis evaluates the product in terms of the buying company's specific needs. It addresses such questions as these:

> How do your product's features, advantages, and benefits compare to the product currently being used?

> Can your product do the same job as your buyer's present product at a lower price?

> Does the buyer's current equipment perform better than is required? (Is equipment too good for present needs?)

> On the other hand, will a higher-priced, better-performing product be more economical in the long run?

As you can see from the examples in this chapter, you are often required to analyze the buyer's present operation carefully before suggesting how your product might improve efficiency, enhance the quality or quantity of the product produced, or save money.

In discussing the presentation of a value analysis to a buyer, Patrick Kamlowsky, who sells drilling bits for oil and gas wells, said:

It's not as simple as it may appear to make a recommendation and have the oil company adhere to it. You must be thorough in the presentation and present the facts in an objective manner. After all, their money is at stake. The presentation must be logical and based on those facts which are known; it must be made with as little speculation as possible.

What is difficult is presenting a recommendation to one who has spent 30 or more years in the oil field and has drilled all over the world. I am confronted with the challenge of explaining to this man that the methods which he has employed for years may not be the best application where he is currently drilling. The presentation of the recommendation must therefore be thorough and to the point. When talking to him, I do not imply that his method is outdated or wrong, but that I believe I can help him improve his method. To be successful, I must establish two things very quickly—his respect and my credibility. Showing him my proposal and supporting evidence, and permitting him the time to evaluate it are vital. I don't wish to come on to him too strong, just show him that I genuinely want to help him.[6]

There are numerous types of value analyses that a salesperson can develop for a prospective buyer. Three types frequently used are (1) product cost versus true value, (2) unit cost, and (3) return on investment.

Compare Product Costs to True Value. All buyers want to know about costs. The value analysis you develop for a customer should present cost in a simple, straightforward manner. A product's costs are always relative to something else; thus cost must be judged in terms of *value* and results. The base cost of your product should never be the determining factor of the sale. Buying a product solely on the basis of cost could cause a customer to lose money.

Costs should never be discussed until you have the opportunity to compare them to the *value* of a product. In this manner, the customer is able to intelligently compare the true worth of the proposed investment in your product to its true monetary cost. In effect, a good purchase involves more than initial cost. It represents an investment, and you must demonstrate that what you sell is a good investment.

Table 2–1 provides an example of how a salesperson might compare the cost of a copier (product X) with that of a competitive copier. The difference between the purchase prices of the two copiers is $305. Product X saves $200 on monthly copy costs, assuming the buyer's firm

Table 2–1

Example of Cost versus Value of a Small Copier

	Product C	Product X
Initial cost	$2,695	$3,000
Type of paper	Treated paper	Plain paper
Copy speed	12 copies per minute	15 copies per minute
Warm up time	Instant	Instant
Cost of each copy	3¢ a copy	1¢ a copy
Monthly cost (assuming 10,000 copies)	$300	$100

Conclusion: The difference in the purchase price of the two copiers is $305 ($3,000 − $2,695). Product X saves $200 on monthly copy costs. The savings on monthly copy costs pays for the higher priced product X in one and one-half months. In 15 months, savings on the monthly copy costs will equal the purchase price of product X.

Product demonstrations, when appropriate, can be magnificent sales aids.

Some salespeople become truly adept. They get to know the product inside out, and they zip through a demonstration in a wondrous way. Buyers are left speechless. A good way to sell—but not the best!

Better? Get the prospect involved in your demonstration. Describe what you're going to do, what the result will be. If there's a lever to be pulled, a button to be pressed, or a switch to be turned, let the **prospect** do it. Give him an active role in the demonstration's success.

Don't dazzle him with hard-to-understand technology. Translate. Simplify. Make him your partner, and see how quickly he stops being the audience and starts becoming a participant in your sales call.

Getting The Prospect To Participate

Speaking of Selling
© 1980, Sales Builders Division of S&MM

makes 10,000 copies a month. The buyer receives a savings of two cents per copy. This savings will make up the difference in the initial purchase price in only six weeks. In 15 months, savings on the monthly copy costs will equal the purchase price of product X. Therefore, product X is less expensive in the long run.

The copier example helps to illustrate how you can demonstrate to your buyer that your product is a better value than one would think from looking only at its purchase price. Another value analysis technique is to further break down a product's price to its **unit cost.**

Unit Costs Break Price Down.   One method of presenting a product's true value to a buyer is to break the product's total costs into several smaller units. Assume you are selling a computer system that costs $1,000 per month and processes 50,000 transactions each month. The cost per transaction is only 2 cents. Figures 2–4 and 2–5 present six additional examples of how value analysis reduces costs.[7]

Return on Investment Is Listened To. **Return on investment** refers to an additional sum of money expected from an investment over and above the original investment. Buyers are very interested in knowing the percentage return on their initial investment. Since the purchase of many industrial products is an investment in that it produces measurable results, you as the salesperson can talk in terms of the percentage return that can be earned by purchasing your product.

Again, assume you are selling computer equipment requiring a $10,000 per month investment. Benefits to the buyer are measured in hours of work saved by employees, plus the resulting salary saving. You first have the buyer agree on an hourly rate, which includes fringe benefit cost; let's say salaries average $5 an hour for employees. The hours saved are then multiplied by this hourly rate to obtain the return on investment. If hours saved amounted to 2,800 per month, this would amount to a savings of $14,000 per month (2,800 hours × $5 hourly rate). You could now develop a table to show the potential return on investment.

Value of hours saved	$14,000 per month
Cost of equipment	− 10,000 per month
Profit	4,000 per month
Return on investment ($14,000 ÷ $10,000)	140 percent

Subtracting the $10,000 cost per month from the return of $14,000 per month provides a $4,000 a month profit or a 140 percent return on investment. This can be taken one step further by considering return on investment after taxes, calculated:

$$\frac{\$14,000 \; (1 \; - \; \text{Tax rate})}{\$10,000}.$$

This return on investment presents the buyer with a logical reason to buy. You should remember to let the customer make the cost esti-

Figure 2–4
How Value Analysis Reduces Costs

Weights mounted on a rotor ring were curved to match the ring curve. Did it need this feature? No. Using a straight piece, the cost dropped from 40 cents to 4 cents.

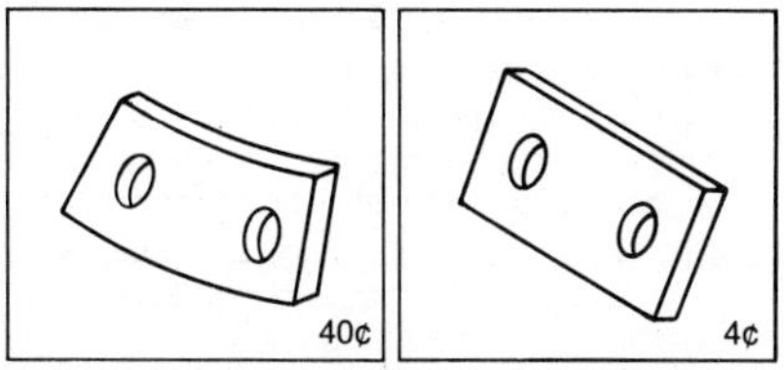

Field coil supports were machined from stock, but the original design blended nicely into a casting operation. The change resulted in lowering the cost from $1.72 to 36 cents each.

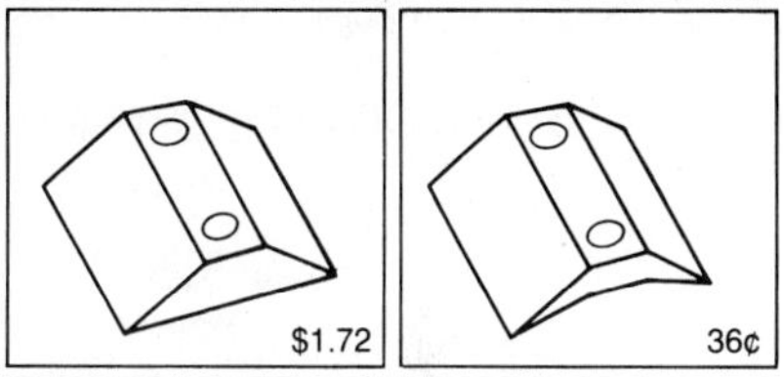

This insulating washer was made from laminated phenolic resin and fiber. Machined from individual pieces of material, it cost $1.23. A supplier with specialty equipment now fly-cuts the parts, nesting them on full sheets, at 24 cents each.

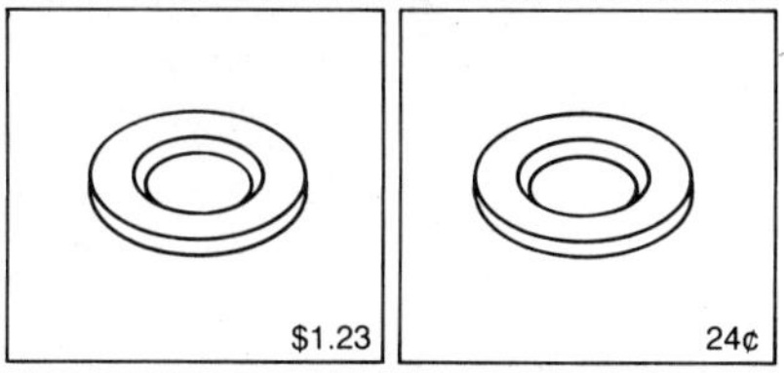

Standard nipple and elbow required special machining to fit a totally enclosed motor. Casting a special street "L" with a lug eliminated machining and a special assembly jig. The cost dropped from 63 cents to 38 cents.

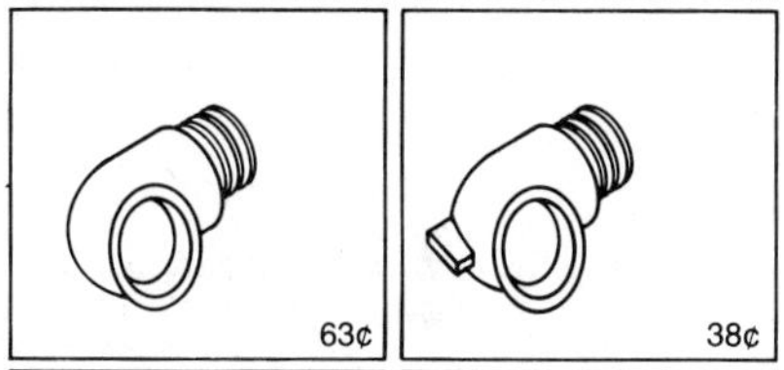

An insulator costing $4.56 was originally porcelain, leaded extra heavy. Now molded from polyester and glass, it is lighter and virtually indestructible. New cost: $3.25.

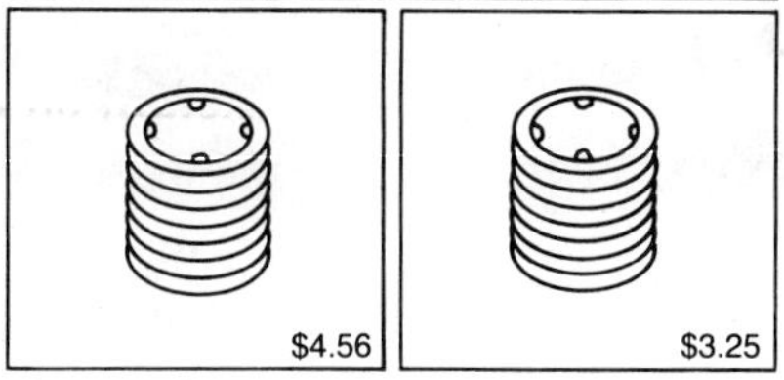

mates. The buyer must agree with the figures used for this to be an effective method of demonstrating the real value of buying your product.

Given that people make a buying decision based on whether they believe a product's benefits will satisfy their needs, how can you uncover a buyer's needs?

Figure 2–5
A Value-Analyzed Assembly for Directing Steel Cable through an Angle Top

1. Left- and right-hand coupling was eliminated.
2. Cover was changed from brass to plastic.
3. Special tapping operation was eliminated by using only one screw captive to cover. Tapped hole was made concentric with body recess.
4. Pulley was made as screw machine piece rather than a machined casting and made captive to body to simplify field installation.
5. Specialty suppliers with high-speed equipment were used.
6. Cost of unit was reduced 60 percent.

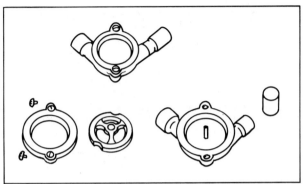

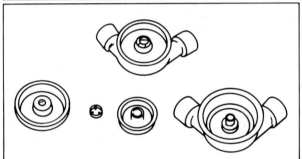

How to Determine Important
Buying Needs—A Key of Success

Your initial task when first meeting the customer is to differentiate between important buying needs and those of lesser or no importance. Figure 2–6 illustrates the concept that buyers have both important needs and needs that are not major reasons for buying a product (relatively unimportant buying needs).

You should determine buyers' important needs and concentrate on emphasizing product benefits that will satisfy these needs. Benefits that would satisfy buyers' unimportant needs should be deemphasized in the sales presentation. If, for example, buyers say that price is important, but you determine that they can afford your product and are also interested in purchasing a stylish, good-quality product, then emphasize the style and quality of your product.

Elmer Wheeler, a famous sales speaker, said, "Sell the sizzle, not the steak!" Wheeler is saying that people buy for reasons other than

Figure 2–6
Match Buyer's Needs to Product's Benefits and Emphasize in Sales Presentation

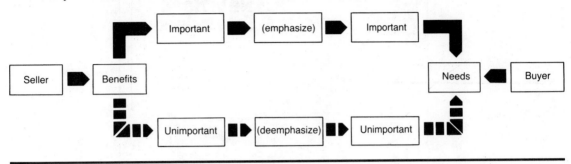

what the product will actually do or its price. They have both practical (rational) and psychological (emotional) reasons for buying. Customers may not buy the product to solve the rational need that the salesperson perceives to be important. They may buy to satisfy an emotional need not so easily recognized. It is important to understand this sales concept and to learn to determine the buyer's important buying needs. The following is a list of some of the most common psychological buying needs:

Fear.	Love of family.
Vanity (keep up with the Joneses).	Personal pleasure.
	Desire to succeed.
Desire for gain or prevention of loss.	Comfort or luxury.
	Self-preservation.
Security.	

It is up to you to determine which buying needs are most important to the customer. How can you do this? Several methods are frequently used to uncover important needs. These methods create the acronym L-O-C-A-T-E.[8]

Listen:	Prospects may drop leading remarks like, "I wish I had a television like this one."
Observe:	Look at prospects; study their surroundings. Experienced salespeople can determine a great deal about people by observing such things as the way they dress or where they live and work.
Combination:	A skillful salesperson may talk to others, listen to a prospect, probe with questions, make careful observations, and empathize—all in an effort to uncover the prospect's needs.
Ask questions:	Questions can often bring out needs that the prospect would not reveal or does not know exist. The salesperson asks, "Is a quiet ceiling fan important to you?" "Yes, it is," says the buyer. "If I could provide you with the quietest ceiling fan on the market, would you be interested?"

A Sale In Need Is A Sale Indeed

Every sale stems from a need. Need is a dissatisfaction on the buyer's part, a feeling of inadequacy or frustration or restlessness, an unsolved problem, a thought that things could be better.

Although some buyers are strongly aware of their own needs, others are only vaguely aware that a need even exists. The successful salesperson is the one who can not only fill the need of the first type, but can develop a need, create an awareness, in the mind of the second.

How can you know the needs of the buyer if he himself doesn't? Sometimes you can't. But turn it around. What are your product's benefits? Every product has a benefit. And every benefit fills a need. Determine that need. Then convince the buyer he has it.

Talk to others: Ask others about a prospect's needs. For instance, ask an office manager's secretary about the manager's satisfaction with a copy machine.

Empathize: Look at the situation from the customer's point of view.

Once the major buying need is determined, you are ready to relate the person's needs to your product's benefits. Like the television camera that transmits images to the television receiver, buyers picture desired products in their minds. Before the picture is focused clearly, buyers often need to be "turned on and tuned in." Once you find their real reasons for wanting to buy a particular type of product, or identify major problems that they want to solve, you have uncovered the key to selling to them.

Uncovering these important buying needs is like pushing a button that turns on a machine. You have just pushed the customer's hot button. You have awakened a need, and customers realize that you understand their problems. *Basically, this is what selling is all about—*

determining needs and skillfully relating your product's benefits to show how its purchase will fulfill customers' needs.

This is not always an easy task. As we have seen, people have a multitude of different needs and may not truly understand or see their unconscious needs or problems. In this situation, your challenge is to convert customers' apparently unconscious needs into recognized and understood needs. Several of the later chapters in this book are devoted to selling techniques aimed at uncovering or smoking out buyer needs. Getting buyers to realize their needs enables them to focus on your sales presentation to determine if your product will meet these needs. Once buyers experience a need, their perceptions of your product become important.

Your Buyer's Perception

Why would two people have the same need but buy different products? Likewise, why might the same individual at different times view your product in diverse ways? The answers to both of these questions involve how the person perceives your product.

Perception is the process by which a person selects, organizes, and interprets information. The buyer receives the salesperson's product information through the senses: sight, hearing, touch, taste, and smell. These senses act as filtering devices through which information must pass before it can be used.

As the definition indicates, perception has three components. Each plays a part in determining buyers' responses to you and to your sales presentation. Buyers often receive large amounts of information in a short period of time, and typically they perceive and use only a small amount of it. Some information is ignored or quickly forgotten because of the difficulty of retaining large amounts of information. This process is known as **selective exposure,** because only a portion of the information an individual is exposed to is selected to be organized, interpreted, and allowed to be exposed to our awareness.

Why does some information reach a buyer's consciousness while other information does not? First, the salesperson may not present the information in a manner that assures its proper reception. For example, there may be too much information given at one time. This causes confusion, and the buyer tunes you out. In some cases, information may be haphazardly presented, causing the buyer to receive it in an unorganized manner.

A sales presentation that appeals to the buyer's five senses helps to penetrate perceptual barriers. It also enhances understanding and reception of the information as you present it. Selling techniques such as asking questions, using visual aids, and demonstrating a product can force buyers to participate in the presentation. This helps you determine if they understand your information.

Second, buyers will tend to allow information to reach consciousness if it relates to needs they recognize and wish to fulfill. If, for example, someone is giving you reasons for purchasing life insurance, and you do not perceive a need for it, there is a good chance that your mind will allow very little of this information to be perceived. However, if you need life insurance, chances are you will listen carefully to the salesperson. If you are uncertain about something, you will ask questions to increase your understanding.

A buyer's perceptual process also may result in **selective distortion,** or the altering of information. It frequently occurs when information is received that is inconsistent with a person's beliefs and attitudes. When buyers listen to a sales presentation on a product that they perceive to be of low quality, they may mentally alter the information to coincide with present beliefs and attitudes, thereby reinforcing themselves. Should buyers believe that the product is of high quality, even when it is not, they may change any negative information about the product into positive information. This distortion can substantially lessen the intended *effect* of a salesperson attempting to compare a product to the product currently used by the individual.

Selective retention also can influence perception. Here buyers may remember only information that supports their attitudes and beliefs, forgetting whatever does not. After a salesperson leaves, buyers may forget the product's advantages stressed by the salesperson because they are not consistent with their beliefs and attitudes.

These perceptions help explain why a buyer may or may not buy. The buyer's perceptional process acts as a filter by determining what part of the sales message is heard, how it is interpreted, and what product information is retained. Therefore, two different sales messages given by two different salespeople, even though they concern very similar products, can be received differently. A buyer can tune out one of the sales presentations and tune in the other, and purchase the perceived product.

While you cannot control a buyer's perceptions, you can often influence and change them. To be successful, you must understand that perceptual barriers can arise during your presentation. You must learn to recognize when they occur and be able to overcome them.

Buyer Perceptions, Attitudes, and Beliefs Are Learned

You make a sales presentation concerning your product's features, advantages, and benefits. Your goal is to provide information that makes your buyer knowledgeable enough to make an educated purchase decision. However, a person's perceptual process may prevent your information from being fully utilized by the buyer. Understanding how people develop their perceptions can help you be more successful in selling.

Perceptions are learned. People develop their perceptions through experience. This is why **learning** is defined as acquiring knowledge or a behavior based on past experiences.

Successful salespeople must help buyers learn about them and their products. If buyers have learned to trust you, they will listen and have faith in what you say, therefore increasing your chance of making sales. If your products perform as you claim they will, buyers will repurchase them more readily. If your presentation provides the information necessary for making a decision, your probability of making the sale increases. Product knowledge influences the buyer's attitude and beliefs about your product.

A person's **attitudes** are learned predispositions toward something. These feelings can be favorable or unfavorable. If a person is neutral toward the product or has no knowledge of the product, no attitude is said to exist. A buyer's attitude is shaped by past and present experience.

Creating a positive attitude is important, but it alone will not result in your making the sale. To sell to someone, you also must convert a buyer's belief into a positive attitude. A **belief** is a state of mind in which trust or confidence is placed in something or someone. The buyer must believe your product will fulfill a need or solve a problem. A favorable attitude toward one product rather than another comes from a belief that one of them is better.

Also, a buyer must believe you are the best person from whom to buy. If you are not trusted as the best source, people will not buy from you. Assume, for example, that someone decides to buy a 19-inch, portable, XL-100 RCA color television. Three RCA dealers are in the trading area, and each dealer offers to sell an XL-100 at approximately the same price. Chances are the purchaser will buy from the salesperson believed to be the best, even though there is no reason not to trust the other two dealers.

If buyers' perceptions create favorable attitudes leading them to believe that your product is best for them and that they should buy from you—you make sales. Often, however, people may not know you or your product. Your job is to provide information about your product that allows buyers to form positive attitudes and beliefs. Should their perception, attitudes, and beliefs be negative, distorted, or incorrect, you must change them. As a salesperson you spend much of your time creating or changing people's learned attitudes and beliefs about your product. This is the most difficult challenge a salesperson faces.

Example of a Buyer's Misperceptions

Assume, as an example, that a woman is shopping for a ceiling fan for her home. The three main features of the product she is interested in are price, quality, and style. While shopping around, she had seen two brands, the Hunter and the Economy brand. The information she received on these two brands has caused her to conclude that all ceiling fans are basically alike. Each brand seems to offer the same features and advantages. Because of this attitude, she has formed the belief that she should purchase a low-price fan, in this case the Economy ceiling fan. Cost is the key factor influencing this purchase decision.

She decides to stop at one more store that sells Casa Blanca fans. She asks the salesperson to see some lower-priced fans. These fans turn out to be more expensive than either the Hunter or Economy models. Noting their prices, she says to the salesperson, "That's not what I had in mind." She walks away as the salesperson says, "Thanks for coming by."

What should the salesperson have done? When the customer walked into the store, the salesperson knew her general need was for a ceiling fan. However, the customer had wrongly assumed that all brands are alike. It was the salesperson's job to first ask the customer fact-finding questions such as, "Where will you use the fan?" "What color do you have in mind?" "Is there a particular style you are interested in?" "What features are you looking for?" "What price range would you like to see?" These questions allow the salesperson to determine the customer's specific needs, attitudes, and beliefs about ceiling fans.

Learning the answers to these questions enables the salesperson to explain the benefits of the Casa Blanca fan as compared to the Hunter and Economy brands. The salesperson can show that fans have different features, advantages, and benefits, and why there are price differences among the three fans. The buyer then can make a decision as to which ceiling fan best suits her specific needs. Knowledge of a buyer's learned attitudes and beliefs can make sales; with this information a salesperson can alter the buyer's perceptions or reinforce them when presenting the benefits of his product.

The Buyer's Personality Should Be Considered _____

People's personalities can also affect buying behavior by influencing the types of products that fulfill their particular needs. **Personality** can be viewed as the individual's distinguishing character traits, attitudes, or habits. While it is difficult to know exactly how personality affects buying behavior, it is generally believed that personality does have some influence on a person's perceptions, attitudes, and beliefs and thus on buying behavior.

Self-Concept

One of the best ways to examine personality is to consider a buyer's **self-concept,** the view of the self.[9] Internal or personal self-evaluation may influence a buyer's attitude toward the products desired or not desired. Some theorists believe that people buy products that match their self-concept.

According to the self-concept theory, buyers possess four images:

1. The **real self**—people as they actually are.
2. The **self-image**—how people see themselves.
3. The **ideal self**—what people would like to be.
4. The **looking-glass self**—how people think others regard them.

As a salesperson you should attempt to understand the buyer's self-concept, for it may be the key to understanding the buyer's attitudes and beliefs. For example, if a man is apparently unsatisfied with his self-image, he might be sold through appeals to his ideal self-image. You might compliment him by saying, "Mr. Buyer, it is obvious that the people in your community think very highly of you. They know you as an ideal family man and good provider for your family [looking-glass self]. Your purchase of this life insurance policy will provide your family the security you want for them [ideal self]." This appeal is targeted at the looking-glass self and the ideal self. Success in sales is often closely linked to the salesperson's knowledge of the buyer's self-concept, rather than the buyer's real self.

Selling Based on Personality

While it is important to know a buyer's self-concept, you should also attempt to uncover any additional aspects of the prospect's personality that might influence a decision to buy so that you can further adjust your sales approach. One way to do this is through personality typing.

Personality Typing. Carl Gustav Jung (1875–1961), with Sigmund Freud, laid the basis of modern psychiatry. Jung divided human awareness into four functions: (1) feeling, (2) sensing, (3) thought, and (4) intuition.* He argued most people can be placed into one of these four groups. Each group, or personality, has certain characteristics formed by their past experiences.

Table 2–2 shows numerous guidelines you can use to identify which personality style someone possesses. You can diagnose styles by (1) identifying the key trait, (2) focusing on time orientation, (3) identifying

---

* There are numerous methods of personality typing. Each is due to the conceptual theory used by the method. Currently, personality typing is a popular sales training technique. I use Jung's classification because of his scientific reputation.

Table 2–2
Guidelines to Identify Personality Style

Guideline	Thinker	Intuitor	Feeler	Senser
How to describe this person	A direct, detail-oriented person. Likes to deal in sequence *on his/her time*. Very precise, sometimes seen as a nit-picker. Fact oriented.	A knowledgeable, future-oriented person. An innovator who likes to abstract principles from a mass of material. Active in community affairs by assisting in policy making, program development, etc.	People-oriented. Very sensitive to people's needs. An emotional person rooted in the past. Enjoys contact with people. Able to read people very well.	Action-oriented person. Deals with the world through his/her senses. Very decisive and has a high energy level.
The person's strengths	Effective communicator, deliberative, prudent, weighs alternatives, stabilizing, objective, rational, analytical, asks questions for more facts.	Original, imaginative, creative, broad-gauged, charismatic, idealistic, intellectual, tenacious, ideological, conceptual, involved.	Spontaneous, persuasive, empathetic, grasps traditional values, probing, introspective, draws out feelings of others, loyal, actions based on what has worked in the past.	Pragmatic, assertive, directional, results-oriented, technically skillful, objective—bases opinions on what he/she actually sees, perfection seeking, decisive, direct and down to earth, action-oriented.
The person's drawbacks	Verbose, indecisive, over-cautious, over-analyzes, unemotional, nondynamic, controlled and controlling, over-serious, rigid, nit-picking.	Unrealistic, "far-out," fantasy-bound, scattered, devious, out-of-touch, dogmatic, impractical, poor listener.	Impulsive, manipulative, over-personalizes, sentimental, postponing, guilt-ridden, stirs up conflict, subjective.	Impatient, doesn't see long-range, status seeking, self-involved, acts first then thinks, lacks trust in others, nit-picking, impulsive, does not delegate to others.
Time orientation	Past, Present, Future	Future	Past	Present
Environment Desk	Usually neat	Reference books, theory books, etc.	Personal plaques and momentos, family pictures.	Chaos
Room	Usually has a calculator and IBM runs, etc.	Abstract art, book cases, trend charts, etc.	Decorated warmly with pictures of scenes or people. Antiques.	Usually a mess with piles of papers, etc. Action pictures or pictures of the manufacturing plant or products on the wall.
Dress	Neat and conservative.	Mod or rumpled.	Current styles or informal.	No jackets; loose tie or functional work clothes.

the environment, and (4) listening to what people say. Imagine that four of your buyers say the following things to you:

- "I'm not interested in all of those details. What's the bottom line?"
- "How did you arrive at your projected sales figure?"
- "I don't think you see how this purchase fits in with our whole operation here."
- "I'm not sure how our people will react to this."

How would you classify their personality styles?† After calling on a buyer several times, it becomes easier to type the person's style. Then you can adjust your presentation to the style.

Adapt Your Presentation to the Buyer's Style

The major challenge faced is to adapt your personal style to best relate to people you deal with. For example, if you consider the customer (or person) that you best relate to, the one that you find it easiest to call on, the odds are that the primary style is similar to yours. The other side of the coin states that the person that is the hardest for you to call on usually has a primary style that differs from yours.

The objective is to increase your skill at recognizing the style of the people you deal with. Once the basic style of a buyer is recognized, for example, it will be possible to modify and adapt your presentation to the buyer's style to achieve the best possible results. While this method is not 100 percent foolproof, it does offer an alternative way of presenting your material if you are not succeeding with your present way. Let's examine a suggested tailored selling method based on the prospect's style preferences.

The Thinker Style. This person places high value on logic, ideas, and systematic inquiry. Completely preplan your presentation with ample facts and supporting data and be precise. Present your material in an orderly and logical manner. When closing the sale, be sure to say, "Think it over, Joe, and I'll get back to you tomorrow," whenever the order does not close on the spot.

The Intuitor Style. This person places high value on ideas, innovation, concepts, theory, and long-range thinking. The main point is to tie your presentation into the buyer's big picture or overview of this person's objectives. Strive to build the buyer's concepts and objectives into your presentation whenever possible. In presenting your material, be sure you have ample time.

In closing the sale, stress time limitations on acting. A good suggestion is to say, "I know you have a lot to do—I'll go to Sam to get the nitty-gritty handled and get this off the ground."

The Feeler Style. This person places high value on being people-oriented and sensitive to people's needs. The main point to include in your presentation is the impact on people that your idea will have. The feeler likes to small talk with you, so engage in conversation and wait for this person's cue to begin your presentation. The buyer will usually ask,

† (A) Senser, (B) Thinker, (C) Intuitor, and (D) Feeler.

"What's on your mind today?" or something similar. Use emotional terms and words, such as, "We're *excited* about this!"

In your presentation, start out with something carried over from your last call or contact. Keep the presentation on a personal note. Whenever possible, get the buyer away from the office (lunch, snack, etc.) on an informal basis, as this is how this person prefers to do business. Force the close by saying something to the effect, "OK, Joe, if there are no objections, let's set it up for next week." Even if the buyer says no, you are not dead. The key with a feeler is to push for the decision.

The Senser Style.   This person places high value on action. The key point with a senser is to be brief and to the point. Graphics, models, samples, and so forth help as the senser can visualize your presentation. With a senser, verbal communication is more effective than written communication.

In presenting, start with conclusions and results and have supporting data to use where and when needed. Suggest an action plan—"Let's move *now*,"—the buyer has to feel you know what to do.

In closing, give one best way. Have options, but do not present them unless you have to. An effective senser close is, "I know you're busy; let's set this up right now."

Each of the four styles is present, in some degree, in all of us. However, one style (the primary style), is usually dominant, and another style (the complementary style) is used as a back-up style. The primary style employed by an individual remains the same in both normal and stress situations, while the secondary style could change.

For some reason or another, some individuals do not have a primary or secondary style but have a personal style comprising all four. Dealing with this type of individual requires strong rapport to isolate this prospect's strong personal likes and dislikes.

You Can Classify Buying Situations _____

Some people may appear to make up their minds quickly and easily either to buy or not to buy. This is not always the case. The quickness and ease of deciding which product to buy typically depends on the type of buying situation. Purchasing a gallon of milk is quite different from buying an automobile. People have more difficulty in selecting, organizing, and interpreting information in purchasing an automobile. Also, their attitudes and beliefs toward the automobile may not be well formed.

True, a few people have the type of personality (and resources) that allows them to quickly purchase an expensive product like an automobile, but this is unusual. When purchasing some types of products, most people carefully compare competing brands. They talk to salespeo-

**Figure 2–7
The Three Classes of
Buying Situations**

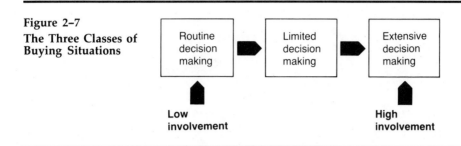

ple. As information is collected, attitudes and beliefs are formed toward each product. People must decide which product has the most desirable features, advantages, and benefits. When considering several brands, people may seek information on each. The more information collected, the greater difficulty they may have in deciding which product to buy.

Purchase decisions can usually be classified as to the difficulty involved in deciding which product to buy. The purchase decision can be viewed as a problem-solving activity falling into one of the three classifications shown in Figure 2–7. These situations are routine decision making, limited decision making, and extensive decision making.

Some Decisions Are Routine

Many products are repeatedly purchased. People are in the habit of buying a particular product. They give little thought or time to the routine purchase; they fully realize the product's benefits. These are called low-involvement goods because they involve a routine buying decision. People's attitudes and beliefs toward the product are already formed and are usually very positive. Cigarettes, cold drinks, beer, and many grocery items are often purchased through **routine decision making.**

For your customer currently making a routine purchase decision, you should reinforce the point that this is a correct buying decision. It is important for you to have the product in stock. If you do not have it, the customer may go to another supplier.

For someone not currently using your product, your challenge is to change this person's product loyalty or normal buying habits. The features, advantages, and benefits of your product should be directly compared to the buyer's preferred brand. Of course, not all purchase decisions are routine.

Some Decisions Are Limited

When buyers are unfamiliar with a particular brand of product, they seek more information in making a purchase decision. In this case, there

The Prospect Who Is Too Friendly

When you go out for a social evening, you want friends. When you make sales calls, you want customers.

Beware of the glad-handing, back-slapping, story-telling buyer who only wants to talk about the ballgame or where you bought your clothes or last night's TV shows—everything but you, your product, your sales call.

Sure he's pleasant to talk to, but that often means "difficult to sell." He's showing you pictures while you're trying to discover his buying needs. Whether he's just naturally gregarious or trying to avoid talking business with you, it may not be until you're in the parking lot that you suddenly realize, "Hey, I never gave my presentation."

Be firm with this type. Politely but resolutely bring him back to the subject at hand—**your** subject at hand.

is **limited decision making**—a moderate level of actual buyer involvement in the decision. The general qualities of goods in the product class are known to the buyer. However, buyers are not familiar with each brand's features, advantages, and benefits. For example, they may perceive that Xerox, 3M, and Canon copiers are the same in performance.

These buyers have more involvement in buying decisions in terms of shopping time, money, and potential dissatisfaction with the purchase than in the routine purchase decision. They seek information to aid them in making the correct decision. A sales presentation should be developed that provides buyers with the necessary knowledge to make brand comparisons and to increase their confidence that the purchase of your product is the correct decision. Occasionally, the purchase of some products requires prospective buyers to go one step further and apply extensive decision making.

Some Decisions Are Extensive

Buyers seeking to purchase products such as insurance, a home, or an automobile can be described as being highly involved in making the buying decision. They may be unfamiliar with a specific brand or type of a product and have difficulty in making the purchase decision. This kind of purchase requires more of an investment in time and money than does the limited decision. This situation demands **extensive decision making** and problem-solving activities.

In making extensive decisions, buyers believe that much more is at stake relative to other buying decisions. They may become frustrated during the decision-making process, especially if a large amount of information is available. They may become confused, not knowing what product features they are interested in because of unfamiliarity with the products. Buying an automobile or a life insurance policy, for example, entails potentially confusing purchase decisions.

You should determine all possible reasons why buyers are interested in a product. Then, in a simple, straightforward manner, present only enough information to allow the buyer to make a decision. At this time, product comparisons can be made, if necessary. You can also help the buyer evaluate alternative products.

In summary, it becomes your job to *provide buyers with product knowledge that allows them to develop positive beliefs that your products fulfill their needs*. Determining the type of decision process a buyer is engaged in is critical to you as a salesperson.

View Buyers as Decision Makers

Buyers, whether private consumers or industrial purchasing agents, are constantly exposed to information about various products. Manufacturers use newspaper, radio, and television advertising; direct-mail offers; and salespeople to stimulate people to buy their products. What steps do people go through in making a purchase decision?

Typically, the buying decision involves the five basic steps shown in Figure 2–8. Buyers recognize a need, collect information provided by the salesperson, evaluate that information, decide to buy, and after the purchase determine whether they are satisfied with the purchase. This sequence reveals that several things occur before and after the purchase, all of which should be considered by the salesperson.

Figure 2–8
Five-Step Model of Buying Process

| Need arousal | → | Collection of information | → | Information evaluation | → | Purchase decision | → | Postpurchase behavior |

Need Arousal

As you remember from the first part of this chapter, buyers may experience a need themselves, or the need can be triggered by the salesperson (**need arousal**). It could be psychological, social, or economic; it could be a need for safety, for self-actualization, or ego fulfillment. It is important to determine a person's needs in order to know what product information to provide. This information should relate the product's benefits to the person's needs.

Collection of Information

If buyers know which product will satisfy a need, they will buy quickly. The salesperson may need only to approach them; they already want to buy the product.

However, when buyers are faced with limited or extensive problem solving, they may want to **collect a great deal of information** about the product. They might visit several retail stores, contact several potential suppliers. They may talk with a number of salespeople about a product's price, advantage, size, and warranty before making a decision.

Information Evaluation

A person's **evaluation of product information** determines what will be purchased. After mentally processing all the information about products that will satisfy a need—and this may or may not include your product—a buyer matches this information with needs, attitudes, and beliefs, as discussed earlier, in making a decision. Only then will a **purchase decision** be made.

This evaluation process includes rating preferences on factors such as price, quality, and brand reputation. Attitudes on different products are based on either psychological or rational reasons.

At this stage, a salesperson can be very effective. Providing information that matches product features, advantages, and benefits with a buyer's needs, attitudes, and beliefs will increase the chances of a favorable evaluation of a product. So the salesperson is charged with the responsibility of uncovering the person's needs, attitudes, and beliefs early in the discussion so as to match the product with the person's needs.

One way to get such information is to determine not only needs, beliefs, and attitudes, but also the type of information a person needs before making a decision. Here are examples of questions you need to know the answers to:

- What product attributes are important in this decision—price, quality, service?
- Of these, what are *most* important?
- What are the prospect's attitudes toward your products?
- What are the prospect's attitudes toward your competitors' products?
- What level of satisfaction is expected from buying the product?

This type of questioning not only tells you about the customer's needs but also involves the customer in the presentation and may convey the idea that you are truly interested in his or her needs. This attitude towards you is in itself enough to create positive attitudes about your product.

Armed with this knowledge about the customer, the salesperson is in a better position to provide the information necessary for a decision and also to help the customer evaluate that information in favor of your product. The information should be provided simply, clearly, and straightforwardly. It should seek to correct any negative information or impressions about your product. Matching information with a customer's needs may enable you to:

- Alter the person's beliefs about your product, for example, by convincing the customer that your product is priced higher than the competition because it is a quality product.
- Alter the person's beliefs about your competitor's products.
- Change the amount of importance a person attaches to a particular product attribute, for example, by getting the customer to consider quality and service rather than price alone.
- Bring out unnoticed attributes of your product.
- Change the search for the ideal product into a more realistic pursuit, such as by substituting a $100,000 home for a $200,000 home, or showing a man whose height is six feet ten inches a mid-sized car rather than a compact.

A company has no better promotional device than having its sales force help their prospects and customers to evaluate products on the market—and not merely their own. The two-way communication between buyer and seller is exceptionally effective in providing the information needed to make the sale on the one hand and to evaluate the product on the other. Salespeople provide knowledge to aid people in their decision-making process. In many respects, salespeople can be viewed as teachers (professors, if you will) who provide helpful information.

Purchase Decision

Is the sale made, once the prospect states an intention to buy? No. You should not consider the sale final until the contract is signed, or you have the buyer's money, because there is still a chance for a change of mind. Even after a customer has selected a product, purchase intentions can be changed by four basic factors. These are:

1. The attitude of others, such as a spouse, friend, or boss. Consideration should be given to both the intensity of another person's attitude and the level of motivation the buyer has to comply with or to resist this other person's attitude.

2. The perceived risk of buying the product—will it give a return on the money?

3. Uncontrollable circumstances, such as not being able to finance the purchase of a house or to pass the physical examination for a large life insurance policy.

4. The salesperson's actions after the decision has been reached. Sometimes it is unwise to continue to talk about a product after this point; something said could change the customer's mind.

The third factor, uncontrollable circumstances, is self-explanatory. However, how can attitudes of others influence a sale? A man may want to buy a dark, conservative business suit, whereas his wife wants him to buy a sport coat and slacks. The buyer's original favorable attitude toward the business suit may have been changed by his wife. A wife's strong disapproval can quite possibly change his mind. In industrial selling, others in the buyer's firm can influence the sale.

Since buyers may not always be sure that they will be satisfied with a purchase, they may perceive a risk and may experience tension and anxiety after buying your product. Haven't we all asked ourselves, "Have I made the correct decision?" The levels of tension and anxiety people experience are related to their perceptions of and attitudes to the products they have had to choose from. Uncertainty about differences between your product and those of your competitors can create anxiety, especially if both products' benefits appear to be very similar, or if your product is more expensive yet promises better benefits. This is especially true for products involving limited or extensive decisions. Prospects might see little difference between products, or may like them all—and thus they can fairly easily change their minds several times before buying.

Finally, many sales have been lost when, after a buyer has said, "I will buy," the salesperson continues to talk. Additional information sometimes causes buyers to change their minds. It is important to finalize the sale as quickly as possible after the buyer makes a decision. Once the prospect decides, stop talking, pack up your bag, and leave.

Postpurchase

No, the decision process does *not* end with the purchase—not for the buyer at least! A product, once purchased, yields certain levels of satisfaction and dissatisfaction. **Purchase satisfaction** comes from receiving benefits expected, or greater than expected, from a product. If buyers' experiences from the use of a product exceed expectations, they are said to be satisfied; but if experiences are below expectations, the customers are said to be dissatisfied.

The buyer can experience **dissonance** after the product's purchase. Dissonance causes tension over whether the right decision was made in buying the product. Some people refer to this as buyer's remorse. Dissonance increases with the importance of the decision and the difficulty of choosing between products. Should dissonance occur, buyers may get rid of a product by returning it or by selling it to someone else. Alternatively, they may seek assurance from the salesperson or friends that the product is a good one and that they made the correct purchase decision (positively reinforcing themselves).

You can help the buyer to be satisfied with the product and lower the level of dissonance in several ways. First, if necessary, show the buyer how to use the product properly. Second, be realistic in your claims made for the product. Exaggerated claims may create dissatisfaction. Third, continually reinforce buyers' decisions by reminding them how well the product actually performs and fulfills their needs. Remember, in some situations buyers can return the product to the seller after purchase. This cancels your sale and hurts your chances of making future sales to this customer.

In summary, you should seek to sell a product that satisfies the buyer's needs. In doing so, remember that the sale is made only when the actual purchase is complete and that you should continue to reinforce the buyer's attitudes about the product at all times, even after the sale. This practice reduces the perceived risk of making a bad buy, which allows buyers to listen to and trust your sales message even though some of your proposals may be out of line with their purchase plans. It also can reduce the buyers' postpurchase dissonance. Buyers who have developed a trust in your product claims believe that you will help them properly use the product.

To Buy or Not to Buy—A Choice Decision _____

Salespeople realize that people buy a product because of a need and that needs can be complex due to the influence of perceptions, attitudes, beliefs, and personality. Furthermore, perceptions, attitudes, and beliefs may differ from one purchase situation to another. How, then, is it possible to state in simple terms why people buy one product and not another?

No, salespeople do not have to be psychologists to understand human behavior. Nor do they need to understand the material covered in the courses taken by a psychology major. Furthermore, the average salesperson cannot be expected to know all that is involved in the psychological and practical processes that a buyer goes through in making a purchase decision.

What the salesperson *does* need to understand are the various factors that can influence the buying decision—the fact that buyers actually examine various factors that can influence these decisions, that buyers actually go through various steps in making these decisions, and how to develop a sales presentation that persuades buyers to purchase the product in order to satisfy needs. To do this, the salesperson should consider the following questions before developing a sales presentation.

- What type of product is desired?
- What type of buying situation is it?
- How will the product be used?
- Who is involved in the buying decision?
- What practical factors may influence the buyer's decision?
- What psychological factors may influence the buyer's decision?
- What are the buyer's important buying needs?

Again, it seems necessary to know a great deal about a person's attitudes and beliefs to answer these questions. Can this be made simpler? Yes. Simply stated, to buy or not to buy is a choice decision. The person's choice takes one of two forms. First, a person has the choice of buying a product or not. Second, the choice can be between competing products. The question salespeople should ask themselves is, "How can I convince a person to choose my product?" The answer to this question involves five things, each of which is necessary to making the sale. People will buy under the following conditions:

1. They perceive a need or problem.
2. They desire to fulfill a need or solve a problem.
3. They decide there is a high probability that your product will fulfill their needs or solve their problems better than your competitor's products.
4. They believe they should buy from you.
5. They have the resources and authority to buy.

What do you do if you know your product can reduce your prospect's manufacturing costs, saving the firm $5,000 a year, for a cost of $4,000, and the prospect says, "No thanks, I like my present equipment"? This buyer does not perceive a need and will not buy. Suppose you make your point about reducing operating costs, but for some reason the prospect is not interested in reducing costs? Chances are, this person will not buy no matter how persuasively you present your product's benefits—because high costs are not seen as an important problem.

Furthermore, even customers who want to solve a problem, but do not like your product, are certainly not going to buy. But if you have convinced them, if they want to solve a problem, and if they perceive your product as solving this problem, the question is still: "Will these customers buy from you?" They will, if they believe you represent the best supplier. If they would rather buy from another supplier, you have lost the sale. Your job is to provide the necessary information so that customers say yes to each of these five questions.

Summary of Major Selling Issues

As a salesperson, you should be knowledgeable about factors that influence your buyer's purchase decision. This knowledge, which helps to increase the salesperson's self-confidence and the buyer's confidence in the salesperson, can be obtained through training and practice.

A firm's marketing effort involves various efforts to create exchanges to satisfy the buyer's needs and wants. Salespeople should understand the characteristics of their target markets (consumer or industrial) and how these characteristics relate to the buyer's behavior in order to better serve and sell to their customers.

The individual goes through various steps or stages in the three buying situations of routine decision making, limited problem solving, and extensive problem solving. You should uncover who is involved in the buying decision and the main factors that influence the decision. These factors include various psychological and practical buying influences.

Psychological factors include the buyer's motives, perceptions, learning, attitudes, beliefs, and personality—all of which influence the individual's needs and result in a search for information on what products to buy to satisfy them. The information is evaluated, resulting in the decision to buy or not to buy. These same two factors influence whether the buyer is satisfied or dissatisfied with the product.

Salespeople should realize that all prospects will not buy their products, at least not all of the time, due to the many factors influencing their buying decisions. You need to be able to uncover buyers' needs and provide the knowledge that allows them to develop personal attitudes toward the product that result in positive beliefs that your products fulfill their needs.

Uncovering prospects' needs is often difficult, since they may be reluctant to tell you their true needs or may not really know what and why they want to buy. You can usually feel confident that people buy for reasons such as to satisfy a need, fulfill a desire, and obtain a value. To determine these important buying needs, you can ask questions, observe prospects, listen to them, and talk to their associates about their needs.

Review and Discussion Questions

1. What three types of buying situations may the buyer be in when contacted by a salesperson? Briefly describe each type.

2. What are the psychological factors that may influence the prospect's buying decision?

3. While you do not have to be a psychologist or understand exactly how the buyer's black box works, you do need to uncover the buyer's motives for buying.
   a. What techniques can be used to uncover the buyer's motives?
   b. The prospect's intention to buy can be influenced by several things. What information does the salesperson need to obtain concerning the prospect's buying intentions before developing a sales presentation?

4. In the following statements, write down each idea that is a benefit:
   a. Counselor talking to student: "In order to improve your science grade, Susie, you must establish better study habits."
   b. Construction supervisor talking to a worker: "That job will be a great deal easier, Joe, and you won't be as tired when you go home nights, if you use that little truck over there."
   c. Father talking to his son: "You will make a lot of friends, Johnny, and be respected at school if you learn how to play the piano."
   d. Banker talking to customer: "If you open this special checking account, Ms. Brown, paying your bills will be much easier."

5. In the following statements, determine what parts of the statements are features, advantages, or benefits.
   a. Hardware sales representative to homeowner: "Blade changing is quick and easy with this saw because it has a push-button blade release."
   b. Consumer sales representative to grocery store buyer: "The king-size package of Tide will bring in additional profits because it is the fastest growing brand and most economical size."
   c. Clothing salesperson to customer: "For long wear and savings

on your clothing costs, you can't beat these slacks. All the seams are double-stitched, and the material is 100 percent Dacron."

6. Indicate which of the following statements are a feature, advantage, or benefit. Write your answer on a sheet of paper.
    a. Made of pure vinyl.
    b. Lasts twice as long as competing brands.
    c. It's quick-frozen at 30° below zero.
    d. Available in small, medium, and large sizes.
    e. New.
    f. No unpleasant aftertaste.
    g. Saves time, work, and money.
    h. Approved by Underwriters' Laboratory.
    i. Gives 20 percent more miles to the gallon.
    j. Contains XR-10.
    k. Baked fresh daily.
    l. Includes a one-year guarantee on parts and labor.
    m. Is packed 48 units or eight 6-packs to the case.
    n. Guaranteed to increase your sales by 10 percent.
    o. Adds variety to your meal planning.

7. Consider the following information:

    The DESKTOP XEROX 2300 copier is a versatile model that delivers the first copy in six seconds. It is also the lowest-priced new Xerox copier available. The 2300 is designed as a general purpose office copier and occupies less than half the top of a standard desk. The new unit copies on a full range of office materials as large as 8½ by 14 inches. A special feature is its ability to reproduce 5½ by 8½-inch billing statements from the same tray used for letter-size or legal-size paper. Selling price of the 2300 will be as low as $3,495 and rentals as low as $60 a month on a two-year contract without a copy allowance.

    What are the features, advantages, and benefits of the DESK-TOP XEROX 2300 copier? What are additional benefits of the copier? List two additional features, advantages, and benefits that a Xerox salesperson could use in presenting the new copier to a prospective buyer.

8. Several features of a car are listed below. Match each feature with its corresponding benefit(s).
    a. Low hoodline:
        (1) Better visibility.
        (2) Economy.
        (3) Quick startup.
    b. Tinted glass:
        (1) Reflects sunlight.
        (2) Reduces eye strain.

        (3) Reduces glare from sun.

    c. Rear window defroster:

        (1) Clears rear windshield, and thus reduces the danger of driving on a cold, foggy day.

        (2) Rear windshield can be de-iced or defogged automatically so you do not have to do it yourself.

        (3) Increases the cost of the car by $250.

    d. Whitewall tires:

        (1) Provide better handling and a more stable ride.

        (2) More appealing to see.

        (3) Increase the life of your tires.

9. In order to convince your customers that your product's benefits are important, you must show how your product's benefits will meet their needs. Suppose your customer says, "I need some kind of gadget that will get me out of bed in the morning." Check the statement below that best relates your product feature, the GE clock radio's snooze alarm, to this customer's need:

    a. "Ms. Jones, this GE radio has a snooze alarm that is very easy to operate. See, all you do is set this button and off it goes. . . ."

    b. "Ms. Jones, the GE radio is the newest radio on the market. It carries a one-year guarantee, and you can trade in your present radio and receive a substantial cut in the price."

    c. "Ms. Jones, since you say you have trouble getting up in the morning, you want an alarm system that will make sure you wake up. Now, GE's snooze alarm will wake you up no matter how often you shut the alarm off. You see, the alarm goes off every seven minutes until you switch off the special 'early bird' knob."

10. A salesperson says, "You expect a pencil sharpener to be durable. Our sharpener is durable because it's constructed with titanium steel bearings. Because of these bearings, our sharpener will not jam up and will last a long time."

    a. In the above example, the "titanium steel bearings" are a

        (1) Benefit.

        (2) Feature.

        (3) Need.

        (4) Advantage.

    b. "Will not jam up" is a

        (1) Benefit.

        (2) Feature.

        (3) Need.

        (4) Advantage.

    c. In the statement, "Will not jam up," the salesperson has

        (1) Converted a product feature into an advantage.

      (2) Converted benefits into a product feature.
      (3) Related a product feature to the customer's need via benefits.
      (4) Numbers (1) and (2) are correct.
      (5) Numbers (1) and (3) are correct.
  d. The statement, "Will last a long time," is a
      (1) Benefit.
      (2) Feature.
      (3) Need.
      (4) Advantage.

11. For each of the following products, determine a potential benefit based on their advantages.

Product	Feature	Advantage
Sony stereo turntable	Direct-drive turntable	More dependable, fewer moving parts
Tab	Only one calorie per 16 oz.	Will not increase your body weight when you drink it
BIC erasable ink pen	Erasable ink	Can erase mistakes
Ceiling fan	Hangs from ceiling, high efficiency	Out of the way, uses less electricity
Sheer panty hose	No dark patches	Looks like real skin
Drilling an oil well	One of our engineers for the entire job	Better service
Hefty trash bags	2-ply	Puncture proof, can overstuff it

12. As a salesperson for Procter & Gamble's soap division, you have been asked by your sales manager to determine the features, advantages, and benefits for Tide detergent and discuss the use of Tide's benefits in a sales presentation at your next sales meeting. You have determined the following four features of Tide. Listed underneath each feature are your ideas of factors that might be of interest to retail grocery buyers. For each, determine the benefit you would emphasize.
  a. Number-one-selling detergent:
      (1) Best traffic-pulling detergent.
      (2) Great brand loyalty.
      (3) High percent of market share.
  b. Four sizes:
      (1) Increases your total detergent sales.
      (2) Boxes are standard sizes.
      (3) Case cost is the same.
  c. Most extensively manufacturer-advertised detergent:
      (1) Continues to attract new customers to your store.
      (2) More customers remember this brand's advertising.

     (3) Produces high repeat business.
  d. Distinctive, colorful package:
     (1) Speeds shopping—easy for shoppers to locate on shelves.
     (2) High visual impact stimulates impulse purchases when on special display.
     (3) Familiar package design easy to recognize in store ads.

13. Value analysis can be an effective sales tool. Define value analysis in your own words and describe its use in a selling situation.

14. As an industrial salesperson, your job often is to present your product to a company's purchasing agent who makes the decision whether or not to buy your product. Often, this purchasing agent must consider many factors other than your product's merits in coming to a final decision to buy your product. Discuss the major nonproduct-related factors that may directly influence the purchasing agent's buying decision.

    Gresham Electric is interested in expanding its sales of small electrical parts to manufacturers of small household appliances. These manufacturers include such companies as General Electric and Westinghouse. Your boss has asked you to study the industrial buying process: (1) recognition of the problem or need, (2) determination of characteristics of the needed product, (3) determination of product specifications, (4) search and qualification of potential sources, (5) acquisition and analysis of proposal, (6) selection of supplier, (7) establishment of an order routine, and (8) evaluation of product performance. What factors affect each step?

    As a salesperson for the Electric Generator Corporation, you have decided to attempt to sell your EG 600 generator to the Universal Construction Corporation. The EG 600 costs $70,000. You estimate that operating and maintenance costs will average $3,000 a year and that the machine will operate satisfactorily for 10 years. You can offer a $65,000 price to Universal, if they purchase 10 to 20 machines. Should they purchase over 21 machines their cost would be $58,000 per generator. The generators they are currently using originally cost them $65,000, have a life of seven years, and cost $5,000 each year to operate. As far as you know, their present supplier cannot offer them a quantity discount.

  a. Develop a value analysis table comparing the two generators.
  b. In your presentation, what are the selling points you would stress?

Projects _____

1. Keep a diary of your purchases for two weeks. Select five or more of the products you purchased during that period and write a short report on why you purchased each product and what you feel are the features, advantages, and benefits of each product.

2. Select two similar industrial products made by different manufacturers and compare their features, advantages, and benefits. Select one of the products and state how you would use the information to show a potential buyer its value over the other product. Make sure the product you select is the highest priced product.

Cases _____

2–1   Economy Ceiling Fans, Inc.

As a salesperson for Economy Ceiling Fans, you have been asked to research and determine your customers' attitudes and beliefs toward your brand of ceiling fans. With this information you will determine if your company has the correct product line and suggest selling points for the company's salespeople when discussing fans with customers who come into their chain of retail stores.

You decide to hold an open house in one of your typical stores located in an upper-income neighborhood on a Sunday and advertise your special prices. During that time you ask everyone to be seated, thank them for coming, and ask them to discuss their attitudes towards your company and ceiling fans in general.

Some people felt that ceiling fans should be shopped for without considering brands, but once a brand is selected, they go to the stores carrying that particular brand and buy from the store with the best price. Most people had collected information on fans from personal sources (such as friends), commercial sources (such as advertising, salespeople, company literature), and public sources (such as consumer rating organizations). Sixty percent had narrowed their choice to fans from Hunter, Casa Blanca, and Economy, and they seemed to look for three things in a ceiling fan: price, quality, and style.

Question:

Given this information on why people buy ceiling fans, what should salespeople be instructed to do when a customer enters their store?

2–2 McDonald's Ford Dealership

The used car salesman for McDonald's Ford, John Alexander, approaches a 25- to 27-year-old female, June Miller, in the car lot and says:

	Can I help you?
Buyer:	20,000 miles on this one—I'll bet a little old lady owned this lemon! What was it, really, before you set it back?
Salesman:	That is the actual mileage. Hi, I'm John Alexander and you are. . . . [*he waits for reply*].
Buyer:	June Miller.
Salesman:	June, what can I help you with?
Buyer:	Oh, I don't know. Something that runs and will get me around.
Salesman:	Do you travel out of town or just drive back and forth to work?
Buyer:	I drive everywhere! I'm even getting in a car pool with my boss.
Salesman:	Good mileage is important then.
Buyer:	Sure is. [*She walks over and looks at a full-size, four-door Ford LTD.*] Say, I like this one! $6,500! You have to be kidding.
Salesman:	Do you need that much room?
Buyer:	Not really, there is just me.
Salesman:	June, are you saying you need a car that is dependable, gets good gas mileage, not too big, and not too expensive?
Buyer:	How did you guess?
Salesman:	Follow me . . . [*he shows her five cars that he feels have these features. Then he asks:*] Which one of these do you like?
Buyer:	Well, they are OK, but I really don't like them. Thanks for your time. I'll shop around a little more. Give me your card, and I'll get back to you later.

Questions:

1. Describe the situation and the buyer's apparent needs.

2. What should the salesman do now that the buyer has said no to the cars he has shown her and is about to leave the car lot?

2–3 Frank's Drilling Service

Frank's Drilling Service specializes in the drilling of oil and gas wells. Scott Atkinson, one of their salesmen, was preparing to contact the drilling engineer at Oilteck, an independent oil company. Scott has learned they are planning to drill approximately 12 new wells in the next six months.

Scott estimates that each oil well will require a drilling depth of approximately 10,000 feet. The drilling service the company is using at present charges 90 cents a foot, plus $1,200 per hour for personnel to operate the equipment. They take about 16 days to drill each well.

Frank's charges $1,200 per hour for personnel, and their costs are $1 a foot. Scott believes his drilling crews save customers time and money because they can drill a 10,000 foot well in 12 days.

Questions:

1. Using the above information, develop a value analysis that could be used by Scott to sell to his customer.

2. What are several features, advantages, and benefits Scott should discuss with Oilteck's drilling engineer?

3 COMMUNICATION AND PERSUASION: IT'S NOT ALL TALK

Learning Objectives

1. To present and discuss the salesperson-buyer communication process.
2. To discuss and illustrate the importance of using nonverbal communications when selling.
3. To review barriers to effective sales communications.
4. To introduce ways of developing persuasive communications.

Key Terms for Selling

Communication
Source
Encoding process
Message
Medium
Decoding process
Receiver
Feedback
Noise
Nonverbal communication
Territorial space
Intimate space
Personal space

Social space
Public space
Space threats
Space invasion
Acceptance signals
Caution signals
Disagreement signals
Persuasion
Empathy
KISS
Listening
Enthusiasm
Source credibility
Proof statements

Profile

C. Edward Tucker
Cannon Financial Institute

C. Edward Tucker is senior vice president and director of marketing for Cannon Financial Institute, Athens, Georgia. In his job, Ed is involved in administration, sales training, and acts as a consultant when selling his firm's services.

Cannon operates trusts schools for bankers held annually at Pepperdine University, the University of North Carolina, and Notre Dame. Cannon also sells numerous services to financial institutions.

Prior to joining Cannon as a consultant to the financial industry, he spent 18 years with the Citizens and Southern National Bank of South Carolina, serving as vice president of sales training and regional marketing. Ed graduated from the University of South Carolina receiving a B.S. degree in banking and finance.

"Sales communications involves exchange of thoughts," says Ed. "Whenever you are communicating to a prospective buyer, there has to be an even flow of information. It is a give and take proposition. I believe many salespeople are still a little overbearing and do not really understand the customer's actual needs. They try to sell the product or service, and when the customer does not buy it, the salesperson cannot believe the customer did not want it. This is a situation where communication was only flowing one way.

"A reverse of this is where the customer knows what he wants (or thinks he does) and walks into the store or bank and places the order. The salesperson takes the order, takes the check for the goods or services purchased, thanks the customer, and the sales process is over. Once again, one-way communication has occurred.

"The most effective sales approach is to let the customer communicate his specific needs. After effective communications from the salesperson (probing, asking specific questions), it can be determined what product or service is best for the customer. Then you are ready to sell the benefits to the customer. That is what is going to make the sale."

"An example of effective and ineffective communications occurred on a flight from Atlanta to Los Angeles, a four-hour trip," said Ed Tucker. "There were two flight attendants serving my cabin. When it was time for the movie, the attendant on my aisle used the following sales pitch: 'Would you like to rent a headset?' I asked, 'How much?' and with that, she responded, '$3.' I said no and thanked her. She went on to her next prospective customer, who also said no. What went wrong here? She never told me what the headset was for, only asked if I wanted one. One would look a little foolish sitting for the remainder of the flight with a headset on without anything to listen to, plus it cost $3 to wear it.

"Now the other attendant used a different approach. She sold the benefits of the movie, which was her core product. She named the movie, the two leading actors, length of time of the movie, and said 'You will be in L.A. before you know it.' 'Sounds good to me,' were most of her responses. 'That will be *just* $3.' And after the exchange of currency took place, the eagerly waiting moviegoer was handed a headset. The difference between the two approaches was the way in which the product was presented."

While there may be many other factors that are crucial to sales success, the ability to communicate effectively, as discussed by Ed Tucker, is certainly of prime importance. In order to convincingly convey this important sales skill, this chapter directly applies a basic communication model to the buyer-seller interaction. Afterward, several factors influencing communication, along with a number of possible barriers to effective communication, are described. The often ignored, though always critical, topic of nonverbal communications is also examined in some depth. The balance of this chapter relates some techniques that can be used to improve sales communications.

Communication: It Takes Two

Communication, in a sales context, is the act of transmitting verbal and nonverbal information and understanding between seller and buyer. This definition presents communication as an exchange process of sending and receiving messages with some type of response expected between the seller and the buyer.

Communication during the sales presentation takes many forms. Ideas and attitudes can be effectively communicated by media other than just language. Actually, in a normal two-person conversation less than 35 percent of the social meaning utilizes verbal components. Said another way, much of the social meaning of what is said in a conversation is conveyed nonverbally.

Research has found that face-to-face communication is composed of *verbal, vocal,* and *facial* communication messages. One equation presents the total impact of communicated messages as equal to 7 percent verbal plus 38 percent vocal plus 55 percent facial.[1] If one recognizes these findings as a reasonable approximation of the total communicative process, then uninformed salespeople are actually ignoring a major part of the communication process that occurs during buyer-seller interaction. We can say that how the sales message is given can often be as important to making the sale as what is said. Thus, nonverbal communications can be very important in communication between buyer and seller. An awareness of nonverbal communication can be a valuable tool in successfully making a sale.

Vocal communication includes such factors as voice quality, pitch, pause, and inflection. Radio newscaster Paul Harvey is famous for *how* he broadcasts the news. His vocal pauses and inflections are masterfully used to obtain and hold the attention of his radio audience. A salesperson's use of vocal factors can aid in sales presentation, too. Along with verbal, vocal, and facial communication, a number of other elements are also involved in sales communications.

Salesperson-Buyer Communication Process Requires Feedback

A basic communication model that depicts how the salesperson-buyer communication process works is shown in Figure 3–1. Basically, communication takes place when a *sender* transmits a *message* through some type of *medium* to a *receiver* who responds to that message. Figure 3–1

Figure 3–1
Salesperson–Buyer Communication Process

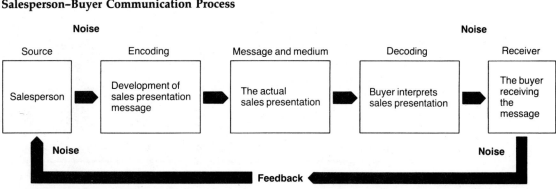

Say What You Mean

There are at least six messages involved in the communication process:

1. What you mean to say.
2. What you really say.
3. What the other person hears.
4. What the other person thinks he heard.
5. What the other person says about what you said.
6. What you think the other person said about what you said.

Gets a bit complicated, doesn't it? Sue and I were looking at a gorgeous moon together under romantic circumstances. As we shared the moment, how was I actually feeling? I was feeling romantic. If we followed the six messages, that incident would have looked something like this:

1.	What you mean to say.	"The moon puts me in a romantic mood."
2.	What you really say.	"Isn't that a brilliant moon?"
3.	What the other person hears.	"The moon is bright."
4.	What the other person thinks she heard.	"Yes, it's bright enough for a walk."
5.	What the other person says about what you said.	"Yes, it's bright enough to shoot a golf ball by."
6.	What you think the other person said about what you said.	"I don't feel romantic."

We can miss each other's wavelengths completely by the time the six messages are completed without even realizing what has happened. All of us are constantly in the process of coding and decoding messages.

We need to learn to ask questions, or restate the point for clarification of meaning. To say what we mean, and say it straight, must be our constant goal in order for those around us to be able to discard all decoding devices.

presents a model that contains eight major communications elements. Each of these elements is defined below.

Source. The source of the communication (also called the communicator); in our case the salesperson.

Encoding Process. The conversion by the salesperson of ideas and concepts into the language and materials used in the sales presentation.

Message. The information conveyed in the sales presentation.

Medium. The form of communication used in the sales presentation and discussion; most frequently words, visual materials, and body language.

Decoding Process. Receipt and translation (interpretation) of the information by the receiver (prospective buyer).

Receiver. The person the communication is intended for; in our case the prospect or buyer.

Feedback. Reaction to the communication as transmitted to the sender. This reaction may be verbal or nonverbal.

Noise. Factors that distort communications between buyer and seller. Noise includes barriers to communications, which will be discussed later.

This model portrays the communication process. A salesperson should know how to develop a sales presentation (encode) so that the buyer obtains maximum understanding of the message (decoding). Communication media that most effectively communicate a specific sales message should be used. Clear verbal discussion, employment of visual aids such as pictures or diagrams, and development of models or samples of the actual product are several types of media a salesperson might use in communicating a particular sales message.

One-way communication occurs when the salesperson talks, and the buyer only listens. The salesperson needs a response or feedback from the buyer to know if communication is taking place. Does the buyer understand the message? Once feedback or interaction and understanding between buyer and seller exist in a communication process, two-way communication has been established.

Two-way communication is essential to you to make the sale. The buyer must understand your message's information in order to make a buying decision. Two-way communication gives the salesperson the ability to present a product's benefits, instantly receive buyer reactions, and answer questions. Buyers usually react both verbally and nonverbally to your presentation.

Nonverbal Communication: Watch for It _____

Amos Skaggs, purchasing agent, stands as a salesperson enters his office. "Hi, Mr. Skaggs," he says, offering his hand. Mr. Skaggs returns a limp, one-second handshake and sits down behind his desk. He begins to open his afternoon mail, almost as though no one else were in the room.

The salesperson sits down and begins his canned sales talk by saying, "Mr. Skaggs, I'm here to show you how your company can lower manufacturing costs by 10 percent." Mr. Skaggs lays his mail down on his desk, leans back in his chair, crosses his arms, and with a growl says: "I'm glad to hear that. You know something, young fellow, pretty soon it won't cost us anything to manufacture our products." "Why is that?" the salesman mumbles, meekly looking down to the floor. "Well, you are the ninth person I've seen today who has offered to save us 10 percent on our costs."

Mr. Skaggs stands up, leans over the table and while peering over his glasses says slowly, "I believe I've heard enough sales pitches for one day." The initially enthusiastic salesperson now apologetically says, "If this is not a good time for you, sir, I can come back at a later date."

In this imaginary sales call, buyer and seller communicated both verbal and nonverbal messages. Here, nonverbal messages conveyed both parties' attitudes better than the actual verbal exchange. The salesperson's negative reactions served to increase Mr. Skaggs's hostile attitude. He could sense the salesperson did not understand his problem and was there to sell him something, not solve his problem. This impression caused a rapid breakdown in communication. The end result, as in this case, is usually NO SALE.

Recognition and analysis of nonverbal communication in sales transactions is relatively new. Only in the past 10 to 15 years has the subject been formally examined in any detail. The presence and use of nonverbal communication, however, have been acknowledged for many years. In the early 1900s Sigmund Freud noted that people cannot keep a secret, even if they do not speak. A person's gestures and actions reveal hidden feelings about something.[2]

People communicate nonverbally in several ways. Four major **nonverbal communication** channels are the physical space between buyer and seller, appearance, handshake, and body movements.

Concept of Space

The concept of **territorial space** refers to the area around the self that a person will not allow another person to enter without consent. Early experiments in territorial space dealt with animals. These experiments determined that higher-status members of a group are often afforded a freedom of movement that is less available to those of lower status.[3] This idea has been applied to socially acceptable distances of space that human beings keep between themselves in certain situations. Territorial space can easily be related to the selling situation.

Space considerations are important to salespeople because violations of territorial space without customer consent may set off the customer's defense mechanisms and create a barrier to communications. A person (buyer) has four types of main distances to consider—intimate (up to 2 feet), personal (2 to 4 feet), social (4 to 12 feet), and public (greater than 12 feet).

Intimate space of up to two feet, or about arm's length, is the most sensitive zone, since it is reserved for very close friends and loved ones. To enter intimate space in the buyer-seller relationship, for some prospects, could be socially unacceptable—possibly offensive.

During the presentation a salesperson should carefully listen and look for signs that indicate the buyer feels uncomfortable, perhaps that the salesperson is too close. A buyer may deduce from such closeness that the salesperson is attempting to dominate or overpower the buyer. This feeling can result in resistance to the salesperson. If such uneasiness is detected, the salesperson should move back, reassuring the customer.

Personal space is the closest zone a stranger or business acquaintance is normally allowed to enter. Even in this zone, a prospect may be uncomfortable. Barriers, such as a desk, are often used to reduce the threat implied when someone enters this zone.

Social space is the area normally used for a sales presentation. Again, the buyer often uses a desk to maintain a distance of four feet or more between buyer and seller. Standing while facing a seated prospect may communicate to the buyer that the salesperson seems too dominating. Thus the salesperson should normally stay seated in order to convey a relaxed manner.

A salesperson should consider beginning a presentation in the middle of the social distance zone, six to eight feet, in order to avoid the prospect's erecting negative mental barriers. This is especially true if the salesperson is not a friend of the prospect.

Public space is often used by the salesperson making a presentation to a group of people. It is similar to the distance between teacher and student in a classroom. People are at ease and thus easy to communicate with at this distance, since they do not feel threatened by the salesperson.

Space Threats.   The territorial imperative causes people to feel that they should defend their space or territory. The salesperson who pulls up a chair too close, takes over all or part of the prospect's desk, leans on or over the desk, or touches objects on the desk runs the risk of invading a prospect's territory. Be careful not to create defensive barriers. However, should you sense a friendliness between yourself and the prospect, use territorial space to your benefit.

Space Invasion. The prospect who allows you to enter or invade personal and even intimate space is saying, "Come on into my space, let's be friends." Now you can use space to your advantage.

In most offices, the salesperson sits directly across the desk from the prospect. The prospect controls the space arrangement. This is one kind of defensive barrier, allowing the prospect to control much of the conversation. Often seating is prearranged, and it could be a space threat if you moved your chair when calling on a prospect for the first time.

However, if you have a choice between a chair across the desk or beside the desk, take the latter seat as shown in Figure 3–2. Sitting at the side lowers the desk communication barrier. If you are friends with the buyer, move your chair to the side of the desk yourself. This helps create a friendly, cooperative environment between you and the buyer.

Communication through Appearance and the Handshake

Other common methods of nonverbal communication are signals conveyed by a person's physical appearance and handshake. Once territorial space has been established, general appearance would be the next medium of nonverbal communication conveyed to a customer by a salesperson. Appearance not only conveys information such as age, sex,

Figure 3–2
Office Arrangements and Territorial Space

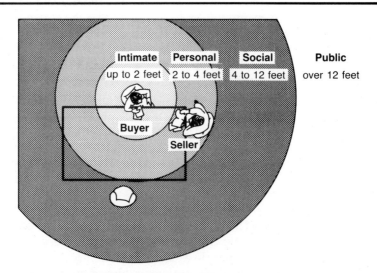

Intimate — up to 2 feet | Personal — 2 to 4 feet | Social — 4 to 12 feet | Public — over 12 feet

Buyer

Seller

height, weight, race, and physical characteristics, but also provides a great deal of data on personality. Hairstyle is one of the first things a buyer notices about a salesperson.

Style Hair Carefully.   Hairstyle has traditionally been an important factor in evaluating personal appearance. Although the longer hairstyles for men that emerged in the late 1960s have gained increased acceptance, longer hair has traditionally been associated with a liberal outlook on life and thus could affect the customer's attitude toward a product. Today's male salespeople might possibly best consider what type of customer they will be calling on and adjust their hairstyles accordingly. This is equally true for the female salesperson.

Though recently decreasing somewhat in popularity, male facial hair is still worn by some male salespeople. For several decades, American males did not sport beards and moustaches to any great extent, but that trend reversed in the 1960s and 70s. A research study in the early 1970s asked people their opinion of facial hair and came up with two very different opinions. One group felt that bearded men are perceived as more sensitive, more masculine, more intelligent, and warmer than clean-shaven men. The other group felt that men with beards are perceived as more deviant, radical, independent, and introverted![4]

Salespeople should carefully consider their grooming and its impact on customer's perceptions. Some companies ask their salesmen to be clean shaven and wear conservative haircuts. And their saleswomen are asked to choose a simple, businesslike, shoulder-length hair style. Other companies leave grooming up to each individual. Your grooming objective is to eliminate communication barriers. It could be your grooming that causes you to convey a favorable first impression. Should your company not have a policy on grooming, examine your customer's grooming before deciding on your own.

Dress as a Professional.   Wardrobe has always been a major determinant of sales success, and today it is emphasized as never before. A variety of books and articles have been written on proper dress for business people. These books espouse the doctrine that male and female sales representatives should wear conservative clothing that projects professionalism, just the right amount of authority, and a desire to please the customer. Sporty clothing is believed to accentuate sales aggressiveness, placing a purchasing agent on the defensive and resulting in lost sales. Too feminine or frivolous clothing for women could project a poor image of a saleswoman.

Many companies believe that decision rules exist for every major clothing item and accessory, but that these are derivatives of one basic commandment—dress in a simple, elegant style. Xerox, IBM, and other large companies have incorporated this idea into their sales training and daily policies. Although they do not have a formal dress code, these firms encourage sales personnel to wear dark, conservative clothing. This practice is designed to project a conservative, stable corporate image to both customers and the general public.

Figure 3–3 illustrates several key considerations for appropriate dress and grooming. If you are uncertain about what to do, visit several retailers. Make sure at least one retailer is a specialty store. They will have the latest styles and will spend time with you. Tell the salespeople what you are looking for and see what they say. Think of this as an investment in yourself because it is expensive to build a wardrobe. However, you are worth it!

Clothes, accessories, and shoes are very important, but do not forget personal grooming, such as skin care and hairstyle. Even men should visit a hairstylist. Learn to recognize image symbols in business dress and use them to your advantage. Be cautious in becoming too individualistic—the unspoken message in most companies is that freedom in dress may be a privilege of rank.

Remember that this material, including the remainder of the chapter, applies to selling *yourself* in job interviews also.

The nonverbal messages that salespeople emit through appearance should be positive in all sales situations. Characteristics of the buyer, cultural aspects of a sales territory, and the type of product being sold are all determinants of mode of dress. In considering these aspects you should create a business wardrobe that will send positive, nonverbal messages in every sales situation. Once you have determined your appropriate dress and hairstyle, the next nonverbal communication channel to consider is your contact with a prospect through your handshake.

Shake Hands Firmly and Look 'em in the Eye.   The handshake is said to have been evolved as a gesture of peace between warriors. By joining hands, two warriors were unable to bear arms against each other (assuming that a shield and not a weapon was held in the left hand).

Today a handshake is the most common way for two people to touch each other in a business situation, and some people feel that it can be a very revealing gesture. A firm handshake is more intense and is indicative of greater liking and warmer feelings. A prolonged handshake is more intimate than a brief one, and it could conceivably cause the customer discomfort, especially in a sales call on a new prospect. A loosely clasped, cold, or limp handshake is usually interpreted as indicating aloofness and unwillingness to become involved. This cold fish handshake is also perceived as being unaffectionate and unfriendly.

General rules for a successful handshake are these: extend your hand first—if appropriate. Remember, however, a few people may be uncomfortable shaking hands with a stranger. At times you may want to allow your customer to initiate the gesture. Maintain eye contact with

Figure 3-3
The Correct Clothes, Grooming, Attitude, and Physical Conditioning All Contribute to Success
This Applies to Your Career As Well As Interviewing and Life

Choose a suit that means business.

Natural fibers, a proper fit, and current styling are important.

A navy pinstripe is a must in anyone's wardrobe.

Keep sports clothes conservative. Find special career lines that retailers offer.

Men and women should consider the looks of their hairstyles and eyewear.

A navy or gray suit, a tailored blouse, jewelry, and a briefcase project a professional image.

Physical fitness produces the stamina and positive mental attitude needed to win in your career and life.

Attention to personal grooming is a must for both men and women.

Correct outerwear is important, too.

your customer during the handshake, gripping the hand firmly. These actions will allow you to initially establish an atmosphere of honesty and mutual respect, starting the presentation in a positive manner.

Body Language Gives You Clues

From birth, people learn to communicate their needs, likes, and dislikes through nonverbal means. The salesperson can learn much from a prospect's raised eyebrow, a smile, a touch, a scowl, or reluctance to make eye contact during a sales presentation. The prospect can communicate with you literally without uttering a word. An ability to interpret these signals can be an invaluable tool to the successful sales professional. In conjunction with interpretation of body language, skillful use and control of the salesperson's own physical actions, gestures, and overall body position can also be helpful.

The buyer can send nonverbal signals via five communciation modes, as shown in Figure 3–4. They are the body angle, facial expression, arm movement or position, hand movements or position, and leg position. Likewise, these modes can generally send three basic types of messages: (1) acceptance, (2) caution, and (3) disagreement.

Acceptance signals indicate that your buyer is favorably inclined towards you and your presentation. These signals give you the green light to proceed. While this may not end in a sale, at the very least the prospect is saying, "I am willing to listen." What you are saying is both acceptable and interesting. Some common acceptance signals are these:

Body angle—leaning forward or upright at attention.

Face—smiling, pleasant expression, relaxed, eyes examining visual aids, direct eye contact, positive voice tones.

Arms—relaxed and generally open.

Body angle

Face

Hands

Arms

Legs

Hands—relaxed and generally open, perhaps performing business calculations on paper, holding on as you attempt to withdraw a product sample or sales materials, firm handshake.

Legs—crossed and pointed toward you or uncrossed.

Salespeople frequently rely only on facial expressions as indicators of acceptance. This practice may be misleading, since buyers may consciously control their facial expressions. You should scan each of the five key body areas to verify your interpretation of facial signals. A buyer who increases eye contact, maintains a relaxed position, and exhibits positive facial expressions is giving you excellent acceptance signals.

Acceptance signals indicate that buyers perceive that they may have a need that your product might meet. You have obtained their attention and interest. You are free to continue with your planned sales presentation.

Caution signals should alert you that buyers are either neutral or skeptical toward what you are saying. Caution signals are indicated by the following:

Body angle—leaning away from you.

Face—puzzled, little or no expression, averted eyes or little eye contact, neutral or questioning voice tone, saying little, and then only asking a few questions.

Arms—crossed, tense.

Hands—moving, fidgeting with something, clasped, weak handshake.

Legs—moving, crossed away from you.

Caution signals are very important for you to recognize and adjust to for two main reasons. First, they indicate blocked communications. Buyers' perceptions, attitudes, and beliefs regarding your presentation may cause them to be skeptical, judgmental, or uninterested in your product. They may not recognize that they need your product or that it can benefit them. Even though you may have their attention, they show very little interest in or desire for your product.

Second, if caution signals are not properly handled, they may evolve into disagreement signals, creating a breakdown in communication and making a sale very difficult to make. Proper handling of caution signals requires that you:

• Adjust to the situation by slowing up or departing from your planned presentation.

• Use open-ended questions to encourage your buyers to talk and express their attitudes and beliefs. "Have you ever been interested in improving efficiency of your workers?" or "What do you think about this benefit?" are examples of open-ended questions.

- Carefully listen to what buyers say and respond directly.
- Project acceptance signals yourself. Be positive, enthusiastic, and smile. Remember, you are glad to be there to help buyers satisfy their needs. Refrain from projecting caution signals even if a buyer does so. If you project a positive image in this situation, there is greater probability that you will change a caution light to a green one and make the sale.

Your objective in using these techniques is to change the caution signal to the green, go-ahead signal. If you continue to receive caution signals, you should proceed carefully with your presentation. Be realistic, alert to the possibility that the buyer may begin to believe your product is not truly beneficial and begin sending disagreement or red light signals.

Disagreement signals tell you immediately to stop your planned presentation and quickly adjust to the situation. Disagreement, or red light signals, indicate you are dealing with a person who is becoming completely uninterested in your product. Anger or hostility may develop if you continue your presentation. Your continuation can cause a buyer to feel 'an unacceptable level of sales pressure resulting in a complete communication breakdown. Disagreement signals may be indicated by these:

Body angle—retracted shoulders, leaning away from you, moving the entire body back from you or wanting to move away.

Face—tense, showing anger, wrinkled face and brow, very little eye contact, negative voice tones, may become suddenly silent.

Arms—tense, crossed over chest.

Hands—motions of rejection or disapproval, tense and clenched, weak handshake.

Legs—crossed and away from you.

You should handle disagreement signals, as you do caution signals, by using open-ended questions and projecting acceptance signals yourself. There are four additional techniques to use. First, stop your planned presentation. There is no use in continuing until you have changed disagreement signals into caution or acceptance signals. Second, temporarily reduce or eliminate any pressure on the person to buy or to participate in the conversation. Let the buyer relax as you slowly move back to selling. Third, let your buyer know you are aware that something upsetting has occurred. Show that you know that you are there to help, not to sell at any cost. Finally, you may wish to use direct questions to determine a buyer's attitudes and beliefs such as, "What do you think of . . . ?" or "Have I said something you do not agree with?"

Body Guidelines. Over a period of time, you should know customers well enough to have a good understanding of the meaning of their body movements. Although a prospect may say no to making a purchase, body movements may indicate uncertainty. As Richard Dreyfuss says in *The Goodbye Girl*, "Your lips say *no, no, no,* but your eyes say *yes, yes, yes!*" This phrase sometimes holds true for selling.

The interpretation of most body language is obvious. However, you should be cautious in interpreting an isolated gesture, such as assuming that very little eye contact means the prospect is displeased with what you are saying. Instead, concentrate on nonverbal cues that are part of a cluster or pattern. Let's say your prospect begins staring at the wall. That is a clue that may mean nothing. You continue your talk. Now the prospect leans back in the chair. That is another clue. By itself it may be meaningless, but in conjunction with the first clue, it begins to take on meaning. Now you see the prospect turn away from you, legs crossed, brow wrinkled. You now have a cluster of clues, all forming a pattern. Now it is time to adjust or change your presentation. Figure 3–5 relates some common nonverbal signals that buyers may give you.[5]

To recapitulate, nonverbal communication is well worth considering in selling. A salesperson ought to

- Be able to recognize nonverbal signals.
- Be able to interpret them correctly.
- Be prepared to alter a selling strategy by slowing, changing, or stopping a planned presentation.
- Respond nonverbally and verbally to a buyer's nonverbal signals.

Effective communication is essential in making a sale. Nonverbal communication signals are an important part of the total communications process between buyer and seller. Professional salespeople seek to learn and understand nonverbal communication as a way of increasing their sales success.

Barriers to Communication

Like the high hurdler, a salesperson often must overcome a multitude of obstacles. These obstacles are more aptly called *barriers to communication*. Consider this example:

Salesperson Joe Jones heard that the XYZ Company buyer, Jake Jackson, was displeased with the company's present supplier. Joe had analyzed XYZ's operation and knew that his product could save the company thousands of dollars a year. Imagine Joe's surprise when Jackson terminated the visit quickly with no sale and no mention of a future appointment.

Figure 3–5
What Nonverbal Signals Are These Buyers Giving to You?

1. When you mention your price, this purchasing agent tilts her head back, raises her hands and her body posture becomes rigid. What nonverbal signals is she communicating and how would you move on with the sale?

2. As you explain your sales features, this buyer looks away, clasps his hands and crosses his legs away from you. What nonverbal signals is he communicating and how would you move on with the sale?

3. As you explain the quality of your product, this company president opens his arms and leans toward you. What nonverbal signals is he communicating and how would you move on with the sale?

Answers to Figure 4–5

1. Your buyer is sending red signals. That means you are facing nearly insurmountable barriers. You've got to stop what you are doing, express understanding, and redirect your approach.
2. This buyer is sending yellow signals that warn you to exercise caution. Your own words and gestures must be aimed at relaxing the buyer or he may soon communicate red signals.
3. This buyer is sending green signals that say: everything is "go." With no obstacles to your selling strategy, simply move on to the close.

Joe told his boss about the interview. "Jackson kept asking me where I went to school, whether I wanted coffee, and how I liked selling, while I was trying to explain to him the features, advantages, and benefits of our product. Suddenly, Jackson stopped the interview." Joe asked the boss, "What did I do wrong? I know he needed our product."

The buyer was sending Joe signals that he likes doing business with people he knows. He did not want to get down to business immediately. He wanted to visit for a while. There was never any true communication established between Jackson and Jones, causing Jones to misread the customer and incorrectly handle the situation.

Salespeople, as illustrated in the above example, often lose a sale after failing to recognize communication barriers between buyer and seller. The main reasons communication breaks down in the sales situation are:

1. **Differences in Perception.** If the buyer and seller do not share a common understanding of information contained in the presentation, communication will break down. The closer a buyer's and seller's perceptions, attitudes, and beliefs, the stronger communication will be between them.

2. **Buyer Does Not Recognize a Need for Product.** Communication barriers exist if the salesperson is unable to convince the buyer of a need and/or that the salesperson represents the best supplier to buy from.

3. **Selling Pressure.** There is a fine line between what is acceptable sales pressure and enthusiasm and what the buyer perceives as a high-pressure sales technique. A pushy, arrogant selling style can quickly cause the prospect to erect a communication barrier.

4. **Information Overload.** You may present the buyer with an excess of information. This overload may cause confusion, perhaps offense, and the buyer will stop listening to you. The engineer making a presentation to a buyer who is not an engineer may concentrate on the technical aspects of a product, while the buyer only wants a small amount of information.

5. **Disorganized Sales Presentation.** Sales presentations that seem unorganized to the buyer tend to cause frustration, even anger. Buyers commonly expect you to understand their needs or problems and to customize your sales presentation to their individual situation. If you fail to do this, communication can break down.

6. **Distractions.** When a buyer receives a telephone call or someone walks into the office, distractions occur. A buyer's thoughts may become sidetracked, and it may be difficult to regain attention and interest.

7. **Poor Listening.** At times the buyer may not actually be listening to you. This often occurs if you do all or most of the talking, not allowing the buyer to participate in the conversation.

The seven barriers to communication listed above are certainly not the only ones that may occur. Mainly, it is important to understand that communication barriers can exist. As in the example of Joe Jones, the buyer may actually need the product, and the salesperson may have excellent product knowledge. He may believe that he made a good sales presentation; yet because of communication barriers, the buyer rejects the salesperson and the product. As a salesperson, you must constantly seek ways of recognizing and overcoming communication barriers, and getting back to identifying and satisfying buyer needs through persuasive communication.

Master Persuasive Communication and You Maintain Control

In order to become a better communicator, you need to consider two major elements of communication. First, you should always strive to improve the message you deliver in the sales presentation. You need to be a capable encoder. Second, you need to improve your ability to determine what the buyer is actually communicating to you. Therefore, you also need to be a good listener or decoder. A good sales communicator knows how to effectively encode *and* decode during a presentation.

Salespeople want to be good communicators in order to persuade people to purchase their products. **Persuasion** means the ability to change a person's belief, position, or course of action. The more effective you are at communicating, the greater are your chances of being successful at persuasion.

The chapters on the selling process will go into greater detail on specific persuasion techniques. For now, let's review several general factors to consider in developing persuasive communications. These factors relate to several components of the simple communication model discussed earlier: feedback, empathy, simplicity, listening, attitude, and proof statements.

Feedback Guides Your Presentation

You need to learn how to generate feedback to determine whether your listener has received your intended message. Feedback does not refer to just any type of listening behavior by the buyer, but to a recognizable response from the buyer. A shake of the head, a frown, or an effort to

Twenty Questions

Communication. It's more than just a word. It's a delicate exercise in which you want to provide information to the buyer, but not too much! You want to befriend him, but not too much! And you want to question him, probe him, but not too much!

Too many questions become an interrogation. However, everyone likes to be asked what they think, especially concerning subjects important to them. So try and phrase your questions as if you're having a conversation with the buyer. Because that's exactly what you're doing.

When you become an especially good questioner, you'll be able to put your answers into the buyer's mouth and lead him down the path to the order: "Doesn't your business thrive on services such as this? ... Wouldn't you say that's a savings well worth considering? ... Isn't your company fighting to hold on to its market share? Then couldn't you use our product at this time? How many can I sign you up for?"

say something are all signals to the salesperson. If the salesperson fails to notice or respond to these signals, no feedback can occur; this means faulty or incomplete communication. A salesperson's observation of feedback is akin to an auto racer's glances at his tachometer. Both aid in ascertaining a receiver's response.

Often feedback must be sought openly because the prospect will not always give it voluntarily. By interjecting into the presentation questions that require the customer to give a particular response, you can stimulate feedback. Questioning, sometimes called probing, allows the salesperson to determine the buyer's attitude toward the sales presentation.

Fisk Telephone Systems, Inc. included this type of feedback in their sales training sessions. Fisk sales trainers suggested to their salespeople that they use questions in their presentations. Some of these questions were:

 Do you think you are paying too much for your telecommunications equipment?

Are you happy with the service now being provided to you?

Are you happy with the equipment your present supplier has installed for your company?

These questions were intended to draw negative responses from the customers concerning their relationship with their present supplier. They provided the Fisk salespeople with a method of determining how the prospect felt about the competitor. These responses allow the salesperson to discuss the specific features, advantages, and benefits of Fisk products relative to the products presently used by the prospect. Thus, in planning your presentation it is important to predetermine when and what feedback-producing questions to ask. One way of creating positive feedback is through empathy.

Empathy Puts You in Your Customer's Shoes

Empathy is the ability to identify and understand the other person's feelings, ideas, and situation. As a salesperson, you need to be interested in what the buyer is saying, not just in giving your sales presentation. Many of the barriers to communication mentioned earlier can be overcome when you place yourself in the buyer's shoes. Empathy is saying to a prospect, "I'm here to help you," or asking, "Tell me your problems and needs so I can help *you*." Empathy is also evidenced by a salesperson's display of sincerity and interest in the buyer's situation.

This may mean acknowledging from time to time that a prospect may not truly need your product. Take, for example, the Scott Paper Company salesperson who finds that the customer still has 90 percent of the paper towels purchased three months ago. There is no reason to sell this customer more paper towels. It is time to help the customer sell the paper towels now on hand by suggesting displays, price reductions, and formats for newspaper advertisements. It is wise always to adopt your customer's point of view in order to meet the customer's needs best.

Keep It Simple, You Silver-Tongued Devil

The new salesperson was sitting in a customer's office waiting for the buyer. Her boss was with her. As they heard the buyer come into the office, the sales manager said, "Remember, a **KISS** for him." No, he was not saying to give the buyer a kiss, but to use the old selling philosophy of *Keep it simple, salesperson.*

The story is told of a little old lady who went into a hardware store. The clerk greeted her and offered her some help. She replied that she was looking for a heater. So the clerk said, "Gee, are you lucky! We've got a big sale on these heaters, and a tremendous selection. Let me show

---

How Can You Simplify the Following Statements?

1. A mass of concentrated earthly material perennially rotating in its axis will not accumulate an accretion of bryophytic vegetation.

2. Individuals who are perforce constrained to be domiciled in vitreous structures of patent frangibility should on no account employ petrous formations as projectiles.

3. A superabundance of talent skilled in the preparation of gastronomic concoctions will impair the quality of a certain potable solution made by immersing a gallinaceous bird in embullient Adam's ale.

Answers:
1. A rolling stone gathers no moss. 2. People who live in glass houses shouldn't throw stones. 3. Too many cooks spoil the broth.

---

you." So after maybe 30 or 45 minutes of discussing duothermic controls, heat induction, and all the factors involved with how a heater operates, including the features and advantages of each of the 12 models, he turned to the little old lady and said, "Now, do you have any questions?" She replied, "Yes, just one, Sonny. Which one of these things will keep a little old lady warm?"

An overcomplex, technical presentation can and should be avoided when it is unnecessary. You should use words and materials that can be understood easily by the buyer. The skilled salesperson can make a prospect feel comfortable with a new product or complex technology through the subtle use of nontechnical information and a respectful attitude.

Creating Mutual Trust Develops Friendship

Salespeople who develop a mutual trust relationship with their customers cannot help being successful. This type of relationship eventually results in high source credibility and even friendship.

The buyer realized that in the past he was not sold products that failed to perform to expectations; the products were worth their price; and the salesperson did everything promised. Building mutual trust is very important to effective long-run communication.

Listening Clues You In

Salespeople often believe that their job is to talk rather than listen. If they will both talk *and* listen, their persuasive powers will increase. Since people can listen (about 400 words per minute) roughly twice as fast as the average rate of speech, it is understandable that a person's mind may wander while listening to a salesperson's presentation. To keep the buyer **listening** to you, ask questions, get the buyer involved in the conversation. Once you ask a question—listen. Carefully listen to what is being said to you. Here are several things to do to improve your listening skills:

- Stop talking.
- Show the prospect you want to listen.
- Watch for nonverbal messages.
- Recognize feelings and emotions.
- Ask questions to clarify meaning.
- If appropriate, restate the prospect's position for clarification.
- Listen to the full story.

It is sometimes difficult, especially for the novice salesperson, to stay calm when a prospect displays favorable signs. The novice may continue to talk on and on about a particular situation or problem. The salesperson must *learn to listen.* Listening implies sincerity and respect. It is a key to sales success.

His thoughts were slow,
  His words were few,
And never made to glisten.
  But he was a joy
Wherever he went.
  You should have heard him listen.
        Author Unknown

Your Attitude Makes the Difference

While a variety of methods and techniques exist in selling, truly effective sales persuasion is based on the salesperson's attitude toward the sales job and his customers. The most important element of this attitude is the salesperson's degree of interest and enthusiasm in helping people to fulfill their needs. This is the foundation for building effective communication techniques. **Enthusiasm** is a condition in which an individual is filled with excitement toward something. Excitement does not mean an aggressive attitude, but rather a positive view toward solving the customers' problems.

You need to sell yourself *on* yourself and *on* being a salesperson. The highly successful salesperson goes all out in helping customers. You should strive to make the buyer feel important. Show the buyer that you are there solely as a problem solver. You can do this by developing methods of expressing true interest such as asking questions, instead of talking at the buyer. This type of attitude will in turn benefit you by allowing you to look at the sales situation from the buyer's viewpoint (empathy).

Salespeople who have established **source credibility** with their customers through continued empathy, willingness to listen to specific needs, and continual enthusiasm toward their work and their customers' business can make claims that their customers will believe. Enthusiasm combined with proof statements greatly improve a salesperson's persuasive ability.

Proof Statements Make You Believable

Salespeople have known for years that the use of highly credible sources can improve persuasiveness of the sales presentation message. **Proof statements** are statements that substantiate claims made by the salesperson. Pharmaceutical companies often quote research studies done by outstanding physicians at prestigious medical schools to validate claims of product benefits. These proof statements add high credibility to a sales message.

Salespeople sometimes quote acknowledged experts in a field on the use of the products. By demonstrating that other customers or respected individuals use the products, they encourage customer belief in the validity of information presented in a sales presentation. People place greater confidence in a trustworthy objective source (particularly one not associated with the salesperson's firm) and are therefore more receptive to what is said by the salesperson.

Summary of Major Selling Issues ⸺⸺⸺⸺⸺⸺

Communication is operationally defined as transmission of verbal and nonverbal information and understanding between salesperson and prospect. Modes of communication commonly used in a sales presentation are words, gestures, visual aids, and nonverbal communication.

A model of the communication process is composed of a sender (encoder) who transmits a specific message via some media to a receiver (decoder) who responds to that message. The effectiveness of this communication process can be hampered by noise, which distorts the message as it travels to the receiver. A sender (encoder) can judge the effectiveness of a message and media choice by monitoring the feedback from the receiver.

Barriers can exist or develop that hinder or prevent constructive communication during a sales presentation. These bariers may relate to the perceptional differences between the sender and receiver, outside distractions, or how sales information is conveyed. Regardless of their source, these barriers must be recognized and either overcome or eliminated if communication is to be effected.

Nonverbal communication has emerged as a critical component of the overall communication process within the past 10 or 15 years. Recognition of nonverbal communication is essential for sales success in today's business environment. Awareness of the prospect's territorial space, a firm and confident handshake, and accurate interpretation of the language of body and limb positioning can be a tremendous aid to a salesperson's success.

A salesperson's overall persuasive power can be enhanced through the development of several key characteristics. The salesperson who creates a relationship based on mutual trust with a customer by displaying true empathy (desire to understand customer's situation and environment), a willing ear (more listening, less talking), and a positive attitude of enthusiastic pursuit of lasting solutions to that customer's needs and problems greatly increases the likelihood of making that sale—not just in the short run, but over the long haul.

Review and Discussion Questions

1. Draw the salesperson-buyer communication process. Describe each step in the process. Why is two-way communication important in this process?

2. This chapter outlined several forms of nonverbal communication.
   a. Give an example of a salesperson making a good first impression through the proper use of an introductory handshake.
   b. What signals should the salesperson look for from a buyer's body language? Give several examples of these signals.

3. A salesperson may spend hours developing a sales presentation, and yet the buyer still does not buy. One reason for losing a sale is that the salesperson and the buyer do not communicate. What barriers to communication may be present between seller and buyer during a sales presentation?

4. When two people are talking, they want the listener to understand what they are saying. They both want to be effective communicators. The same is true of the salesperson who wants the buyer to listen to a sales presentation. What can the salesperson do to help ensure that the buyer is listening?

5. You arrive at the industrial purchasing agent's office on time. This is

your first meeting. After you have waited five minutes, the agent's secretary says, "She will see you." After the initial greeting, she asks you to sit down. For each of the three following situations determine:

a. What nonverbal signals is she communicating?
b. How would you respond nonverbally?
c. What would you say to her?

   (1) She sits down behind her desk. She sits up straight in her chair. She clasps her hands together and with little expression on her face says, "What can I do for you?"

   (2) She sits down behind her desk. She moves slightly backwards in her chair, crosses her arms, and while looking around the room says, "What can I do for you?"

   (3) She sits down behind her desk. She moves slightly forward in her chair, seems hurried, yet relaxed toward your presence. Her arms are uncrossed. She looks you squarely in the eye, and with a pleasant look on her face says, "What can I do for you?"

6. In each of the following selling situations determine:

a. What nonverbal signals is the buyer communicating?
b. How would you respond nonverbally?
c. What would you say?

   (1) The buyer seems happy to see you. Because you have been calling on him for several years, the two of you have become business friends. In the middle of your presentation, you notice the buyer slowly lean back in his chair. As you continue to talk, a puzzled look comes over his face.

   (2) As you begin the main part of your presentation, the buyer reaches for the telephone and says, "Keep going, I need to tell my secretary something."

   (3) As a salesperson with only six months' experience, you are somewhat nervous about calling on an important buyer who has been a purchasing agent for almost 20 years. Three minutes after you have begun your presentation, he rapidly raises his arms straight up into the air and slowly clasps his hands behind his head. He leans so far back in his chair that you think he is going to fall backward on the floor. At the same time, he crosses his legs away from you and slowly closes his eyes. You keep on talking. Slowly the buyer opens his eyes, uncrosses his legs, and sits up in his chair. He leans forward, placing his elbows on the desk top, seemingly propping his head up with his hands. He seems relaxed as he says, "Let me see what you have here." He reaches his hand out for you to give him the presentation materials you have developed for him.

(4) At the end of your presentation, the buyer leans forward, his arms open, and smiles as he says, "You really don't expect me to buy that piece of junk, do you?"

Project

The use of questions by the salesperson is an effective method of obtaining feedback from a buyer. This statement applies to conversation between two people. For the next two days, try using questions in your conversations with other people and report on your results. These questions should reflect an interest in the person you are conversing with and the topic being discussed. Use of the second person (you, your, yours) should increase feedback and create an atmosphere of trust.

For example, questions such as, "What do you mean?" "What do you think?" or "How does that sound?" can be used by you in your conversation to have other people participate and to help you to determine how they feel toward your topic of conversation.

Asking people's opinions can also result in a positive response, since they may feel flattered that you care about their opinion. Questions can also help you guide the direction of topics discussed in your conversation. Try to determine people's reactions to your questions and report on your findings in class.

Cases

3–1 Skaggs Manufacturing

John Andrews arrived promptly for his 10 A.M. meeting with Martha Gillespie, the buyer for Skaggs Manufacturing. At 10:15, when Ms. Gillespie hadn't arrived, John asked her secretary if she was out of the office for the morning. The secretary smiled and said, "She'll probably be a few minutes late." John resented this delay and was convinced that Gillespie had forgotten the appointment.

Finally, at 10:20 Gillespie entered her office, walked over to John, said hello, and promptly excused herself to talk to the secretary about a tennis game scheduled for that afternoon. Ten minutes later, Gillespie led John into her office. At the same time, a competing salesperson entered the office for a 10:30 appointment. With the door open, Gillespie asked John, "What's new today?" As John began to talk, Gillespie began reading letters on her desk and signing them. Shortly after that, the telephone began to ring, whereupon Gillespie talked to her husband for 10 minutes.

As she hung up, Gillespie looked at John and suddenly realized his frustration. She promptly buzzed her secretary and said, "Hold all calls." She got up and shut the door. John again began his presentation when Gillespie leaned backward in her chair, pulled her golf shoes out of a desk drawer, and began to brush them.

About that time, the secretary entered the office and said, "Martha, your 10:30 appointment is about to leave. What should I tell him?" "Tell him to wait, I need to see him." Then she said, "John, I wish we had more time. Look, I think I have enough of your product to last until your next visit. I'll see you then. Thanks for coming by."

John quickly rose to his feet, did not shake hands, said OK, and left.

Questions:

1. What nonverbal cues did the salesperson, John Andrews, experience when contacting Martha Gillespie?

2. If you were John, how would you have handled the situation?

3–2 Lanier Dictaphone (A)

Judy Allison, the Lanier Dictaphone saleswoman in Alabama, entered the office of Bill Taylor, purchasing agent for a large manufacturing firm. Two weeks earlier, she had made her first sales call and had left a demonstrater dictaphone for Taylor to have executives of the company try out. The previous evening Taylor had called Judy and asked her to see him so that he could give her an order. After the initial hellos, the conversation went like this:

Buyer:	Judy, thanks for coming by today. Our executives really liked your equipment. Here is an order for four dictaphones. When can you deliver them?
Salesperson:	Is tomorrow too soon?
Buyer:	That is perfect. Leave them with Joyce, my secretary. Joyce [*Bill says over the intercom*], Judy will deliver the dictaphones tomorrow and go ahead and take them to Sally, Anne, and Sherri. Women sure understand the use of modern equipment!
Salesperson:	Bill, thanks for your help.
Buyer:	Forget it, Judy. I wish I could have helped more. Your dictaphones can reduce the number of secretaries in the typing pool, resulting in big savings to our company.
Salesperson:	You're right; many of my customers are going to them for that very reason.
Buyer:	I know, but some executives still feel people cannot be replaced by machines.

Question:

Analyze and describe the conversation between Judy and Bill. What should Judy do now?

4 SO, WHAT DO I NEED TO KNOW?

Learning Objectives

1. To discuss the major body of knowledge needed for increased sales success.

2. To illustrate how this knowledge can be used during the sales presentation.

3. To show how sales aids are used by people selling consumer and industrial goods.

Key Terms for Selling

Sales training
National advertising
Retail advertising
Cooperative advertising
Trade advertising
Industrial advertising
Direct-mail advertising
Consumer sales
  promotion
Trade sales promotion
Point-of-purchase
  displays
Shelf positioning
Shelf facings
SAMI data
Premiums
Contests and
  sweepstakes

Consumer premiums
Dealer premiums
Price
List price
Net price
Zone price
FOB shipping point
FOB destination
Noncumulative quantity
  discount
Cumulative quantity
  discount
Cash discounts
Trade discounts
Consumer discounts
Markup
Gross profit
Net profit

Profile

Michael Bevan
Parbron International

My name is Michael Bevan, and I'm 31 years old. I went to the University of Toronto for one year. I chose to go into business in 1975, and from then until December 1984 I held a variety of positions with Coronet Carpets, Ltd., Ivac Canada, and Milliken Contract Carpets. In December 1984 I began my current position as executive vice president of Parbron International in Canada. In the year and a half I've been with Parbron, sales have risen from $85,000 to $3 million.

We are currently in the commercial carpet and floor systems business. We install raised computer floors for the marketplace and also commercial carpet to many of the Fortune 500 companies in Canada. We represent every major brand in Canada.

I think a college degree gives more discipline to a person, but I can prove that you don't need it if you have the innate ability to sell. I think that a four-year program at a university helps you to develop the discipline required to do a job properly. Personally, if I had an option, I would have preferred to finish my degree.

One reason students should choose a career in sales is that, without the sale, nothing goes. If you don't sell something, nothing gets manufactured or bought, and the whole cycle stops. To be a sales representative for any company is exciting because you are the reason that company will become successful, and you're only held back by your abilities. The career path is endless.

Long hours are a part of sales. When I put in long hours to build something, it's very fulfilling. I don't have difficulty with long hours; I probably work from 6:30 in the morning until 6:30 or 7:00 at night. That's a full 12-hour day; and it's not with a two-hour executive lunch. It's on-hand all the time. If a customer wants to see me on a weekend, I'm there because I have to be there; he needs me. I don't like to do it; I don't want to compromise my family—but they also recognize that I have to build a business, and that takes commitment.

"We'll do things like design carpets and work on the colorations with the interior design firms," says Michael Bevan. "We develop specifications, and design custom products and logos. We're capable of doing virtually anything that can go on floors. We'll work very closely with someone like Crosby-Caristan Carpets. We'll bring them into it and develop a pricing scheme and product deliveries, and work directly for the end user.

"In our business, being successful takes a lot of knowledge. The key, first of all, is understanding every aspect of the business. This involves working with the design concept (developing a color, texture, and style for the interior design) and working with the architectural company (meeting the architect's requirements). It also involves working with the end user and assuring him that the other two steps are correct because he's the one who has to live with that whole scenario.

"Finally we are involved in installing the product. We have on our staff 65 installers who will complete the job for the end user. We must understand every single stage from the beginning right through to the end much better than our competition.

"Since I have a background in manufacturing, I think I have a lead against my competitors in the marketplace because I understand how a manufacturer works. That alone, encompassed with a lot of knowledge, will allow us to have an edge against competition."

Successful salespeople, such as Michael Bevan, learn of and keep current on information concerning the company, product, distribution, promotion, pricing, competition, industry trends, and the economy. This chapter examines areas of information that are essential to the success of all salespeople.

Where'd You Learn That?
Sources of Sales Knowledge

Knowledge for selling is obtained in two ways. First, most companies provide some form of formal sales training. This information is taught through preliminary training programs and sales meetings. Second, the salesperson learns by being on the job. Experience is surely the best teacher for the beginning salesperson.

Sales training is the effort put forth by an employer to provide the opportunity for the salesperson to receive job-related culture, skills, knowledge, and attitudes that result in improved performance in the selling environment.

John H. Patterson, founder of the National Cash Register Company and known as the father of sales training, used to say, "At NCR our salesmen never stop learning."[1] This philosophy is the reason that successful companies thoroughly train new salespeople and maintain ongoing training programs for their experienced sales personnel.

Companies are interested in training primarily to increase sales volume, salesperson productivity, and profitability. This emphasis on sales training for *results* has been expressed by the chairman and chief executive officer of U.S. Steel:

We support training and development activities to get results . . . . We're interested in the specific things that provide greater rewards to the employee, increased return to the stockholder, and enable reinvestment of sales revenue to meet the growing needs of the business. In other words, [we're interested in] those things which affect the "bottom line."[2]

Like many professional careers, selling is a skill that can truly be developed only through *experience*. Sales knowledge obtained through education, reading, formalized sales training, and word-of-mouth is helpful in enhancing overall sales ability, but actual experience is the critical source of sales knowledge. Some sales managers will hire only experienced people to fill entry-level selling slots. Indeed, some corporations will not allow people to fill marketing staff positions unless they have had field sales experience with the company or a major competitor.

Sales experience makes for a better salesperson by showing how buyers perceive a product or product line; revealing unrecognized or undervalued product benefits or shortcomings; voicing a multitude of unanticipated protests and objections; showing a great number of prospect moods and attitudes over a short period of time; generally, providing a challenge that makes selling a skill never to be truly mastered, only improved. No author or sales trainer can simulate the almost infinite variety of situations that a salesperson will confront over the span of a career. Authors and trainers can provide only general guidelines as a framework for action. Actual selling experience alone gives a person direct feedback on how to function in a specific selling situation.

The sales knowledge gained through periodic sales training and actual experience benefits not only the salesperson but also the firm and its customers.

Why Salespeople Require Knowledge _____

A knowledgeable salesperson will be able to provide better service to customers. Knowledge based on experience should result in increased sales. However, there are also two other important reasons for the salesperson to have selling knowledge. These are (1) to increase the salesperson's self-confidence, and (2) to build the buyer's confidence in the salesperson. For the salesperson, these are the major reasons for acquiring sales knowledge.

Knowledge Increases Confidence in Salespeople

Salespeople who are calling on, for example, computer systems engineers, university professors, or aerospace experts may be at a disadvantage. In many cases they will have less education and experience than their prospects in their fields of expertise.

Imagine yourself making a sales call on Dr. Michael DeBakey, the distinguished heart surgeon. Can you educate him in the use of your company's synthetic heart valves? Not really, but you can offer your help in supplying product information from your firm's medical department. This personal service, your product knowledge, and his specific needs are what will make the sale for you. Knowledge about your company, its market, and your buyer will enable you to acquire confidence in yourself, ultimately resulting in increased sales.

...And in Buyers

Futhermore, prospects and customers want to do business with salespeople who know their business and the products they sell. When a prospect has confidence in the salesperson's expertise, a sales presentation becomes more acceptable and believable to the prospect.

You should strive to be *the* expert on all aspects of your product. Knowledge of your product and its uses will also allow you to confidently answer questions and field objections raised by prospects. You can explain better how a product suits a customer's needs. But product knowledge alone may not be enough to convince every buyer.

Know Your Firm

Knowledge of your firm can sometimes aid you in projecting an expert image to the prospect. Company knowledge includes information of the history, policies, procedures, distribution systems, promotional activities, and pricing practices that have guided the firm to its present status.

The type and extent of company knowledge to be used depends on the company, its product lines, and the industry. In general, consumer goods salespeople require little information about the technical nature of their products; however, selling high-technology products (computers, complex machinery, etc.) to highly knowledgeable industrial buyers requires extensive knowledge.

General Company Information

All salespeople need to be aware of the background and present operating policies of their company. These policies are your guidelines, and you must understand them to do your job effectively. Information on company growth, policies, procedures, production, and service facilities may often be of use in your sales presentation. Here are four examples:

Company Growth and Accomplishment. Knowledge of your firm's development since its origin provides you with promotional material and builds your confidence in your company.

An IBM office products salesperson might say to a buyer,

In 1952, IBM placed its first commercial electronic computer on the market. That year our sales were $342 million. Currently, our sales are projected to be over $30 billion. IBM has reached these high sales figures because our advanced, technological office equipment and information processors are the best available at any price. This IBM "Star Trek I" system I am showing you is the most advanced piece of equipment on the market today. It is five years ahead of any other computer!

Policies and Procedures. To give good service, you should be able to tell a customer how an order is processed, how long it takes for orders to be filled, your firm's returned goods policy, how to open a new account, and what to do in the event of a shipping error. If you handle these situations quickly and fairly, your buyer will gain confidence in you and your firm.

Production Facilities. Many companies require their new salespeople to tour their production facilities to give them a first-hand look at the company's operations. This is a good opportunity to gain product knowledge. For example, the Bigelow-Sanford Carpet Company salesperson can say, "When I was visiting our production plant, I viewed each step of the carpet production process. The research and development department allowed us to watch comparison tests between our carpets and competitor's carpets. Our carpets did everything but fly— but they are working on that!"

Service Facilities. Many companies have both service facilities and service representatives to help their customers. Being able to say, "We can have a service representative here the same day you call our service center," strengthens a sales presentation, especially if service is important for the customer (as it is in the office copier and computer industries).

Know Your Product

Knowledge about your company's products and those of your competitors is a major component of sales knowledge. You should become an expert on your company's products. You should understand how they are produced and their level of quality. This type of product knowledge is important to the buyer.

Your product knowledge may include such technical details as these:

- Performance data.
- Physical size and characteristics.
- How the product operates.
- Specific features, advantages, and benefits of the product.
- How well the product is selling in the marketplace.

Many companies have their new salespeople work in a manufacturing plant (for example, on the assembly line) or in the warehouse (filling orders and receiving stock). This hands-on experience may cost the salesperson a lot of sweat and sore muscles for a couple of weeks or months, but the payoff is a world of product knowledge and help in future selling that could not be earned in any other way. U.S. Steel, for example, has its new salespeople spend several weeks in a production plant. Often new salespeople in the oil and gas industry find themselves roughnecking and driving trucks during the first few months on the job. Also, a sales representative for McKesson Chemical is apt to spend the first two or three weeks on the job in a warehouse unloading freight cars and flatbed trucks and filling 55-gallon drums with various liquid chemicals.

Much can be learned at periodic company sales meetings. At sales meetings a consumer goods manufacturer may concentrate on developing sales presentations for the products to receive special emphasis during the company sales period. Company advertising programs, price discounts, and promotional allowances for these products are discussed. Although little time is spent on the technical aspects of consumer products, much time is devoted to discussing the marketing mix for these products (product type, promotion, distribution, and price).

Sales managers for technical products might spend as much as 75 percent of a sales meeting discussing product information. The remaining time might be allotted to sales techniques.

In many cases, distributors of low-priced, high-volume products (food retailers, for instance) or users of high-priced critical components (tires for autos) are equally or more concerned with how quickly and by what means they will receive a product. This involves a very important kind of information: knowledge of your firm's channels of distribution.

A Little Knowledge of Distribution Can Go a Long Way

It is essential to understand the channel of distribution used by your company to move its products to the final consumer. Knowledge of each channel member is also vital. Wholesalers and retailers often stock thousands of products, and each may have hundreds of salespeople, like you, from a multitude of companies calling on its buyers. You should know as much about each channel member as possible. Some important information you will need is:

- Likes and dislikes of each channel member's customers.
- Product lines and assortment each one carries.
- When each member sees salespeople.
- Their distribution, promotion, and pricing policies.
- What and how much of a product each has purchased in the past.

While most of your channel members will have similar policies concerning salespeople, you should keep abreast of the differences between them.

Conflict and Cooperation in Distribution Channels

A trade channel can be ideally viewed as a group of firms acting together to move goods from the manufacturer to users. Yet power struggles do exist in distribution channels. Wholesalers may resist buying a new product until it is actually demanded by their retail customers. Supermarket retailers may already have 12 different brands of hand soap, toothpaste, or cookies. Why should they buy another brand that comes in three sizes? If they were to buy this new product, would a present product need to be dropped?

What about the large retailer, such as Sears or Safeway, that typically demands special favors such as products built to specifications, lower prices, and special delivery from the manufacturer? The manufacturer selling to mass merchandisers who discount their products may find it difficult to convince nondiscounters, like Sears, to help sell these products.

These are just a few examples of the type of channel conflicts you may have to face. If the problem turns into a stalemate, the channel member affected by the problem may be forced to take an alternative course of action. If wholesalers will not cooperate as the manufacturer wishes, the manufacturer may sell only to retailers. If a manufacturer will not cooperate with a wholesaler or retailer, that wholesaler or retailer may begin manufacturing its own house brand products.

These alternative solutions can be costly to both parties involved in terms of lost sales, or the additional costs incurred. Both manufacturers and middlemen can promote a spirit of cooperation by establishing policies and taking actions to benefit their channel counterparts.

Cooperation from the Manufacturer.   The manufacturer should enable its salespeople to offer their middlemen:

- A reasonable assortment of products, properly designed, reasonably priced, and available in the quantities requested.
- Deletion of individual products from the product line when needed.
- A fair or proportionate amount of advertising for new products (when applicable) to build product demand.
- A pledge to honor service guarantees and to refund or replace damaged merchandise.
- Regular sales call schedule on middlemen.
- Reasonable estimates of quantities of product to stock or order.
- Useful market information.

By treating each middleman as a partner rather than an adversary and considering his viewpoint, you can reduce channel conflicts for the manufacturer.

Cooperation from the Middleman.   Likewise, wholesalers and retailers should consider the manufacturer's point of view. Often a manufacturer has spent years developing a product and is prepared to spend millions of promotional dollars to introduce the product to the market. Failure by middlemen to stock a new product, or in some cases to carry adequate quantities of a new product, can jeopardize the tremendous investment in time, capital, and human resources that the manufacturer has made.

What can the middlemen do to cooperate with the manufacturer? They can:

- Give careful consideration to the sale proposal of a manufacturer's salesperson, especially those representing large suppliers.
- Provide their employees with essential product information.
- Carry an adequate supply of a product.
- Properly display and price products to avoid consumer confusion.
- Advertise and promote as agreed on with manufacturer's salesperson.
- Honor manufacturer's warranties and coupons.
- Pay bills on time.

While periodic channel conflicts are almost unavoidable, cooperation between channel members is important for efficient movement of goods from manufacturer to end user. Although they may seem fairly obvious, the actions and policies suggested here are important to stress. They can aid channel members in avoiding costly conflicts, thereby furthering the efficient diffusion of industrial and consumer goods.

In many cases, the manufacturer or middleman's sales representative is the medium through which such channel-smoothing policies are administered. In this important function, effective salespeople can benefit not only employers and customers, but also themselves. Channel cooperation aids salespeople by increasing sales revenue and maintaining long-run supplier relationships. Another help comes from advertising.

Advertising Aids Salespeople

Personal selling, advertising, publicity, and sales promotion are the main components of a firm's promotional effort. Companies sometimes coordinate these three promotional tools in a promotional campaign. A sales force may be asked by the corporate marketing manager to concentrate on selling product A for the months of April and May. Meanwhile, product A is simultaneously promoted on television and in magazines, and direct-mail samples or cents-off coupons for product A are being sent to consumers.

Keeping abreast of your company's advertising and sales promotion activities is a must. By incorporating this data into your sales presentation, you can provide your customers with a world of information that they probably knew little about, and that could secure you the sale. Figure 4–1 illustrates the type of advertising and sales promotion you would use when making a sales presentation for a mouthwash called Fresh Mouth. Suppose Fresh Mouth was a new product and had just emerged from the test market. As a lead-in to the information in Figure 4–1, you might say:

Mr. Buyer, Fresh Mouth was a proven success in our Eastern test markets. Fresh Mouth had a 9.8 percent market share only nine months after the start of advertising. Laboratory tests proved that the Fresh Mouth formula is superior to that of the leading competition. Consumer panels significantly preferred Fresh Mouth to leading competing brands. There was a repurchase rate of 50 percent after sampling. The trade (retailers) gave enthusiastic support in the test market areas.

[Now you would discuss the information contained in Figure 4–1.]

Figure 4–1

Example of Advertising and Sales Promotion Information Salesperson Tells Buyer

1. Massive sampling and couponing:
   - There will be a blanketing of the top 300 markets with 4.4 oz. sample plus eight-cents-off coupon. Your market is included.
   - There will be a 75 percent coverage of homes in the top 100 markets. Your market is included.
2. Heavy advertising:
   - Nighttime network TV.
   - Daytime network TV.
   - Saturation spot TV.
   - Newspapers.
   - The total network and spot advertising will reach 85 percent of all homes in the United States five times each week, based on a four-week average. This means that, in four weeks, Fresh Mouth will have attained 150 million home impressions—130 million of these will be women.
   - There will be half-page, two-color inserts in local newspapers in 50 markets, including yours. This is more than 20 million circulation. Scheduled to tie in with saturation sampling is a couponing program.
   - $15 million will be spent on promotion to ensure consumer acceptance.
3. TV advertising theme—the salesperson would show pictures or drawings of the advertisements:
   - The commercial with POWER to sell!
   - "POWER to kill mouth odor—POWER to kill germs—POWER to give FRESH MOUTH."
   - The commercial shows a young male, about 20 years of age, walking up to a young girl, saying, "Hi, Susan!" They kiss and she says, "My, you have a fresh mouth, Bill!" He looks at the camera with a smile and says, "It works!" The announcer closes the commercial by saying "FRESH MOUTH—it has the POWER!"
4. Display materials:
   - Shelf display tag.
   - Small floor stand for end-of-aisle display—holds two dozen 12 oz. bottles.
   - Large floor stand—holds four dozen 12 oz. bottles.

Types of Advertising Differ

The development and timing of an advertising campaign for a product or service is handled by a firm's advertising department or by an outside advertising agency. The result of this effort is the television commercial, radio spot, print media (newspaper or magazine), or other form of advertisement (billboard, transit placard, etc.). Following the development of the actual ad, the firm itself must establish and coordinate a plan for tying in sales force efforts with the new ad campaign. There are six basic types of advertising programs that a company can use: national, retail, cooperative, trade, industrial, and direct-mail advertising.

National advertising: Designed to reach all users of the product, whether consumers or industrial buyers. These ads are shown across the country. In some cases, national advertisers may restrict their expenditures to the top 100 markets. *Top 100* refers to the 100 largest major metropolitan areas where most of the U.S. population is concentrated. Therefore, the advertiser gets more punch per ad dollar. Giant marketing companies like Procter & Gamble, IBM, Ford, Holiday Inn, and Coca-Cola commonly use national advertising.

Retail advertising: Used by a retailer to reach customers within its geographic trading area. Local supermarkets and department stores regularly advertise nationally distributed brand products. National-brand advertising may be totally paid for by the retailer, or its costs may be partially picked up by the manufacturer.

Cooperative or **co-op advertising:** Refers to advertising conducted by the retailer with cost paid for by the manufacturer or shared by the manufacturer and retailer. It is obviously an attractive selling aid for the salesperson to be able to give the buyer an advertising allowance to promote a firm's goods.

Figure 4–2 shows an advertising agreement between a retailer and a manufacturer. The agreement provides for *these items:*

Figure 4–2

BACTERIA FIGHTERS INCORPORATED
Advertising Agreement
between
Bacteria Fighters Inc.
and
the Undersigned Account

1. APPLICABILITY: This agreement provides for special advertising services on **Fresh Mouth.**
2. AVAILABILITY: This agreement is available on proportionally equal terms to all competing accounts who purchase **Fresh Mouth** during the period December 1, 1988, to January 31, 1989, on one order with split shipments acceptable straight stock purchases of the 6 Fl. Oz., 12 Fl. Oz., 15 Fl. Oz., 24 Fl. Oz. (1 Pt. 4 Fl. Oz. Marked Weight) sizes may be applied to the total advertising fund.
3. AMOUNT OF EARNINGS AVAILABLE:

	No. of Dozens Purchased		Adv. Allowance Rate per Dozen		Total Fund
Fresh Mouth 24 Fl. Oz. Size	_____	×	40¢	=	_____
Fresh Mouth 18 Fl. Oz. Size	_____	×	30¢	=	_____
Fresh Mouth 12 Fl. Oz. Size	_____	×	20¢	=	_____
Fresh Mouth 6 Fl. Oz. Size	_____	×	10¢	=	_____
			TOTAL FUND	=	_____

4. ADVERTISING SERVICES REQUIRED: Account agrees to advertise **Fresh Mouth** in print and/or radio and/or television at least once during the period January 31, 1989, to April 30, 1989, subject to the following terms and conditions:
   a. For the purpose of this agreement the term "print" means newspapers and/or other print media having a circulation or not less than 3,000.
   b. Radio and/or television advertising is also acceptable under this agreement.
   c. Advertising must include retail price, and/or number of Bonus Trading Stamps, and/or other special consumer incentive.
   d. Any advertising furnished under this agreement shall not be considered as advertising furnished under any other agreement.
5. RATES OF PAYMENT: Subject to the maximum fund available. **B.F. Inc.** will pay to accounts the allowances as set forth in #3 above for Account's print and/or radio and/or television advertising of any size(s) **Fresh Mouth.**

Figure 4–2 *(concluded)*

6. CERTIFICATION AND PAYMENT:

    a. Print Media—Payment for newspaper and other print media features will be made after receipt by **Fresh Mouth** of a properly executed certificate of performance accompanied by newspaper advertising tear sheets or copies of other print media used, together with an affidavit indicating the date, method and extent of circulation.

    b. Radio and/or Television—Payment for radio and/or television features will be made after receipt by **B.F. Inc.** of a properly executed certificate of performance and Account's statement certifying the number, date, time and type of radio and/or television features run, accompanied by affidavits from an authorized representative of the station(s), or other satisfactory proof, that such announcements were so broadcast over said station(s).

7. CANCELLATION: Any funds for which payment has not been applied by June 30, 1989, shall be cancelled and **B.F. Inc.** shall have no further liability to account with respect thereto. No amount claimed to be due hereunder is to be deducted from any invoice.

8. TERMINATION: This agreement may be terminated at any time by either party on fifteen (15) days' written notice.

9. MODIFICATION: **B.F. Inc.** representatives are not authorized to modify or waive any provisions of this agreement.

Bacteria Fighters Inc.

B.F. Inc. Representative's Signature	Print Account's Name
Region Unit No.	Account's Signature
Date _____, 198___	Advertising As
	Street Address
	City State

....

CERTIFICATE OF PERFORMANCE

This is to certify that we have accepted delivery of the goods and have performed the services required under the **B.F. Inc.** agreement dated _____ and are entitled to $_____ Total.

	Dealer's Name IBM No.
B.F. Inc. Representative's Signature	Dealer's Signature
Date _____, 198___	

- The duration (time period) of the advertisement.
- The product(s) to be advertised.
- The amount of money to be paid to the retailer for advertising purposes (based on amount and sizes of product purchased).
- The type of advertising agreed on.
- Proof by the retailer that the product has actually been advertised as agreed (a copy of the advertisement).

Cooperative advertising follows a fairly simple cycle. After agreeing on the size of the order, you (the salesperson) and your buyer complete the advertising agreement, and you both sign it. You then give the buyer a copy of the signed agreement. On your next sales visit the retailer gives you a copy of the advertisement. Again, both of you sign the bottom of the agreement, and you send the signed agreement and advertisement to the appropriate company personnel. In response, your office sends you the reimbursement check, and on your next sales call you give the check to the buyer. The cycle is ended.

An advertising agreement, skillfully employed, can be an effective selling tool. The salesperson with a positive attitude toward making the sale will already have an advertising agreement filled out before seeing a retail buyer. Based on past sales and future sales potential, and using this advertising money, the salesperson can present a "suggested order" for the buyer. After discussing the information in Figure 4–2 the salesperson might close the sale by saying:

Considering the size of your store, your past purchases, and the promotional campaign my company has suggested for Fresh Mouth, I suggest you buy 12 dozen of the 24 oz. size, 14 dozen of the 18 oz. size, 24 dozen of the 12 oz. size, and 12 dozen of the 6 oz. size. Let's reduce the price of the 18 oz. size and advertise it. I will build you a display over on that wall and pay $54 of your advertising cost. (The salesperson hands the filled out contract to the buyer.)

Generally, national and retail advertising is aimed at the final consumers of a product. But not all advertising is directed toward consumers. Trade and industrial advertising are aimed at other members in the channel of distribution and other manufacturers.

Trade advertising: Undertaken by the manufacturer and directed toward the wholesaler or retailer. Such an advertisement appears in trade magazines serving only the wholesaler or retailer. Figure 4–6 is an example of a manufacturer advertising to retail pharmacies in the popular trade magazine *American Druggist*.

Industrial advertising: Aimed at individuals and organizations who purchase products for use in manufacturing other products. General Electric may advertise small electric motors in magazines read by buyers employed by firms such as Whirlpool or Sears.

Direct-mail advertising: Mailed directly to the consumer or industrial user. This can be an effective method of exposing these users to a product, or act as a reminder that the product is available to meet a specific need. Often, trial samples or coupons accompany the direct-mail piece.

Direct-mail advertising can solicit a response from a current user of a product. For example, the user may be asked to fill out and mail in a questionnaire. In return, the manufacturer sends the user a sample of the product or information about the product.

Table 4–1	Rank	Company Name	Total Advertising Dollars ($000)
Top 10 U.S. Advertisers	1	Procter & Gamble	$1,600,000
	2	Philip Morris Cos.	1,400,000
	3	RJR/Nabisco	1,093,000
	4	Sears, Roebuck & Co.	800,000
	5	General Motors Corp.	799,000
	6	Beatrice Cos.	684,000
	7	Ford Motor Co.	614,600
	8	K mart Corp.	567,000
	9	McDonald's Corp.	550,000
	10	Anheuser-Busch Cos.	522,900

Why Spend Money on Advertising?

Table 4–1 lists the 10 U.S. companies that spent most on advertising in 1985. Why would a company spend so many millions on advertising? Companies advertise because they hope to:

- Increase overall sales as well as sales of a specific product.
- Pave the way for their salespeople by building product and/or company recognition.
- Give salespeople additional selling information to use in their sales presentations.
- Develop leads for their salespeople (through mail-ins, ad response, etc.).
- Increase cooperation from middlemen (through co-op advertising and promotional campaigns).
- Help educate the customer about the company's products.
- Inform prospects that a product is on the market and where to buy it.
- Aid in reducing cognitive dissonance over the purchase.
- Create sales or presell customers between a salesperson's calls.

Advertising serves a variety of purposes, depending on the nature of a product or industry. The majority of the 10 top advertisers listed in Table 4–1 are well-known manufacturers of consumer goods.[3] This indicates that more advertising dollars are lavished on consumer items. However, as industrial advertising has more specified channels of communication (such as trade periodicals and trade shows) and a smaller number of potential customers, advertising costs tend to be lower. In either case, advertising, carefully employed, can benefit both a firm and its sales force. Sales promotion is another potential aid to a company and its sales force.

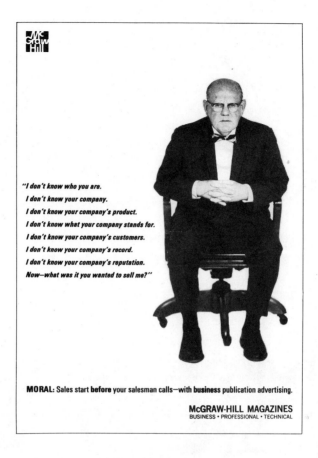

"*I don't know who you are.*
I don't know your company.
I don't know your company's product.
I don't know what your company stands for.
I don't know your company's customers.
I don't know your company's record.
I don't know your company's reputation.
Now—what was it you wanted to sell me?"

MORAL: Sales start **before** your salesman calls—with **business** publication advertising.

McGRAW-HILL MAGAZINES
BUSINESS • PROFESSIONAL • TECHNICAL

Sales Promotion Generates Sales for You

Sales promotion involves activities or materials other than personal selling, advertising, and publicity used to create sales for goods or services. Sales promotion can be divided into consumer and trade sales promotion. **Consumer sales promotion** includes free samples, coupons, contests, and demonstrations to consumers. **Trade sales promotion** encourages resellers to purchase and aggressively sell a manufacturer's products by offering incentives like sales contests, displays, special purchase prices, and free merchandise (for example, buy 10 cases of a product and get 1 case free).

The company's promotional efforts can be a useful sales tool for an enterprising salesperson. Sales promotion offers may prove to the retailer or wholesaler that the selling firm will actively assist in creating consumer demand. This in turn improves the salesperson's probability of making the sale. Some of the more popular sales promotion items, which we will briefly discuss, are point-of-purchase displays, shelf positioning, premiums, contests and sweepstakes, and consumer premiums.

Point-of-Purchase Displays: Get 'em Out There

Point-of-purchase (POP) displays allow a product to be easily seen and purchased. A product POP display may include photographs, banners, drawings, coupons, a giant-sized product carton, aisle dumps, counter displays, or floor stands. POP displays greatly increase product sales. It is up to the salesperson to obtain the retailer's cooperation to allow the use of the POP display in the store.

Figure 4–3 shows Mark Failor of General Mills making a giant display of Cheerios. People are attracted to displays. They catch the customer's attention and make products easy to purchase, which results in increased product sales.

Figure 4–3
Examples of Point-of-Purchase Displays

General Mills' Mark Failor made two sales. He sold this Kroger grocery store a promotional size order of Cheerios and he had to sell the store manager on allowing him to build this giant display.

This Noxell salesman's Cover Girl floor stand draws shoppers to it.

Counter displays are very effective because they allow a product to be easily seen and purchased.

Get the Buyer Interested!

Kathyleen Paynter of Campbell Soup believes that a large part of her job involves getting retailers to promote her products in their stores. Kathyleen says:

"Aside from basic selling skills, I think two very important selling aids are enthusiasm and imagination to get the buyer interested in the sale. Using imaginative selling ideas will get the buyer's attention and make him interested in the sale. Dare to do something different or crazy to get his attention. If applicable, sampling your product—in my case, out of a thermos—is a great way to get even the busiest buyer to talk with you.

"Here are some unusual selling ideas I've had success with:

- I once made a cookie shaped like the V-8 trademark to sell a 50-case display, advertisement and feature of V-8 products.

- I made a 6½ foot Chunky Soup Robot out of excess point-of-sale material to sell a large Chunky Soup display.

- I helped a product manager win a Caribbean cruise by designing a Soup'n'Celery tie-in display and by dressing up as a can of soup and getting his wife to dress as a stalk of celery."

The use of unusual display pieces and costumes gets the store personnel and customers interested in a display and, therefore, increases sales and that helps everyone.

Shelf Positioning Is Important to Your Success

Another important sales stimulator you can use is the shelf positioning of your products. **Shelf positioning** refers to the physical placement of the product within the retailer's store. **Shelf facings** are the number of individual products placed beside each other on the shelf. You should determine where a store's customers can easily find and examine your company's products, and place your products in that space or position with as many shelf-facings as the store will allow. Figure 4–4 shows how a General Mills' salesman has effectively obtained excellent shelf positioning and multiple shelf facings in a retail grocery outlet.

The major obstacle you must face when attempting to obtain shelf space for your products is limited space. A retail store has only a fixed amount of display space—and thousands of products to stock. You are competing for shelf space with other salespeople and with the retailer's own brands.

Figure 4–4
Shelf Positioning and Shelf Facings Will Stimulate Sales

Mark Failor of General Mills obtained excellent shelf positioning and shelf facings. He knows this will boost his sales. Mark also places a 79-cent shelf-talker by his product to help attract shoppers' attention.

It is often up to the salesperson to sell the store manager on purchasing different sizes of a particular product. Also, the salesperson may want a product displayed at several locations in the store. A Johnson & Johnson salesperson may want his J&J baby powder and baby shampoo displayed with both baby products and adult toiletries.

SAMI Data Helps Get You Shelf Space. **SAMI (Selling Areas—Marketing, Inc.)** is a company that supplies sales data to manufacturers who sell through retail food stores. This data shows manufacturers the movement of products to retail food stores from warehouses of wholesalers in 54 major television market areas containing about 88 percent of national food sales. These warehouses contract to provide SAMI with this information every four weeks on computer cards or tapes. This service provides manufacturers who sell to warehouses with sales data both for their brands and for those of their competitors.

Manufacturers, in turn, relay this information to their salespeople to aid them in promoting certain products to their retail buyers and to improve shelf positioning for their products. The Quaker Oats Company is one of many food companies who provide their salespeople with SAMI information.

Suppose a Quaker salesperson finds that a supermarket has 100 feet of shelf space allocated to dog food and that Quaker Ken-L-Ration Kibbles'n'Bits has 5 feet of this shelf space. In checking his SAMI data, the salesperson finds that Kibbles'n'Bits has a 10 percent market share in the retailer's trading area. Given this discrepancy, the Quaker salesperson now has a logical reason as to why the store buyer should allow an increase in shelf space for this product from 5 to 10 feet. Such a move could increase Kibbles'n'Bits sales in that store, benefiting both the retailer and Quaker.

Premiums

The premium has come a long way from being just a trinket in a Cracker Jack box. Today it is a major marketing tool. In 1988 American businesses will spend well over $10 billion on consumer and trade premiums and incentives.[4] Premiums create sales.

A **premium** is an article of merchandise offered as an incentive to the user to take some action. The premium may act as an incentive to buy, sample the product, come into the retail store, or simply stir up interest so the user will request further information. Premiums serve a number of purposes: to promote consumer sampling of a new product, to introduce a new product, to encourage point-of-purchase displays, and to boost sales of slow products. Figure 4–5 presents the three major categories of premiums: (1) contests and sweepstakes, (2) consumer premiums, and (3) dealer premiums.

Contests and Sweepstakes Are Fun.   **Contests and sweepstakes** are popular premium offers. Coca-Cola, for example, offered consumers the chance to win up to $1,000 by completing the phrase "Coke, The Real Thing" with words found under Coke, Tab, and Sprite bottle caps marked with the number 1. General Mills once offered a one-week family vacation in Nashville, Tennessee, plus $5,000 to consumers who redeemed 10 cents off coupons on the back of boxes of Golden Grahams cereal.

Consumer Premiums Get Cooperation.   The widest variety of premiums are those directed at consumers. When a company has offered a premium for a product, its salespeople can use that premium in their sales presentations for two reasons. First, the premium can be used to help make a sale. Second, the premium can be used to urge the customer to buy a larger than normal quantity of the product. Six types of **consumer premiums** commonly used by companies are shown in Figure 4–5.

The consumer can mail in for a premium or receive the premium (a direct premium) when the product is purchased. The third type of consumer premiums are called self-liquidators. These are an offer to sell a second product, usually at a reduced cost, when the consumer sends in proof of purchase of buying a first product. The salesperson says to

Figure 4–5
Examples of Premiums

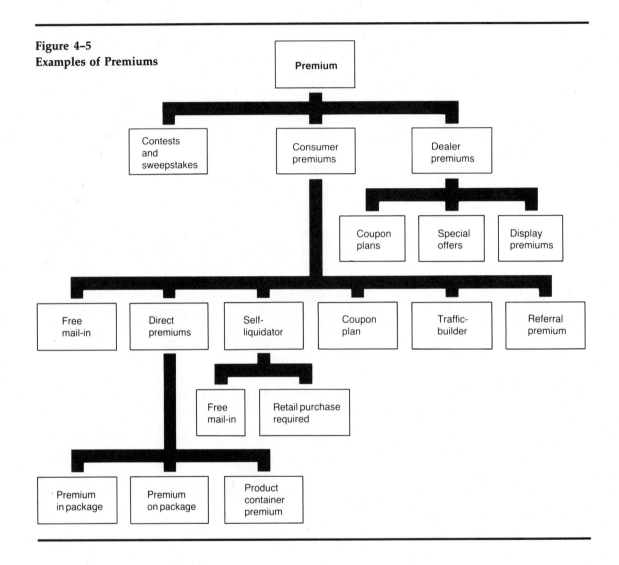

the buyer, "This month we have a self-liquidator with Gillette Foamy Shave Cream. Your customer buys Foamy and sends in your sales receipt, and for $1 they will receive a Gillette Trac II shaver and blades. This should increase your normal sales 10 percent." In another instance, Gillette has attached razors to cans of Foamy, making it a direct premium.

Coupon plans, the fourth type of consumer premium, require the buyer to save each coupon received from the purchase of a product and trade in accumulated coupons for merchandise. For example, the Betty Crocker coupon program promotes Gold Medal Flour, Wheaties, and Bisquick. Coupons taken from packages of these goods can be exchanged for silver-plated flatware.

Free products offered to customers who come in to see a product demonstration are called traffic-builders. For example, an appliance dealer might offer a plastic laundry basket to homeowners who come into the store to examine a line of washers and dryers. An auto dealership may give a free U.S. road map to individuals who test-drive a new model of automobile.

Many people believe that the best form of advertising is a satisfied customer. This type of customer can positively influence someone else's attitude toward a product. The referral premium plan works this way: You have sold your product to Ms. Young. She liked it. You ask her for the names of one or more friends who have seen the product and might be prospective buyers. You offer her an attractive premium if any of her friends or neighbors buys your product.

If carefully designed and administered, consumer premiums can benefit all parties involved—consumer, wholesaler, retailer, sponsoring firm, and salesperson. Premiums also work when directed at distributors.

Dealer Premiums. Premiums are usually consumer-oriented. Yet many companies also offer premiums to middlemen. There are three principal types of **dealer premiums** in use today:

1. The *coupon plan* offers the dealer a choice of items from a catalog in return for coupons included with purchases of the manufacturer's products.

2. The *special offer* is a one-shot premium tied to the purchase of products.

3. The *display premium* allows the retailer who buys a product to get and keep a store display. The salesperson tells the buyer, "With your purchase of 20 dozen assorted toothbrushes you will receive free this beautiful, high-quality display rack worth $50. You can place it on this shelf, and it will hold all of your various brands of toothbrushes."

The grocery, drug and toiletries, and automotive supply industries are several major users of dealer premiums.

Although promotional devices are often extremely effective selling aids, customers are still to a great extent concerned with unit price, quantity discounts, and credit terms. Therefore, these are key areas of selling knowledge.

What's It Worth? Pricing Your Product _____

An important part of a comprehensive marketing strategy for a product is establishing its price. **Price** refers to the value or worth of a product that attracts the buyer to exchange money or something of value for the product or service. A product has some want-satisfying attributes for which the prospect is willing to exchange something of value. The person's wants assign a value to the item offered for sale. For instance, a golfer who wants to purchase a dozen golf balls has already conceived some estimated measure of the product's value. Of course, the sporting goods store may have set a price higher than his estimate. This could diminish want somewhat, depending on the difference between the two. Should the golfer then find the same brand of golf balls on sale at a discount store, at a price more in line with a preconceived idea of the product's value, the want may be strong enough to stimulate purchase of the product.

Many companies offer their customers various types of discounts from their normal price to entice them to buy. These discounts become an important part of the firm's marketing effort. They are usually developed at the corporate level by the firm's marketing managers. Immediately before the sales period when the product's promotion begins, the sales force is informed of special discounts they may offer their customers. This discount information becomes an important part of their sales presentation. It is extremely important for salespeople to familiarize themselves with the company's price, discount, and credit policies so that they can use them to competitive advantage, as well as enhance their professional image in the eyes of the buyer.

Types of Prices

While a firm may engage in any number of pricing practices, all companies have a list price, net price, and prices based on transportation terms. Five of the more commonly quoted types of prices are defined as follows:

List price—the standard price charged to customers.

Net price—price after allowance for all discounts.

Zone price—price based on geographical location or zone of customers.

FOB shipping point—FOB (free on board) means the buyer pays transportation charges on the goods—title to goods passes to customer when they are loaded on shipping vehicles.

FOB destination—seller pays all shipping costs.

These prices are established by the company. The salesperson is not normally involved in pricing the product. This type of pricing allows the salesperson to quote prices according to company guidelines.

Selling the same quantity of like products at different prices to two different industrial users or resellers is illegal. Laws such as the Robinson-Patman Act of 1936 forbid price discrimination in *interstate* commerce that will injure competition. While the law does not apply to sales within a state (intrastate sales), a majority of states have similar laws.

A company can justify different prices if it can prove to the courts that its price differentials do not substantially reduce competition. Often companies can justify price differentials by showing the courts one of two things. First, take the case of one customer buying more of a product than another. For the customer purchasing larger quantities, a firm can manufacture and market the products at a lower cost. These lower costs are passed on to the customer in the form of reduced prices. Second, price differentials can be justified when a company must lower prices to meet competition. Thus, if justified, companies can offer their customers different prices. They typically do this through discounts.

Discounts Lower the Price

Discounts are a reduction in price from the list price. In developing a program to sell a product line over a specified period of time, marketing managers consider discounts along with the advertising and personal selling efforts engaged in by the firm. The main types of discounts allowed to buyers are quantity, cash, trade, and consumer discounts.

Quantity Discounts: Buy More, Pay Less. Quantity discounts result from the manufacturer's saving in production costs because it can produce large quantities of the product. As shown in Figure 4–6, these savings are passed on to customers who buy in large quantities using discounts. Quantity discounts can either be noncumulative or cumulative.

One-time reductions in prices are **noncumulative quantity discounts** and are commonly used in the sale of both consumer and industrial goods. The Schering salesperson might offer the buyer of Coricidin "D" a 16⅔ percent price reduction. The Colgate salesperson may be able to offer the retailer free 2 dozen of the king-size Colgate toothpaste for every 10 dozen purchased.

The salesperson is expected to use these discounts as inducements for the retailer to buy in large quantities. The sales goal is to get the customer to display and locally advertise the product at a price lower than normal. Ideally, the retailer's selling price should reflect the price reduction allowed because of the quantity discount.

Cumulative quantity discounts are discounts received for buying a certain amount of a product over a stated period of time, such as one

Figure 4–6
Various Types of Promotional Allowances Available to Resellers

GREAT NEW DEAL!
Four double-strength sizes to strengthen your profits!

Promotional Allowances					Promotional Support
Free-goods* allowance	Plus advertising allowance†		Plus merchandising allowance		Direct to consumer national TV promotion . . . 1.705 GRPs
	Option A	Option B‡	Reduced price feature	Display	
12 oz liquid 8⅓% off invoice	Up to $1.25 per dozen	$1.00 per dozen	$.75 per dozen reduced price feature	$.75 per dozen floor or end cap display	88% reach 1.7 billion impressions
5 oz liquid 8⅓% off invoice	Up to $.75 per dozen	$.50 per dozen	$.50 per dozen reduced price feature	$.50 per dozen floor or end cap display	Year-round physician detailing and sampling
60s tablets 8⅓% off invoice	Up to $1.25 per dozen	$1.00 per dozen	$.75 per dozen reduced price feature	$.75 per dozen floor or end cap display	Major trade and medical journal advertising support
24s tablets 8⅓% off invoice	Up to $.75 per dozen	$.50 per dozen	$.50 per dozen reduced price feature	$.50 per dozen floor or end cap display	

Also available—up to 2% billback allowance for four-color roto advertising or consumer coupon programs.
Unlimited purchases allowed for claiming billback allowances.
Retail buy-in period: July 15 through August 30, 1988.
Advertising performance period: July 15 through November 8, 1988.
Claim deadline: 45 days following appearance of ad.
Contact your Representative for complete details.

*Through participating wholesaler.
†All ads should feature both liquid and tablets.
‡Provided advertising coverage is in at least 75% of the applicant's trading area.

year. Again, these discounts reflect savings in manufacturing and marketing costs.

To receive a 10 percent discount, a buyer may have to purchase 12,000 units of the product. Under the cumulative discount, the buyer would not be required to purchase the 12,000 units at the same time. He could buy 1,000 units each month, for example. As long as the agreed-on amount is purchased within the specified time, the 10 percent discount on each purchase applies. A cumulative discount allows the buyer to purchase the products as needed rather than in a single order.

Cash Discounts: Get the Customer to Pay on Time. Cash discounts are earned by buyers who pay bills within a stated period of time. For example, if the customer purchases $10,000 worth of goods on June 1 and the cash discount is *2/10 net 30,* the customer pays $9,800 instead of $10,000. This 2/10 net 30 can be translated into a 2 percent discount if the bill is completely paid within 10 days of the sale. If the payment is not made within 10 days, the full $10,000 is due in 30 days. The salesperson might ask the buyer to reduce the price of the product to its net invoice costs and advertise it. The buyer's gross margin (profit) would be the 2 percent cash discount.

Trade Discounts Get Middlemen's Attention.   The manufacturer may reduce prices to middlemen to compensate them for the services they perform. This is a **trade discount.** The trade discount is usually stated as a percentage off of the list retail price. A wholesaler may be offered a 50 percent discount and the retailer a 40 percent discount off the list price. The wholesaler's price to its retail customers is 10 percent above its cost or 40 percent off the list price. The wholesaler earns a 10 percent gross margin on sales to retail customers. Middlemen are still eligible to earn the quantity and cash discounts.

Consumer Discounts Increase Sales. Consumer discounts are one-time price reductions passed on from the manufacturer to the middlemen or directly to the consumer. *Cents-off* product labels are price reductions passed directly to the consumer. A package marked 15 cents off each product, or $1.80 a dozen, uses a consumer discount.

The manufacturer expects middlemen to reduce the price from their normal price. A mass merchandiser might normally sell a product with a list price of $2.50 for $1.98. The manufacturer would want its salespeople to persuade the retailer to price the product 15 cents lower than the $1.98, or at a price of $1.83.

Cents-off coupons, which the consumer brings to the retail store, are another example of a temporary price discount. In both the cents-off and coupon examples, the manufacturer is ensuring that the price reduction is passed on to the consumer. This is done because the middlemen may not have promoted the product or reduced the price, keeping the quantity or off-invoice savings for themselves. An offer of a cents-off product label and coupons are used by the salesperson to sell larger quantities to customers. A summary of discounts, and examples of each, is provided in Figure 4–7.

Markup Represents Gross Profit _____

Markup refers to the dollar amount added to the cost of the product to get its selling price. Markup is often expressed as a percentage and represents gross profit, not net profit. **Gross profit** is the money avail-

Figure 4–7	Types of Discounts	Discount Examples
Types and Examples of Discounts	Quantity discount	
	Noncumulative	Buy 11 dozen, get 1 dozen free.
	(one-time offer)	20 percent off on all purchases.
		$5 off invoice for each floor-stand purchase.
	Cumulative	5 percent discount with purchase of 8,000 units.
	(yearly purchases)	8 percent discount with purchase of 10,000 units.
		10 percent discount with purchase of 12,000 units.
	Cash discounts	2/10 end-of-month.
		2/10 net 30.
	Trade discounts	40 percent off to retailers.
		50 percent off to wholesalers.
	Consumer discounts	15 cents off regular price marked on product's package.
		10-cents-off coupon.

able to cover the costs of marketing the product, operating the business, and profit. **Net profit** is the money remaining after the costs of marketing and operating the business are paid.

Figure 4–8 presents an example of markup based on a product's selling price for each channel-of-distribution member. Each channel member has a different percentage markup. The product that costs the manufacturer $3 to produce eventually costs the consumer $12. The manufacturer's selling price represents the wholesaler's cost. Price markups enable the wholesaler to pay business operating costs, to cover the product's cost, and to make a profit. The wholesaler's selling price of $6 becomes the retailer's cost. In turn, the retailer marks the product up to cover its cost and the associated costs of doing business (such as stocking the product and allocation of *fixed costs* per square foot) and to maintain a desired level of profit.

The percentage markup can be based on either the product's selling price or its cost. It is important to know which method of determining markup is to be used. Using the manufacturer's cost of $3, markup of $2, and selling price of $5 shown in Figure 4–8, the methods of determining percentage markup can have different results as shown below:

$$\text{Percentage markup on selling price} = \frac{\text{amount added to cost}}{\text{selling price}} = \frac{\$2.00}{\$5.00} = 40 \text{ percent}$$

$$\text{Percentage markup on cost} = \frac{\text{amount added to cost}}{\text{cost}} = \frac{\$2.00}{\$3.00} = 66.6 \text{ percent}$$

Figure 4–8
Example of Markup on Selling Price in Channel of Distribution

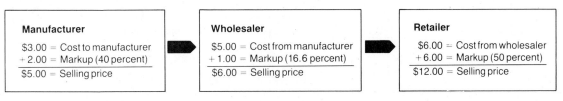

In general, middlemen want to buy goods at low prices and establish selling prices at a competitive level that will allow for a reasonable profit. Such objectives result in retailers having different markups on different goods. For example, a retailer may have markups of 10 percent on groceries, 30 percent on cameras, and 50 percent on houseware items. Too, based on type of store (discount—high volume; specialty—low volume; department—high service), markups may vary greatly depending on volume of sales and degree of service rendered.

In preparing the sales presentation for an individual customer, the salesperson should consider all of the various discounts available to suggest a promotional plan for the retailer. For example, the advertisement shown in Figure 4–6 illustrates several of the various discounts a retailer can receive with the purchase of three decongestants. The salesperson can use these discounts in the sales presentation by suggesting that the retailer advertise the products at a reduced price and place the promotional displays by each of the store's cash registers.

Be Creative in Your Pricing Techniques

Salespeople often use creative pricing techniques when selling to retailers and helping them to resell the products they have purchased. Take, for example, the RCA salesperson who presented a retailer his $100 promotional discount and suggested the retailer purchase 30 units and sell an $800 color television for $599. The salesperson pointed out that the retailer would still make the normal 50 percent markup as shown in Figure 4–9. The retailer said no, since even though the percentage gross profit (markup) would be the same, the actual dollar return would be too low. (Compare "Normal cost and profit" box with "Salesperson's first suggestion" in Figure 4–9.)

The salesperson wasn't finished yet, however. After leaving the store briefly to visit a local appliance retailer who agreed to sell 30 ceiling fans (at a retail price of $99) for $50 each, the salesperson returned with a second suggestion: advertise the televisions for $799 and offer a "free"

Figure 4–9
Examples of Creative Pricing

Normal cost and profit
$800 = Television retail price
−400 = Normal cost
$400 = Markup (400/800 = 50 percent of retail price)

Deal cost and profit
$400 = Normal cost
−100 = Promotional allowance
$300 = Deal Cost

Salesperson's first suggestion:
$599 = Promotional selling price
−300 = Deal cost
$299 = Markup (299/599 = 50 percent of selling price)

Salesperson's second suggestion:
$799 = Advertised price
−350 = Total cost ($300 deal cost plus $50 fan)
$449 = Markup (449/800 = 56 percent of selling price)

ceiling fan with each purchase. As shown in Figure 4–9, the retailer would make a higher percentage markup of 56 percent and receive more actual cash—$450. The retailer agreed and purchased the fans. All 30 TV sets were sold in a single weekend! The salesperson used this same creative pricing technique for six other customers in different cities. The moral of this story is to look for new, creative ways to sell your product. If you combine a little extra effort with a little ingenuity, any sale is possible.

Customer Credit: Get 'em to Pay on Time

It is often the salesperson's responsibility to open up new accounts, see that customers pay on time, and collect overdue bills. Table 4–2 shows an example of a salesperson's customer accounts receivable and aged trial balance. Five customers are 30 days or more past due on paying their account balances.

The next time the salesperson calls, Jones Lumber and Hardware Unlimited may be required to pay at least their 90-day balance before any more products can be ordered. Otherwise, it is quite possible that friction could develop. The salesperson's credit department may prohibit further sales to overdue customers.

The salesperson should know the company's credit policies and be provided a statement of the customer's accounts receivable. Given this information, this salesperson can be prepared when the buyer from Jones Lumber says:

Jill, send me $300 worth of your product.

Salesperson: Mr. Jones, you will have it next Friday. Would you have your bookkeeper make out a check for $336.76? I'll send it in with your order.

The $336.76 is the total past due amount owed by Jones Lumber to the salesperson's company, as shown in Table 4–2. The salesperson can get in a tough spot between serving her customer and her company. However, she must avoid bad-debt losses, and she should politely get straight to the point with customers who are not paying their bills.

The sale is not complete until the product is paid for. If it is not paid for, both the salesperson and the company lose. The salesperson must know the customer's past and future ability to pay. Credit and payment cooperation between salesperson and customer results in better service to the customer and profitable sales for the salesperson.

Know Your Competition, Industry, and Economy

Today's successful salespeople understand their *competitors'* products, policies, and practices just as well as they do their own. It is quite common for a buyer to ask a salesperson, "How does your product compare to the one I'm presently using?" If unable to confidently answer such a question, a salesperson will lose ground in the selling race. A salesperson needs to be prepared to discuss product features, advantages, and benefits in comparison to those of other products and confidently show why the salesperson's product will fulfill the buyer's needs better than competitive products.

Table 4–2

Example of a Salesperson's Customer Accounts Receivable and Aged Trial Balance

Territory Number	Customer Number	Customer Name	Total Balance	Current Balance	30 Days	60 Days	90 Days	Sales to Date
043	00035	Ace Hardware	$ 943.65	$ 943.65				$ 5,628.11
043	00605	Jones Lumber	584.54	247.78	$ 85.55	$ 154.30	$ 96.91	626.76
043	01426	ABC Fix-it	1,103.69	377.04	435.14	291.51		1,434.17
043	39782	Hardware Unlimited	2,932.59	743.04	846.50	773.44	569.61	3,387.99
043	04568	McNeal Supplies	72.02		72.02			952.81
043	04569	Building Supplies	400.41	392.37	8.04			1,422.82
	Territory total or grand total		6,036.90	2,703.88	1,447.25	1,219.25	666.52	13,452.66

The Secret of the Slight Edge

Selling, like sports, is often a game of inches. You succeed by being just a little bit better. If you have even the smallest advantage, seize it. Capitalize on it.

Everything has an advantage, a quality that sets it apart from the competition. Your product does, your company does, and you do.

Study your product. Compare it to the others.

What makes it different—what makes it better? Maybe it's stronger. Maybe it's made with better materials. Maybe it's less expensive. Maybe you can guarantee to have it in the customer's plant the day after tomorrow. Maybe it confers status. Maybe it's convenient to operate. Maybe it's attractive. Maybe it's one of a hundred things. But it's there.

One method to obtain information on competitors is through advertisement. From the advertising of a competitor, Joe Mitchell, a salesperson representing a large business machines firm, developed a chart for comparing the sales points of his various machines against those of the competition. Joe does not do this for fun, nor does he name the competitive equipment on the chart. Instead, he just calls them Machine A, Machine B, Machine C, and so forth. When he finds a claimed benefit in one of the other machines, which his product does not have, he works to find a better benefit to balance it off. "Maybe the chart isn't always useful," Joe says, "but it certainly has prepared me to face a customer. I know just what other machines have and what they do not have that my prospect might be interested in. I know the principal sales arguments that will be used in selling these machines and also the benefits I must bring up to offset and surpass competition.

"Many times a prospect will mention an advertisement of another company and ask about some statement or other," Joe goes on to say. "Because I've studied those ads and taken the time to find out what's behind the claims, I can give an honest answer and also can point out how my machine has the same feature or quality, and then offer additional benefits. Of course, I never run down a competitor's product. I just try to run ahead of it."

The salesperson selling industrial goods and the industrial buyer work for different companies, but both are in the same industry. The industrial buyer often seeks information from salespeople on the *industry* itself and how economic trends might influence the industry *and* both of their companies. Thus, the salesperson should be well informed on the industry and the economy. The salesperson can get this type of information from the company, newspapers, television, radio, *The Wall Street Journal*, industrial and trade periodicals, and magazines such as *Business Week* and *U.S. News and World Report*. The salesperson who is well informed will generally be more successful than the poorly informed salesperson.

Summary of Major Selling Issues _____

Company knowledge includes information on a firm's history, development policies, procedures, products, distribution, promotion, and pricing. A salesperson should also be knowledgeable about the competition, the firm's industry, and the economy. This type of knowledge can even be used as an aid in improving one's self-concept. A high degree of such knowledge helps the salesperson to build a positive self-image and to feel thoroughly prepared to interact with customers.

Wholesalers and retailers stock thousands of products, often making it difficult for them to support any one manufacturer's products as wanted by the manufacturer. This situation may result in conflicts between members of the channel of distribution. To reduce these conflicts and aid middlemen in selling its products, manufacturers offer assistance in advertising, sales promotion aids, and pricing allowances. In addition, many manufacturers spend millions of dollars to compel consumers and industrial buyers to purchase from the middlemen and the manufacturer.

National, retail, trade, industrial, and direct-mail advertising are used to create demand for products and can be used as a powerful selling tool for the salesperson to use in the sales presentation. Sales promotion activities and materials are another potential selling tool for the salesperson to use in selling consumer and industrial buyers. Samples, coupons, contests, premiums, demonstrations, and displays are effective sales promotion techniques that can be employed to help sell merchandise.

Price, discounts, and credit policies are additional facts the salesperson should be able to discuss confidently with customers. Each day the salesperson is involved in informing or answering questions posed by customers in these three areas. Customers always want to know the salesperson's list and net price, and if there are any transportation charges. Discounts (whether quantity, cash, trade, or consumer) represent important buying incentives offered by the manufacturer to the buyer. The buyer will want to know the terms of payment. The salesperson will need to understand company credit policies in order to open new accounts, see that customers pay on time, and collect overdue bills.

Review and Discussion Questions

1. A salesperson's knowledge needs to extend into many areas such as general company knowledge, product knowledge, knowledge of upcoming advertising and promotional campaigns, knowledge about company price, discount, and credit policies, and knowledge about the competition, the industry, and the economy. These are all vital for sales success. For each of the above-mentioned categories, explain how a salesperson's knowledge can lay the groundwork for successful selling.

2. How do salespeople generally acquire their sales knowledge?

3. At times a manufacturer may experience conflicts between itself and members of its channel of distribution. What types of conflicts may arise? Why? What type of cooperation is needed on the part of the manufacturer to reduce channel conflict? From middlemen?

4. Explain how a salesperson's knowledge can be converted into selling points to be used in the sales presentation. Give two examples.

5. A salesperson should have a good understanding of the competition, customers, and everything connected with his or her company. Why, however, should a salesperson take the time to be up-to-date on facts about the economy and his or her industry?

6. What is the difference between a product's shelf positioning and its shelf facing? How can a salesperson maximize both shelf positioning and shelf facings? Why is it important to do this?

7. What is meant by the term SAMI? How can a salesperson use SAMI information to advantage in a sales presentation?

8. Companies use numerous types of premiums in their efforts to market their products. Why? What types of premiums do they use? How can a salesperson use a premium offer in a sales presentation to a reseller?

9. Many companies offer their customers various types of discounts from their normal, or list, price to entice them to buy. Discuss the main types of discounts that can be offered. Should the salesperson

mention a discount at the beginning, middle, or end of a sales presentation? Why?

10. It cost a company $6 to manufacture a product that it sold for $10 to a wholesaler who in turn sold it to a retailer for $12. A customer of the retailer bought it for $24. What was the markup on selling price for each member of this product's channel of distribution?

11. Determine the markup of a product that cost your customer $1, with the following potential suggested resell prices: $1.25, $1.50, $2.00. How much profit would the reseller make selling your product at each of the three suggested resell prices?

12. What are the major types of advertising a manufacturer might use to promote its products? How can a salesperson use information about the company's advertising in the sales presentation?

13. Before firms, such as General Foods and Quaker Oats, introduce a new consumer product nationally, they frequently first place the product in a test market to see how it will sell. How can a salesperson use test information in a sales presentation?

14. Assume you sell hardware supplies to grocery, drug, and hardware retailers. Tomorrow, December 15, you plan to call on the ACE Hardware chain—your largest customer. To reach your sales quota for this year, you must get a large order. You know they will buy something; however you want them to purchase an extra amount. Furthermore, you know they are 120 days overdue on paying what you shipped them months ago, and your company's credit manager will not ship them more merchandise until they pay their bill. How would you handle the sales call? Include in your answer where you would bring up the overdue bill problem in your sales presentation. Also include what you would do if the buyer said, "I haven't paid for my last order yet! How can I buy from you today?"

15. What is cooperative advertising? Explain the steps involved.

16. Why do companies advertise?

17. Consumer sales promotion and trade sales promotion try to increase sales to consumers and resellers, respectively. Listed below are several promotional techniques. Classify each as a consumer or trade promotional technique and give an example for each. Can any of the promotions be used for both consumers and the trade?
  a. Coupons on or inside packages.
  b. Free installation (premium).
  c. Displays.
  d. Sales contests.
  e. Drawings for gifts.
  f. Demonstrations.
  g. Samples.

h. Special pricing (buy three, get one free).

i. Sweepstakes.

18. List and define five commonly quoted types of prices.

19. Following are examples of several different types of discounts. In each situation (*a*) explain what type of discount is being used, (*b*) determine by what percentage the *cost* of the product has been reduced and the savings per unit, and (*c*) answer all other questions asked for each situation.

a. Bustwell Inc., a regional business computer sales firm, is attempting to sell a convenience store chain (Gas 'N' Go) a new computer operated gasoline pump meter. The device will help reduce gasoline theft, give an extremely accurate record of each sale, and aid in determining when Gas 'N' Go should order more gasoline. Mr. Gas, of the convenience chain, seems interested in your initial proposal but believes the price may be too high. The cost of each computer is $1,000, but you could sell Mr. Gas 50 computers for $45,000. The Gas 'N' Go chain owns 43 stores and is building 8 more, which will open in about one month.

b. The Storage Bin Warehouse in your territory has reported a number of break-ins in the past three months. As a salesperson for No-Doubt Security Products, you believe your extensive line of alarm systems and locks could greatly benefit the warehouse. You make an appointment with the manager at the Storage Bin for early next week. During your preparation for the sales call, you discover that the warehouse at present uses poor quality locks and has no security system. You plan to offer the manager a security package consisting of 150 Sure-Bolt dead locks (for his 150 private storage rooms) at a price of $10 each and a new alarm system costing $5,000. The terms of the sale are 2/10 net 30. How would the total cost change if the terms of the alarm system alone where changed to 5/10 net 30 (and the locks remained 2/10 net 30)? What is the cost of the security package if the Storage Bin takes 25 days to pay for the purchase?

c. You are a salesperson for Madcap Arcade Games, selling video games and pinball machines. A local business wants to open an arcade and would like to buy a new game about every two weeks. A new game costs $3,000. You can offer a 5 percent discount (in the form of an end-of-year rebate) if at least 25 games are purchased from you during the next one-year period. What will the discount (in dollars) now be?

d. The XYZ company is having its year-end sales push. As a salesperson for XYZ, a manufacturer of consumer goods such as toothpaste, shampoo, and razor blades, you have been instructed to give a "buy eleven get one free" discount to half of your accounts. The remainder of your accounts, because of their small volume, are to be offered 10 percent off on all purchases. Compare the two situations. Who is getting the better deal?

Project

To complete this project you will need to visit two places. First, visit your local library. Examine magazines, such as the *American Druggist, Incentive Marketing, Journal of the American Medical Association, Purchasing, Sales & Marketing Management,* and report on the type of promotions companies are offering their customers. Second, visit local retailers, such as a supermarket, and report on merchandising techniques being used to promote individual products. Once you have collected information on several products, pick one product and describe how this information could become part of a sales presentation.

Cases

4–1 Claire Cosmetics

Jane Thompson has recently been hired by a national cosmetics manufacturer. She has just graduated from college. Having had no previous work experience, she has always felt nervous about making sales presentations. Her large-volume customers make her especially nervous. However, for the one month that she had been in her territory, Jane was really only taking orders, which took off much of the pressure. Also, the salespeople whom Jane replaced did an excellent job, and customers seemed to accept Jane because of this.

In today's mail Jane receives information on products the company wants the sales force to emphasize next month. She is instructed to review the material and come to next week's sales meeting prepared to discuss the information. Of the four products to concentrate on, one product will receive special emphasis.

Claire Super Hold hair spray will have the following sales promotion aids and price allowances.

- Floor stand containing 12 eight-ounce and 36 twelve-ounce sizes.
- Counter display containing 6 eight-ounce and 6 twelve-ounce sizes.
- $1 floor stand and counter display off-invoice allowance.
- 10 percent co-op advertising allowance, requiring proof of advertising.
- 10 percent off-invoice discount for each dozen of each size purchased.

The 8-ounce size has a suggested retail price of $1.39 and has a normal invoice cost of 83 cents or $9.96 a dozen. The more popular 12-ounce size retails for $1.99 and costs $1.19 each or $14.28 a dozen. Jane knows that she, like each salesperson, will be called on at the meeting to give her ideas on how to sell this product in front of the 10 salespeople in her district. Her boss will be there, and, it is rumored, the national sales manager will be in the area and may attend. This really makes her nervous.

Questions:

1. What can Jane do to prepare herself for the meeting to reduce her nervousness?
2. If you were attending the meeting what ideas would you present?

4–2 McBath Feminine Apparel

Getting a new, improved product into a chain of stores that has never carried her line of ladies' apparel is a new experience for Lynn Morris. Lynn has just been promoted to key account sales representative for McBath Feminine Apparel in the past month.

She has worked for McBath since graduating from college three years earlier. As a novice salesperson in a large metropolitan market, she had inherited a sales territory where virtually all of the major department stores in her area carried the popular McBath line. By displaying a service attitude, Lynn kept all her original accounts, and even managed to help several of these outlets increase their sales of her McBath products, but she was never really given the opportunity to sell to new accounts.

Now, she has accepted the key account (a key account is one that generates a large volume of sales for the company) sales position in another region of the country. Further, she has been given the responsibility of selling to a large chain of department stores (Federale) that has never carried McBath products. Vice president of marketing at McBath, Maurice Leverett, is counting heavily on adding the Federale chain because James McBath, the company's hard-driving president, is intent on continuing McBath's rapid sales growth.

Lynn firmly believes that her products are the best on the market. She is concerned, however, about the sales interview she has scheduled with the chief purchasing agent at Federale, Mary Bruce. Despite McBath's high-quality image and its reputation for having a dependable, hard-working sales force, Mary Bruce has turned down other McBath salespeople several times over the past six years, saying, "We already stock four manufacturers' undergarments and lingerie. We are quite happy with the lines we now carry and with the service their salespeople provide us. Besides, we only have so much floor space to devote to bras (McBath's major item), and we don't want to confuse our customers with another line."

Lynn has decided to make her company's new display system her major selling point for several reasons:

- Several high-ranking McBath executives (including vice president of marketing Leverette) are strong backers of the new display and want it in all retail outlets.

- The stores currently using the display for test marketing purposes have shown an increase in sales for McBath products of 50 percent.

- Federale will not have to set aside very much space for the new system, and it can be installed, stocked, and ready for use in less than one hour.

- The display will increase shopping convenience by allowing shoppers easy access to the well-known, trusted line of McBath products with the aid of clear, soft-shell plastic packaging and easy-to-understand sizing.

- A new advertising campaign will start in a few weeks and will emphasize the revolutionary display. Other promotions, such as coupons and special introductory sales, will also be tried.

Questions:

1. Lynn believes a good presentation will be critical for her to sell Ms. Bruce the new display. How should she structure her presentation? What are the key selling points she should discuss?

2. Assume you are Maurice Leverett (vice president of marketing for McBath). Give an example of each of the four major types of discounts discussed in this chapter that you could have your salespeople use to help them get the new display into retail stores. What type of discount do you think will be the most effective? The least effective? Explain your reasoning.

3. How can Lynn use quantity (cumulative and noncumulative), cash, trade, and consumer discounts to her advantage?

III THE DYNAMICS OF SELLING

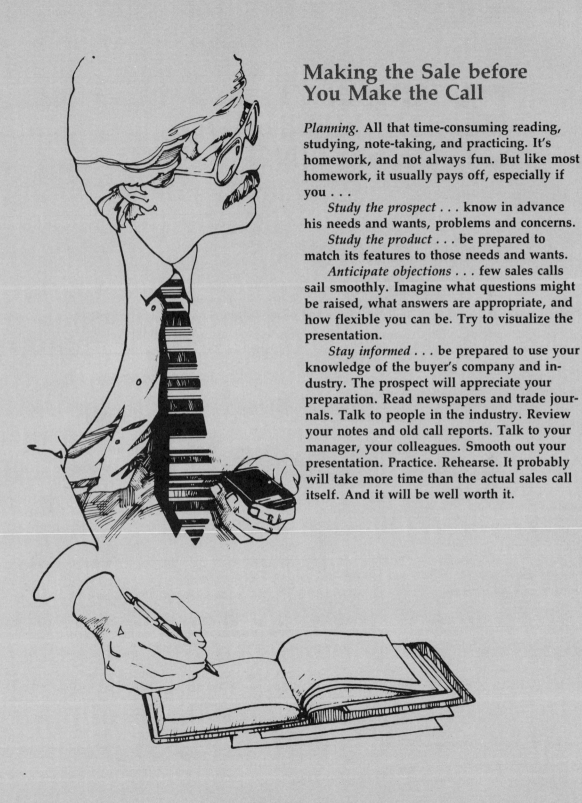

Making the Sale before You Make the Call

Planning. All that time-consuming reading, studying, note-taking, and practicing. It's homework, and not always fun. But like most homework, it usually pays off, especially if you . . .

Study the prospect . . . know in advance his needs and wants, problems and concerns.

Study the product . . . be prepared to match its features to those needs and wants.

Anticipate objections . . . few sales calls sail smoothly. Imagine what questions might be raised, what answers are appropriate, and how flexible you can be. Try to visualize the presentation.

Stay informed . . . be prepared to use your knowledge of the buyer's company and industry. The prospect will appreciate your preparation. Read newspapers and trade journals. Talk to people in the industry. Review your notes and old call reports. Talk to your manager, your colleagues. Smooth out your presentation. Practice. Rehearse. It probably will take more time than the actual sales call itself. And it will be well worth it.

5 PROSPECTING— THE LIFEBLOOD OF SELLING

Learning Objectives

1. To begin discussion of the 10 steps of the sales process.
2. To convey the importance of sales prospecting.
3. To illustrate how to make an appointment with the prospect.

Key Terms for Selling

Sales process	Endless chain method
Prospect	Exhibitions and demonstrations
Prospecting	Center of influence method
Lead	Direct mail prospecting
Qualified prospect	Telephone prospecting
Gatekeepers	Telemarketing
Cold canvas method	Observation method

Profile

Vikki Morrison
FirstTeam Walk-In Realty

Vikki's company has four offices in Orange County, California, which are currently closing escrow on between $70 and $80 million a month in volume. Her office is in Huntington Beach, California. FirstTeam has over 200 agents, and Vikki is their top producer. From 1981 to 1985 she closed on over $48 million. By June of 1986 Vikki had sold $9 million, well on her way to reaching her goal of $19 million for the year. This would earn her $570,000.

Vikki strongly believes in effective sales prospecting. "Prospecting for business is the only way you can obtain clientele," says Vikki. "Each person you meet is a potential client—everyone, from your dry cleaner and your grocer to local gas station owners, as well as my individual geographical residential areas that I call a 'farm.' In my field I contact a household on a once-a-month basis in hopes of establishing face-to-face contact and a chance to chat with the homeowner." Vikki often knocks on doors of some 400 homes each month.

"After four or five contacts with the same individuals, and hopefully a positive response, I actually build a relationship with these people based on friendship. I don't discuss selling real estate with them unless they bring up the subject. We are friends. We discuss everything else, and I especially enjoy learning about their different talents and hobbies. There are some very unique people in the world if you take the time to find out about them.

"I plan each day in advance. I have a daytimer that I follow religiously. I go into my farm with 3 x 5 cards containing each person's name, address, and any other pertinent information about them. I have been doing it for so long that if someone from my farm telephones and says, 'Hi, this is Sally Jones,' I can immediately picture her house and the street on which she lives. I can usually recall the names of her children and sometimes even that of her dog. I provide a number of services for these people throughout the year, and when they decide to sell their homes, they many times call me.

"Selling, to me, is the lifeblood of our economy. Salespeople lead the way for all forms of business. I love selling real estate, but I could sell anything I believe in."

"Planned sales calls are a must" says IBM's Matt Suffoletto. "I begin my planning by carefully examining the account's situation and what product they will probably need. Then I review the latest trade journals for that industry's current trends. With this information I develop several sales presentation scenarios with potential questions and answers that the consumer may wish me to discuss.

"While it is important to plan the presentation, you must be prepared to be flexible and anticipate the need to change your plan. A sales call must be fluid and dynamic based on your customer's actual situation and needs at the time of the call which is difficult to plan."

The first two parts of this book give you much of the background a salesperson needs for making an actual presentation. You can be the most knowledgeable person on topics such as buyer behavior, competitors, and product information, yet still have difficulty being a successful salesperson unless you are thoroughly prepared for each part of the sales call. Part III of this book examines the various elements of the sales process and sales presentation.

Vikki Morrison has introduced you to the importance of prospects and methods to obtain an appointment with the prospect. Later in this chapter, Matt Suffoletto's remarks on planning the sales call will be closely examined in a discussion of the four steps in planning. Let's begin by explaining what is meant by the sales process.

The Sales Process Has 10 Steps

As discussed in Chapter 1, the **sales process** refers to a sequential series of actions by the salesperson that leads toward the customer taking a desired action and ends with a follow-up to ensure purchase satisfaction. Although many factors may influence how a salesperson makes a presentation in any one situation, there does exist a logical, sequential series of actions that, if followed, can greatly increase the chances of making a sale. This selling process involves 10 basic steps as briefly listed in Figure 5–1. Steps 1 and 2 will be discussed in this chapter, and all steps will be discussed in greater detail in the following chapters. Steps 3 through 9 compose the sales presentation itself. Before a sales presentation can be attempted, several important preparatory activities should be carried out.

Steps before the Sales Presentation

As indicated in Figure 5–2, a successful salesperson is involved in prospecting, obtaining an appointment with the prospect, and planning

Figure 5–1
The Selling Process Has Ten Important Steps

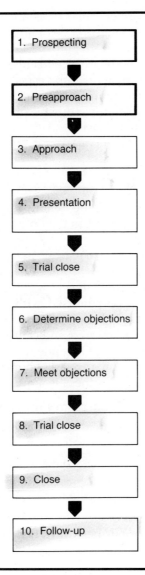

1. Prospecting
2. Preapproach
3. Approach
4. Presentation
5. Trial close
6. Determine objections
7. Meet objections
8. Trial close
9. Close
10. Follow-up

Figure 5–2
Before the Sales Presentation

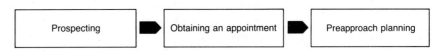

Prospecting → Obtaining an appointment → Preapproach planning

the sales interview prior to ever actually meeting with the prospect. Like a successful lawyer, the salesperson does a great amount of background work before meeting the judge—the prospect. One rule of thumb states that a good sales process involves 20 percent presentation, 40 percent preparation, and 40 percent follow-up, especially when selling large accounts. As in most professions, success in selling often requires as much or more preparation before and between calls than is involved in actually making the calls themselves.

Prospecting—Lifeblood of Selling

Prospecting is the first step in the selling process. A **prospect** is a qualified person or business that has the potential to buy your product or service. **Prospecting** is the lifeblood of sales because it identifies potential customers. There are two reasons that a salesperson must look constantly for new prospects: (1) to increase sales, and (2) to replace customers that will be lost over time.

A prospect should not be confused with a lead. The name of a person or business who might be a prospect is referred to as a **lead.** A lead can also be referred to as a *suspect*, indicating the person or business is suspected of being a prospect. Once the lead has been qualified, the lead becomes a prospect. You can ask yourself seven questions to determine if an individual or business is a **qualified prospect.**

1. Does this individual or business *need* my services or products?
2. Does this individual or business *perceive* a *need* or *problem* that may be satisfied by my product or *service?*
3. Does the individual or business have a sincere *desire* to fulfill this need or solve this problem?
4. Can this person's desire to fulfill needs or solve problems be converted into a *belief* that my product is needed?
5. Does this individual or business have the *financial resources* to pay?
6. Does the individual have the *authority* to buy?
7. Will this potential prospect's purchase be large enough to be *profitable?*

The majority of salespeople operate in single sales territories containing customers, prospects, and leads. Although locating leads and qualifying prospects are important activities for all salespeople, those selling products directly to the consumer, such as life insurance, automobiles, or real estate, rely more heavily on prospecting than their industrial and retail store counterparts. Yet prospecting is also important to the latter.

Take, for example, Matt Suffoletto's (IBM) comments on prospecting:

Prospecting is the process of acquiring basic demographic knowledge of potential customers for your product. Lists are available from many vendors which break down businesses in a given geography by industry, revenue, and number of employees. These lists can provide an approach to mass marketing, via either mailings or telephone canvassing. That canvassing is either done by the salesperson or through an administrative sales support person. No matter who performs the canvass or how it is done, it is an important element in increasing sales productivity. The next step of qualifying the potential customer is often included in the prospecting process. Qualification is a means of quickly determining two facts. First, is there potential need for your product and second, is the prospect capable of making a purchase decision? Specifically, does he or she have the decision authority and the financial ability to acquire your product?

Where to Find Prospects

Sources of prospects can be many and varied or few and similar, depending on the service or product provided by the salesperson. Basically, these sources can be categorized as follows:

- Personal acquaintances.
- "Bird dogs," who are people who know about area residents, such as a real estate salesperson, bank clerk, gas station attendant, etc.
- Newspaper leads.
- Lists and directories, such as the telephone directory.
- Old accounts.

Naturally, persons selling different services and products might not use the same sources for prospects. A salesperson of oil field pipe supplies would most likely make extensive use of various industry directories in a search for names of drilling companies. A life insurance salesperson could, and should, use personal acquaintances, "bird dogs," and old accounts as sources of prospects. A pharmaceutical salesperson would scan the local newspaper looking for announcements of new physicians, hospital, medical office, and clinical laboratory openings, whereas a sales representative for a company such as General Mills or Quaker Oats would watch for announcements of the construction of new grocery stores and shopping centers.

Top real estate salesperson Vikki Morrison feels that prospecting, which for her means knowing people in her neighborhood, has greatly aided her in becoming a successful salesperson. She strives to become her prospect's friend.

"In my area, most of the people I see are wives—and any woman who tried to farm in this tract in high heels and a dress, dripping with jewelry, would never make it," she believes. "I'm not trying to impress anybody. These people either know me or they know about me from the neighbors. I'm no threat—especially in my tennies, polyester pants, and T-shirt!" she laughs.

"Usually, I never meet the husband until the actual listing—then he wants to meet me to find out if I really know what I'm doing in real estate. As far as he's concerned, I'm just a friend of his wife's. These are the people I care about," she explains. "If someone needs a plumber or babysitter or a dentist, they call me. If I need a closing gift and someone on the block does creative things, I call them. We're all in this together!"

Who Makes the Industrial Buying Decisions?

Industrial goods have market and product characteristics different from those of consumer goods. Therefore, the buying decision is somewhat different for industrial goods than for consumer goods. The industrial buying process, like the consumer buying process, can be viewed as a series of steps. The eight steps involved in purchasing industrial products are (1) recognition of the problem or need, (2) determination of the characteristics of the needed product, (3) determination of product specifications, (4) search and qualification of potential sources, (5) acquisition and analysis of proposal, (6) selection of supplier(s), (7) establishment of an order routine, and (8) evaluation of product performance.

Figure 5–3 shows the steps in the industrial buying process, along with each of the three industrial buying situations. For the straight rebuy, steps 2 through 7 can be eliminated. In this situation a need is recognized, such as a low inventory of a product, and the order is automatically processed. The salesperson supplying a product on a

Figure 5–3
Industrial Buying Process and Situations

| | Type of Buying Situation | | |
Steps in Industrial Buying Process	New Task	Modified Rebuy	Straight Rebuy
1. Recognition of a problem or need	yes	yes	yes
2. Determination of characteristics of the needed product	yes	yes	no
3. Determination of product specifications	yes	yes	no
4. Search and qualification of potential sources	yes	yes	no
5. Acquisition and analysis of proposal	yes	yes	no
6. Selection of supplier(s)	yes	yes	no
7. Selection of an order routine	yes	yes	no
8. Evaluation of product performance	yes	yes	yes

straight rebuy basis should contact the customer periodically to check inventory, and to make sure that the order is being quickly processed. This procedure will strengthen a customer's loyalty to and reliance on a seller, indirectly warding off competition. Salespeople should be continually on the alert for the possibility that present customers may reassess their needs and find some problem with a product, and thus seek another supplier. By routinely contacting the customer, the salesperson becomes aware of changes in the buyer's attitude.

In the new task and modified buying situations, several competing suppliers' salespeople may be presenting the prospect with information. The salesperson helps to determine the buyer's needs and shows the buyer how they can be fulfilled by a product. The salesperson needs to work closely with everyone who has an influence on the buying decision. When no firm has an initial edge on an industrial order, the salesperson who spends the *right* amount of time with the *right* people often walks away with the order. This person probably spent some time learning *whom* to talk to. Knowing the right people in an organization is vital to a salesperson's existence. With experience, most good salespeople learn whom they need to contact. But how does the beginning salesperson find these influential people? The next section should help provide some answers.

Who Should I Talk To?

Salespeople must locate those people in the buying firm who will influence and make the buying decision. Industrial salespeople may talk with several people about the product before making a sale.

Emmett Reagan of Xerox is an excellent example of a person who finds the decision maker. As shown in Figure 5–4, the salesman (Emmett Reagan) approaches the receptionist, signs in, and asks to see the purchasing agent. As he greets her he presents his business card. In this situation the purchasing agent does not permit the salesperson to come to his office. Instead, he comes to the lobby where the business will be discussed. This is a defense mechanism often employed by purchasers.

The salesman is seated in the lobby going over details of his presentation while waiting for the prospect. The prospect arrives in the lobby and is greeted by the salesman. Then the prospect and salesman discuss the proposed transaction, after which the purchaser agrees to witness a product demonstration. He also makes it clear at this time that the ultimate decision will be made by the vice president of finance.

After the product is demonstrated to the purchasing agent, he agrees that the product has merit and that the vice president of finance may be interested. Now the purchasing agent and the salesman make a joint presentation to the vice president of finance.

Figure 5–4
Xerox Salesman Emmett Reagan Illustrates Initial Industrial Sales Call

Emmett signs in at the reception desk.

Asks to see the purchasing agent.

Reviews his presentation while waiting.

Meets the purchasing agent.

Discusses the proposed transaction.

Demonstrates the product.

Meets the company's vice president of finance (the decision maker).

Again discusses the proposed transaction.

The purchasing agent and vice president talk it over.

Figure 5–4 *(concluded)*

Emmett asks the vice president to see a demonstration.

Emmett answers all questions . . .

and carefully shows and discusses features, advantages, and benefits.

In determining whom to see and how much time to spend with each person, the salesperson should learn who influences the purchase decision and the *strength of each person's influence.* People who may influence the purchase of a product include the following:

- Initiator—the person proposing to buy or replace the product.
- Deciders—the people who are involved in making the actual decision—such as the plant engineer, purchasing agent, and perhaps someone from top management.
- Influencers—plant engineer, plant workers, and research and development personnel who develop specifications needed for the product.
- Buyers—the purchasing agent.
- Gatekeepers—people who influence where information from salespeople goes and with whom salespeople will be allowed to talk. Receptionists, secretaries, and purchasing agents can be gatekeepers.
- Users—those people that must work with or use the product—for example, plant workers or secretaries.

It is crucial that the salesperson get by the **gatekeepers** and talk to the initiator and to users, influencers, buyers, and deciders. For example, users of a company's copy machine (initiators) may become dissatisfied with its quality of copies. A secretary (influencer) mentions that Xerox makes an excellent copier that the firm can afford. After a conference with several major users of the present duplicating machine, the office manager (decider) confers with the representatives of several competing copy machine firms and decides to lease the Xerox machine. A purchase order is forwarded to the corporate home office where a purchasing agent (buyer) approves these purchases. Which person should the Xerox salesperson have visited in selling the machine? In this example, each person who participates in the purchase decision should have been contacted—the secretary, major users, and office manager—and the salesperson should have explained the product's benefits to each one.

Often a new salesperson is not allowed in the plant or allowed to talk to people within the company other than the purchasing agent. Hundreds of other salespeople may have already called on the company, wanting to do the same thing. Large manufacturers, like General Motors, have salespeople stop at the receptionist's desk. Whoever the salesperson has asked to see is telephoned. Purchasing agents and other influential individuals will often see only those salespeople who have appointments, or with whom they are well acquainted. A new salesperson calling on GM must plan ahead. It will be necessary to call ahead for an appointment, not just drop by.

If a buyer's secretary is reluctant to make an appointment, or if the buyer refuses to establish a meeting time, the salesperson must either give up or use creativity and charm. Sending a reluctant buyer a personalized novelty, such as a small figure of a salesperson holding his sample case along with a note saying: "This salesperson has something that will benefit you" is a creative way of gaining an appointment.

Take another example. After being turned away by a head nurse (gatekeeper), a pharmaceutical salesman put a stethoscope around his neck, obtained a small doctor's bag and proceeded to work his way up to the 10th floor of a large hospital to see the hospital's chief of surgery about a new drug. He told the doctor what he had done and why, and he was asked not to do it again. All was not for naught, however, because he arranged to have future conferences with the surgeon in the doctor's lounge on request. This salesman would not take no for an answer. While you do not want to offend any possible future clients with your persistence, you may be able to open the door on a sale that a gatekeeper tried to keep closed.

Ask yourself, when you do something creative like this, how many others have been stopped by the gatekeeper! Buyers, like all of us, appreciate people who give them special attention, or go out of their way for them, especially if they believe someone understands ..ir needs, sincerely wants to help them, and acts in a professional manner.

Planning a Prospective Strategy

Prospecting, like other sales activities, is a skill that can be constantly improved by a dedicated salesperson. Some salespeople charge themselves with finding X number of prospects per week. Indeed, Burroughs Corp. (a large manufacturer of computers and other types of business equipment) asks its sales force to allocate a portion of each working day to finding and contacting several new prospects. A successful salesperson continually evaluates prospecting methods, comparing results and records with the mode of prospecting used, in pursuit of a prospecting strategy that will result in the most effective contact rate.

Prospecting Methods

The actual method by which a salesperson obtains prospects may vary. Several of the more popular prospecting methods, as shown in Figure 5–5, are the cold canvas method, the endless chain method, group prospecting, public exhibitions and demonstrations, finding and getting the help of centers of influence, direct mail, telephone prospecting, telemarketing, and observation.

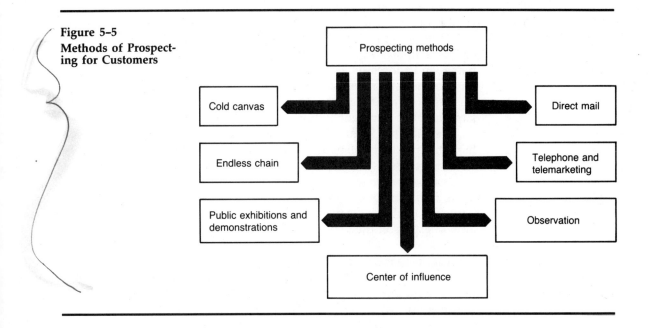

Figure 5–5
Methods of Prospecting for Customers

The **cold canvas prospecting method** is based on the law of averages. For example, if past experience reveals that 1 person out of 10 will buy a product, then 50 sales calls could result in five sales. Thus the salesperson contacts as many leads as possible, recognizing that a certain percentage of people approached will buy. There is normally no knowledge about the individual or business called on. This form of prospecting relies solely on the volume of cold calls made.

The door-to-door and the telephone salesperson both employ cold canvas prospectors. For example, each summer the Southwestern Company hires college students to sell their medical books, children's books, and bibles. These salespeople go into a town and knock on the door of every person living on each block they work, often contacting up to 50 people each day. They frequently ask people if they know of others who might like to purchase their products.

Another popular method of obtaining prospects is the **endless chain referral method.** After every sale (or contact with a person), the salesperson asks the customer for a list of several friends who might also be interested in the product. The salesperson then approaches these prospects, attempts to sell to them, and also asks them for the names of potential prospects. The salesperson says, "Ms. Jones, who of your friends can you recommend for me to contact?" Ideally, this procedure provides the salesperson with a constant supply of prospects. The endless chain is widely used in the sale of such services as insurance and products such as Tupperware and Avon cosmetics.

Exhibitions and demonstrations frequently take place at trade shows and other types of special interest gatherings. Many times, related firms will sponsor a booth at such shows, and staff it with one or more salespeople. As people walk up to the booth to examine the products, a salesperson has only a few minutes to qualify leads, get their names and addresses so as to later contact them at their homes or offices for demonstrations. Although salesperson-buyer contact is usually brief, this type of gathering does give a salesperson extensive contact with a large number of potential buyers over a fairly brief period of time.

For example, Figure 5–6 shows a Richard D. Irwin, Inc. trade exhibit. Irwin exhibits all of their college textbooks at meetings attended by college professors. Irwin sales manager Ray Lesikar, second from left, and sales rep Tim Anderson, third from left, talk to professors about using Irwin textbooks in their classes. The professors interested in a particular textbook are mailed a complimentary copy of the text, and the local salesperson then contacts the professor in his or her office.

Prospecting via the **center of influence method** involves finding and cultivating people in a community or territory who are willing to cooperate in helping to find prospects. They typically have a particular position that gives them some form of influence over other people, as well as information that allows the salesperson to identify good prospects. For

Figure 5–6

Irwin Salespeople Staff Their Booth at a Trade Show Aimed at Selling Their Textbooks to College Professors

example, a person who graduates from a college and begins work for a local real estate firm might contact professors and administrators at his alma mater to obtain the names of teachers who have taken a job at another university and will be moving out of town. He wants to help them sell their homes.

Clergy, salespeople who are selling noncompeting products, officers of community organizations such as the Chamber of Commerce, and members of organizations such as the Lions Club or a country club are other individuals who may function as a center of influence. Be sure to show your appreciation for this person's assistance. Keeping such influential persons informed on the outcome of your contact with the prospect helps to secure future aid.

In cases where there are a large number of prospects for a product, **direct mail** can sometimes be effectively used to contact individuals and businesses. Direct-mail advertisements have the advantage of contacting large numbers of people, who may be spread across an extended geographical area, at a relatively low cost as compared to using salespeople. People who request more information from the company can subsequently be contacted by a salesperson.

Like direct mailing, use of **telephone prospecting** to contact a large number of prospects across a vast area can be far less costly than the use of a canvasing sales force, though this method is usually more costly than mailouts.

Effective Use Of The Telephone

You often can accomplish as much in a few minutes on the telephone as you can in a full-length sales call. The phone can be an effective time-saver in making appointments, following up on personal visits, handling complaints, prospecting for new business, even taking orders or reorders. Its value increases as the cost of a field sales call rises.

The secrets to phone selling are few, and relatively obvious. Speak up. Don't mumble. Be courteous. Be direct. Be forceful.

Remember, you have no sales aids over the phone. You can't impress the buyer with your clothes, your appearance, your smile, or your handshake. You can't hand him a cigar, give him literature, show him a visual, demonstrate the product. Your only means of persuasion is your voice—make the most of it.

This person-to-person contact afforded by the telephone allows for interaction on the part of the lead and caller, enabling a lead to be quickly qualified or rejected. Salespeople can even contact their local telephone company for aid in incorporating the telephone into their sales program.

One example of telephone prospecting is the aluminum siding salesperson who telephones a lead and asks two questions that quickly determine if that person is or is not a prospect. The questions are these:

Telephone Salesperson: Sir, how old is your home?

Lead: One year old.

Telephone Salesperson: Is your home brick or wood?

Lead: Brick!

Telephone Salesperson: Since you do not need siding, would you recommend we contact any of your neighbors or friends who can use a high-quality siding at a competitive price? [Endless chain technique]

The biggest sales buzzword of the 1990s is **telemarketing.** Tele-marketing is a marketing communication system using telecommunication technology and trained personnel to conduct planned, measurable marketing activities directed at targeted groups of consumers.

The internal processes of a telemarketing center are shown in Figure 5–7. Many firms initiate their telemarketing venture by featuring an 800 number in some advertisement. In print ads a coupon may be made available for the reader to use. When the coupon response or a telephone call comes in to the center, a trained specialist calls the respondent (in the case of coupons) or answers the incoming call. The telemarketing center specialist fulfills the request and, in many cases, determines whether the customer has sufficient potential to warrant a face-to-face sales call.

From thousands of such contacts with the public, a firm can develop a valuable data base that produces many informational reports. Many

Figure 5–7
The Processing System within a Telemarketing Center

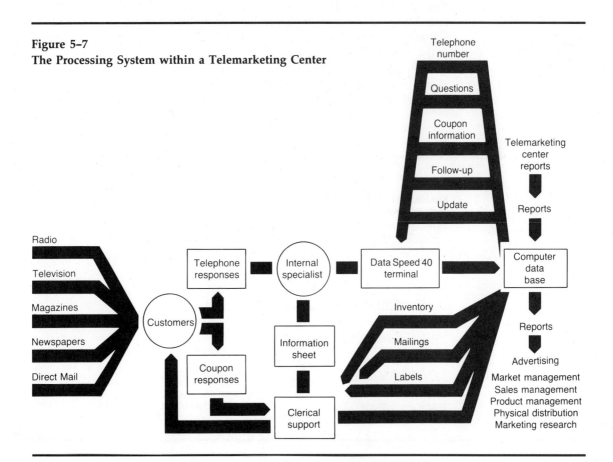

Fortune 500 companies, a few of which are discussed below, use tele-marketing centers in this way. Figure 5–8 describes some of their informational reports.

Examples of Firms Using Telemarketing. The B. F. Goodrich Chemical Group uses a telemarketing center for order taking, customer service, and information dissemination. When customers call, a center specialist brings up the customer's file on a data terminal screen, records the order, checks inventory, and when necessary, talks with production and shipping to schedule the shipment. Field sales personnel are also provided current inventory data and estimated arrival times. High-volume accounts are scheduled for field visits, thereby increasing the number and quality of contacts between B. F. Goodrich and its best customers.

The Fotomat Company is another successful adopter of telemarketing. They introduced a new product—videotape sales and rentals—through their media advertising, which featured an 800 number to encourage call-in orders. They closely coordinated their distribution activities with the telemarketing system and have realized cost savings and improved customer service.

The 3M Company relies on a telemarketing center to assist customers with equipment trouble. After calling 3M's 800 number, the customer describes the problem to a skilled technician with access to an on-

Figure 5–8

Reports from a Tele-marketing Center to Other Marketing Groups within the Firm

Advertising	Physical Distribution
Inquiries per advertisement	Consumers' orders
Profiles of respondents	Distributors' orders
Sales conversion rates per advertisement	Tracing and dispatching
	Shipment requirements
	Inventory requirements
	Product return needs
	Customer service needs

Market Management	Product Management
Segment analyses	Sales per product
Marginal account identification	Questions and complaints
	Consumer profiles

Marketing Research	Sales Management
Demographic data	Lead qualification
Image and attitude	Marginal account status
Forecasting data	

line computer system. On more than 30 percent of the calls, 3M has found the equipment difficulty can be solved in minutes without having to dispatch a service technician. This has improved customer service activities and provided a valuable service at a very reasonable cost to 3M.

Westinghouse Credit Corporation uses telemarketing to qualify leads and develop good prospects for field salespeople. Calls are made from the telemarketing center to determine interest, verify mailing information, and transmit leads to branch offices. Results are used for planning future distribution needs such as volumes and locations.

The publication of an 800 number on packages, information sheets, and sale displays invites a two-way information exchange between customers and the telemarketing centers for Procter & Gamble and Johnson & Johnson. This exchange not only facilitates effective distribution activities but also encourages the use of a familiar channel for future or repeat sales. Clairol and Scott's also offer follow-up services for their hair-tinting products and lawn products, respectively.

Telemarketing is not only for prospecting. It is also great for maintaining contact with regular customers and providing salespeople with up-to-date information.

A salesperson can often find prospects by constantly watching what is happening in the sales area—the **observation method.** Office furniture, computer, and copier salespeople look for new business construction in their territories. New families moving into town are excellent leads for real estate and insurance salespeople. No matter what prospecting method used, it is always important to keep your eyes and ears open for information on who needs your product.

What Is the Best Prospecting Method?

Like many other components of the selling process, prospecting methods should be chosen in light of the major factors defining a particular selling situation. As in most other optional situations discussed in this text, there is *no one* optimal mode of prospecting to fit all situations. Generalizations can be made, however, regarding the criteria used in choosing an optimal prospecting method for a particular selling situation. Three criteria that should be used in developing the *best* prospecting method for you should have you:

1. *Customize* or choose a prospecting method that fits the specific needs of your individual firm. Do not copy another company's method.

2. Concentrate on *high potential* customers first, leaving for later prospects of lower potential.

Successful Selling Secrets: Vikki Morrison

"There are no secrets to successful selling. There is only hard work from 7 in the morning to 10 at night. The biggest secret is total honesty at all times, with all parties. You should act with integrity and treat clients with the same respect you want from them.

"Never call clients with anything but calm assurance in your voice, because if they feel you are panicked, they will become panicked. Your walk, speech, mannerisms, and eye-to-eye contact say more about you than you'll ever know, so practice all forms of your presentation every day in every way. I suppose a secret is to save the best house for last. I just try to do the best job for the client, even when it means turning them over to another agent who would have a more suitable property in a different area."

Vikki does not work alone; she uses her available resources in selling. A computer terminal in Vikki's office gives her up-to-date information on listing and analysis of proposed transactions. She personally employs three assistants to help her keep up with the listings and shoppers. Vikki knows the value of the real estate in her area and can give free market analysis with less than one hour's notice.

"An important part of my job is providing customers personal service via constant follow-up, before the appointment, during, and after the sale. I have periodic follow-ups to see how they like their new home or investments. Anniversary flowers and cards on their birthday are a specialty of mine. I try to eliminate any and all of their buying fears when I can, and be available to reassure them.

"I sell on emotional appeal. No matter what the facts, most people still buy based on emotion. The trigger for someone's emotional side can be quite varied. For example, for some men, their families are their hot button; for others, the greed appeal of a good deal is more important. Every person is different and should be handled as the very important individual that they are.

"Another factor in my selling is that I care about my clients. They know it, I know it, and they feel it when I'm working with them and long after the escrow is closed. These people are my good friends, and we have fun together."

3. Always *call back* on prospects who did not buy. With new products, do not restrict yourself to present customers only. A business may not have purchased your present products because they did not fit their present needs; however, your new product may be exactly what they need.

Always keep knocking on your customers' doors in order to help them solve their problems through the purchase of your product.

Obtaining the Sales Interview

Given a satisfactory method of sales prospecting and an understanding of the psychology of buying, a key factor in the selling process that has yet to be addressed is actually obtaining a sales interview. Although cold calling (approaching a prospect without prior notice) is quite suitable in a number of selling situations, industrial buyers and some other types of individuals may have neither the time nor the desire to consult with a sales representative who has not first secured an appointment.

The Benefits of Appointment Making

The practice of making an appointment before calling on a prospect can save a salesperson literally hours in time wasted in traveling and waiting to see someone who is busy or even absent, as seen in Figure 5–9. When an appointment is made, a buyer knows you are coming. People are normally in a more receptive mood when they expect someone than when an unfamiliar salesperson pops in. Appointment making is often

Figure 5–9
Steve Ellis of General Mills Finds that Scheduling Appointments by Telephone Is a Time Saver

Getting an Appointment Is Not Always Easy

The owner of an oil field supply house in Kansas City was Jack Cooper's toughest customer. He was always on the run, and Jack had trouble just getting to see him, much less getting him to listen to a sales presentation. Jack would have liked to take him to lunch so he could talk to him, but the owner never had time. Every day he called a local hamburger stand and had a hamburger sent to his office so he wouldn't have to waste time sitting down to eat.

Jack wanted to get the owner interested in a power crimp machine that would enable him to make his own hose assemblies. By making them himself, the owner could save about 45 percent of his assembly costs—and Jack would make a nice commission.

The morning Jack was going to make his next call, his wife was making sandwiches for their children to take to school. Jack had a sudden inspiration. He asked his wife to make two deluxe bag lunches for him to take with him.

Jack arrived at the supply house just before lunchtime. "I know you're too busy to go out for lunch," he told the owner, "so I brought it with me. I thought you might like something different for a change."

The owner was delighted. He even took time to sit down and talk while they ate. And after lunch, Jack left with an order for the crimper—plus a standing order for hose and fittings to go with it!

associated with a serious, professional image, and it is sometimes taken as an outward gesture of respect toward a prospect.

From the salesperson's point of view, an appointment provides a time set aside for the buyer to listen to a sales presentation. This is important since adequate time to explain a proposition improves the chance of making the sale. In addition, a list of appointments aids a salesperson in optimally allocating each day's selling time. Appointments can be arranged by telephone or by contacting the prospect's office personally.

Telephone Appointment. For obvious reasons of time and cost, the telephone is often used to make sales appointments. Though seemingly a simple task, obtaining an appointment over the telephone is frequently not easy to do. Business executives are generally busy, and their time is scarce. However, there are a number of practices that can aid in successfully making an appointment over the telephone:

- Plan and write down what you will say. This will help you organize and concisely present your message.
- Clearly identify yourself and your company.
- State the purpose of your call and briefly outline how the prospect may benefit from the interview.
- Prepare a brief sales message, stressing product benefits over features. Present only enough information to stimulate interest.
- Do not take no for an answer. You should be persistent even if there is a negative reaction to the call.
- Ask for an interview so that you can further explain product benefits.
- Phrase your appointment request as a question. Your prospect should be given a choice, such as: "Would nine or one o'clock Tuesday be better for you?"

Successful use of the telephone in appointment scheduling requires an organized, clear message that will capture interest quickly. Before you dial a prospect's number, you should mentally or physically sketch out exactly what you plan to say. While on the telephone you should get to the point quickly (as you may have only a minute), disclosing just enough information to stimulate the prospect's interest. For example:

Mr. West, this is Sally Irwin of On-Line Computer Company calling you from Birmingham, Alabama. Businessmen such as yourself are saving the costs of rental or purchase of computer systems, while receiving the same benefits they get from the computer they presently have. May I explain how they are doing this on Tuesday at nine o'clock in the morning or would one o'clock in the afternoon be preferable?

One method for obtaining an appointment with anyone in the world is for you to have someone else make it for you. Now, that sounds simple enough, doesn't it? However, I do not mean just have anyone make the appointment. It should be a satisfied customer. Say, "Listen, you must have a couple of people who could use my product. Would you mind telling me who they are? I'd like you to call them up and say I'm on my way over." Or, "Would you just call them up and ask them if they would meet with me?" This simple technique frequently works. In some situations an opportunity to make an appointment personally arises or is necessitated by circumstances.

Personally Making the Appointment.   Many business executives are constantly bombarded with an unending procession of interorganizational memos, correspondence, reports, forms, and *salespeople*. In order to use their time optimally, many executives establish policies to aid them in determining whom to see, what to read, and so on. They maintain gatekeepers (secretaries, receptionists, or other subordinates) who execute established time-use policies by acting as filters for all correspondence, telephone messages, and people seeking entry to the executive suite. Successful navigation of this filtration system often requires a professional salesperson who (1) is determined to see the executive and believes it can be done, (2) develops friends within the firm (many times including the gatekeepers), and (3) optimizes time by calling only on those individuals who make or participate in the purchase decision.

Believe in Yourself.   As a salesperson you should believe that you can obtain interviews because you have a good offer for your prospects. You can develop confidence in yourself by knowing your products and by knowing your prospects, their business, and their needs. Speak and carry yourself as though you expect to get in to see the prospect. Instead of saying, "May I see Ms. Vickery?" you say, while handing the secretary your card, "Could you please tell Ms. Vickery that Mr. Baker from XYZ Corporation is here?"

Develop Friends in the Prospect's Firm.   Successful salespeople know that people within the prospect's firm can often indirectly help in arranging for an interview and influence buyers to purchase a product. A successful Cadillac salesperson states:

To do business with the boss, you must sell yourself to everyone on his staff. I sincerely like people—so it came naturally to me. I treat secretaries and chauffeurs as equals and friends. Ditto for switchboard operators and maids. I regularly sent small gifts to them all. An outstanding investment.

The little people are great allies. They can't buy the product. But they can kill the sale. Who needs influential enemies? The champ doesn't want anyone standing behind him throwing rocks.

In many cases, all you do is treat people decently—an act that sets you apart from 70 percent of your competitors.

Matt Suffoletto, the IBM sales representative profiled in Chapter 1, says it another way:

I have observed one common distinction of successful salespeople. They not only call on the normal chain of people within the customer's organization, but they have periodic contact with higher level decision-makers to communicate the added value which their products and services have provided. This concept, when exercised judiciously, can have a tremendous impact on your effectiveness.

Respect, trust, and friendship are three key elements in any salesperson's success. Timing is also important.

Call at the Right Time on the Right Person. Both gatekeepers and busy executives appreciate salespeople who do not waste their time. Using past sales call records or by calling the prospect's receptionist, a salesperson can determine when the prospect prefers to receive visitors. Direct questions such as asking the receptionist, "Does Mr. Smith purchase your firm's office supplies?" or "Whom should I see concerning the purchase of office supplies?" can be used to determine whom to see.

Do Not Waste Time Waiting. Once you have asked the receptionist if the prospect can see you today, you should (1) determine how long you will have to wait, and if you can afford to wait that length of time; (2) be productive while waiting by reviewing how you will make the sales presentation to the prospect; and (3) once an acceptable amount of waiting time has passed, tell the receptionist, "I have another appointment and must leave in a moment." When politely approached, the receptionist will usually attempt to get you in. If still unable to enter the office, you can ask for an appointment as follows: "Will you please see if I can get an appointment for 10 on Tuesday?" If this request does not result in an immediate interview, it implies the establishment of another interview time. If you establish a positive relationship with a prospect and with gatekeepers, waiting time will normally decrease while your priority will increase.

Summary of Major Selling Issues

The sales process involves a series of actions beginning with prospecting for customers. The sales presentation is the major element of this process. Before making the presentation, the salesperson must find prospects to contact, obtain appointments, and plan the entire sales presentation.

Prospecting involves locating and qualifying the individuals or businesses that have the potential to buy a product. A person or business who might be a prospect is a *lead*. Questions that are used to determine if someone is qualified are "Is there a real need?" "Is the prospect aware of that need?" "Is there a desire to fulfill the need?" "Does the prospect believe a certain product can be of benefit?" "Does the prospect have the

A Foot In The Door Is Not Always A Foot In The Door

Here he comes again. A flashing smile, the right bon mot, a carload of promises, a pocketful of miracles. It's Supersalesman.

Nothing stops him. A hard-nosed receptionist? He charms her. A buyer without any time? This gold pen has your name engraved on it. An unsmiling purchasing agent? Let me take you to lunch. He always gets his foot in the door.

But does he always get the sale? Far from it. In the end it's the salesman who does his homework, plans ahead, and knows his business who will walk out with a higher percentage of orders.

Flowers for the secretary is a nice touch. So is a gold pen, if appropriate. And entertaining a prospect is okay, too. Just don't depend on them to make the sale.

finances and authority to buy?'' and ''Are potential sales large enough to be profitable to me?''

Several of the more popular prospecting methods are cold canvas and endless chain methods, public exhibitions and demonstrations, locating centers of influence, direct mailouts, telephone, and observation prospecting. To obtain a continual supply of prospects, the salesperson should develop a prospecting method suitable for each situation.

Once a lead has been located and qualified as a prospect, the salesperson can make an appointment with that prospect by telephone or in person. At times it is difficult to arrange an appointment, so the salesperson must develop ways of getting to see the prospect. One of the best ways to see the prospect is to develop friends within the prospect's firm who can help arrange for an interview. Believing in yourself and feeling that you have a product needed by the prospect is important.

Review and Discussion Questions _____

1. Real estate saleswoman Vikki Morrison was profiled in Chapter 5. Discuss what Vikki said about the importance of prospecting and the methods she uses.

2. What is the difference between a lead and a prospect? What should you, as a salesperson, do to qualify a potential customer?

3. This chapter termed prospecting the *lifeblood of selling*.
   a. Where do salespeople find prospects?
   b. List and briefly explain seven prospecting methods discussed in this chapter. Can you think of any other ways to find prospects?

4. Assume you have started your own business to manufacture and market a product line selling for between $5,000 and $10,000. Your primary customers appear to be small retailers. How would you uncover leads and convert them into prospects without personally contacting them?

5. Assume you had determined that John Firestone, vice president of Pierce Chemicals, was a prospect for your paper and metal containers. You decide to call Mr. Firestone to see if he can see you this week. When his secretary answers the telephone, you say, "May I speak to Mr. Firestone, please," and she says, "What is it you wish to talk to him about?" How would you answer her question? Now what would you say if you were told, "I'm sorry, but Mr. Firestone is too busy to talk with you"?

6. You are a new salesperson. Next week your regional sales manager will be in town to check on the progress you have made in searching for new clients for your line of industrial chemicals. You have learned that Big Industries, Inc., a high technology company, is in need of a supplier of your product. Also, a friend has told you about 12 local manufacturing firms that could possibly use your product. The sales potential of each of these firms is about one tenth that of Big Industries. Knowing that your sales manager expects results, explain:
   a. How you will qualify each lead (assuming the 12 smaller firms are similar).
   b. After you have obtained interviews, develop a customer benefit plan for each case.

Project _____

Contact several salespeople in your community and ask them to discuss their prospecting system, plus the steps they go through in planning their sales call. Write a short paper on your results and be prepared to discuss it in class.

Cases

5–1 Lanier Dictaphone (B)

You work for the Lanier Dictaphone Equipment Corporation selling recording equipment. Imagine yourself as just entering the lobby and reception room of a small manufacturing company. You hand the receptionist your business card and ask to see the purchasing agent. "What is this in reference to?" the secretary asks, as two other salespeople approach.

Question:

Which of the following alternatives would you use and why?

a. Give a quick explanation of your equipment, ask whether the secretary has heard of your company, or used your equipment, and again ask to see the purchasing agent.

b. "I would like to discuss our dictating equipment."

c. "I sell dictating equipment designed to save your company money and provide greater efficiency. Companies like yours really like our products. Could you help me get in to see your purchasing agent?"

d. Give a complete presentation and demonstration.

5–2 Micro-Office Electronics System

Larry Long, John Alexander, and Kathryn Reece just sat down for their weekly sales meeting when Larry said, "Selling Apple's new Macintosh personal computer in our market will not be easy for us. The city only has 200,000 people; the county has 275,000. Yet there are 20 or more companies selling personal computers in the area. Radio Shack, IBM, Digital, and the others are tough competitors. I'm not sure where to begin."

"Larry, our best prospects, and the ones to begin seeing this afternoon, are our present customers—not only the ones presently using our Apple PCs, but customers who buy our equipment and office supplies," said John. "These people know us and already have accounts set up."

"That's OK for you," replied Kathryn, "however, many of my present customers already have PCs. So I'm not sure I can count on selling many to them. I'm going to have to explore new territories, knock on doors, and dial-for-dollars to even come up with leads."

Larry broke in with, "Let's go after the IBM customers. IBM has the biggest market share in our area. We need to hit them head-on."

"No way," replied John, "we could get creamed if we got into a war by attacking IBM or any of our other competitors."

"But with all of our advertising," Larry continued, "the company's service, and our fair price on a state-of-the-art PC, we can regain our market share."

"Hold it, hold it," Kathryn said, "let's start over and develop a plan that will allow us to uncover as many prospects as quickly as we can. After all, we need to push this new product and get the competitive edge before competition knows what hit 'em."

Questions:

1. Evaluate each of the prospecting methods proposed by Larry, John, and Kathryn.

2. What prospecting system would you recommend? Why?

6 PLANNING THE SALES CALL IS A MUST!

Learning Objectives

1. To discuss reasons for planning the sales call.
2. To present the four elements of sales call planning.
3. To introduce the prospect's mental steps in making a buying decision.

Key Terms for Selling

Sales planning	Attention
Sales call objective	Interest
Customer profile	Desire
Customer benefit plan	Conviction
Sales presentation	Action
Prospect's mental steps	

Profile

Bill Frost
AT&T

Bill Frost received his Bachelor of Science degree in engineering from Texas A&M University. He earned a Master of Science degree in management from Pace University in New York. Frost's career with the Bell System began in 1962 with Southwestern Bell. He was named to his current position as AT&T communications sales vice president in 1983—prior to the divestiture of AT&T and its operating companies.

Preparation, personal selling, and people management are the elements of Frost's success in the competitive telecommunications environment. "You've got to be out there in the marketplace. As a sales vice president with responsibility for five states and more than 300 employees, I am continually their support. I am there to help them in any way I can."

This Texas native doesn't believe in "howdy" calls—where you go out, shake hands, and tell a client to call if they ever need you. Frost maintains that planning before a contact is essential. "I go with a purpose. Whether it's a telephone call or a personal visit, you must think through the strategy and tactical plan. Then you go out and perform your plan."

The follow-up is just as crucial, Frost says. "After the contact is over, then you need to critique it. You ask yourself questions—like what went right or what didn't go well at all. You must be very honest with yourself and recognize whether or not you accomplished what you set out to do."

For Frost, building long-term personal relationships is another key element to successful selling. "It's important to be seen as a friend instead of a sales type who's simply there for personal gain." Frost works for this type of relationship at the bottom, the top, and every level in between in his client organizations.

Bill Frost and every salesperson profiled in this text feel planning the sales call is one of the key elements of being successful in sales. This chapter examines why and how to plan the sales call.

Once the prospect has been located and qualified, the salesperson is ready to plan the sales interview. To illustrate why planning is important, let's first review an actual sales call using disguised names.

Dan Roberts was a salesperson for University Press, a publisher of college textbooks. He called on professors at colleges and universities to show his press's new books and to remind them of the backlist of older books. Dan entered the office of Elizabeth Johnston, a professor at a school in his territory. The conversation went like this:

Salesperson: Hello, Professor Johnson? [Pronouncing the name incorrectly.]

Buyer: Yes, I am Professor Johnston. Can I help you?

Salesperson: I'm Dan Roberts, with University Press.

Buyer: I'm off to class. I can see you during my office hours.

Salesperson: Office hours. Oh, well, I wanted to talk to you about our new salesmanship book. Do you teach a course on selling?

Buyer: [abruptly] That's my favorite subject. Who is the author?

Salesperson: Oh, I'm not sure, let me check my catalog. Yes, here it is, it's . . . Johnston. Say, that is you!

Dan Roberts was certainly unprepared for the call. He did not know how to pronounce Professor Johnston's name; he did not find out the professor's office hours; he was not aware that the professor taught the course in selling; and he did not know his product. He was really embarrassed to find out that the professor had written the very book he was promoting. The one thing Dan did do correctly was to have an objective for the call—to visit with professors who teach good sales procedure. However, he should have looked at the school's class schedule to determine who was teaching the course and at what time. Dan's lack of preparation implied to Professor Johnston that he was not a good salesperson and that he did not regard the call as worthy of preparation. These shortcomings got Dan off to a bad start with Professor Johnston.

Reasons for Planning the Sales Call

While salespeople would say there are numerous reasons for planning the sales call, four of the most frequently mentioned reasons are these: planning aids in building confidence; it develops an atmosphere of good will between the buyer and seller; it reflects professionalism; and it generally increases sales. Each of these claims is certainly worthy of consideration.

Builds Self-Confidence. If you are to give a speech before a large group of people, you tend to be nervous. This nervousness can be

Matt Suffoletto of IBM: Planning the Sales Call

"The sales call is still the key to most sales efforts, and planning a sales call is the foundation of a successful sale. You would never consider going on a long distance trip without looking at a roadmap. Similarly, you should plan what you want to accomplish on a sales call and later measure yourself against that plan.

"If I were to ask you to describe the best salesperson you have ever encountered, you would probably respond that he or she was convincing and impressive. You can prepare yourself to be both convincing and impressive. First, you must know your product and more importantly, the product's application for your customer. Second, you must know your customer. You can gain a wealth of background knowledge about your customer's business from such sources as corporate annual reports, *Dunn & Bradstreet* directories, and the local Chamber of Commerce. Overall, planning shows up and pays off in increased sales when you do your homework."

greatly reduced and your self-confidence increased simply by planning what you will say and practicing your talk. The same is true in making a sales presentation. By carefully planning your presentation, you will have increased confidence in yourself and your ability as a salesperson. This is why planning the sales call is especially important.

Develops an Atmosphere of Goodwill. The salesperson who understands a customer's needs and is prepared to discuss how a product will benefit the prospect is appreciated and respected by the buyer. Knowledge of a prospect and concern for the prospect's needs demonstrates a sincere interest in a prospect, which is generally rewarded with an attitude of goodwill on the part of the prospect. This goodwill gradually aids in building the buyer's confidence and results in a belief that the salesperson can be trusted to fulfill obligations.

Creates Professionalism. Good business relationships are built on your knowledge of your company, your industry, and your customers' needs. Show prospects that you are calling on them to help solve their problems or satisfy their needs. These factors are the mark of a professional salesperson who uses specialized knowledge in an ethical manner to aid customers.

Increases Sales.   A confident salesperson who is well prepared to discuss how products will solve particular needs will always be more successful than the unprepared salesperson. Careful planning ensures that you have diagnosed a situation and have a remedy for your customer's problem. Planning assures that a sales presentation is well thought out and will be appropriately presented.

Like other beneficial presales call activities, planning is most effective (and time efficient) when done logically and methodically. Some salespeople try what they consider to be planning, later discarding the process because it took too much time. In many cases, these individuals were not aware of the basic elements of sales planning.

Elements of Sales Call Planning

Figure 6–1 depicts the four facets for consideration in **sales planning.** These are (1) determination of the sales call objective, (2) development or review of the customer profile, (3) development of a customer benefit

Computer Information with Your Bacon and Eggs

Tomorrow's traveling salesperson will start the day by hooking a portable computer-printer-plotter combination to the motel-room telephone. While he shaves and showers, or has breakfast in bed, the computer will receive from the home office the newest sales leads that came in the day before, along with special messages put on the system by the sales manager such as price changes, advice on how to counter a new competitive product that will debut that week, and improvements made in the delivery schedule that would be a strong selling point.

The printer will also churn out the leads the salesperson is scheduled to call on that day, including a profile of the prospect's product application, interfaces with the company, and buying potential. A recap of the salesperson's last visit, and his comments, along with any problems the prospect may be having, will also be printed. The plotter will provide a map of the territory he will cover, with information on the location of each call, travel time, and an estimate of the time he should spend based on each account's buying potential.

The computer will also remind him that tomorrow is the manager's birthday and that he has switched from cigars to pipes.[1]

Figure 6–1
Steps in Planning the Sales Call

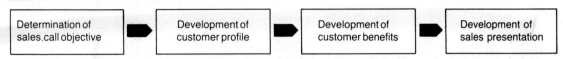

plan, and (4) the development of the individual sales presentation based on the sales call objective, customer profile, and customer benefit plan.

Always Have a Sales Call Objective. A salesperson should meet with a prospect or customer with an objective in mind. The **sales call objective** should be (1) specific, (2) measurable, and (3) directly beneficial to the customer. For example, the Colgate salesperson might have objectives of checking all merchandise and having the customer make a routine reorder on merchandise and sell promotional quantities of Colgate toothpaste.

The Colgate salesperson might call on a chain store manager with the multiple objectives of making sure that Colgate products are placed where they will sell most rapidly, replenishing the store's stock of Colgate products so that customers will not leave the store disgruntled due to stockouts, and aiding the manager in deciding how much promotional Colgate toothpaste and Rapid Shave shaving cream should be displayed.

Industrial salespeople develop similar objectives to determine if their present customers need to reorder and also to sell new products. A customer profile sheet, such as shown in Figure 6–2, can be used as a guide for determining the appropriate strategy to use in contacting each customer.

Customer Profile Provides Insight. As much relevant information as possible should be reviewed regarding the firm, the buyer, and the individuals who influence the buying decision before a sales call is made in order to properly develop a customized presentation, as seen in Figure 6–3. The material discussed in Chapters 3 and 13 concerning the various factors on why the buyer buys should also be considered by the salesperson at this time. A **customer profile** should tell you:

- Who makes the buying decisions in the organization—an individual or committee?

- What is the buyer's background? The background of the buyer's company? The buyer's expectations of you?

Figure 6–2

Example of Information Used in a Profile and for Planning

Customer Profile and Planning Sheet

1. Name: _____
   Address: _____
2. Type of business: _____
   Name of buyer: _____
3. People who influence buying decision or aid in using or selling our product: _____
4. Buying hours and best time to see buyer: _____
5. Receptionist's name: _____
6. Buyer's profile: _____
7. Sales call objectives: _____
8. What are customer's important buying needs? _____
9. Sales presentation
   a. Sales approach: _____
   b. Features, advantages, benefits: _____
   c. Method of demonstrating FAB: _____
   d. How to relate benefits to customer's needs: _____
   e. Trial close to use: _____
   f. Anticipated objections: _____
   g. Trial close to use: _____
   h. How to close this customer: _____
   i. Hard or soft close: _____
10. Sales made—product use/promotional plan agreed on: _____
11. Post sales call comments (reason did-did not buy; what to do on next call; follow-up promised): _____

- What are the desired business terms and needs of the account, such as delivery, credit, technical service?

- What competitors successfully do business with the account? Why?

- What are the purchasing policies and practices of the account? For example, does the customer buy special price offer promotions, or only see salespeople on Tuesday and Thursday?

- What is the past history of the account? For example, past purchases of our products, inventory turnover, profit per shelf foot, our brand's volume sales growth, payment practices, and attitude toward resale prices.

You can determine this information from a review of records on the company or through personal contact with the company.

Customer Benefit Plan: What It's All About! Beginning with your sales call objectives and what you know or have learned about your prospect, you are now ready to develop your **customer benefit plan.** The customer benefit plan contains the nucleus of the information you will use in your sales presentation; thus it should be developed to the

Figure 6–3

The Telephone and Computer Aid in Planning Sales Calls

This Xerox salesman uses the telephone and computer to make appointments and plan sales calls. By examining an account's past sales, sales potential, and the buyer's profile information stored on the computer, customer sales call planning can be improved.

Why your product should be purchased!

best of your ability. Creating a customer benefit plan can be approached as a four-step process:

Step 1. Select the *features, advantages,* and *benefits* of your product to present to your prospect. This addresses the issue of *why* your product should be purchased. The main reason your product should be purchased by your prospect is that its benefits fulfill certain needs or solve certain problems. Carefully determine the benefits you wish to present.

Step 2. Develop your *marketing plan*. If selling to a wholesaler or retailer, your marketing plan should include how, once they buy your product, they will sell your product to their customers. An effective marketing plan would include your suggestions on how a retailer, for example, should promote the product through displays, advertising, proper shelf space and positioning, and pricing. For an end user of the product, such as the company who buys your manufacturing equipment, computer, or photocopier, you should develop a program showing how your product can be most effectively used or coordinated with existing equipment.

Step 3. Develop your *business proposition*, which includes items such as your price, percent markup, forecasted profit per square foot of shelf space, return-on-investment, and payment plan. Value analysis is an example of a business proposition for an industrial product.

Step 4. Develop a *suggested purchase order* based on your customer benefit plan. A proper presentation of your analysis of customer needs and your product's ability to fulfill these needs, along with a satisfactory business proposition and marketing plan, should allow you to justify to the prospect how much of your product to purchase. This suggestion may also have to include, depending on the nature of your product, such things as what to buy, how much to buy, the assortment to buy, and when to ship the product to the customer.

Visual aids should be developed to effectively communicate the information developed in these four steps. The visuals should be organized in the order you will discuss them. Your next step is to plan all aspects of the sales presentation itself.

The Sales Presentation Is Where It All Comes Together. It is now time to plan your **sales presentation** from the beginning to end. (This process involves developing the steps of the sales presentation described earlier in Figure 5–1.) These are the approach, presentation, trial close method to uncover objections, ways to overcome objections, additional trial closes, and the close of the sales presentation. Each of these steps will be discussed in detail in the following chapters.

Figure 6–4 summarizes the steps relevant to planning a sales presentation. First you should develop your sales call objective by determining which product or products you will be presenting to your prospect. Based on your call objective and what you know about your prospect (customer profile), you determine which specific product benefits to present, a market plan for your prospect, the business proposition you will discuss with the prospect, and your suggestion of what and how much the prospect should buy. This information is sequenced as you wish to present it. Visual aids and demonstrations can be developed to help you create an informative and persuasive sales presentation. As was mentioned earlier, the *last step* in planning your sales call is the development and rehearsal of your sales presentation.

In developing the sales presentation it is helpful to think in terms of leading the prospect through five steps or phases that many salespeople believe make up a purchase decision. These are referred to as the prospect's mental steps.

The Prospect's Mental Steps

In making a sales presentation, you need to quickly obtain the prospect's full attention, develop interest in your product, create a desire to fulfill a need, establish the prospect's conviction the product will fill

Figure 6–4

A Sequence of Events to Complete in Developing a Sales Presentation

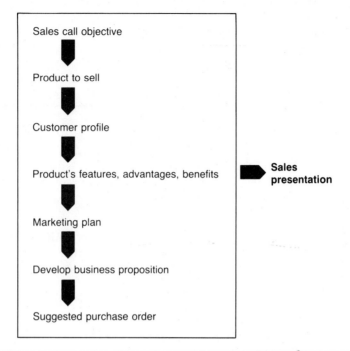

Sales call objective

Product to sell

Customer profile

Product's features, advantages, benefits   **Sales presentation**

Marketing plan

Develop business proposition

Suggested purchase order

the need, and finally get action by having the prospect actually purchase the product. As in Figure 6–5, the **prospect's mental steps** occur in the following order.

Attention

From the first moment you begin to talk, you should quickly capture and maintain the prospect's **attention.** This may be difficult at times because of distractions, pressing demands on the prospect's time, or simply lack of interest. You should carefully plan what to say and how to say it. Since attention getters have only temporary effect, you must be ready to quickly move to Step 2, sustaining the prospect's interest.

Interest

Before meeting with prospects, you should determine their important buying motives. These can be used in capturing their **interest.** If not, you may have to determine them at the first of your presentation by asking questions. Prospects enter the interest stage if they listen to and enter into a discussion with you. You should quickly strive to link your

Figure 6–5
The Prospect's Five Mental Steps in Buying

product's benefits to prospects' needs. If this link is completed, prospects usually express a desire for the product.

Desire

Using FAB formula (Chapter 2), you should strive to bring prospects from lukewarm interest to a boiling desire for your product. **Desire** is created when prospects express a wish or wanting for a product like yours.

To better determine if the product should be purchased, prospects may have questions for you and may present objections to your product. You should anticipate prospects' objections and provide information to maintain their desire.

Conviction

While prospects may desire a product, they still have to be convinced that your product is the best for their needs and that you are the best supplier of the product. In the **conviction** step you strive to develop a strong *belief* that the product is best suited to prospects' specific needs. Conviction is established when no doubts remain about purchasing the product from you.

Purchase or Action

Once the prospect is convinced, you must plan the most appropriate method of asking the prospect to buy or to take **action.** If each of the preceding steps has been carried out correctly, closing the sale is the easiest step in the sales presentation.

Overview of the Sales Process

We have briefly discussed the various steps in the selling process, reviewed the sales presentation, and examined the five mental steps a prospect moves through toward purchasing a product. Each step will ⌐ examined in more depth later, along with methods and techniques that successful salespeople use to lead the prospect to make the correct purchase decision. Figure 6–6 presents an overview of the selling process and gives corresponding examples of the prospect's mental stages and questions that may be posed at various points during the presentation.

You see that the approach is used to get the prospect's attention and interest by having the prospect recognize a need or problem and by stating a wish to fulfill the need or solve the problem. The presentation

Figure 6–6

The Selling Process and Examples of Prospect's Mental Thoughts and Questions

Steps in the Selling Process	Prospect's Mental Steps	Prospect's Potential Verbal and Mental Questions

1. Prospecting
  Salesperson locates and
  qualifies prospects.		

2. Preapproach
  Salesperson obtains
  interview, determines sales
  call objective, develops
  customer profile, customer
  benefit program, and selling
  strategies. Customer's
  needs are determined.		

3. Approach
  Salesperson meets
  prospect and begins
  individualized sales
  presentation.
 	
  Needs are further
  uncovered.
	Attention due to arousal of
	  potential need or problem.
	Interest due to recognized need or
	  problem and the desire to fulfill
	  the need or solve the problem.
		Should I see salesperson?
		Should I continue to listen,
		  interact, devote much time to a
		  salesperson?
		What's in it for me?

4. Presentation
  Salesperson relates product
  benefits to needs, using
  demonstration,
  dramatizations, visuals, and
  proof statements.
	Interest in information that
	  provides knowledge and
	  influences perceptions and
	  attitude.
	Desire begins to develop based
	  on information evaluation of
	  product features, advantages,
	  and benefits. This is due to
	  forming positive attitudes that
	  product may fulfill need or solve
	  problem. Positive attitudes
	  brought about by knowledge
	  obtained from presentation.
		Is the salesperson prepared? Are
		  my needs understood? Is the
		  seller interested in my needs?
		Should I continue to listen and
		  interact?
		So what? (to statements about
		  features)
		Prove it! (to statements about
		  advantages)
		Are the benefits of this product
		  the best to fulfill my needs?

5. Trial close
  Salesperson asks
  prospect's opinion on
  benefits during and after
  presentation.
	Desire continues based on
	  information evaluation.	

Figure 6–6 *(concluded)*

Steps in the Selling Process	Prospect's Mental Steps	Prospect's Potential Verbal and Mental Questions
6. Objections Salesperson uncovers objections.	*Desire* continues based on information evaluation.	Do I understand the salesperson's marketing plan and business position? I need more information to make a decision. Can you meet my conditions?
7. Meet objections Salesperson satisfactorily answers objections.	*Desire* begins to be transformed into belief. *Conviction* established due to belief product and salesperson can solve needs or problems better than competitive products. Appears ready to buy.	Let me see the reaction when I give the salesperson a hard time. I have a minor/major objection to what you are saying. Is something nonverbal being communicated? Did I get a reasonable answer to my objection?
8. Trial close Salesperson uses another trial close to see if objections have been overcome; or if presentation went smoothly before the close, to determine if the prospect is ready to buy.	*Conviction* becomes stronger.	Can I believe and trust this person? Should I reveal my real concerns?
9. Close Salesperson has determined prospect is ready to buy and now asks for the order.	*Action* (purchase) occurs based on positive beliefs that the product will fulfill needs or solve problems.	I am asked to make a buying decision now. If I buy and I am dissatisfied, what can I do? Will I receive after-the-sale service as promised? What are my expectations toward this purchase? Why don't you ask me to buy? Ask one more time and I'll buy.
10. Follow-up Salesperson provides customer service after the sale.	Satisfaction—dissatisfaction	Did the product meet my expectations? Am I experiencing dissonance? How is the service associated with this product? Should I buy again from this salesperson?

constantly maintains interest in the information you present and generates desires for the product.

Uncovering and answering the prospect's questions and revealing and meeting or overcoming objections result in more intense desire. This desire is transformed into the conviction that your product can fulfill the prospect's needs or solve problems. Once you have determined the prospect is in the conviction stage, you are ready for the close.

The importance of carefully planning the sales call cannot be over-emphasized. Plan your sales call in order to build your self-confidence, to develop goodwill between yourself and your prospect, to create an image of professionalism in the prospect's mind, and of course, to increase your sales. In planning the sales call, the salesperson should determine the objective for contacting the prospect, develop or review the customer's profile, develop a customer benefit plan, and finally, create an individualized sales presentation. Once these are accomplished, you are ready to meet the prospect.

Summary of Major Selling Issues

Most salespeople agree that careful planning of the sales call is absolutely essential to success in selling. Among many reasons why planning is so important, four of the most frequently mentioned are that planning builds self-confidence, develops an atmosphere of goodwill, creates professionalism, and increases sales. By having a logical and methodical plan, you can decide what you wish to accomplish and then later measure your accomplishments with your plan.

There are four basic elements of sales call planning. First, you must always have a sales call objective—one that is specific, measurable, and directly beneficial to the customer. Second, as a salesperson, you should also work on developing or reviewing the customer profile. By having relevant information about your customer, you can properly develop a customized presentation. Information on the background, needs, and competitors of your potential buyer can be found by reviewing your company's records or by personally contacting the buyer and his company.

The third step in planning your sales call involves developing your customer benefit plan. In order to do this, you must look at why your product should be purchased and develop a marketing plan to convey these reasons and benefits to your prospect. You can then develop a *business proposition* by listing your price, percent markup, return-on-investment, and other quantitative data about your product in relation to your prospect. Last, you must develop a *suggested purchase order* and present your analysis, which might include suggestions on what to buy, how much to buy, what assortment to buy, and when to ship the product.

Finally, you should plan your whole sales presentation. Visual aids can help you make your presentation informative and creative. In making your call, it helps to think in terms of the phases that make up a purchase decision—the mental steps. The steps involved are capturing the prospect's attention, determining buying motives, creating desire, convincing the person that your product is best suited to his needs, and then closing the sale.

By adhering to these guidelines for planning your sales presentation, you may spend more time than the actual sales call itself. However, it will be well worth it.

Review and Discussion Questions _____

1. What are the elements to consider when planning a sales call? Explain each.

2. An important part of planning a sales call is the development of a customer benefit plan. First, what are the major components of the customer benefit plan? Second, what is the difference in developing a customer benefit plan for a General Foods salesperson selling consumer products versus an industrial salesperson for a company such as IBM?

3. Many salespeople feel a prospect goes through several mental steps in making a decision to purchase a product. Discuss each of these steps.

4. Outline and discuss the sequence of events involved in developing a sales presentation.

5. Some salespeople feel a person should not be asked to buy a product until the prospect's mind has entered the conviction step of the mental process. Why?

6. What is the difference, if any, between the selling process and the sales presentation?

7. First, define the term *the selling process*. Second, list the major steps in the selling process on the left side of a page of paper. Third, beside each step of the selling process write the corresponding mental step a prospect should be experiencing.

8. Below are 13 situations commonly faced by the salespeople. For each situation, determine which mental buying stage your prospect is experiencing. Give your reason why you feel the prospect is at that stage.
   a. "Come on in; I can only visit with you for about five minutes."
   b. "That sounds good, but how can I be sure it will do what you say it will?"
   c. "Yes, I see your copier can make 20 copies a minute and copy on both sides of the page. Big deal!"
   d. The buyer thinks, "Will the purchase of this equipment help my standing with my boss?"
   e. "I didn't know there were products like this on the market."
   f. The buyer thinks, "I'm not sure if I should listen or not."
   g. "I wish my equipment could do what yours does."

h. "Well, that sounds good, but I'm not sure."

i. What kind of great deal do you have for me today?"

j. "When can you ship it?"

k. You discuss your business proposition with your buyer, and you get a favorable nonverbal response.

l. "I like what you have to say. Your deal sounds good. But I'd better check with my other suppliers first."

m. You have completed your presentation. The buyer has said almost nothing to you, including asking no questions and giving no objections. You wonder if you should close.

9. Think of a product sold through one of your local supermarkets. Assume you had recently been hired by the product's manufacturer to contact the store's buyer to purchase a promotional quantity of your product and to arrange for display and advertising. What information do you need for planning your sales call, and what features, advantages, and benefits would you consider appropriate to use in your sales presentation?

Project

Ask a buyer for a business in your community what salespeople should do when calling on a buyer. Find out if the salespeople this buyer sees are prepared for each sales call. Ask why or why not something is purchased. Do salespeople use the FAB as discussed in this chapter? Does the buyer think privately, "So what?" "Prove it!" and "What's in it for me?" Finally, ask what superiors expect of a buyer in the buyer's dealings with salespeople.

Cases

6-1 Ms. Hansen's Mental Steps in Buying Your Product

Picture yourself as a Procter & Gamble salesperson who plans to call upon Ms. Hansen, a buyer for your largest independent grocery store. Your sales call objective is to convince Ms. Hansen that she should buy your family size of Tide detergent. Her store now carries the three smaller sizes. You have developed a marketing plan that you feel will help convince her that she is losing sales and profits by not stocking Tide's family size.

You enter the grocery store, check your present merchandise, and quickly develop a suggested order. As Ms. Hansen walks down the aisle toward you, she appears to be in her normal grumpy mood. After your greeting and handshake, your conversation goes like this:

Salesperson:	Your sales are really up! I've checked your stock in the warehouse and on your shelf. This is what it looks like you need. [You discuss sales of each of your products and their various sizes, suggesting a quantity she should purchase based upon her past sales and present inventory.]
Buyer:	Ok, that looks good. Go ahead and ship it.
Salesperson:	Thank you. Say, Ms. Hansen, you've said before that the shortage of shelf space prevents you from stocking our family size Tide—though you admit you may be losing some sales as a result. If we could determine how much volume you're missing, I think you'd be willing to *make* space for it, wouldn't you?
Buyer:	Yes, but I don't see how that can be done.
Salesperson:	Well, I'd like to suggest a test—a weekend display of all four sizes of Tide.
Buyer:	What do you mean?
Salesperson:	My thought was to run all sizes at regular shelf price without any ad support. This would give us a pure test. Six cases of each size should let us compare sales of the various sizes and see what you're missing by regularly stocking only the smaller sizes. I think the additional sales and profits you'll get on the family size will convince you to start stocking it on a regular basis. What do you think?
Buyer:	Well, maybe.

Questions:

1. Examine each of the things you said to Ms. Hansen, stating what part of the customer benefit plan each of your comments is concerned with.

2. What are the features, advantages, and benefits you have in your sales presentation?

3. Examine each of Ms. Hansen's replies to you, stating which of the mental buying steps she is in at that particular time during your sales presentation.

4. At the end of your conversation, Ms. Hansen said, "Well, maybe." What should you do now?
    a. Continue to explain your features, advantages, and benefits.
    b. Ask a trial close question.
    c. Ask for the order.
    d. Back off and try again on the next sales call.
    e. Wait for Ms. Hansen to say, "OK, ship it."

6–2 Machinery Lubricants, Inc.

Ralph Jackson sells industrial lubricants to manufacturing plants. The lubricants are used to lubricate the plants' machinery. Tomorrow, Ralph plans to call upon the purchasing agent for Acme Manufacturing Company.

For the last two years, Ralph has been selling Hydraulic Oil 65 to Acme in drums. Ralph's sales call objective is to persuade Acme to switch from purchasing his oil in drums to a bulk oil system. Last year Acme bought approximately 364 drums or 20,000 gallons at a cost of $1.39 a gallon, or $27,800. A deposit of $20 was made for each drum. Traditionally, many drums are lost and from one to two gallons of oil may be left in each drum when returned by customers. This is a loss to the company.

Ralph wants to sell Acme two 3,000-gallon storage tanks for a cost of $1,700. He has arranged with Pump Supply Company to install the tanks for $1,095. Thus the total cost of the system will be $2,795. This system reduces the cost of the oil from $1.39 to $1.25 per gallon, which will allow it to pay for itself over time. Other advantages include having fewer orders to process each year, a reduction in storage space, and less handling of the oil by workers.

Question:

If you were Ralph, how would you plan the sales call?

Whole Chapter!

7 CAREFULLY SELECT WHICH SALES PRESENTATION METHOD TO USE

Learning Objectives

1. To explain why you have the right to present your product.

2. To discuss and illustrate four sales presentation methods.

3. To examine the question of which is the best presentation method.

4. To understand why you first select your sales presentation method and then your approach.

Key Terms for Selling

Sales presentation
Memorized presentation
Formula presentation
Need-satisfaction presentation

Need development
Need awareness
Need fulfillment
Problem-solution presentation

Profile

Emmett Reagan
Senior Training Analyst, Xerox Corporation

Emmett Reagan is a senior training analyst at the Xerox International Center for Training and Management Development at Leesburg, Virginia. He joined Xerox Corporation in 1963 after graduating from the University of Alabama. Following basic sales training he was assigned to a geographic sales territory in southeast Virginia. Emmett was subsequently promoted to the position of sales manager in Richmond, Virginia, where he remained until the summer of 1971. He was then transferred to Rochester, N.Y., where he became school manager for advanced sales training. In 1973 he moved to northern Virginia as part of the group responsible for planning and development of the Xerox International Training Center.

With respect to the sales presentation, Emmett feels that "at the outset it's important to understand that the most productive behavior in which we can engage is that which uncovers, refines, and develops needs. This is what the professional salesperson does best. It is also what the professional does first.

"Unless we are able to gather sufficient information, there is little likelihood that we will be able to uncover problems for which our product could become the solution. Obviously, the best way to do this is by asking questions.

"The most basic questions we would ask early in the presentation would be those that would provide general information about the customer as an individual and the company in general. To develop a need further, we must then make a transition from the gathering of general information to the point where the information is specific. Often a great deal of mutual trust is required before the prospect will open up.

"You should make sure you understand the prospect's concern. Clarify it. Restate it several times if necessary. Also, help the customer resolve the issue. Ask how it should be handled. Once the prospect identifies an appropriate solution, build on it and extend or expand the benefit of what you are selling. After all of the above steps have been completed, we should now be in a position to ask for the order. We will probably be successful."

"Once a strong need has been clearly identified," says Xerox's Emmett Reagan, "there is often a tendency to become smug. The new or inexperienced salesperson is often guilty of this particular sin. Needs development is often the most difficult period of the entire cycle. It is, as often as not, also the most productive. Many times the seller, feeling good because of knowing that a good job was done of needs development, simply goes back to the office and waits for the telephone to ring, or for the big order to come in the mail.

"Often this conduct is encouraged by the buyer who makes statements like, 'This looks good. I'll be in touch.' What the buyer neglects to tell our enterprising seller is that he'll also be in touch with everybody else in town who might have a solution for this need that we have worked so diligently to uncover. The salesperson is often critical of buyers who take such steps. We often forget that in addition to finding solutions to problems, our customer is also charged with the responsibility for protecting the corporate assets. To do this he must explore all the options at his disposal.

"It is this point that establishes the criteria for making the decision. So rather than skipping blithely back to the office and waiting for the order to fall, we would do well to spend some time influencing these criteria in our own behalf. Some call it *writing the specs,* others refer to it as *guidelines for decision,* but regardless of what we call it we must understand that our prospect goes through this agonizing exercise in every big-ticket transaction.

"The agony is in direct proportion to the dollar amount of the sale. The main point here is not to quit after the need has been developed. Begin working to assist the buyer in developing criteria for the decision-making process. Remember, too, that it is at this point in the cycle that competition is likely to be most active."

Salespeople, sales trainers, and sales managers agree that the most challenging, rewarding, and enjoyable aspect of the buyer-seller interaction is the sales presentation. An effective sales presentation completely and clearly explains all aspects of a salesperson's proposition as it relates to a buyer's needs. Surprisingly, or perhaps not so surprisingly, attaining this objective is not as easy as you might think. Few successful salespeople will claim that they had little trouble developing a good presentation, or mastering the art of giving the sales presentation. How then can you, as a novice, develop a sales presentation that will improve your chances of making the sale?

You must select a sales presentation method according to your prior knowledge of the customer, your sales call objective, and your customer benefit plan. You are now ready to begin developing your sales presen-

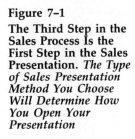

Figure 7–1
The Third Step in the Sales Process Is the First Step in the Sales Presentation. *The Type of Sales Presentation Method You Choose Will Determine How You Open Your Presentation*

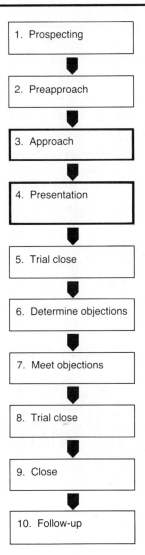

tation. The particular sales presentation method you have selected will make an excellent framework on which to build your specific presentation. The sales opener, or approach, as shown in Figure 7–1 is the first major part of the sales presentation.

This chapter discusses four sales presentation methods. The reasons successful salespeople develop special approaches for the sales interview are examined next along with objectives of the approach, several types of approaches, and applied examples of each type of approach.

Matching the proper approach to the situation and how to handle a prospect that shows little or no interest are then reviewed. The chapter begins by examining a question frequently pondered by new salespeople—"Do I have the right to present my product to a prospect?"

The Right to Approach

You have the right (or duty) to present your product if you can show that it will definitely benefit the prospect. In essence, you have to prove that *you* are worthy of the prospect's time and serious attention. You may earn the right to this attention in a number of ways:

- By exhibiting specific product or business knowledge.
- By expressing a sincere desire to solve a buyer's problem and satisfy a need.
- By stating or implying that your product will save money or increase the firm's profit margin.
- By displaying a service attitude.

Basically, prospects want to know how you and your product will benefit *them* and *the companies* they represent. Your sales approach should initially establish and thereafter concentrate on your product's key benefits for each prospect.

This strategy is especially important during the approach stage of a presentation because it aids in securing the prospect's interest in you and your product. At this point you, at the very least, want this unspoken reaction from the prospect: "Well, I'd better hear this salesperson out. I may hear something that will be of use to me." Now that you have justified your right to sell to a prospect, you must determine just how to present your product.

Sales Presentation Methods— Select One Carefully

The **sales presentation** involves a persuasive vocal and visual explanation of a business proposition. While there are many ways of making a presentation, only four will be discussed here. These four methods are presented to highlight the alternatives available to help you sell your products.

As shown on the continuum in Figure 7–2, these four sales presentation methods are the (1) memorized (or stimulus-response), (2) formula, (3) need-satisfaction, and (4) problem-solution selling methods. The basic difference in the four methods concerns what percentage of the

most useful.

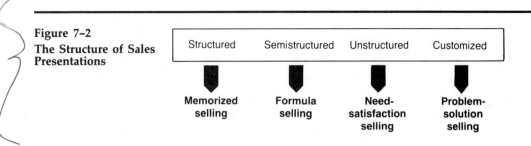

Figure 7–2
The Structure of Sales Presentations

conversation is controlled by the salesperson. In the more structured memorized and formula selling techniques, the salesperson normally requires a monopoly on the conversation, while the less structured methods allow for a much greater degree of buyer-seller interaction in which both parties participate equally in the conversation.

Memorized Sales Presentation

The **memorized presentation** (or stimulus-response method) is based on either of two assumptions: that a prospect's needs can be stimulated by direct exposure to the product, via the sales presentation, or that these needs have already been stimulated because the prospect has made the effort to seek out the product. In either case, the salesperson's role is to develop this initial stimulus into an affirmative response to an eventual purchase request.

The salesperson does 80 to 90 percent of the talking during a memorized sales presentation, only occasionally allowing the prospect to respond to predetermined questions, as shown in Figure 7–3.[1] Notably, the salesperson does not attempt to determine the prospect's needs during the interview, but just gives the same canned sales talk to all prospects. Since no attempt is made at this point to learn what goes on in the consumer's mind (remember the black box), the salesperson concentrates on discussing the product and its benefits, concluding the pitch with a purchase request. It is hoped that a convincing presentation of product benefits (stimulus) will cause the prospect to buy (response).

National Cash Register Co. (now NCR Corp.) pioneered the use of canned sales presentations. An analysis of the sales approaches of some of its top salespeople done during the 1920s revealed to NCR that they were saying basically the same things. The firm proceeded to prepare a series of standardized sales presentations based on the findings of their sales approach analysis, ultimately requiring its sales force to memorize these approaches for use during sales calls. The method worked quite well for NCR and was later adopted by a number of other firms. Canned sales presentations are still in use today, mainly in telephone and door-to-door selling.

Figure 7–3

Example of a Memorized Sales Presentation and Participation Time by the Customer and Salesperson

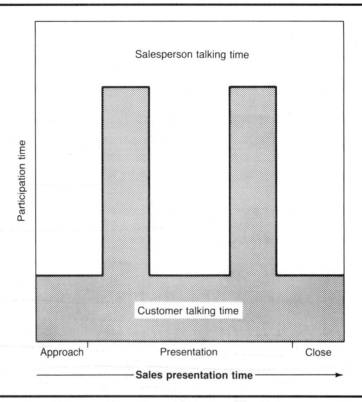

Pro's

However, parts of any type of presentation may be canned, yet linked with freeform conversation. Over time most salespeople develop proven selling sentences, phrases, and sequences in which to discuss information. They tend to use these in all of their presentations.

Despite its impersonal aura, the canned or memorized sales presentation has a number of distinct advantages, as seen in Figure 7–4:

It ensures that the salesperson will give a well-planned presentation and that the same information will be discussed by all of the company's salespeople.

It both aids and lends confidence to the inexperienced salesperson.

It is effective when selling time is short, as in door-to-door or telephone selling.

It is effective when the product is a nontechnical one, such as books, cooking utensils, and cosmetics.

As may be apparent, the memorized sales presentation method has several major drawbacks:

Figure 7–4
Dyno Electric Cart Memorized Presentation

Situation: You are calling on a purchasing manager to try to elicit an order for some electric cars (like a golf cart) to be used at a plant for transportation in and around the buildings and grounds. The major benefit you wish to emphasize in your presentation is that these carts save time, so you incorporate this concept into your approach. For this product you are able to use the memorized stimulus-response presentation.[2]

Salesperson:	Hello, Mr. Pride, my name is Karen Nordstrom, and I'd like to talk with you about how to save your company executives time. By the way, thanks for taking time to talk with me.
Buyer:	What's on your mind?
Salesperson:	As a busy executive, you know time is a valuable commodity. Nearly everyone would like to have a few extra minutes each day and that is the business I'm in, selling time. While I can't actually sell you time, I do have a product that is the next best thing . . . a Dyno electric cart—a real time-saver for your executives.
Buyer:	Yeah, well, sure everyone would like to have extra time. However, I don't think we need any golf carts. [First objection.]
Salesperson:	Dyno electric cart is more than a golf cart. It is an electric car designed for use in industrial plants. It has been engineered to give comfortable, rapid transportation in warehouses, plants, and across open areas.
Buyer:	They probably cost too much for us to use. [Positive buying signal phrased as an objection.]
Salesperson:	First of all, they cost only $2,200 each. With their five-year normal life that is only $400 per year plus a few cents electricity and a few dollars for maintenance. Under normal use and care, these carts only require about $100 of service in their five-year life. Thus, for about $50 a month you can save your key people a lot of time. [Creative pricing—show photographs of carts in use.]
Buyer:	It would be nice to save time, but I don't think management would go for the idea. [Third objection, but still showing interest.]
Salesperson:	That is exactly why I am here. Your executives will appreciate what you have done for them. You will look good in their eyes if you give them an opportunity to look at a product that will save time and energy. Saving time is only part of our story. Dyno cars also save energy and thus keep you sharper toward the end of the day. Would you want a demonstration today or Tuesday? [Alternative close.]
Buyer:	How long would your demonstration take? [Positive buying signal.]
Salesperson:	I only need one hour. When would it be convenient for me to bring the car in for your executives to try out?
Buyer:	There really isn't any good time. [Objection.]
Salesperson:	That's true. Therefore, the sooner we get to show you a Dyno car, the sooner your management group can see its benefits. How about next Tuesday? I could be here at 8:00, and we could go over this item just before your weekly management group meeting. I know you usually have a meeting Tuesdays at 9 because I tried to call on you a few weeks ago and your secretary told me you were in the weekly management meeting. [Close of the sale.]
Buyer:	Well, we could do it then.
Salesperson:	Fine, I'll be here. Your executives will really be happy! [Positive reinforcement.]

Con's

It presents features, advantages and benefits that may not be important to the buyer.

It allows for little prospect participation.

It is impractical to use when selling technical products that require prospect input and discussion.

It proceeds quickly through the sales presentation to the close, requiring the salesperson to close or ask for the order several times. This may be interpreted by the prospect as high-pressure selling.

The story is told of the new salesperson who was halfway through a canned presentation when the prospect had to answer the telephone. When the prospect finished the telephone conversation, the salesperson had forgotten the stopping point and, therefore, started all over again. The prospect naturally became angry.

In telling of his early selling experiences, consumer goods salesman John Anderson remembers that he was once so intent on presenting his memorized presentation that halfway through it the prospect yelled, "Enough, John, I've been waiting for you to see me. I'm ready to buy. I know all about your products." John was so intent on giving his canned presentation, and listening to himself talk, that he did not recognize the prospect's buying signals.

The point can be made that for some selling situations a highly structured presentation can be used successfully. Its advantages and disadvantages should be examined to determine if it is appropriate for your prospects and your types of products.

Some situations may seem partially appropriate for the memorized approach, but require a more personal touch. Such circumstances warrant the examination of formula selling.

The Formula Presentation

The **formula presentation,** often referred to as the *persuasive selling presentation*, is akin to the stimulus-response method: it is based on the assumption that similar prospects in similar situations can be approached with similar presentations. However, in order for the formula method to apply, the salesperson must first know something about the prospective buyer. The salesperson follows a less structured, general outline in making a presentation, allowing more flexibility and less direction.

The salesperson generally controls the conversation during the sales talk, especially at the beginning. Figure 7–5 illustrates how a salesperson should take charge during a formula selling situation.[3] For example, the salesperson might make a sales opener (approach); discuss the product's features, advantages, and benefits; and then start to solicit comments from the buyer through the use of trial closes, answering questions, and handling objections. At the end of the participation curve, the salesperson regains control over the discussion and moves in to close the sale.

The formula selling approach obtains its name from the salesperson using the attention, interest, desire, and action (AIDA) procedure of developing and giving the sales presentation. We earlier added *conviction* to the procedure because the prospect may want or desire the product, yet he or she may not be convinced this is the best product or the best salesperson from whom to buy.

Straight rebuy and modified rebuy situations, especially with con-

Figure 7–5

Example of a Formula Sales Presentation and Participation Time by the Customer and Salesperson

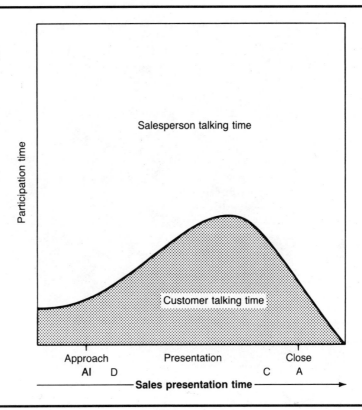

Salesperson talking time

Participation time

Customer talking time

| Approach | Presentation | Close |
| AI   D | | C   A |

Sales presentation time

sumer goods, lend themselves to this method. Many prospects or customers are going to buy because they are familiar with the salesperson's company. The question is, "How can a salesperson for Quaker Oats, Revlon, Gillette, Procter & Gamble, or any other well-known manufacturer develop a presentation that will convince a customer to purchase promotional quantities of a product, participate in a local advertising campaign, or stock a new untried product?"

Beecham Products, a consumer goods manufacturer, has developed a sequence, or formula, for their salespeople to follow. They refer to it as the "10-step productive retail sales call." The Beecham salesperson shown in Figure 7–6 is headed into the grocery store to find his buyer for his products such as Cling Free Sheets, Aqua-Fresh toothpaste, Aqua Velva, and Sucrets. The 10 steps and their major components are:

Step 1. Plan the call:
- Review the situation.
- Analyze problems and appointments.
- Set objectives.

Figure 7–6
This Beecham
Salesperson Will Use
the Formula Sales
Presentation to Sell
His Buyer.

- Plan the presentation.
- Check your sales materials.

Step 2. Review plans:
- Before you leave your car review your plans, call objectives, suggested order forms, etc.

Step 3. Greet personnel:
- Give a friendly greeting to all store personnel you see.
- Alert the store manager for sales action.

Step 4. Check conditions in store:
- Note appearance of stock on shelf.
- Check distribution and pricing.
- Note out-of-stocks.
- Perform "quick fix" by straightening shelf stock.
- Report competitive activity.
- Check back room (store room):
  - Locate product to correct out-of-stocks.
  - Use reserve stock for special display.
- Update sales plan, if needed.

Step 5. Approach:
  - Keep it short.

Step 6. Presentation:
  - Logical, clear, interesting.
  - Tailor to dealer's style.
  - Present from dealer's point of view.
  - Use sales tools.

Step 7. Close:
  - Present a suggested order (ask for the order).
  - Offer a choice.
  - Answer questions and handle objections.
  - Get a "real" order.

Step 8. Merchandising:
  - Build displays.
  - Dress up the shelves.

Step 9. Records and reports:
  - Complete immediately after the call.

Step 10. Analyze the call:
  - Review the call to spot strong and weak points. How could the sales call have been improved? How can the next call be improved?

Formula selling can be a very effective method for calling on customers, who are currently buying, and prospects, about whose operation the salesperson has learned a great deal. In such situations, formula selling offers a number of significant advantages:

It ensures that all information is presented in a logical manner.

It allows for a reasonable amount of buyer-seller interaction.

It allows for smooth handling of *anticipated* questions and objections.

When executed in a smooth, conversational manner, the formula method of selling has no major flaws, as long as the salesperson has correctly identified the prospect's needs and wants. The Procter & Gamble formula sales presentation given as an example in Figure 7–7 can be given to any retailer who is not selling all available sizes of Tide (or of any other product). In this situation a formula approach is used in calling on a customer the salesperson has sold to previously. If, on the other hand, the salesperson had not known a customer's needs and used this Tide presentation, chances are customer objections would arise early in the presentation—as they sometimes do with the stimulus-response (memorized) sales presentation method. Still, the formula technique is not adaptable to a number of complex selling situations. These require still another sales presentation.

Figure 7–7

Example of a Formula Approach Sales Presentation

Formula Steps	Buyer-Seller Roles	Sales Presentation
Summarize the situation for *attention* and *interest*	*Salesperson:*	Ms. Hanson, you've said before that the shortage of shelf space prevents you from stocking our family-size Tide—though you admit you may be losing some sales as a result. If we could determine *how much* volume you're missing, I think you'd be willing to *make* space for it, wouldn't you? [Trial close.]
State your marketing plan for *interest*	*Buyer:*	Yes, but I don't see how that can be done.
	Salesperson:	Well, I'd like to suggest a test—a weekend display of all four sizes of Tide.
	Buyer:	What do you mean?
Explain your marketing plan for *interest* and *desire*	*Salesperson:*	My thought was to run all sizes at regular shelf price *without* any ad support. This would give us a pure test. Six cases of each size should let us compare sales of the various sizes and see what you're missing by regularly stocking only the smaller sizes. I think the additional sales and profits you'll get on the family size will convince you to start stocking it on a regular basis. [Reinforce key benefits.] What do you think? [Trial close.]
Buyer appears in *conviction* stage	*Buyer:*	Well, maybe. [Positive reaction to trial close.]
Suggest an easy next step *action*	*Salesperson:*	May I enter the six cases of family-size Tide in the order book now? [Close.]

The Need-Satisfaction Presentation

The **need-satisfaction presentation** is different from the stimulus-response and the formalized approaches in that it is designed as a relatively flexible, *interactive* sales presentation. It is the most challenging and creative form of selling.

The salesperson will typically start the presentation with a probing question such as, "What are you looking for in investment property?" or, "What type of computer needs does your company have?" This opening brings up a discussion of the prospect's needs, and it also gives the salesperson an opportunity to determine whether any of the products being offered might be beneficial. When something the prospect has said is not understood by the salesperson, it can be clarified by a question or by restating what the buyer has said. The need-satisfaction

Figure 7–8

Example of a Need-Satisfaction Sales Presentation and Participation Time by the Customer and Salesperson

format is especially suited to the sale of industrial and technical goods with stringent specifications and high price tags.

Often, as shown in Figure 7–8, the first 50 to 60 percent of conversation time (referred to as the **need-development** phase) is devoted to a discussion of the buyer's needs.[4] Once aware of the prospect's needs (the **need-awareness** phase), the salesperson begins to take control of the conversation by restating the prospect's needs to clarify the situation. During the last stage of the presentation, the **need-fulfillment** phase, the salesperson shows how the product will satisfy mutually agreed-on needs. As you can see in Figure 7–9, the salesperson selling the Dyno Electric Cart begins the interview with the prospect by using a planned series of questions to uncover problems and to determine whether the prospect is interested in solving them.[5]

Should you have to come back a second time to see the prospect, as is often the case in selling industrial products, you would use the formula sales presentation method in calling on the same prospect. You might begin with a benefit statement such as this:

Figure 7–9

Example of a Need-Satisfaction Presentation

Salesperson:	Mr. Pride, you really have a large manufacturing facility. How large is it?
Buyer:	We have approximately 50 acres under roof, with our main production building being almost 25 acres under one roof. There are a total of six buildings used for production.
Salesperson:	How far is it from your executives' offices here to your plant area? It looks like it must be two miles over to there.
Buyer:	Well, it does, but it's only one mile.
Salesperson:	How do your executives get over to the plant area?
Buyer:	They walk over through our underground tunnel. Some walk on the road when we have good weather.
Salesperson:	When they get to the plant area, how do they get around in the plant?
Buyer:	Well, they walk or catch a ride on one of the small tractors the workers use in the plant.
Salesperson:	Have your executives ever complained about their having to do all of that walking?
Buyer:	All of the time!
Salesperson:	What is it they don't like about their long walks?
Buyer:	Well, I hear everything from "It wears out my shoe leather," to "It's hard on my pace-maker." The main complaints are the time it takes them and that some of the older executives are exhausted by the time they get back to their offices. Many people need to go over to the plant but don't.
Salesperson:	It sounds as if your executives would have an interest in reducing their travel time and not having to exert so much energy. By doing so, doesn't it seem they would get to the plant as they need to, saving them time and energy and the company money?
Buyer:	I guess so.
Salesperson:	Mr. Pride, on the average how much salary would you say your executives make an hour?
Buyer:	Maybe $20 an hour.
Salesperson:	If I could show you how you can save your executives time in getting to and from your plant, would you be interested?
Buyer:	Yes, I would. [Now the salesperson moves into the presentation.]

"Mr. Pride, when we talked last week you were interested in saving your executives time and energy in getting to and from your plant, and you felt the Dyno Electric Cart could do this for you." (You could pause and let him answer or say, "Is that correct?")

From the buyer's response to your question, you can quickly determine what to do. If an objection is raised, you can respond to it. If more information is asked for, you can provide it. If what you have said about your product has pleased the buyer, you simply ask for the order.

You should be cautious when uncovering a prospect's needs. Too many questions can alienate the prospect. Remember, many prospects do not want to initially open up to salespeople. Actually, some salespeople are uncomfortable with the need-satisfaction approach because they feel less in control of the selling situation than with a canned or formula presentation. A good point to remember is that you are not a performer on a stage, but that rather, your job is to meet your prospect's needs—not your own. Eventually, you can learn to anticipate customer reactions to this presentation method and learn to welcome the challenge of the interaction between you and the buyer.

The Problem-Solution Presentation

In selling highly complex or technical products such as insurance, industrial equipment, accounting systems, office equipment, and computers, salespeople are often required to make several sales calls in order to develop a detailed analysis of a prospect's needs. After completing this analysis, the salesperson arrives at a solution to the prospect's problems and usually uses both a written analysis and an oral presentation. The **problem-solution presentation** usually consists of six steps:

1. Convincing the prospect to allow the salesperson to conduct the analysis.
2. Actually making the analysis.
3. Buyer and seller mutually agreeing on the problems and determining that the buyer wants to solve them.
4. Preparing the proposal for a solution to the prospect's needs.
5. Preparing the sales presentation based on the analysis and proposal.
6. Making the sales presentation.

The problem-solution presentation is a flexible, customized approach involving an in-depth study of a prospect's needs and requiring a well-planned presentation. The salesperson may find it necessary to present the proposal to a group of individuals. In some cases, a *selling team* may be required for the presentation of a technical, high-dollar investment solution to a problem. The salesperson may lead the interview, allowing team members to present information in their areas of expertise (such as computer software or financial analysis). Team selling requires an immense amount of coordinated interaction between sales, financial, and technical areas, offering a true challenge to the salesperson with managerial aspirations.

Step 3 cannot be overemphasized, for it is important to determine whether you and the prospect share the same perceptions of the buyer's needs and problems. You should be wary of saying, "My survey has shown these problems, and this is what I suggest you need to buy." Instead, you should develop a question approach to determine if the prospect believes them to be real and important problems. Once both of you agree on the problems and you determine that the buyer is interested in solving them, you may proceed with your presentation.

Which Is the Best Presentation Method?

Each of the four sales presentation methods can be the best one when the method is properly matched with the *situation*. For example, the stimulus-response method can be used when time is short and the product is simple. Formula selling is effective in repeat purchases or

Matt Suffoletto of IBM Uses the Problem-Solution Presentation Method

"A successful salesperson has expertise in the products he or she sells, as well as an in-depth knowledge of the customer's business. The salesperson often makes recommendations which alter the mainstream of the customer's business process. Recognizing the requirement for business skills, IBM provides training in both the technical aspects of our products, as well as their industrial application.

"My territory consists of manufacturing customers; hence I pride myself in understanding concepts such as inventory control, time-phased requirements planning, and shop floor control. Typically, I work with customer user department and data processing people to do application surveys and detailed justification analysis. After the background work is completed, I make proposals and presentations to educate the chain of decision makers on the IBM recommendations.

"Selling involves the transformation of the features of your product into benefits for the customer. The principal vehicles for that communication are the sales call, formal presentations, and proposals. The larger the magnitude of the sale, the more time and effort is spent on presentations and proposals. A proposal may range from a simple one-page letter and attachment with prices, terms, and conditions, to multi-volume binders with detailed information on the product, including its use, detailed justification, implementation schedules, and contracts. The wide range of comprehensiveness implies an equal range in time commitment of the salesperson.

"Very few sales are made in a single call. At the first sales call the salesperson generally searches for additional information that needs to be brought back, analysis that needs to be done, or questions to be answered. These are opportunities to demonstrate responsiveness to the customer. Getting back to the customer in a very timely and professional manner is a way to build trust and confidence into a business relationship."

when you know or have already determined the needs of the prospect.

The need-satisfaction method is most appropriate when information needs to be first gathered from the prospect as is often the case in selling industrial products. Finally, the problem-solution presentation is excellent for selling high-cost technical products or services, and especially for system selling involving several sales calls and a business tion. To help improve sales, the salesperson should understand and be able to use each method based on each situation.

You should always be prepared to change any part of your sales presentation to meet the particular characteristics of a specific selling situation or environment.

Select the Presentation Method, Then the Approach

Before you can develop your presentation, you must know which presentation method you will use. Once you determine which presentation method is best for your situation you can then plan what you will do when talking with your prospect. The first consideration should be how to begin your sales presentation. This is discussed in the next chapter.

Summary of Major Selling Issues

In order to improve your chances of making a sale, as a salesperson you must master the art of giving a good sales presentation. An effective presentation will work toward specifically solving the customer's problems. The particular sales presentation method you select should be based on your prior knowledge of the customer, your sales call objective, and your customer benefit plan.

Because prospects want to know how you and your product will benefit them and the companies they represent, you must show them you have a right to present your product as it has key benefits for them. Many different sales presentation methods are available. They differ from one another depending on what percentage of the conversation is controlled by the salesperson. The salesperson usually does most of the talking in the more structured memorized and formula selling techniques, while there is more buyer-seller interaction in the less structured methods.

In the memorized presentation, or stimulus-response method, the salesperson does 80 percent to 90 percent of the talking, with each customer receiving the same sales pitch. Although this method ensures a well-planned presentation and is good for certain nontechnical products, it is also somewhat inflexible, allowing little prospect participation. The formula presentation, a persuasive selling presentation, is similar to the first method, but it takes the prospect into account by answering questions and handling objections.

The most challenging and creative form of selling uses the need-satisfaction presentation. This flexible method begins by raising questions about what the customer specifically needs. After you are aware of the customer's needs, you can then show how your product fits these needs. You must be cautious because many people don't want to open up to the salesperson.

When selling highly complex or technical products like computers or insurance, a problem-solution presentation consisting of six steps is a good sales method. This method involves a detailed analysis of the buyer's specific needs and problems and designing a proposal and presentation to fit these needs. This customized method often uses a selling team to present the specialized information to the buyer.

In comparing the four presentation methods, there is no one best method. Each one must be tailored to meet the particular characteristics of a specific selling situation or environment.

Review and Discussion Questions

1. What are the four sales presentation methods discussed in this chapter? Briefly explain each method. Be sure to include any similarities and differences in your answer.

2. One salesperson profiled in your textbook stated that he concentrates on the need-fulfillment phase of the sales presentation. Do you feel he is correct in his approach? Why?

3. Assume a salesperson already knows the customer's needs. Instead of developing the customer's needs as a part of the sales presentation, he goes directly to the close. What are your feelings on this type of sales presentation?

4. To properly use the formula sales presentation, what information is needed by the salesperson?

5. What steps are required to develop and use the need-satisfaction presentation?

6. Assume you are selling a product requiring you to typically use the problem-solving sales presentation method. You have completed your study of a prospect's business and are getting ready to present your recommendation to him. What would be your selling strategy?

Project

Assume you are a salesperson selling a consumer item, such as a wristwatch. Without any preparation, make a sales presentation to a friend. If possible, record your sales presentation on a tape recorder. Analyze the recording and determine the approximate conversation time of your prospect. On the basis of your analysis, which of the four sales presentation methods discussed in Chapter 7 did you use? How early in the sales presentation did your prospect begin to give you objections?

Cases

7-1   Cascade Soap Company

Mike Bowers sells soap products to grocery wholesalers and large retail grocery chains. The following presentation occurred during a call he made on Bill Reese, the soap buyer for a grocery store.

Salesperson: Bill, you have stated several times that the types of promotions or brands that really turn you on are ones that carry the best profit. Is that right?

Customer: Yes, it is. I'm really getting pressure to increase my profit per square foot in my department.

Salesperson: Bill, I recommend that you begin carrying the king size of Cascade. Let's review the benefits and economics of this proposal. King-size Cascade would cost you 86.8¢ a box. The average resale in this market is 99¢. That means that you would make 12.2¢ every time you sell a box of king-size Cascade. Based on my estimated volume for your store of $40,000 per week, you would sell approximately two cases of king-size Cascade per week. That is $19.80 in new sales and $2.44 in new profits per week for your store. As you can see, the addition of Cascade 10 to your auto dishwash department will increase your sales and, even more important, increase your profits—and this is what you said you wanted to do, right?

Customer: Yes, I am interested in increasing profits.

Salesperson: Do you want me to give this information to the head stock clerk so that he can make arrangements to put Cascade 10s on the shelf? Or would you like me to put it on the shelf on my next call?

Questions:

1.   What sales presentation method was Mike using?

2.   Evaluate Mike's handling of this situation.

7-2   A Retail Sales Presentation

Customer is looking at a display of Cross gold pens and pencils.

Salesperson: *[giving a big smile]* Hello. My name is Laura Hurst. Are you looking for a pen and pencil set for yourself or for a gift?

Customer: I'm looking for a graduation gift for my brother, but I'm not necessarily looking for a pen and pencil set.

Salesperson: Is your brother graduating from college or high school?

Customer: He is graduating from college this spring.

Salesperson: I can show you quite a few things that would be appropriate gifts. Let's start by taking a look at this elegant Cross pen and pencil set. Don't they look impressive?

Customer: They look too expensive. Besides, a pen and pencil set doesn't seem like an appropriate gift for a college graduate.

Salesperson: You're right, a Cross pen and pencil set *does* look expensive. Just imagine how impressed your brother will be when he opens your gift package and finds these beautiful writing instruments. Even though Cross pen and pencil sets look expensive, they are actually quite reasonably priced, considering the total value you are getting.

Customer: How much does this set cost?

Salesperson: You can buy a Cross pen and pencil set for anywhere from $15 to $300. The one I am showing you is gold-plated and costs only $28. For this modest amount you can purchase a gift for your brother that will be attractive, useful, will last a lifetime, and show him that you truly think he is deserving of the very best. Don't you think that is what a graduation gift should be?

Customer: You make it sound pretty good, but frankly I hadn't intended to spend that much money.

Salesperson: Naturally, I can show you something else. However, before I do that, pick up this Cross pen and write your name on this pad of paper. Notice that in addition to good looks, Cross pens offer good writing. Cross is widely acclaimed as one of the best ball point pens on the market. It is nicely balanced, has a point that allows the ink to flow on the paper smoothly, and rides over the paper with ease.

Customer: You're right, the pen writes really well.

Salesperson: Each time your brother writes with this pen he will remember that you gave him this fine writing instrument for graduation. In addition, Cross offers prestige. Many customers tell us that Cross is one of the few pens they have used that is so outstanding that people often comment on it by brand name. Your brother will enjoy having others notice the pen he uses is high in quality.

Customer: You're right. I do tend to notice when someone is using a Cross pen.

Salesperson: You just can't go wrong with a Cross pen and pencil set for a gift. Shall I wrap it for you?

Customer: It's a hard decision.

Salesperson: Your brother will be very happy with this gift.

Customer: Okay. Go ahead and wrap it for me.

Salesperson: Fine. Would you like me to wrap up another set for you to give yourself?

Customer: No, one is enough. Maybe someone will buy one for me someday.

Questions:

1. Describe the selling techniques being used by the retail salesperson.

2. Evaluate the salesperson's handling of this situation.

8 BEGIN YOUR PRESENTATION STRATEGICALLY

Learning Objectives

1. To explain the importance of a salesperson using an approach to open the sales presentation and provide examples of approaches that open with statements, questions, and demonstrations.

2. To illustrate why the approach should have a theme that is related to the presentation and the prospect's important buying motives.

3. To present four types of questioning techniques for use throughout the presentation.

Key Terms for Selling

Creative imagery
Introductory approach
Complimentary approach
Referral approach
Premium approach
Product approach
Showmanship approach
Customer benefit approach
Curiosity approach

Opinion approach
Shock approach
Multiple question approach (SPIN)
Direct question
Nondirective question
Rephrasing question
Redirect question

Jack Pruett
Bailey Banks & Biddle

Profile

Jack Pruett is a sales specialist with Bailey Banks & Biddle, a division of the Zale Corporation, the world's largest retailer of fine jewelry. He works in Atlanta, Georgia. Jack has his sales responsibility and assists others in the store. I asked him about his sales and he said, "My customers typically spend a minimum of $2,500 to $5,000. The largest sale to a single customer I have so far was $120,000 in diamonds, rings, and a gold and diamond bracelet. My highest sales for one month has been $278,000 and for a year $820,000. I expect to sell over $1 million this year."

Jack's previous job was that of a Pepsi-Cola truck driver, driving from Augusta, Georgia, into South Carolina. Jack says, "This is where I learned a lot about people, and this attributed to my sales success. I learned to deal with people equally and fairly no matter who they are, where they come from, or what their background is.

"Sales is a joy to me. I would really rather sell jewelry than anything in the world. It is both personally and financially rewarding. It takes hard work to earn serious money. Today, retailers recognize the importance of salespeople to their success and many are compensating on a commission basis, which allows good salespeople to make high salaries.

"I realize there are sales techniques, and many of us use parts of some techniques. But selling is a people business, and there are no two people with the same fingerprints or needs. So you can't treat people exactly the same. The most important factor to my success is my belief that I can do the best job taking care of a person's needs. I've studied hard, worked hard, and developed a selling process that works for me. It didn't happen overnight—it was my second year in the business before I became comfortable in jewelry sales."

"Many professions offer personal and financial rewards," says Jack Pruett. "A salesperson doesn't save lives, like a physician, or build the largest bridge in the world, like an engineer. But we do receive a tremendous amount of joy out of what we do.

"Sales is really personally and financially rewarding. I know people selling shoes who earn $60,000 a year, who sell men's clothes and earn $70,000, who sell jewelry and earn more than $100,000. These people are professionals making a substantial salary. The secret is to believe in what you're doing and what you're selling—then develop a method to serve your customers.

"Another secret of my success is that I've learned how to create business. One afternoon a young couple came in. We looked awhile, and they weren't really interested in buying anything. So I asked them if they knew anyone who might need one of our products. The man said, 'Yes, I have a friend who has expressed an interest in an 18-carat Rolex watch.' 'That sells for over $9,000,' I replied. This shopper felt comfortable enough to say, 'Why don't you call him,' before I could ask if I could contact his friend.

"So I called him and got him to come into the store. He bought the watch, plus a ladies diamond watch for $12,000, a $30,000 three-carat diamond, and two gold watches for his children. Without farming (prospecting) I'd never have found this customer. This happens to me more than you think. Actually, it doesn't just happen. I make it happen."

Jack puts major emphasis on understanding buyers' needs, qualifying customers, becoming their friend, having customers introduce him to prospects, giving personal service, and playing down features and advantages while concentrating on benefits. Having made a sale, he shows customers he is thankful for their business and provides all of the service they need to be satisfied with their purchase. These are some of the things that have made him successful.

Salespeople profiled throughout this text stress the importance of the *approach*. The salesperson needs to have a good beginning in order to have a good ending to the sales presentation. This is illustrated by the following example.

The Approach—Opening the Sales Presentation _____

Raleigh Johnson had spent days qualifying the prospect, arranging for an appointment, planning every aspect of the sales presentation; and in the first 60 seconds of the sales presentation he realized his chance of selling was excellent. He was quickly able to determine the prospect's needs and evoke attention and interest in his product because of the technique he used to begin the sales interview.

... Is not an accidental process. Every step—from the greeting to the handshake to the opening statement—should be taken with an eye toward gaining attention.

Moreover, you want **favorable** attention. Get the buyer in your corner and he'll be willing—even eager—to listen to you. Lose him, and he'll barely hear a word you say. The challenge is to win him over within the first ten seconds that you're in his office.

Your handshake should be firm and brief. Always remember his name and pronounce it right. Make sure your opening statement is bright, forceful, persuasive, and focuses directly on his buying needs.

Once you've worked hard at gaining his attention, work just as hard at reinforcing it. Customers have notoriously short attention spans.

A buyer's reactions to the salesperson in the early minutes of the sales presentation are critical to a successful sale. This short time period is so important that it is treated as an individual step in selling referred to as the approach. Part of any approach is the prospect's first impression of you.

Your Attitude during the Approach

As shown in Figure 8–1, it is not uncommon for a salesperson to experience tension in various forms when contacting a prospect. Often this is brought on when the salesperson has preconceived ideas that things may go wrong during the sale. Prospects may be viewed as having negative characteristics, which will make the sales call difficult.

All salespeople experience some degree of stress at times. Yet successful salespeople have learned a relaxation and concentration technique, called **creative imagery,** which allows them to cope with stress. The salesperson envisions "what is the worst that can possibly hap-

Figure 8–1
Make Sure Your Attitude Is Positive

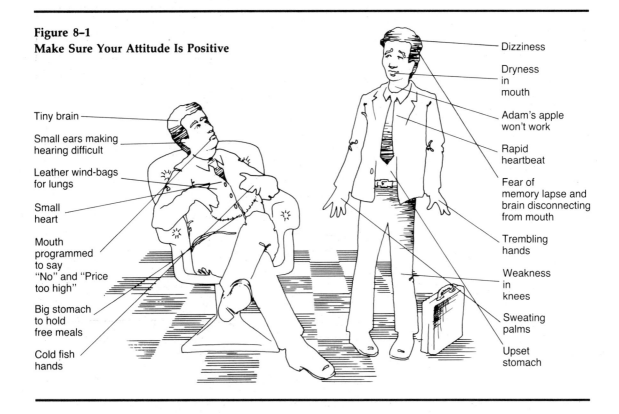

Tiny brain

Small ears making
hearing difficult

Leather wind-bags
for lungs

Small
heart

Mouth
programmed
to say
"No" and "Price
too high"

Big stomach
to hold
free meals

Cold fish
hands

Dizziness

Dryness
in
mouth

Adam's apple
won't work

Rapid
heartbeat

Fear of
memory lapse and
brain disconnecting
from mouth

Trembling
hands

Weakness
in
knees

Sweating
palms

Upset
stomach

pen?" Then preparation is made to react to it and even accept it if need
be. The best that can happen is also envisioned, as seen in Figure 8–2.
Furthermore, contingency plans are mentally prepared should the
planned sales talk need to be abandoned.

The last question the salesperson should ask is "what are the
chances that things will go wrong?" Chances are the answer involves a
very low probability. Usually there is less than a 1 percent chance that
things will really go wrong, especially when careful planning has taken
place before the sales call. A greater than 99 percent probability that
things will go as planned should dim the fears of the most worrisome of
salespeople.

The First Impression of You Is Critical to Success

When you first meet your prospect, the initial impression you make is
based on appearances. If this impression is favorable, your prospect is
more likely to listen to you, but if it is not favorable, your prospect may
erect communication barriers that can be difficult to overcome.

Figure 8–2

Creative Imagery Is a Great Way to Relax While Psyching Yourself Up before Seeing Your Prospect

Picture worst and best that can happen, plus success.

The first impression is centered on the image projected by your (1) appearance and (2) attitude. Here are some suggestions for making a favorable first impression.

- Wear business clothes that are appropriate and fairly conservative.
- Be neat in dress and grooming.
- Refrain from smoking, chewing gum, or drinking when in your prospect's office.
- Keep an erect posture to project confidence.
- Leave all unnecessary materials outside the office (overcoat, umbrella, or newspaper).
- If possible, sit down. Should the prospect not offer a chair, ask, "May I sit here?"
- Be enthusiastic and positive toward the interview.
- Smile, always smile! (Try to be sincere with your smile; it will aid you in being enthusiastic and positive toward your prospect.)
- Do not apologize for taking the prospect's time.
- Do not imply that you were just passing by and that the sales call was not planned.
- Maintain eye contact with the prospect.
- If the prospect offers to shake hands, do so with a firm, positive grip, while continuing to maintain eye contact.
- If possible, before the interview, learn how to pronounce your

228

Figure 8–3

Five Ways to Remember Prospect's Name

1. Be sure to hear the person's name and use it, "It's good to meet you, Mr. Firestone."
2. Spell it out in your mind, or if it is an unusual name, ask the person to spell the name.
3. Relate the name to something you are familiar with, such as relating the name Firestone to Firestone automobile tires.
4. Use the name in the conversation.
5. Repeat the name at the end of the conversation, such as "Goodbye, Mr. Firestone."

prospect's name correctly and use it throughout the interview. Should the prospect introduce you to other people, remember their names by using the five ways to remember names shown in Figure 8–3.

Like an actor, the salesperson must learn how to project and maintain a positive, confident, and enthusiastic first impression no matter what mood the prospect is in when first encountered by the salesperson.

The Situational Approach

The situation you face will determine what approach technique you should use to begin your sales presentation. The situation is dictated by a number of variables, which only you can truly identify. Some of the more common situational variables are these:

- The type of *product* you are selling.
- Whether this is a *repeat call* on the same person.
- Your degree of knowledge about the *customer's needs*.
- The *time* you have in which to make your sales presentation.
- Whether the customer *is aware of a problem*.
- Your sales call *objective*.
- The *type of approach* you believe will be well received by the customer.
- Your *customer benefit plan*.

These factors must be examined and assigned a degree of importance before you ever step into your customer's office. This approach selection process can greatly aid you in making a satisfactory impression.

Approach Techniques and Objectives. Approach techniques can be grouped into three general categories: (1) opening with a statement; (2) opening with a demonstration; and (3) opening with a question or questions.

[handwritten margin note: 1. Approach →3 types depend on which type of presentation you are going to make (4)]

Jack Pruett on the Retail Approach

"A lot of times," says Jack Pruett, "customers come in and say 'I'm just looking.' It's OK to look, but why is it they are just looking? What is it that they might need? Is it something they would like to have that they feel like they can't afford? We might have the perfect terms. Without talking to the customer and getting close to them, making them feel comfortable, feel at home, and not pressured, you will never find out. You have to work at learning how to do that—and that comes with trying it and with experience."

Your choice of approach technique depends on which of the four sales presentation methods you have selected based on your situation and sales presentation plan. Figure 8–4 presents one way of determining which approach technique to use. Using questions in a sales approach is feasible with any of the four presentation methods, whereas statements and demonstrations typically should be reserved for either the stimulus-response or formula sales presentation methods. Because of their customer-oriented nature, the need-satisfaction and problem-solving sales presentation methods should always employ questions at the outset. The following three sections will review each of these approach techniques, giving examples to increase understanding of their use and particular beneficial aspects.

Both the *statement* and *demonstration* approach techniques have three basic objectives. The objectives are as follows:

1. To capture the *attention* of the prospect.
2. To stimulate the prospect's *interest*.
3. To provide a *transition* into the sales presentation.

You should imagine the prospect silently asking three questions: (1) "Shall I see this person?" (2) "Shall I listen, talk with, and devote more

Figure 8–4

The Approach Technique to Use for Each of the Four Sales Presentation Methods

Sales Presentation Methods	Approach Techniques		
	Statement	Demonstration	Questions
Memorized ("canned")	✔	✔	✔
Formula (persuasive selling)	✔	✔	✔
Need-satisfaction			✔
Problem-solving			✔

time to this person?" and (3) "What's in it for *me*?" The answers to these questions will help determine the outcome of the sale. If you choose to use either of these two approaches, you should create a statement or demonstration approach that will cause the prospect to say yes to each of these three questions.

The sales approach can be a frightening, lonely, heart-stopping experience. It can easily lead to ego-bruising rejection. Your challenge is to move the prospect from an often cold, indifferent, or sometimes even hostile frame of mind to an aroused excitement about the product. By quickly obtaining the prospect's attention and interest, the conversation can make a smooth transition into the presentation, which greatly improves the probability of making the sale by allowing you to quickly lead into the sales presentation, shown in Figure 8–5.

In addition to creating attention, stimulating interest, and providing for transition, the use of questions in your approach should have the following objectives:

1. To *uncover* the needs or problems *important* to the prospect.

2. To determine if the prospect wishes to *fulfill* these needs or *solve* these problems.

3. To have the prospect *tell you* about these needs or problems and the intention to do something about them.

Since people buy to fulfill needs or solve problems, the use of questions in your approach is preferable to the use of statements or demonstrations. Questions allow you to uncover needs, whereas statements and demonstrations are used when you assume you already know the prospect's needs. However, all three approach techniques can be used by the salesperson in the proper situation.

Openings with Statements

Opening statements can be effective if properly planned, especially if the salesperson has been able to uncover the prospect's needs before entering the office. Four statement approaches frequently used are the (1) introductory approach, (2) complimentary approach, (3) referral approach, and (4) premium approach.

The **introductory approach** is the most common and the least powerful because it does little to capture the prospect's attention and

---

Figure 8–5
The Approach Leads Quickly into the Sales Presentation

interest. It opens with the salesperson's name and business: "Hello, Ms. Crompton, my name is John Gladstone, representing the Pierce Chemical Company."

The introductory approach is needed when meeting a prospect for the first time. In most cases, though, the introductory approach should be used in conjunction with another approach. This additional approach could quite easily be the complimentary approach.

Everyone likes a compliment. If the **complimentary approach** is sincere, it can be an effective beginning to a sales interview.

> "Ms. Rosenberg, you certainly have a thriving restaurant business. I have enjoyed many lunches here. While doing so, I have thought of several products that could make your business even better and make things easier for you and your employees."

> "Mr. Davidson, I was just visiting with your boss who commented that you were doing a good job in keeping the company's printing costs down. I have a couple of ideas that may help you further reduce your costs!"

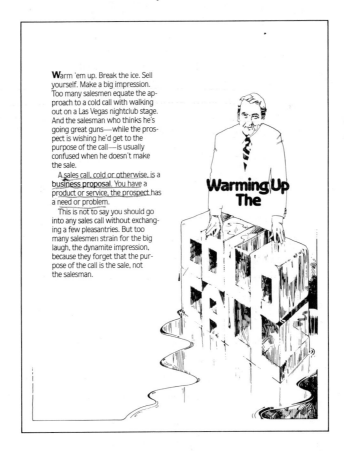

Warm 'em up. Break the ice. Sell yourself. Make a big impression. Too many salesmen equate the approach to a cold call with walking out on a Las Vegas nightclub stage. And the salesman who thinks he's going great guns—while the prospect is wishing he'd get to the purpose of the call—is usually confused when he doesn't make the sale.

A sales call, cold or otherwise, is a business proposal. You have a product or service, the prospect has a need or problem.

This is not to say you should go into any sales call without exchanging a few pleasantries. But too many salesmen strain for the big laugh, the dynamite impression, because they forget that the purpose of the call is the sale, not the salesman.

Warming Up The

Sometimes a suitable compliment is not in order, or just cannot be generated. Another way to get the buyer's attention is to mention a mutual acquaintance as a reference.

The use of another person's name, the **referral approach,** can be effective if the prospect respects that person. It is important to remember, however, that the referral approach can have a negative effect if the prospect does not like the person.

> "Ms. Rosenburg, my name is Carlos Ramirez, with the Restaurant Supply Corporation. When I talked to your brother last week, he wanted me to give you the opportunity to see Restaurant Supply's line of paper products for your restaurant."

> "Hello, Mr. Gillespie—Linda Crawford with the Ramada Inn suggested that I contact you concerning our new Xerox table copier."

One salesperson tells of asking the customer to tape-record a brief introduction to a friend. When calling on the friend, the salesperson placed the recorder on the desk and said, "Amos McDonald has a message for you, Ms. James . . . let's listen."

Few people can obtain a reference for every prospect they intend to contact (this may be especially true for a beginning salesperson). Even if you don't know "all the right people," you can still get on track by offering the buyer something for nothing—a premium.

A **premium approach** is effective because everyone likes to receive something free. When appropriate, you can use free samples and novelty items in a premium approach.

> Early in the morning of her first day on a new campus, one textbook salesperson makes a practice of leaving a dozen doughnuts in the faculty lounge with her card stapled to the box. She claims that prospects actually come looking for her!

> "Mr. Jones, here is a beautiful desk calendar with your name engraved on it. Each month I will place a new calendar in the holder, which, by the way, will feature one of our products. This month's calendar, for example, features our lubricating oil."

> "Ms. Rogers, this high-quality Fuller hair brush is yours, free, for just giving me five minutes of your time."

> "Ms. McCall [*handing her the product to examine*], I want to leave samples for you, your cosmetic representatives, and your best customers of Revlon's newest addition to our perfume line."

Creative use of premiums can be an effective sales approach. Demonstrations can also leave a favorable impression with a prospect.

Demonstration Openings

Openings using demonstrations and dramatics can be effective because of their ability to force the prospect into participating in the interview. Of the two methods discussed here, the product approach is more frequently used by itself or in combination with statements and questions.

In the **product approach,** the salesperson places the product on the counter or hands it to the customer, saying nothing. The salesperson waits for the prospect to begin the conversation. The product approach is useful if the product is new, unique, colorful, or if it is an existing product that has been noticeably changed.

If, for example, Pepsi-Cola completely changed the shape of its bottle and label, the salesperson would simply hand the new product to the retail buyer and wait for a reaction. In marketing a new pocket calculator for college students, the Texas Instruments salesperson might simply lay the product on the buyer's desk and wait. It is possible to effectively combine the product approach with the showmanship approach.

The **showmanship approach** involves doing something unusual to catch the prospect's attention and interest. This should be done carefully so that the approach does not backfire, which can happen if the demonstration does not work or is so flamboyant as to be inappropriate for the situation.

> "Ms. Rosenburg, our paper plates are the strongest on the market, making them drip-free, a quality your customers will appreciate." [*The salesperson places a paper plate on her lap and pours cooking grease or motor oil onto it while speaking to the prospect.*]

> As she hands the buyer a plate from a new line of china, she lets it drop onto the floor. It does not break. While picking it up, she says, "Our new technique in treating quality china will revolutionize the industry. Your customers, especially new brides, will love this feature. Don't you think so?"

> The salesperson selling Super Glue would repeat the television advertisement for the prospect. In the prospect's office, the salesperson glues two objects together, such as a broken handle back onto a coffee cup, waits one minute, hands the cup to the buyer for a test, and then begins the sales presentation. The mended cup can be left with the buyer as a gift and a reminder.

Opening with Questions

Questions are the most common openers because they allow the salesperson to better determine the prospect's needs and to force the

A Successful Saleswoman's Approach

Sheila Fisher, a middle-aged widow, lived in California for 25 years before returning to her native England three years ago. She wanted to move back to California and wanted a home of her own. She had some cash available for a down payment, but her income was fixed and she was not sure what she could make if she went back to work as a hair stylist. However, she did know what she did not want. "I don't want exotic financing," Sheila told Vikki Morrison. "I want to keep my life simple. I don't want to get in a situation where, in three years, I'll have to sell."

This encounter was their first face-to-face meeting. Vikki has a formula for such situations. In a previous telephone conversation, she had gotten a rough idea of what Ms. Fisher wanted: A three-bedroom home with a formal dining room and assumable financing that will keep her monthly payments at or below $600 after a $50,000 down payment.

Before the meeting, Vikki had combed the multiple listing book for condominiums that matched Fisher's needs and compiled a list of addresses. If she had viewed the home before, she simply called the owners to warn them she would be dropping in. If she hadn't visited the home, Vikki put it on the list of homes to screen before Ms. Fisher's arrival.

By the time the two women met, Vikki had mapped out a tour of five homes, building up to a spacious condominium with a $144,000 price tag that the realtor thought was the best of the lot. But she didn't really expect to sell any of them that day.

"This is our getting-acquainted day," Vikki told Sheila as she turned into traffic on busy Golden West Avenue. "So be very blunt, very up-front. That's the only way I can learn your tastes. Okay?"

Ms. Fisher agreed. She had already decided that she liked Vikki Morrison, the fourth real estate agent whom she had consulted.

"I think she's listening to me," she confided in Vikki's absence. "I think she understands."

prospect to participate in the sales interview. Only questions that the salesperson knows from experience and preplanning will receive a positive reaction from the buyer should be used, since a negative reaction would be hard to overcome.

Like opening statements, opening questions can be synt[...] suit a number of selling situations. In the following sections, several basic questioning approaches will be introduced. This listing is by no means exclusive, but serves only to introduce the reader to a smattering of questioning frameworks. With experience, a salesperson can develop a knack for determining what question to ask what prospect.

Customer Benefit Approach. Using this approach, the salesperson asks a question that implies that the product will benefit the prospect. If it is their initial meeting, the salesperson can include both his/her name and the company's name.

> "Hi, I'm Charles Foster of ABC Shipping and Storage Company! Mr. McDaniel, would you be interested in a new storage and shipping container that will reduce your transfer costs by 10 to 20 percent?"

> "Would you be interested in saving 20 percent on the purchase of our IBM typewriters?"

> "Ms. Johnson, did you know that several thousand companies like yours have saved 10 to 20 percent of their manufacturing cost as described in this *Newsweek* article? [Continue, not waiting for a response.] They did it by installing our computerized assembly system! Is that of interest to you?"

Your **customer benefit approach** statement should be carefully constructed so as to anticipate the buyer's response. However, you should always be prepared for the unexpected, as when the salesperson said, "This office machine will pay for itself in no time at all." "Fine," the buyer said. "As soon as it does, send it to us."

A customer benefit approach can also be implemented through the use of a direct statement of product benefits. While the customer benefit approach begins with a question, it can be used with a statement showing how the product can benefit the prospect. The three customer benefit questions shown earlier can be converted into benefit statements.

> "Mr. McDaniel, I want to talk with you about our new storage and shipping container that will reduce your costs by 10 to 20 percent."

> "I'm here to show you how to save 20 percent on the purchase of our IBM typewriters."

> "Mr. Johnson, several thousand companies—like yours—have saved 10 to 20 percent on their manufacturing cost by installing our computerized assembly system! I'd like 15 minutes of your time to show you how we can reduce your manufacturing costs."

Benefit statements are useful in situations in which you are aware of the prospect's or customer's critical needs and know you have a short time to make your presentation. However, to assure a positive atmosphere, statements can be followed by a short question— "Is that of interest to you?"—to help ensure that the benefits are important to the buyer. Even if you know of the buyer's interest, a positive response to your question is a commitment; the buyer will listen to your presentation because of the possible benefits offered by your product.

Furthermore, you can use the buyer's response to this question as a reference point, something to refer to, throughout your presentation. Continuation of an earlier example will illustrate the use of a reference point.

> "Mr. McDaniel, earlier you mentioned your interest in reducing your shipping cost. The [Now mention your product's feature.] enables you to [Now discuss your product's advantages.] And the benefit to you is the reduction of manufacturing costs."

Sometimes salespeople have to prepare an approach that temporarily baffles a prospect. One of the more common ways of baffling entails the exploitation of human curiosity.

Curiosity Approach.   The salesperson asks a question or does something to make the prospect curious about the product or service. For example, a salesperson for Richard D. Irwin, Inc., the company that publishes this text, might use the **curiosity approach** by saying,

> "Do you know why college professors such as yourself have made this [as she hands the book to the prospect] the best-selling book about how to sell on the market?"

> "Do you know why a recent *Newsweek* article described our new computerized assembly system as revolutionary?" [The salesperson briefly displays the *Newsweek* issue, then puts it away before the customer can request to look at the article. Interrupting a sales presentation by urging a prospect to review an article would lose the prospect's attention for the rest of the interview.]

One manufacturer's salesperson sent a telegram to a customer saying, "Tomorrow is the big day for you and your company." When the salesperson arrived for the interview, the prospect could not wait to find out what the salesperson's message meant.

In calling on a male buyer who liked to smoke cigars, a consumer goods saleswoman set a cigar box on the buyer's desk. After some chat, the buyer said, "What's in the box?" The saleswoman handed the box to the buyer and said, "Open it." Inside was one of her products that she wanted to sell him. After he bought, she gave him the cigars. Selling can be fun, especially if the salesperson enjoys being creative.

Opinion Approach. People are usually flattered when asked their opinion on a subject. Most prospects are happy to discuss their needs if asked correctly. Here are some examples:

> "I'm new at this business, so I wonder if you could help me? My company says our Model 100 copier is the best product on the market for the money. What do you think?"

> "Mr. Jackson, I've been trying to sell you for months on using our products. What is your honest opinion about our line of electric motors?"

The **opinion approach** is especially good for the new salesperson because it shows that you value the buyer's opinion. Opinion questioning also shows that you are not going to attempt to challenge a potential buyer's expertise by spouting a memorized pitch.

Shock Approach. As its title implies, the **shock approach** uses a question designed to make the prospect think seriously about a subject related to the salesperson's product. For example:

> "Did you know that you have a 20 percent chance of having a heart attack this year?" (Life insurance.)

> "Did you know that home burglary, according to the FBI, has increased this year by 15 percent over last year?" (Alarm system.)

> "Shoplifting costs store owners millions of dollars each year! Did you know that there is a good chance you have a shoplifter in your store right now?" (Store cameras and mirrors.)

This type of question must be used carefully, as some prospects may feel you are merely trying to pressure them into a purchase by making alarming remarks.

Multiple Question Approach (SPIN). In many selling situations it is wise to use questions to determine the prospect's needs. A series of questions can be an effective sales interview opener. Multiple questions force the prospect to immediately participate in the sales interview, and quickly develop two-way communication. Carefully listening to the prospect's needs will aid in determining what features, advantages, and benefits to use in the sales presentation itself.

A relatively new method of using **multiple questions** is the **SPIN approach,** which involves using a series of four types of questions in a specific sequence.[1] SPIN stands for (1) Situation, (2) Problem, (3) Implication, and (4) Need-payoff questions. Since SPIN requires questions to be asked in their proper sequence, its steps will be carefully described in the following four sections.

Step 1. <u>Situation questions.</u> Ask about the prospect's general situation as it relates to your product.

Industrial examples: Dyno Electric Cart salesperson to purchasing agent: "How large are your manufacturing plant facilities?"

IBM typewriter salesperson to purchasing agent: "How many secretaries do you have in your company?"

Consumer examples: Real estate salesperson to prospect: "How many people do you have in your family?"

Appliance salesperson selling a microwave oven to prospect: "Do you like to cook? Do you and your family eat out much?"

As the name of this question implies, the salesperson first asks a "situation" question that helps provide a general understanding of the buyer's needs. Situation questioning allows the salesperson to move smoothly into questions on specific problem areas. Also, beginning an approach using specific questions may make the prospect uncomfortable and unwilling to talk to you about problems, and may even make the buyer deny them. These are warm-up questions enabling you to get a better understanding of the prospect's business.

Step 2. <u>Problem questions.</u> Ask about specific problems, dissatisfactions, or difficulties perceived by the prospect relative to your situation question.

Industrial examples: Dyno Electric Cart salesperson to purchasing agent: "Have your executives ever complained about having to do so much walking in and around the plant?"

IBM typewriter salesperson to purchasing agent: "Do your Royal typewriters do all that your secretaries want them to do?" (You may have previously asked the secretaries this question and know that they are dissatisfied.)

Consumer examples: Real estate salesperson to prospect: "Has your family grown so that you need more space?"

Appliance salesperson selling microwave oven to prospect, "Are you happy with your present oven? Are there times when you must quickly prepare meals?"

Problem questions should be asked early in the presentation to bring out the needs or problems of the prospect. Your goal is to have the prospect admit, "Yes, I do have a problem."

To maximize your chance of making the sale, you must determine which of the prospect's needs or problems are important (explicit needs) and which are unimportant. The more explicit needs you can discover, the more vividly you can relate your products' benefits to areas the prospect is actually interested in, and thus, the higher your probability of making the sale.

An important or explicit need or problem is recognized as such by the prospect. There is a desire to fulfill the need or solve the problem. Problem questions are useful in developing explicit needs.

If the prospect should state a specific need after your situation or problem questions, do not move directly into your sales presentation. Continue with the next two steps to increase your chance of making the sale. A prospect may sometimes not appreciate all the ramifications of a problem.

Step 3. *Implication questions.* Ask about the implications of the prospect's problems or how a problem affects various related operational aspects of a home, life, or business.

Industrial examples: Dyno Electric Cart salesperson to purchasing agent: "It sounds as if your executives would have an interest in reducing their travel time and not having to exert so much energy in transit. Doesn't it seem that if they could do so, they would get to the plant as quickly as they need to, saving themselves time and energy, and the company money?"

IBM typewriter salesperson to purchasing agent: "Does this problem mean your secretaries are not as efficient as they should be, thus increasing your costs per page typed?"

Consumer examples: Real estate salesperson to prospect: "So with the new baby and your needing a room as an office in your home, what problems does your present residence create for you?"

Appliance salesperson to prospect: "With both of you working, does your present kitchen oven mean . . . inconvenience for you? . . . that you have to eat out more than you want to? . . . that you have to eat junk foods instead of well-balanced meals?"

Implication questions seek to help the prospect realize the true dimensions of a problem. The phrasing of the question is important in getting the prospect to discuss problems or areas for improvement and in fixing them in the prospect's mind. In this situation, the prospect is personally motivated to fulfill this need or solve this problem.

If possible attach a bottom line figure to the implication question. You want the prospect to state, or agree with you, that the implications of the problem are causing such things as production slowdowns of 1 percent, resulting in increased costs of 25 cents per unit; increased reproduction costs of one cent per copy; loss of customers; or the adding of personnel to make service calls, costing an extra $500 a week.

You use this hard data later in your discussion of the business proposition. Using the prospect's data, you can show how your product can influence his costs, productivity, or customers.

S-P-I questions do not have to be asked in exact order, and you can ask more than one of each type of question. You will generally begin with a situation question(s) and follow with a problem question. However, you could ask a situation question, then a problem question, and then another situation question, for example. The need-payoff question is always last.

Step 4. Need-payoff questions. Ask if the prospect has an important, explicit need.

Industrial examples: Dyno Electric Cart salesperson to purchasing agent: "If I could show you how you can solve your executive's problems in getting to and from your plant, and at the same time save your company money, would you have an interest?"

IBM office products salesperson to purchasing agent: "Would you be interested in a method to improve your secretaries' efficiency at a lower cost than you now incur?"

Consumer examples: Real estate salesperson to prospect: "If I could show you how to cover your space problems at the same cost per square foot, would you be interested?"

Appliance salesperson to prospect: "Do you need a convenient way to prepare well-balanced, nutritious meals at home?"

Phrasing the need-payoff question is the same as opening with a benefit statement. However, in using the SPIN approach, the prospect defines the need. If the prospect responds positively to the need-payoff questions, you know this is an important (explicit) need. You may have to repeat the P-I-N questions to fully develop all of the prospect's important needs.

The Procter & Gamble, Tide, sales presentation shown in Figure 7–7 is an example of using the P-I-N approach for a customer with whom you are very familiar. Let's say your customer says yes to your need-payoff question: "If we could determine how much volume you're missing, I think you'd be willing to make space for the large size, wouldn't you?" Then you move directly into your brief sales presentation.

If the answer is no, you know that this is not an important need. Start over again by asking *Problem*, *Implication*, and *Need-payoff* questions to determine important needs.

 Product Not Mentioned in SPIN Approach. As you see from the SPIN examples, the product is not mentioned in the approach. This allows you to develop the prospect's need without revealing exactly what you are selling.

When a salesperson first walks into the buyer's office and says, "I want to talk about Product X," the chances of a negative response greatly increase because the buyer does not perceive a need for the product. SPIN questions allow you to better determine the buyer's needs before you begin your presentation.

The Use of Questions Results in Sales Success

Since this is the first chapter in which you have been exposed to the use of questioning techniques, and since properly questioning your prospect or customer is so important to your sales success, you should now be exposed to the many uses and types of questions.

Asking questions, sometimes called *probes*, is an excellent technique for (1) obtaining information from the prospect, (2) developing two-way communication, and (3) increasing prospect participation.

When using questions in selling, you need to know or to be able to anticipate the answer you want to your question. Once you know the answer you want, you can develop the question. This procedure can be used to request information you do not have, and to confirm information you already know.

An ideal question is one a prospect is willing and able to answer. Only questions that can help make the sale should be asked, so use questions sparingly and wisely.

Is It Selling Or Is It Telling?

It's **your** sales presentation, and you spend a lot of time on it—shaping it, smoothing it, rehearsing it, memorizing it. It's just the way you want it—so why isn't it working?

Have you forgotten that there's a person at the other end?

A pro. Good at his job. A buyer who knows his business. He has opinions, ideas, suggestions. And maybe he doesn't like to be lectured at.

There's often a fine line between selling and telling. Include the buyer in your scenario. Ask him what he thinks, what his problems are. Relate your facts to his business. Discuss what you have to say with him.

Always take the attitude that you're *informing* the buyer by imparting some valuable new facts to him. Nobody likes to be lectured at—but everyone welcomes being informed.

Why would asking a question get the prospect's attention? Because to give an answer a prospect must think about the topic to some extent. There are four basic categories of questions that can be used at any point during your presentation. These categories are (1) direct, (2) nondirective, (3) rephrasing, and (4) redirect questions.

The Direct Question

The **direct question** or closed-ended question can be answered with very few words. A simple yes or no will answer most direct questions. They are especially useful in moving a customer toward a specific topic. Examples the salesperson might use are "Mr. Berger, are you interested in saving 20 percent on your manufacturing costs?" or, "Reducing manufacturing costs are important, aren't they?" You should be able to anticipate a yes response from these questions.

Never phrase the direct question as a direct negative-no question. A *direct negative-no question* is any question that can be answered in a manner that cuts you completely off. The retail salesperson says, "May I help you?" and the reply usually is, "No, I'm just looking." It's like hanging up the telephone on you. You are completely cut off.

Other types of direct questions ask "what kind" or "how many?" These questions also ask for a limited, short answer from the prospect. The implication and need-payoff questions used in SPIN are examples of direct questions used for the approach.

However, the answer to a direct question does not really tell you much, because there is little feedback involved. You may need more information to determine the buyer's needs and problems, especially if you could not find them out before making the sales call. Nondirective questioning can aid you in your quest for information.

The Nondirective Question

To open up two-way communication, the salesperson can use an open-ended or **nondirective question** by beginning the question with one of six words: Who, what, where, when, how, and why. Examples include the following:

- Who will use this product?
- What features are you looking for in a product like this?
- Where will you use this product?
- When will you need the product?
- How often will you use the product?
- Why do you need or want to buy this type of product?

One word questions such as "Oh?" or "Really?" can also be useful in some situations. One-word questions should be said so that the tone increases or is emphasized: "Oh?!" This prompts the customer to continue talking. Try it—it works.

To practice using the open-ended questioning technique, ask a friend a question—any question—beginning with one of these six words, or use a one-word question, and see what answer you get. Chances are, the response will consist of several sentences. In a selling situation, this type of response allows the salesperson to better determine the prospect's needs.

The purpose of using a nondirective question is to obtain unknown or additional information, to draw out clues to hidden or future needs and problems, and to leave the situation open for free discussion of what is on the customer's mind. Situation and implication questions are examples of the nondirective question.

phrasing Question

The third type of question is called a **rephrasing question**. At times, the prospect's meaning is not clearly stated. In this situation, if appropriate, the salesperson might say:

> Are you saying that price is the most important thing you are interested in? (sincerely, not too aggressively)

> Then what you are saying is, if I can improve the delivery time you would be interested in buying?

This form of restatement allows for clarification of meaning and determination of the prospect's needs. If the prospect answers yes to the second question, you would work out a way to improve delivery. Should no be the answer to the delivery question, you know delivery time is not an important buying motive, and you can continue to probe for the true problem.

The Redirect Question

The fourth type of question is the **redirect question**. This is used to redirect the prospect to selling points that both parties agree on. There are always areas of agreement between buyer and seller even if the prospect is opposed to purchasing the product. The redirect question is an excellent alternative or backup opener. An example will clarify the concept of redirective questioning.

Imagine you walk into a prospect's office, introduce yourself, and get this response, "I'm sorry, but there is no use in us talking. We are satisfied with our present suppliers. Thanks for coming by." Respond by replacing your planned opener with a redirecting question. You might say:

> We do agree that having a supplier that can reduce your costs is important.

> You will agree that manufacturers must use the most cost efficient equipment to stay competitive these days, wouldn't you?

> Wouldn't you agree that you need to continually find new ways to increase your company's sales?

Using a redirect question moves the conversation from a negative position to a positive or neutral one, while reestablishing communications between two people. The ability to redirect a seemingly terminated conversation through the use of a well-placed question may impress the prospect simply by showing that you are not a run-of-the-mill order taker, but a professional salesperson who sincerely believes in the beneficial qualities of your product.

Three Rules for Using Questions

The first rule is to use only questions that you can anticipate the answer to or that will not lead you into a situation from which you cannot escape. While questions are a powerful selling technique, they can easily backfire on you.

The second rule in using a question is to pause or wait after submitting a question to allow the prospect time to respond to it. Waiting for an answer to a well-planned question is sometimes an excruciating process—seconds may seem like minutes. A salesperson must allow the prospect time to consider the question, and hope for a response. Failing to allow a prospect enough time defeats the major purpose of questioning, which is to establish two-way communication between the prospect and the salesperson.

The third rule is to listen. Many salespeople are so intent on talking that they forget to listen to what the prospect says (or disregard his nonverbal signals). Salespeople need to listen consciously to prospects so that they can ask intelligent, meaningful questions that will aid both themselves and their prospects in determining what needs and problems exist and how to solve them. Prospects appreciate a good listener and view a willingness to listen as an indication that the salesperson is truly interested in their situation.

Keep Quiet and Get the Order

Dennis DeMaria, Branch Manager, Westvaco, Folcroft, PA, says "One of the biggest single weapons you as a salesperson can use in getting an order from a customer or prospect is keeping quiet and patiently waiting for the buyer to answer your questions. A general rule in the selling profession is that the person who asks the questions is the person who has control of the interview. The information obtained from asking questions is the necessary ammunition you use to find the buyer's likes, dislikes, hot buttons, and areas to avoid. This valuable information also informs the salesperson whether the customer is ready to buy or whether he or she should continue selling.

"Experience has shown that salespeople *do* ask questions, but they forget the most important part of this sales principle: *after you ask a question you must be patient, don't talk and let the buyer answer*. It does not matter how long it takes for the buyer to respond, keep quiet and wait for the answer. Remember, the first person to speak after a question has been asked, loses."[2]

He Is Still Not Listening? _____

What happens when you give your best opening approach, and as you continue to talk you realize your prospect is not listening? What about prospects who open mail, who fold their arms while looking at the wall or seem to be looking beyond you into the hallway, who make telephone calls in your presence, or who may even doze off, as shown in Figure 8–6.

This is the time to use one of your alternative openers, which will tune him into your message. The prospect must be forced to participate in the talk by using either the question or demonstration approach. By handing the person something, showing him something, or asking a question, attention can be briefly recaptured, no matter how indifferent a prospect is to your presence.

If you can overcome such preoccupation or indifference in the early minutes of your interview by quickly capturing the prospect's attention and interest, the probability of your making a sale will greatly improve. This is why the approach is so important to the success of a sales call.

It is crucial that you never become flustered or confused when a communication problem arises during your approach. As was mentioned earlier, the salesperson who can capture another person's imag-

Figure 8–6
What Does It Take to Get Your Prospect's Attention?

ination earns the right to a prospect's full attention and interest. Your prospect should not be handled as an adversary, for in that type of situation you will seldom, if ever, gain the sale.

You Need to Be Flexible in Your Approach

Picture yourself as a salesperson getting ready to come face-to-face with an important prospect, Ellen Myerson. You have planned exactly what to say in the sales presentation, but how can you be sure to get Ms. Myerson to listen to your sales presentation? You realize she is busy and may be indifferent to your being in the office; she probably is preoccupied with her own business-related situation and several of your competitors may already have seen her today.

You have planned to open your presentation with a statement on how successful your memory typewriter has been in helping secretaries save time and eliminate errors in their typing. When you enter the office, Ms. Myerson comments on how efficient her secretaries are and how they produce error-free work. From her remarks, you quickly determine that your planned statement approach is inappropriate. What do you do now?

You might begin by remarking how lucky she is to have such conscientious secretaries. Then proceed into the SPIN question approach, first asking questions to determine general problems that she may have, and then using further questions to uncover specific problem areas she might like to solve. Once you have determined specific problems, you could ascertain whether they are important enough for her to want to solve them in the near future. If so, you can make a statement that summarizes how your product's benefits will solve her critical needs and test for a positive response. A positive response will allow you to conditionally move into your sales presentation.

You should always be prepared to change any part of your sales presentation to meet the particular characteristics of a specific selling situation or environment.

Summary of Major Selling Issues

As the first real step in your sales presentation, your approach is an extremely critical factor. To assure your prospects' attention and interest during a memorized or formula mode of presentation, you may want to use a statement or demonstration approach. In more technically oriented situations where you and the prospects must agree on needs and problems, a questioning approach (SPIN, for instance) is in order. Generally, in developing your approach you should imagine your prospects asking themselves: "Do I have time to listen, talk with, or devote to this person? What's in it for me?"

Words alone will not assure you a hearing. The first impression that you make on a prospect can negate your otherwise positive and sincere opening. To assure a favorable impression in most selling situations, you should generally dress conservatively, be well groomed, and act as though you are truly glad to meet this person.

Your approach statement should be especially designed for each prospect. You can choose to open with a statement, question, or demonstration by using any one of many techniques. Several alternative approaches should be held in readiness should you feel the need to alter your plans for a specific situation.

Carefully phrased questions are extremely useful at any point in a sales presentation. Questions should display a sincere interest in prospects and their situations. Skillfully handled questions employed in a sales approach can wrest a prospects' attention from distractions, centering it on you and your presentation. Questions can generally be of use in determining prospect wants and needs, and thereby increasing prospect participation in the sales presentation. Four basic types of questions discussed in this chapter are direct, nondirective, rephrasing, and redirect questions.

In using questions, you should be sure to ask the type of questions that you can anticipate the answer to. Also, remember to allow prospects time to completely answer the question and be sure to listen carefully to their answers for a guide as to how well you are progressing toward selling to them. Should you determine that your prospect is not listening to you, do something to recapture attention. Techniques such as offering something or asking questions can refocus the prospect's attention long enough for you to move back into your presentation.

Review and Discussion Questions

1. Explain the reasons for using questions when making a sales presentation. Discuss the rules for questioning that should be followed by the salesperson when using questions.

2. What are three general categories of the approach? Give an example of each.

3. What is SPIN? Give an example of a salesperson using SPIN.

4. In each of the following instances determine if a direct, nondirective, rephrasing, or redirect question is being used. Also, discuss each of the four types of questions.

    a. "Now let's see if I have this right; you are looking for a high quality product and price is no object?"

    b. "What type of clothes are you looking for?"

    c. "Are you interested in Model 101 or Model 921?"

    d. "Well, I can appreciate your beliefs, but you would agree that price is not the only thing to consider when buying a copier, wouldn't you?"

    e. "When would you like to have your new Xerox 9000 installed?"

    f. "Are you saying that *where* you go for vacation is more important than the cost of getting there?"

    g. "You would agree that saving time is important to a busy executive like yourself, wouldn't you?"

5. Which of the following approaches do you think is the best? Why?

    a. "Ms. Jones, in the past you've made it a practice to reduce the facings on heavy-duty household detergents in the winter months because of slower movement."

    b. "Mr. Brown, you'll recall that last time I was in, you expressed concern over the fact that your store labor was running higher than the industry average of 8 percent of sales."

    c. "Hi! I'm Jeanette Smith of Procter & Gamble, and I'd like to talk to you about Cheer. How's it selling?"

6. Assume you are a salesperson for NCR (the National Cash Register Corporation) and you want to sell the owner/manager (Mr. Johnson) of a large independent supermarket your computerized customer check-out system. You have just met Mr. Johnson inside the front door of the supermarket, and after your initial introduction the conversation goes as follows:

Salesperson: Mr. Johnson, your customers are really backed up at your cash registers, aren't they?

Buyer: Yeah, it's a real problem.

Salesperson: Do your checkers ever make mistakes when they are in a rush?

Buyer: They sure do!

Salesperson: Have you ever thought about shortening checkout time while reducing checker errors?

Buyer: Yes, but those methods are too expensive!

Salesperson: Does your supermarket generate over $1 million in sales each month?

Buyer: Oh, yes—why?

Salesperson: Would you be interested in discussing a method of decreasing customer check-out time 100 percent and greatly lessening the number of errors made by your checkers, if I can show you that the costs of solving your problems will be more than offset by your savings?

    a. Using the framework of the SPIN approach technique, determine whether each of the above questions asked by the sales-person is a Situation, Problem, Implication, or Need-payoff question.

b. If Mr. Johnson says yes to your last question, what should you do next?

c. If Mr. Johnson says no to your last question, what should you do next?

7. As a salesman for Gatti's Electric Company, Cliff Defee is interested in selling John Bonham more of his portable electric generators. John is a construction foreman for a firm specializing in building large buildings such as shopping centers, office buildings, and manufacturing plants. He is currently using three of Cliff's newest models. Cliff has just learned John will be building a new manufacturing plant. As Cliff examines the specifications for the new plant, he feels John will require several additional generators. Two types of approaches Cliff might make are depicted in the following situations:

Situation A

Salesperson:	I see you got the Jonesville job.
Buyer:	Sure did.
Salesperson:	Are the specs ok?
Buyer:	Yes.
Salesperson:	Will you need more machines?
Buyer:	Yes, but not yours!

Situation B

Salesperson:	I understand you have three of our electric sets.
Buyer:	Yes I do.
Salesperson:	I'm sure you'll need additional units on your next job.
Buyer:	You're right, I will.
Salesperson:	Well, I've gone over your plant specifications and put together products just like you need.
Buyer:	What I don't *need* are any of your lousy generators.
Salesperson:	Well, that's impossible. It's a brand new design.
Buyer:	Sorry, I've got to go.

a. Briefly describe both approaches in Situation A and B. In both situations Cliff finds himself in a tough spot. What should he do now?

b. What type of approach could Cliff have made that would have allowed him to uncover John's dissatisfaction? Would the approach you are suggesting also be appropriate if John had been satisfied with the generators?

8. This is a cold call on the warehouse manager for Coats Western Wear, a retailer with four stores. You know most of the manager's work consists of deliveries from the warehouse to the four stores. Based on your past experience, you suspect that the volume of shipments to the warehouse fluctuates, with certain seasons of the year being extremely busy.

As a salesperson for Hercules Shelving, you want to sell the manager your heavy-duty gauge steel shelving for use in the warehouse. Since this is a relatively small sale, you decide to go in cold, relying only on your questioning ability to uncover potential problems and make the prospect aware of them.

You are now face-to-face with the warehouse manager. You have introduced yourself and after some small talk you feel it is time to begin your approach. Which of the following questions would serve your purpose best?

a. "Have you had any recent storage problems?"

b. "How do you take care of your extra storage need during your busy seasons such as Christmas?"

c. "Can you tell me a little about your storage problems?"

Projects

1. Television advertisements are constructed to quickly capture the viewer's attention and interest in order to sell a product or service. Examine at least five commercials and report on the method each one used to get your attention, stimulate your interest, and move you from this attention-interest phase into discussing the product. Determine whether the first few seconds of the commercial related to the product's features, advantages, or benefits, and if so, how? You may wish to use a tape recorder.

2. Assume that you are scheduled for a 30-minute job interview next week with a representative of a company you are really interested in working for. How would you prepare for the interview and what could you do during the first few minutes of the interview to get the recruiter interested in hiring you? Can you see any differences between this interview situation and the environment of a salesperson making a sales call on a prospect?

Cases

8–1 The Thompson Company

Before making a cold call on the Thompson Company, you did some research on the account. Barbara Thompson is both president and chief purchasing officer. In this dual capacity she is often so rushed that she is normally impatient with salespeople. She is known for her habit of quickly turning down the salesperson and shutting off the discussion by turning and walking away. In looking over Ms. Thompson's operation, you notice that the inefficient metal shelving she is using in her warehouse is starting to collapse. Warehouse employees have attempted to remedy the situation by building wooden shelves and reinforcing the weakened metal shelves with lumber. They have also begun stacking boxes on the floor, requiring much more space.

You recognize the importance of getting off to a fast start with Ms. Thompson. You must capture her attention and interest quickly, or she may not talk with you.

Question:
Which of the following attention-getters would you choose:
a. "Ms. Thompson, I'd like to show you how Hercules shelving can save you both time and money."
b. "Ms. Thompson, can you spare a few moments of your time to talk about new shelving for your warehouse?"
c. "Ms. Thompson, how would you like to double your storage space?"

8–2 The Copy Corporation

Assume you are contacting the purchasing agent for office supplies of a large chain of retail department stores. After hearing that the company is opening 10 new stores, you determine they will need a copier for each store. Three months earlier you had sold this purchasing agent a lease agreement on two of your larger machines. The buyer wanted to try your machines in the company's new stores. If they liked them, you would get the account. Unknown to you, one of the machines was not working properly, causing the purchasing agent to be pressured by a store manager to replace it immediately. As you walk into the purchasing agent's office, you say:

Salesperson:	I understand you are opening 10 new stores in the next six months.
Buyer:	I don't know who told you, but you seem to know!
Salesperson:	If you'll let me know when you want a copier at each store, I'll arrange for it to be there!
Buyer:	Look, I don't want anymore of your lousy copiers! When the leases expire, I want you here to pick them up, or I'll throw them out in the street! I've got a meeting now. I want to see you in three months.

Questions:

1. Describe this situation, commenting on what the salesperson did correctly and what was done incorrectly.
2. Develop another approach the salesperson could use to uncover the problems experienced by the purchasing agent.

8–3 Electronic Office Security Corporation

Ann Saroyan is a salesperson for the Electric Office Security Corporation. She sells industrial security systems that detect intruders and activate an alarm. When Ann first began selling, she used to make brief opening remarks to her prospects and then move quickly into her presentation. While this resulted in selling many of her security systems, she felt there must be a better method.

Ann began to analyze the reasons prospects would not buy. Her conclusion was that even after her presentation, prospects still did not feel they needed a security alarm system. She decided to develop a multiple-question approach that would allow her to determine the prospect's attitude toward a need for a security system. If the prospect does not initially feel a need for her product, she wants her approach to help convince the prospect of a need for a security system.

Ann developed and carefully rehearsed her new sales presentation. Her first sales call using her multiple-question approach was with a large accounting firm. She asked the receptionist who she should see and was referred to Joe Bell. After she waited 20 minutes, Mr. Bell asked her to come into his office. The conversation went like this:

Salesperson:	This is a beautiful old building, Mr. Bell. Have you been here long?
Buyer:	About 10 years. Before we moved here we were in one of those ugly glass and concrete towers. Now, you wanted to talk to me about office security.
Salesperson:	Yes, Mr. Bell. Tell me, do you have a burglar alarm system at present?
Buyer:	No, we don't. We've never had a break in here.
Salesperson:	I see. Could you tell me what's the most valuable item in your building?
Buyer:	Probably the computer.
Salesperson:	And is it fairly small?
Buyer:	Yes, amazingly, it's not much bigger than a typewriter.
Salesperson:	Would it be difficult to run your business without it—if it were stolen for example?
Buyer:	Oh yes, that would be quite awkward.

Salesperson: Could you tell me a bit more about the problem you would face without your computer?

Buyer: It would be inconvenient in the short term for our accounts and records people, but I suppose we could manage until our insurance gave us a replacement.

Salesperson: But without a computer wouldn't your billing to customers suffer?

Buyer: Not if we got the replacement quickly.

Salesperson: You said the computer itself is insured. Do you happen to know if the software—the programs, your customer files—is insured too?

Buyer: I don't believe so; our insurance covers the equipment only.

Salesperson: And do you keep back-up records somewhere else—in the bank, for example?

Buyer: No, we don't.

Salesperson: Mr. Bell, in my experience, software isn't left behind after a theft. Wouldn't it be a very serious problem to you if that software were taken?

Buyer: Yes, you're right, I suppose. Redevelopment would certainly cost a lot. The original programs were very expensive.

Salesperson: And even worse, because software development can take a long time, wouldn't that hold up your billing to customers?

Buyer: We could always do that manually.

Salesperson: What effect would that have on your processing costs?

Buyer: I see your point. It would certainly be expensive, as well as inconvenient, to run a manual system.

Salesperson: And if you lost your software, wouldn't it also make it harder to process customer orders?

Buyer: Yes. I don't have much contact with that part of the business, but without order processing and stock control I'm sure we would grind to a halt in a matter of days.

Salesperson: Are there any other items in the building that would be hard to replace if stolen?

Buyer: Some of the furnishings. I would hate to lose this antique clock, for example. In fact, most of our furnishings would be very hard to replace in the same style.

Salesperson: So if you lost them, wouldn't it hurt the character of your office?

Buyer: Yes, it would be damaging. We've built a gracious, civilized image here, and without it we would be like dozens of other people in our business, the glass and concrete image.

Salesperson: This may sound like an odd question, but how many doors do you have at ground level?

Buyer: Let me see . . . uh . . . six.

Salesperson: And ground level windows?

Buyer:	About 10 or a dozen.
Salesperson:	So there are 16 or 18 points where a thief could break in, compared with one or two points in the average glass and concrete office. Doesn't that concern you?
Buyer:	Put that way, it does. I suppose we're not very secure.

Questions:

1. Did the dialogue between buyer and seller seem natural to you?

2. Did the salesperson use too many questions in her approach?

3. Analyze each of the salesperson's questions and state whether it is a Situation, Problem, Implication, or Need-payoff type of question.

4. Analyze each of the buyer's responses to the salesperson's questions and state what type of need the salesperson's question uncovered. Was it an implied or minor need response or was it an explicit or important need response? Why?

5. How would you improve on this salesperson's approach?

6. After the buyer's last statement what would you do?
   a. Move into the presentation.
   b. Ask a Problem question.
   c. Ask a Need-payoff question.
   d. Ask for an appointment to fully discuss your system.

9 ELEMENTS OF MAKING A GREAT PRESENTATION

Learning Objectives

1. To present the purpose and essential steps of the sales presentation.
2. To discuss the six elements of the sales presentation mix.
3. To review difficulties that may arise during the sales presentation.
4. To emphasize the need to properly diagnose the prospect in order to determine how to design the sales presentation.

Key Terms for Selling

Sales presentation mix
Logical reasoning
Suggestive propositions
Prestige suggestion
Autosuggestion
Direct suggestion
Indirect suggestion
Counter suggestion
Paul Harvey dialogue
Simile

Metaphor
Analogy
Proof statements
Visuals
Dramatization
Demonstration
Trial close
Interruptions
Competition
Detailed comparison

Profile

Linda M. Slaby-Baker
Quaker Oats

My career in the food industry began during my sophomore year in college. I decided the best way to learn the industry was to start at the grassroots level. I deduced that by my senior year, I should know which career in the industry was best suited for me. During my college years, I worked as a dietary supervisor at Hermann Hospital, as a food intern for the catering department of the Brasewood Marriott Hotel, and as an order clerk for the product buying office of Fleming Foods. These jobs taught me valuable human relation skills, and a good appreciation for people at all levels of an operation. The experience also paved the way for my first career opportunity with the Quaker Oats Company.

I began my career with the Quaker Oats Company in February 1980 as an account representative. This position required servicing 50 to 60 independent grocery operations. In the grocery industry, selling time is a valuable commodity. The typical grocery manager gives you 5 to 10 minutes to sell new items, book promotional cases, or suggest space management improvements. Needless to say, your presentation must be short, persuasive, concise, and organized.

My presentation experience was a key factor in determining the success of my next two positions: account supervisor and account manager. These two positions entailed calling on divisional or independent direct accounts. The presentations were given to one or more buyers for 30 or more retail stores. My presentation time of 5 to 10 minutes was increased to 15 to 60 minutes; but, ironically, the same presentation principles applied. My buyer was constantly interrupted by the phone or his/her secretary. My biggest problem was bringing the buyer back into the presentation. During the presentation, I needed to immediately catch the buyer's attention, meet his/her needs, and close the sale. These were the essentials to a successful presentation.

"**Y**our presentation," says Linda Slaby-Baker, "should be a give-and-take of mutually beneficial information between you and your buyer. Probe your buyer with questions and then let him talk. Asking questions invites the buyer into your presentation, and you quickly learn what he wants to hear. Buyers are human; they love to give their viewpoints. Ask the buyer for his input into the structuring of trade deals, the spending of advertising dollars, or how to increase the sales on a slow product.

"Visual aids bring life to your presentations. Visuals take the buyer's mind off you and on a graph, a chart, an advertisement, or a sample. Samples of the product are a must in consumer product presentation. Always leave a sample for the buyer to try.

"In my presentations, I use a number of bar graphs to illustrate the sales growth of products and indexing charts to illustrate shares of the market. Since I am in a business where the products are edible, I bring samples for my buyers to taste. To sell a new syrup, I brought in a small toaster and heated up some frozen waffles. I poured the syrup over the warm waffles and the buyer sampled the product in his office. The result was, I sold all three sizes of the syrup."

This chapter discusses the elements of the presentation—the fourth step in the sales process (see Figure 9–1). We begin by examining the purpose and essential steps in the presentation. Next, we review and expand on presentation techniques used by salespeople such as Linda Slaby-Baker of the Quaker Oats Company. We end the chapter discussing the importance of the proper use of trial closes and difficulties that may arise in the presentation, along with the need to design your presentation around an individual situation and buyer.

The Purpose of the Presentation

Certainly the main goal of your presentation is to sell your product to your customer. However, we know that a prospective buyer considers many things before making a decision on which product to buy. As we have seen, the approach or first few minutes of the interview should be constructed to do such things as determine the prospect's need, capture attention and interest, while allowing for a smooth transition into the presentation.

The presentation itself is a continuation of the approach. What then should be the purpose of the presentation? Basically, the purpose of the presentation is to provide *knowledge* via the features, advantages, and benefits of your product, your marketing plan and business proposal. This allows the buyer to develop positive personal *beliefs* toward your product. The beliefs result in *desire* (or *need*) for the type of product you are selling. Your job, as a salesperson, is to convert that need into a

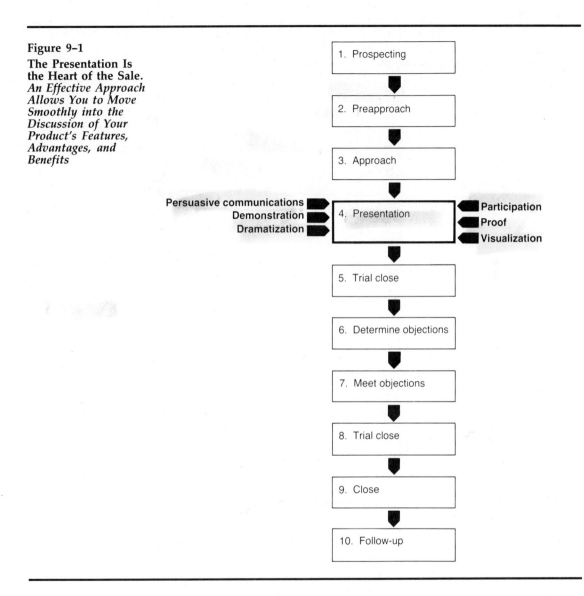

Figure 9–1

The Presentation Is the Heart of the Sale. *An Effective Approach Allows You to Move Smoothly into the Discussion of Your Product's Features, Advantages, and Benefits*

1. Prospecting
2. Preapproach
3. Approach

Persuasive communications
Demonstration
Dramatization

4. Presentation

Participation
Proof
Visualization

5. Trial close
6. Determine objections
7. Meet objections
8. Trial close
9. Close
10. Follow-up

want, and into the *attitude* that your specific product is the best product to fulfill a certain need. Furthermore, you must convince the buyer that not only is your product the best but also you are the best source to buy from. When this occurs, your prospect has moved into the *conviction* stage of the mental buying process.

A real need is established, the buyer wants to fulfill that need, and there is a high probability your product is best for the purpose. This results in your making a sale, as shown in Figure 9–2. Whether to buy or

Figure 9–2
The Five Purposes of the Presentation

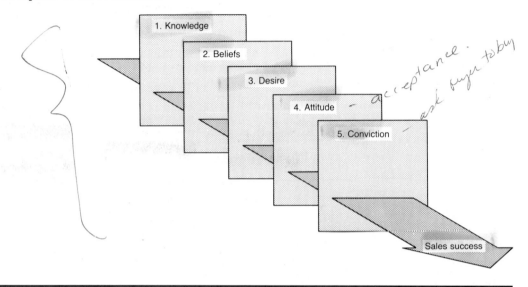

not is a choice decision, and you have provided the necessary information so that the customer chooses to buy from you.

Let us assume, for example, you are a salesperson for IBM, and you wish to sell a company 10 of your new memory electric typewriters costing $5,000 each. The prospect's company is at present using your competitor's electric typewriters, which cost $3,000 each. How should you conceptualize the prospect's thought processes regarding whether to buy or not buy from you in order to develop your presentation as shown in Figure 9–1?

First, you should realize that the prospect has certain attitudes toward present equipment (typewriters). The prospect's job performance is judged according to the management of certain responsibilities. Thus, improving the performance of company employees is important. However, the prospect knows nothing about you, your product, or your product's benefits. The prospect may feel that IBM products are good, high-quality products, but expensive. However, you cannot be sure about the buyer's present attitudes.

You should develop a SPIN approach to determine the buyer's attitudes toward typewriters in general and the memory typewriter specifically. Once you have gone through each of the four SPIN questions, and you feel more information about your product is in order, you begin your presentation.

You present the product information you feel will allow the buyer to develop a positive attitude toward your product. Next, using possibly a value analysis type of proposal, you show how a memory typewriter can increase a secretary's efficiency, reduce costs per item typed, and pay for itself in one year, using a return-on-investment technique. A positive reaction from your prospect indicates that the desire stage of the mental buying process has been reached. There is a need for some brand of memory typewriter.

Now you show why your IBM memory typewriter is the best solution to the buyer's need and show that you will provide service after the sale. A positive response on these two items now indicates that the prospect believes your product is best and that the conviction stage has been reached. The prospect wants to buy the IBM memory typewriter.

Up to this point, you have discussed your product's features, advantages, and benefits, your marketing plan, and your business proposition. You have *not* asked the prospect to buy. Rather, you have developed a presentation to lead the prospect through four of the five mental buying steps: the attention, interest, desire, and conviction steps. It may take you five minutes, two hours, or several weeks of repeat calls to move the prospect into the conviction stage.

You should realize that you must move the prospect into the conviction stage before a sale is made. So hold off asking the prospect to buy until the conviction stage. Otherwise, this usually results in objections and failure to listen to your whole story, thus fewer sales. The sales presentation has seven major steps. Each step is taken in order to logically and sequentially move the prospect into the conviction stage of the buying process.

When a person buys something, did you ever stop to think what is actually being purchased? Is the customer really buying your product? Not really. What is actually being bought is a mental picture of the future in which your product helps to fulfill some expectation. The buyer has mentally conceived of certain needs. Your presentation must create mental images that move your prospect into the conviction stage.

Three Essential Steps within the Presentation

No matter which of the four sales presentation methods you use, your presentation should follow the three essential steps shown in Figure 9–3.* These are:

 Step 1. Fully discuss the features, advantages, and *benefits* of your product. Tell your whole story. Inside retail salespeople often include a discussion of the company. (See Figure 9–3.)

---

* These three steps are discussed in Chapter 6 under the topic "Customer Benefit Plan."

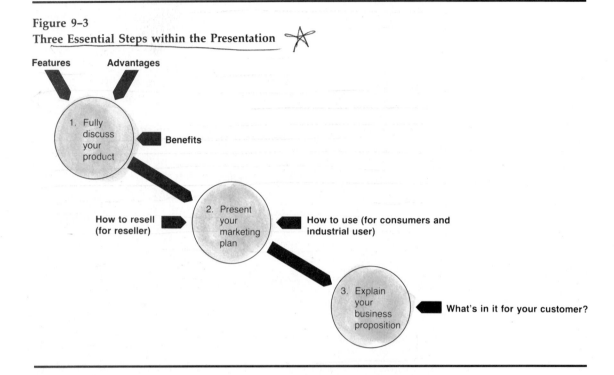

Figure 9–3
Three Essential Steps within the Presentation

Features   Advantages

1. Fully discuss your product

Benefits

How to resell (for reseller)

2. Present your marketing plan

How to use (for consumers and industrial user)

3. Explain your business proposition

What's in it for your customer?

Step 2. Present your marketing plan. For your wholesalers and re-tailers, this is your suggestion on how they should *resell* the product. For end users, it is your suggestion on how they can *use* the product.

Step 3. Explain your business proposition. This step relates the *value* of your product to its *cost*. It should be discussed last, since you always want to present your product's benefits and marketing plan relative to your product's price.

Ideally, information in each of these steps should be presented in such a manner as to create a visual picture in the prospect's mind of the benefits of the purchase. To do this, you should use persuasive communication and participation techniques, proof statements, visual aids, dramatization, and demonstrations in your talk as you move through each of the three steps.

The Sales Presentation Mix

Salespeople sell different products in many different ways, but all use six broad classes of presentation elements to some degree in their pre-

Successful Retail Salespeople Sell the Store

Retail salespeople should be aware that many customers have concerns about the store they buy from. It is common to wonder if a store will go out of business, change ownership, or stop carrying a line of merchandise. To buy an item, we want to know that it is quality merchandise and that we will receive our money's worth.

Because of customer concerns such as these, salespeople should "sell their store." "I always talk about my company and reputation" says Jack Pruett of Bailey Banks & Biddle. "We started out as silversmiths. We made the first class rings for West Point and the Naval Academy. We designed the Purple Heart, the Medal of Honor, and the United States Seal as it is today. We are cutting a stone today that's helped me in a lot of sales because it will be the largest single cut diamond in the world—it's called the Zale diamond, and I tell customers about it.

"I take a lot of time to discuss the credibility of the company and the history of the company. This makes the customer more interested in who they are doing business with and helps them want to do business with us and me. They are far less likely to go down the mall and buy from another store. If they do shop around, they will remember me, my interest in them, and our organization because other retail salespeople don't do this. I greatly increase my chances of a prospect coming back to me by selling them on my store." (See Figure 9–4.)

Figure 9–4
Jack Pruett Sells the Customer on Himself, His Product, the Store, and His Company

sentations to provide information in a meaningful way to the prospect or customer. For this reason, I refer to these elements as the *presentation mix.*

The **sales presentation mix** refers to the elements the salesperson assembles to sell to prospects and customers. While all elements should be part of the presentation, it is up to the individual to determine the extent to which each element is emphasized. This determination should be primarily based on the sales call objective, customer profile, and customer benefit plan. Let's now examine each of these six elements, as shown in Figure 9–5.

Persuasive Communications

To be a successful salesperson, do you need to be a smooth talker? No, but you do need to consider and use factors that aid in clearly communicating your message. As shown in Table 9–1, sales managers in 44 major manufacturing firms ranked three factors (enthusiasm, per-

Figure 9–5
The Salesperson's Presentation Mix

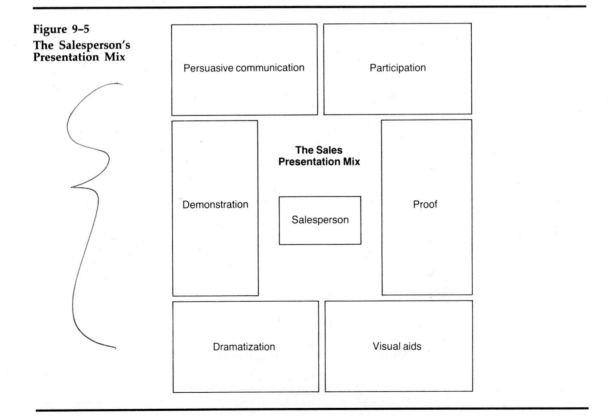

Table 9–1
Sales Managers' Ranking of Characteristics for Salespeople

Attribute	Rank Assigned by Respondents*										Total Points
	1 (10)	2 (9)	3 (8)	4 (7)	5 (6)	6 (5)	7 (4)	8 (3)	9 (2)	10 (1)	
1. Enthusiasm	16	5	8	5	1	5	—	1	—	—	338
2. Well organized	6	8	11	3	5	5	1	2	—	—	304
3. Obvious ambition	8	6	5	7	4	3	2	3	3	—	285
4. High persuasiveness	2	10	3	1	10	4	5	3	1	2	254
5. General sales experience	3	2	4	6	6	2	8	8	5	4	226
6. High verbal skill	2	3	3	6	2	7	7	6	4	1	215
7. Specific sales experience	2	4	2	8	6	1	5	4	4	5	214
8. Highly recommended	1	—	1	4	3	3	7	2	7	2	149
9. Follows instructions	—	2	—	3	4	4	2	9	9	8	142
10. Sociability	—	1	1	2	—	7	6	6	8	10	134

* The top numeral in each column is the ranking given by executives, with 1 being most important and 10 least important. Numbers in parentheses are point ratings assigned to each rank. Numbers in the table show the number of respondents who assigned each rank to each attribute.

suasiveness, and verbal skill) as important attributes for salespeople.[1] Enthusiasm was ranked most important, with high persuasiveness and high verbal skill ranking fourth and sixth, respectively.

In Chapter 3 we discussed seven factors which, if used, will help you to be a better communicator. The factors were these:

1. Using questions.
2. Having empathy.
3. Keeping the message simple.
4. Creating mutual trust.
5. Listening.
6. Having a positive attitude and enthusiasm.
7. Being believable.

Additional persuasive factors to consider in the presentation are logical reasoning, persuasive suggestions, a sense of fun, personalized relationships, trust, body language, a controlled presentation, diplomacy, and the "Paul Harvey dialogue" or conversation style.

Logical Reasoning. The application of logic through reasoning is an effective persuasive technique that appeals to prospects' common sense by requiring them to think about the proposition and to compare alternative solutions to problems. It can have excellent results when applied to selling computers, heavy equipment, and communication systems.

This is especially so when selling complicated proposals involving comparative cost data, when price versus benefits must be judged, and when the product is a radically new concept.

Logical reasoning involves a presentation constructed around three parts: a major premise, a minor premise, and a conclusion. Here is an example:

1. Major premise: All manufacturers wish to reduce costs and increase efficiency.

2. Minor premise: My equipment will reduce your costs and increase your efficiency.

3. Conclusion: Therefore you should buy my equipment.

If presented exactly in the straightforward manner as above, the logical formula may be too blunt; the prospect may raise defenses. However, you can develop the framework or outline of the presentation to first determine if the prospect is interested in reducing costs and increasing manufacturing efficiency. If so, then a value analysis can be presented showing the benefits of your product over other alternatives. Information such as performance data, costs, service, and delivery information can be presented in a persuasive manner using various elements of the presentation mix.

Persuasion through Suggestion. Suggestion, like logical reasoning, can be effectively used to persuade prospects. The skilled use of suggestions can arouse attention, interest, desire, conviction, and action. Types of suggestions that may be considered for incorporation into the presentation are:

1. **Suggestive propositions** imply that the prospect should act now, such as, "Shouldn't you go ahead and buy now before the price goes up next month?" Prospects often like to postpone their buying decisions, so the suggestive approach can help overcome this problem.

2. **Prestige suggestions** are used to get the prospect to visualize using products that famous people, companies, or someone the prospect might trust uses, such as, "The National Professional Engineers' Association has endorsed our equipment. That's the reason several hundred of the Fortune 500 manufacturers are using our products. This elite group of manufacturers are finding the equipment is further helping them to increase their profits, sales, and market share. Is this of interest to you?"

3. **Autosuggestion** attempts to have prospects imagine themselves using the product. Television advertisements frequently use this

form of suggestion. The salesperson visualizes the product, saying, "Just imagine how this equipment will look and operate in your store. Your employees will perform much better and will thank you."

4. The **direct suggestion** is widely used by professional salespeople in all industries because it does not tell, but *suggests* they buy, which does not offend the buyer. Such a suggestion might go thus: "Based on our survey of your needs, I suggest you purchase. . . ." or "Let's consider this: we ship you three train carloads of Whirlpool washers and dryers of the following colors and models. . . ."

5. The **indirect suggestion** can be used at various times for some prospects when it is better not to be direct in suggesting a recommended course of action. Indirect suggestions help instill in prospects' minds factors such as doubt about a competitor's products or desire for your product, which makes it seem as if it is their idea: "Should you buy 50 or 75 dozen 12-oz. Revlon hairspray for your promotion?" or, "Have you talked with anyone who has used that product?"

6. The **counter suggestion** is used to get an opposite response from the prospect: "Do you really want such a high-quality product?" Often the buyer will begin expanding on why a high-quality product is needed. This is an especially effective technique to include in the presentation if you have already determined the prospect wants a high-quality product.

Make the Presentation Fun. Selling is fun, not a battle between the prospect and salesperson, so loosen up and enjoy the presentation. This is easy to do, once you realize that you believe in yourself and what you are selling—so sound like it! Have the *right mental attitude* and you can be successful.

Personalize Your Relationship. When I worked for a large national industrial manufacturer, my sales manager taught me to personalize my presentation. He would say, "Charles, you are enthusiastic; you believe in yourself, your products, your company; and you give a very good presentation. To improve, however, you need to personalize your relationship with each of your customers. In some manner let them know during your presentation that you have their best interests at heart." He would always say, "Show 'em that you love 'em."

I came up with the short phrase, "You have me." Once I incorporated this into my presentation at the appropriate time, I saw a significant increase in my total sales and sales-to-customer-call ratio by saying something such as: "You are not only buying my products but also me. You have me on call 24 hours a day to help you in any way I can."

Yes, it does sound somewhat corny, but it helped show my customers that I cared for them and that they could believe in me. This helped to build trust between us. You might choose a different way, yet it is important to tell and show them that you are looking out for their interests.

Building Trust. Two of the best and easiest ways to build your persuasive powers with prospects is to be *honest* and *do what you say* you will. This results in building trust, which increases sales. Most professional buyers have elephant-like memories that can be used to your advantage if you follow through after the sale and do what you said you would do when presenting your proposal.

Honesty is always the best policy and is an effective way to build trust. The salesperson should never claim more than the product can actually accomplish. If the product does not live up to expectations, then apologize, return the product for credit, or trade the product for another product. This is extremely important in obtaining repeat sales. This builds trust; the next time the prospect is reluctant to buy, then you say, "Haven't I always taken care of you? Trust me, this product is what you need. I guarantee it!"

Use Your Own Body Language. Just as you watch for buying signals from a prospect, so too the prospect watches your facial expressions and body movements. The salesperson's own nonverbal communications should project a positive image to the prospect, one that shows you know what you are talking about and understand the buyer's needs. Your customer will think, I can trust this person.

The best nonverbal selling technique to use is the smile. As my sales manager said, "It's often not what you say but how you say it, and you can say almost anything to anyone if you do it with a smile. So practice your facial expressions and smile—always smile."

Control the Presentation. In making the presentation, you always need to be able to direct the conversation as planned in order to lead the prospect through your presentation and proposal. The salesperson is often faced with how to maintain control and what to do should the prospect take control of the conversation. For example, what do you do if the prospect likes to talk about hobbies, attacks your company or products for poor service or credit mix-ups, or is a kidder and likes to poke fun at your products, which he might call "dogs"?

When this happens, the salesperson should stay with a planned presentation if at all possible. If there is some complaint, this should be addressed first. If the prospect likes to talk about other things, then do so only for a brief period. When the prospect's attention and interest are hard to maintain, questions or some manner of getting participation in the presentation are the two best methods to rechannel the conversation.

Be sure to keep control of the visual aids and any materials you use in your presentation. New salespeople often make the mistake of handing prospects their catalog, price list, or brochures showing several products. When buyers are looking through all of this information, chances are they are not listening to you. Too much information can cause frustration, and they will not buy. So hold on to your product materials with one hand and discuss the points of information you wish to present while prospects look and listen to you.

Be a Diplomat.   All salespeople will face the situation where the prospects feel they are right, or know it all, and the salesperson has different opinions. For example, the salesperson may have previously sold the prospect's company a machine that is always breaking down due to its operator, not the piece of equipment, yet the salesperson's company gets the blame. What to do?

The salesperson has to be a diplomat in cases where tempers rise and prospects are wrong but feel they are correct and will not change their opinions. Retreat may be the best option; otherwise, you run the risk of destroying the relationship. If you challenge the prospect, you could win the battle only to lose the war. This is a decision the salesperson must make based on the individual situation.

Use the Paul Harvey Dialogue.   Paul Harvey has the most listened-to radio news broadcast in America because of what he says and how he says it. Listen to him yourself. Then use the **Paul Harvey dialogue.** Construct your presentation to incorporate his excellent methods of speech, delivery, and particularly how he builds suspense into his stories. With these techniques, your talk comes alive, rather than sounding like a dull, monotone, memorized presentation.

Simile, Metaphor, and Analogy.   Words can be used as selling tools. Similes, metaphors, analogies, pauses, silence, and changes in the rate of speaking, tone, and pitch can be extremely effective methods of gaining prospects' attention and capturing their interest in a proposal.

A **simile** is a direct comparison statement using the words *like* or *as:* A poorly manicured lawn is *like* a bad haircut. Our Sylvania safeline bulbs are *like* a car's shatterproof windshield. Shaklee diet drinks are *like* a chocolate milkshake. The carton folds *as flat as* a pancake for storage.

A **metaphor** is an *implied* comparison that uses a contrasting word or phrase to evoke a vivid image: Our power mowers *sculpt* your lawn. Our cabin cruiser *plows* the waves smoothly. The computer's *memory* stores your data. The components *telescope* into a two-inch-thick disk.

The **analogy** compares two different situations that have something in common such as, "our Sun Screen for your home will stop the sun's heat and glare before it hits your window. It's like having a shade tree in front of your window without blocking the view." Remember to talk the prospect's language by using familiar terminology and buzz words in a conversational tone.

Participation Is Essential to Success

The second major part of the presentation involves techniques for getting the prospect to participate in the presentation. You can induce participation through the use of:

1. Questions.
2. Product use.
3. Visuals.
4. Demonstrations.

We have already discussed the use of questions and will discuss the use of visuals and demonstrations later, so let's briefly consider having prospects actually use the product.

- If you are selling stereos, let them see, hear, feel them!
- If you are selling food, let them see, smell, taste it!
- If you are selling clothes, let them feel and wear them!

By letting prospects use the product, you can appeal to their senses of sight, sound, touch, and smell. The presentation should be developed to appeal to the senses since people often buy because of emotional needs and the senses are keys to developing emotional appeals.

Proof Statements Build Believability

Prospects often say to themselves, before I buy, you must *prove it!* Prove it is a thought everyone has from time to time. Salespeople must therefore prove they will do what they promise to do, such as helping to make product displays when the merchandise arrives. Usually, *prove it* means proving to a prospect during a presentation that the product's benefits and the salesperson's proposal are legitimate.

Because salespeople often have a reputation for exaggeration, prospects are at times skeptical of the salesperson's claims. By incorporating **proof statements** into the presentation, the salesperson can increase the prospect's confidence and trust that product claims are accurate. Several useful proof techniques are customers' past sales figures, the guarantee, testimonials, company proof results, and independent research results, as seen in Figure 9–6.

Figure 9–6
Researching Proof
Statements before a
Sales Presentation

Quaker Oats' Eli Jones uses his
personal computer to keep track of
customer information such as past
sales and customer profile data. This
helps him develop his suggested
purchase order.

Past Sales Help Predict the Future.   Customers' past sales proof statements are frequently used by the salesperson when contacting present customers. Customers keep records of their past purchases from each of their suppliers that can be used by the salesperson to suggest what quantities of which products to purchase. For example, the Colgate salesperson would check a customer's present inventory of all products carried, determine the number of products sold in a month, subtract inventory from forecasted sales, and suggest the customer purchase that amount. It is difficult for buyers to refuse to buy when presentations are based on their own sales records. If they are offered a price discount and promotional allowances, they might purchase 3 to 10 times the normal amount (a promotional purchase).

Assume, for example, that a food store normally carries 10 dozen of the king-size Colgate toothpaste in inventory with 3 dozen on the shelf, and sells approximately 20 dozen a month. The salesperson would produce the buyer's past sales record and simply say, "You should buy 7 to 10 dozen king-size Colgate toothpaste." If offering promotional allowances, the salesperson might say:

The king-size Colgate is your most profitable and best-selling item. You normally sell 20 dozen king-size Colgate each month with a 30 percent gross profit. With our 15 percent price reduction this month only and our advertising allowances, I suggest, based on your normal sales, that you buy either 80 to 100 dozen, reduce the price 15 percent, display it, and advertise the discount in your newspaper specials. This will attract people to your store, help increase store sales, and allow you to make your normal profit.

The salesperson now stops talking to see the buyer's reaction. A suggested order plus an alternative on the quantity to purchase have been proposed. Does the quantity seem high to you? It may be high, just right, or low, but it is the buyer's decision. The salesperson is saying, given your past sales and with my customer benefit plan I believe you can sell *x* amount.

Be realistic about your suggested increase in order size. Some salespeople double the size of the order, expecting the prospect to cut it in half. Your honesty builds credibility with the buyer.

The Colgate salesperson (like comparable consumer goods salespeople such as Quaker Oats' Linda Slaby-Baker) might suggest purchases not only of toothpaste but of all Colgate products. That same sales call could involve multiple presentations of several products that have promotional allowances, plus the recommendation of the purchase of 10 or more items based on present inventories and the previous month's sales.

The Guarantee. The guarantee is a powerful proof technique because it assures prospects that if they are dissatisfied with their purchase, the salesperson or the company will stand behind a product. The manufacturer has certain product warranties that the retail salesperson can use in a presentation.

Furthermore, the consumer goods salesperson selling to retailers may say, "I'll guarantee this product will sell for you. If not, we can return what you do not sell." The industrial salesperson may explain the equipment's warranties and service policies and state, "This is the best equipment for your situation that you can buy. If after you have used it for three months and you are not 100 percent satisfied, I will return it for you."

Testimonials. Use of testimonials in the presentation as proof of the product's features, advantages, and benefits is an excellent method to build trust and confidence. Today we see manufacturers effectively advertising their consumer products using testimonials, such as Roger Staubach, the ex-Dallas Cowboys football star, asking people, "How do you spell *relief?*" Professional buyers are impressed by testimonials from prominent people, experts, and satisfied customers as to a product's features, advantages, and benefits.

Using Testimonials and Recommendations

To sell a new account, you have to overcome the buyer's basic fear —that he or she will be ridiculed by superiors and peers, accused of overpaying or of buying something that doesn't work.

Nothing breaks down that fear like evidence that another buyer at another company has bought, used, paid for, and been satisfied with the product.

Get letters of recommendation when you can, or just permission to use a customer's name during a sales call. Then you can subtly drop a third-party name into the conversation: "You know, that's just why Ernie Jones at ABC Co. is so pleased with our product." If the sale hangs in the balance, though, drop the subtlety and simply announce that "ABC Co. has been using it for years!"

Company Proof Results. Companies routinely furnish data concerning their products. Consumer goods salespeople can use sales data, such as test market information and current sales data. Industrial salespeople use performance data and facts based on company research as proof of their products' performance.

A consumer goods manufacturer gave its salespeople test market sales information to use in their presentation on a new product that was being introduced nationally. Using this information, a salesperson might say:

Our new product will begin to sell as soon as you put it on your shelf. The product was a success in our eastern test market. It had 9.8 percent market share only nine months after the start of advertising. Laboratory tests proved our formula superior to that of the leading competition in our consumer product tests. There was a high repurchase rate of 50 percent after sampling. This means increased sales and profits for you.

Independent Research Results. Proof furnished by reputable sources outside the company usually have more credibility than company-generated data. Pharmaceutical salespeople frequently tell physicians about medical research findings on their products that are published in leading medical journals by medical research authorities.

"On a typical day," says Sandra Snow of the Upjohn Company, "I see as many physicians as possible and initiate a discussion with them about one of our products that will have importance to them in their fields of medicine. I attempt to point out advantages that our drugs have in various states, by using third-party documentation published in current medical journals and texts. The information has much more meaning to a physician who knows that it is not me or the Upjohn Company that has shown our drug to have an advantage, but rather a group of researchers who have conducted a scientific study. All of the material that we give to the physician has previously been approved for our use by the Food and Drug Administration."

Publications such as *Road Test Magazine, Consumer Reports*, newspaper stories, and governmental reports, such as the Environmental Protection Agency publications, may contain information the salesperson can use in the presentation. For a proof statement referring to independent research results to be most effective, it should contain (1) a restatement of the benefit before proving it, (2) the proof source and relevant facts or figures about the product, and (3) expansion of the benefit. Consider the following example of a salesperson's proof statement:

I'm sure that you want a radio that's really going to sell and be profitable for you (benefit restatement). Figures in Consumer Guide *and* Consumer Sales *magazine indicate that the Sony XL 100 radios, although the newest on the market, are the third largest in sales (source and facts). Therefore, when you handle the Sony XL line, you'll find that your radio sales and profits will increase, and you will see more customers coming into your store (benefit expansion).*

Proof statements should be incorporated into the presentation. They provide a logical answer to the buyer's challenge to "prove it!" Quite often proof statements can be presented through the use of visual aids.

The Visual Presentation—Show and Tell

In giving a sales presentation, salespeople do two things: They *show* and *tell* the prospect about a proposal. They *tell*, using persuasive communications, participation techniques, and proof statements. They *show* by using visual aids.

People retain approximately 10 percent of what they hear, but 50 percent of what they see. Consequently, there is five times the chance of making a lasting impression with an illustrated sales presentation rather than with words alone.

Visuals are most effective when you believe in them and have woven them into the message of your sales presentation. You use them to:

- Increase retention.
- Reinforce message.
- Reduce misunderstanding.
- Create a unique and lasting impression.
- Show your buyer you are a professional.

The visual presentation (showing) incorporates the three remaining elements of the presentation mix: visual aids, dramatization, and demonstration. Certainly there is some overlap between the three, for a demonstration does use visuals and can be considered to have some dramatics. Let's examine each of the elements to consider how they can be used separately or combined into a selling presentation.

Visual Aids Help Tell the Story

Visuals, or visual aids, refer to devices that appeal chiefly to the prospect's vision with the intent of producing mental images of the product's features, advantages, and benefits. Many companies routinely supply their salespeople visuals for their products. Some of the common visuals are:

- The product itself.
- Charts and graphics illustrating product features and advantages, such as performance and sales data.
- Photographs of the product and its uses.
- Models of the products, especially for large, bulky products.
- Audiovisual equipment such as films, slides, and tape cassettes.
- Sales manuals and product catalogs.
- Order forms.

Figure 9–7 is an illustration of an Uarco Business Forms salesperson making a video-slide presentation to company executives.[2] Many sales organizations supply their salespeople with video equipment to show things such as examples of their advertisements or their products in operation.

Most visual aids are carried in the salesperson's bag. The sales bag should be checked before each sales call to ensure all visuals necessary for the presentation are organized in the sales bag in such a manner to allow the salesperson to easily reach into the bag and pull out needed

Figure 9–7
A Saleswoman
Making a Slide
Presentation for Uarco
Business Forms

visuals. Only new, top-quality, professionally developed visuals should be used. Tattered, torn, or smudged visuals should be routinely discarded. The best visual aid is your showing the buyer the actual product.

Quaker Oats salesperson Linda Slaby-Baker illustrates in Figure 9–8 the use of visual aids when calling on customers. After planning her sales call, she packs her sales bag, enthusiastically greets her buyer, and begins her sales presentation. Her visual aids consist of the product itself, visuals she has created tailored to this particular buyer, and visuals furnished to her by Quaker Oats. The use of visuals allows Linda to give her sales presentation in a persuasive manner. As you see in Figure 9–8, Linda uses different visuals, different body positions, and different conversational techniques to actively bring her buyer into their conversation. This provides her sales presentation with a dramatic element, which greatly improves her probability of making the sale.

Dramatization Improves Your Chances

Dramatics refers to talking or presenting the product in a striking, showy, or extravagant manner. Thus, salesmanship can involve **drama-**

Figure 9–8
Quaker Oats Saleswoman Linda Slaby-Baker Illustrates the Use of Visual Aids

1. *Linda reviews call plan before seeing buyer.*

2. *Products and sales aids placed in and arranged in her sales bag.*

3. *Enters buyer's office.*

4. *Greets buyer with firm handshake, smile, eye contact.*

tization or theatrical presentation of products. However, dramatics should be incorporated into the presentation only when you are 100 percent sure that the dramatics can be carried out acceptably. This was not considered by the salesperson who set the buyer's trash can on fire. The salesperson had difficulty extinguishing the fire with his new fire extinguisher and ran the buyer out of the room because of extensive smoke. However, if carried out correctly, dramatics can be very effective. One of the best methods of developing ideas for the dramatization of a product is to watch television commercials. Products are presented using visuals, many are demonstrated, and certainly most are dramatized. Take, for example, the following television advertisements.

"We challenged the competition . . . and they ran!" says the Heinz tomato ketchup advertisement. Two national brands of ketchup

Figure 9–8 *(concluded)*

5. *Begins presentation using products and sales aids in bag.*

6. *Uses her personally developed sales aids customized to her buyer.*

7. *Shows facts, figures, reasons to buy.*

8. *Linda uses company sales aids to get buyer involved in presentation.*

and Heinz Ketchup are poured into a paper coffee filter held up by a tea strainer. The competition's ketchup begins to drip, then to run through the filter. The Heinz ketchup does not drip or run, indicating the high quality of the Heinz ketchup relative to their competition.

Bounty paper towel advertisement shows coffee spilled and shows how quickly the product absorbs the coffee relative to the competitive paper towel.

The STP motor oil additive advertisement shows a person dipping one screwdriver into STP motor oil additive and another screwdriver into a plain motor oil. The person can pick up and hold with two fingers the end of the screwdriver covered with plain motor oil. The screwdriver covered with STP motor oil additive slips out of the fingers indicating STP provides better lubrication for an automobile engine.

You can use your dramatic demonstration to set you apart from the many, many salespeople that buyers see each day. Buyers, such as industrial purchasing agents, like to see you, for they know you will have an informative and often entertaining sales presentation. One salesperson known for his effective presentations was George Wynn. George was an industrial salesperson for Exxon U.S.A. responsible for the sales of machine lubricating oils and greases in Dayton, Cincinnati, and Columbus, Ohio.

One group of products sold by George consisted of oils and greases sold to the food processing industry. These lubricants had to be approved by the Federal Food and Drug Administration for incidental food contact. One of the products sold was a lubricating grease, Carum 280. George ordered a number of one-pound cans for customer samples. As George started his sales presentation of these FDA approved products, he would take one of the cans from his sample case, open it, and spread this grease on a slice of bread also removed from his sample case. After taking a bite of the bread spread with the grease, he then offered a bite to the buyer. The buyer generally refused the offer. However, in the mind of the buyer, this dramatic demonstration set George's presentation apart from others. It helped prove to the buyer the product was safe to use in a food processing plant.

Another dramatic demonstration used by George involved lubricating greases used by the steel industry. Greases that are resistant to high temperatures are desirable for most applications in the steel industry. Exxon developed a line of temperature-resistant greases that made use of a new thickener that held the oil in suspension better than competitive products. In order to demonstrate this product attribute, George used a pie tin held at a 45° angle centered over a small lighted alcohol lamp. A small glob of the Exxon grease as well as globs of several better-known competitors were placed on the pie tin. As the pie tin was heated, the oil separated from each of the competitive greases and ran down the pie tin. The oil did not separate from the Exxon product, thus dramatically demonstrating the high temperature resistance of this steel mill grease when compared to the leading competitive products.

Demonstrations Prove It! _____

One of the best ways to convince a prospect that a product is needed is to show the merits of the product through a **demonstration,** as did George Wynn. If a picture is worth a thousand words, then a demonstration is worth a thousand pictures. Therefore, it is best to show the product, if possible, and to actually have the prospect use it. If this is not feasible, then pictures, models, motion pictures, or slides are the next best alternative. Whatever the salesperson is attempting to sell, the prospect should be able to see it.

Psychological studies have shown that people receive 87 percent of their information on the outside world through their eyes and only 13 percent through the other four senses. What this says to the salesperson is to make a product visible. Also let the prospect feel, see, hear, smell, and use the product. The dynamic demonstration appeals to human senses by telling, showing, and creating buyer-seller interaction.

Demonstrations are part of the dramatization and fun of your presentation. Do not underestimate their ability to make sales for you, no matter how simple they may appear. For example, a glass company some years ago came out with a shatterproof glass. This was not standard equipment in automobiles then, as it is now. They had their salesmen going around the country trying to sell this shatterproof glass. One of the salespeople completely outsold the rest of the sales force. When they had their convention, they said, "Joe, how come you sell so much glass?" He replied, "Well, what I've been doing is taking little chunks of glass and a ball peen hammer along with me on my sales calls. I take the little chunk of glass, and I hit it with the hammer. This shows that it's shatterproof. It splinters, but doesn't shatter and fall all over the ground. This has been helping me to sell a lot of glass."

So the next year they equipped every one of their salespeople with a little ball peen hammer and little chunks of glass. But an interesting thing happened. Joe still far outsold the rest of the sales force in his sales. So, when the convention came around again the next year, they asked, "Joe, how is it you're selling so much? You told us what you did last year. What are you doing different?" He replied, "Well, this year, I gave the glass *and* the hammer to the customer and let *him* hit it." You see, the first year he had dramatization in his demonstration. The second year Joe had dramatization and participation in his demonstration. Again, it's often not what you say but how you say it that makes the sale for you.

A Demonstration Checklist.   There are seven points to keep in mind as you prepare your demonstration. These points are shown in Figure 9–9. First, is the demonstration really needed and appropriate for your prospects? Certainly every sale does not need a demonstration nor will all products lend themselves to a demonstration.

If the demonstration is appropriate, what is its objective? What should the demonstration accomplish? Next, you should be sure you have properly planned and organized the demonstration. It is important to rehearse it so that the demonstration flows smoothly and appears to be natural. Take your time in talking and going through your demonstration so as to make it look easy. Remember, if you, the expert, cannot operate the machine, for example, imagine how difficult it will be for the prospect.

The only way to ensure a smooth demonstration is to practice. Yet there is always the possibility that the demonstration will not go as

Figure 9–9

Sales Demonstration Checklist
☑ Is the demonstration *needed* and *appropriate*?
☑ Have I developed a specific demonstration *objective*?
☑ Have I properly *planned* and *organized* the demonstration?
☑ Have I rehearsed to the point that the demonstration *flows smoothly* and appears to be *natural*?
☑ What is the probability the demonstration will *go as planned*?
☑ What is the probability the demonstration will *backfire*?
☑ Does my demonstration present my product in an *ethical* and *professional* manner?

planned or will backfire no matter how simple it may be. You need to be prepared for this. An example was an ex-student of mine who was demonstrating his new Kodak slide projector. Two bulbs in a row burned out as he demonstrated the product to a buyer for a large discount chain. He anticipated what could go wrong and always carried extra parts in his sales bag. When the first bulb went out, he began talking of how easy it was to exchange bulbs, and when the second one blew, he said "I want to show you that again," with a smile. He always carried two spare bulbs, but now he carries three.

Lastly, you should make sure your demonstration presents the product in an ethical and professional manner. You do not want to misrepresent the product or proposal. A complex product, such as a large computer system, can be presented as simple to install with a few start-up problems, yet the buyer may find the computer system difficult to get into operation.

Get Participation in Your Demonstration.   By getting the prospect to participate in the demonstration, you can be assured not only that you have obtained a buyer's attention but also that you can direct it where you want it. It also helps the prospect visualize owning and operating the product. The successful demonstration aids in reducing buying uncertainties and thus resistance to its purchase. The salesperson can have the prospect do four things to have a successful demonstration:

1. Let the prospect do something simple.
2. Let the prospect work an important feature.
3. Let the prospect do something routine, frequently repeated.
4. Ask the prospect questions throughout the demonstration.

First, get the prospect to do something which is simple, easy to do with a low probability of foul-up. Second, in planning the demonstra-

282

tion, select the main features you will stress in the interview and allow the prospect to participate on the feature that relates most to an important buying motive. Again, you need to keep it simple.

A third way to a have a successful demonstration is to get the prospect to do something with the product that is frequently done. Finally, be sure to get feedback from the prospect throughout the demonstration by asking questions or pausing in your conversation. This is extremely important since it will accomplish the following:

- Determine the prospect's attitude toward the product.
- Allow you to progress in the demonstration or wait and answer any questions or address any objections.
- Aid in getting the prospect into the positive yes mood.
- Set the stage for the close of the sale.

Little agreements lead to the big agreement to say yes. Be sure to phrase the questions in a positive manner, such as, "That is really easy to operate, isn't it?" instead of, "This isn't hard to operate, is it?" They ask the same thing, yet the response to the first question is positive instead of negative. The best questions force the prospect to mentally place the product in use, such as the question phrased, "Do you feel this feature could increase your employee's production?" The answer yes commits the buyer to the idea that the feature will increase employee production. Remember, it is often not what you say, but how you say it.

Reasons for Using Visual Aids, Dramatics, and Demonstrations

As we have seen, visual aids, dramatics, and demonstrations are important to the salesperson's success in selling a prospect. The reasons for using them are that they:

- Capture attention and interest.
- Create two-way communications.
- Involve the prospect through participation.
- Afford a more complete, clearer explanation of products.
- Increase a salesperson's persuasive powers by obtaining positive commitments on a product's single feature, advantage, or benefit.

Guidelines for Using Visual Aids, Dramatics, and Demonstrations

While visual aids, dramatics, and demonstrations are important, their proper use is critical if they are to be effective. When using them, you should consider:

Figure 9–10

Beecham's Santo Laquatra Uses Videotaping to Prepare His Salespeople to Sell

- Rehearsing by practicing in front of a mirror, on a tape recorder, and to a friend. Figure 9–10 shows Santo Laquatra, the national sales training manager for Beecham Products, videotaping two salespeople roleplaying their sales presentation. He plays it back so everyone can critique the presentation. Then, once you are ready to make your actual presentation, first see your less important prospects. This allows you to refine the presentation further before contacting your large accounts.

- Customizing them to the sales call objective, prospect's customer profile, and customer benefit plan. Concentrate on the prospect's important buying motives and use appropriate multiple appeals to sight, touch, hearing, and smell.

- Making them *simple, clear,* and *straightforward.*

- Being sure to *control* the demonstration in order not to let the prospect take from you your selling aids. It can be disastrous to have the prospect not listen or pass up major selling points you wished to present.

- Making them *true to life.*

- Encouraging *prospect participation*.
- Incorporating *trial closes* (questions) after showing or demonstrating a major feature, advantage, or benefit in order to determine if it is believed and important to the prospect.

The Trial Close—
A Major Step in the Sales Presentation

The **trial close** is one of the best selling techniques that you can use in your sales presentation. It is used to check the "pulse" or attitude of your prospect toward your sales presentation. The trial close should be used at the following four important times:

1. After making a *strong selling point* in the presentation.
2. After the *presentation*.
3. After answering an *objection*.
4. *Immediately before* you move to *close* the sale.

The trial close allows you to determine (1) whether the prospect likes your product's feature, advantage, or benefit (the strong selling point); (2) whether you have successfully answered the objection; (3) whether any objections remain; and (4) whether the prospect is ready for you to close the sale. It is a powerful technique to induce two-way communication (feedback) and participation from the prospect.

If, for example, the prospect says little while you make your presentation, and if you get a no answer when you come to the close, you may find it difficult to change the prospect's mind. You have not learned the real reasons why the prospect says no. To help avoid this, salespeople use the trial close to determine the prospect's attitude toward the product throughout the presentation.

The trial close asks for the prospect's *opinion*, not a decision to buy. It is a direct question that can be answered with very few words.* These are examples of a trial close:

"How does that sound to you?"

"Are these the features you are looking for?"

"Is this what you are interested in?"

"That's great—isn't it?"

"Is this important to you?"

If the prospect responds favorably to your trial close, then you know that you are in agreement or that you have satisfactorily answered an

---

* See Chapter 8 for other uses and examples of direct questions.

objection. Thus the prospect may be ready to buy. However, if you get a negative response, you know not to close. Either you have not answered some objection or the prospect is not interested in the feature, advantage, or benefit you are discussing. This type of feedback allows you to better uncover what your prospect thinks about your product's potential for satisfying needs.

Sell Sequence

One way to remember to incorporate a trial close into your presentation is the use of the *Sell Sequence*. Each letter of the word *sell* stands for a sequence of things to do and say in order to stress benefits important to the customer.

S	E	L	L
Show	Explain	Lead	Let
feature	advantage	into benefit	customer talk

Showing the product

By remembering the word *sell;* you can remember to *show the feature, explain the advantage, lead into the benefit, and then let customer talk by asking a question about the benefit (trial close).*

Example: Industrial salesperson to industrial purchasing agent: "This equipment is made of stainless steel [feature], which means it won't rust [advantage]. The real benefit is that it reduces your replacement costs, thus saving you money! [benefit] That's what you're interested in—right?" [trial close]

Example: Beecham salesperson to consumer goods buyer: "Beecham will spend an extra $1 million in the next two months advertising Cling Free fabric softener [feature]. Plus, you can take advantage of this month's $1.20 per dozen price reduction [feature]. This means you will sell 15 to 20 percent more Cling Free in the next two months [advantage], thus making you higher profits and pulling more customers into your store [benefits]. How does that sound?" [trial close]

Once you attempt your trial close, carefully listen to what the customer says and watch for nonverbal signals to determine if what you have said has made an impact. If you get a positive response to your trial close, consider asking the customer to buy at once.

Remember, the trial close does not ask the customer to buy or make any type of purchase decision. It asks only for an opinion. The trial close is a trial question to determine the customer's opinion towards the salesperson's proposition in order to know if it is time to close the sale. Thus, its main purpose is to induce feedback from the buyer.

The Ideal Presentation

In the ideal presentation, your approach technique quickly captures your prospect's interest and immediately gets signals that the prospect has a need for your product and is ready to listen. The ideal prospect is friendly, polite, relaxed, will not allow anyone to interrupt you, asks questions, and participates in your demonstration as you had planned. This allows you to move skillfully through your presentation.

The ideal customer cheerfully and positively answers each of your questions, allowing you to anticipate just the correct moment to ask for the order. You are completely relaxed and sure of yourself when you come to the close. The customer says yes and enthusiastically thanks you for your valuable time. Several weeks later, you receive a copy of the letter your customer wrote your company's president glowing with praise for your professionalism and sincere concern for the customer.

Be Prepared for Presentation Difficulties

Yes, a few sales presentations go somewhat like that, yet most have one or more hurdles you should be prepared for. Refer back to Linda Slaby-Baker's profile for her example of interruptions. While certainly not all of the difficulties you might face can be discussed here, three main problems that are possible to encounter during your sales presentation are interruptions, how to handle the discussion of competition, and the necessity oftentimes of making the presentation in a less than ideal situation.

How to Handle Interruptions

It is quite common for **interruptions** to occur during the presentation. The secretary comes into the office or the telephone rings, distracting the prospect. What should you do?

First, you should determine if the discussion that interrupted your presentation is personal or confidential. If so, by gesture or voice you can offer to leave the room—which is always appreciated by the prospect. While waiting, you should regroup your thoughts and mentally review how you will move back into the presentation. Once the discussion is over, you can try these approaches:

Interruptions

1. Wait quietly and patiently until you have completely regained the prospect's attention.

2. Briefly restate the selling points that had interested the prospect, as, for example, "We were discussing your needs for a product such as ours, and you seemed especially interested in knowing about our service, delivery, and installation. Is that right?"

3. Do something to increase the prospect's participation, such as showing the product, using other visuals, or asking questions. Watch closely to determine if you have regained the prospect's interest.

4. If interest is regained, you can move deeper into the presentation.

Should You Discuss Your Competition?

Competition is something all salespeople must contend with every day. If you are selling a product, you must compete with others selling comparable products. How should you handle competition? Basically, you should keep in mind three considerations: (1) do not refer to a competitor unless absolutely necessary, (2) acknowledge your competitor only briefly, and (3) make a detailed comparison of your product and that of your competitor.

1. Do Not Refer to Competition. First of all, you can lessen any surprises the buyer may present by properly planning for the sales call. In developing your customer profile, chances are you will find out what competing products are being used, and your prospect's attitude toward your products and those of your competitors. Based on your findings, the presentation can be developed without specifically referring to competition.

2. Acknowledge Competition and Drop It. Many salespeople feel their competition should not be discussed unless the prospect brings it up. Then acknowledge competition only briefly and return to your

Selling Against the Competition

You're **always** selling against the competition. The prospect either already uses a competitive product or service, has used one, would like to use one, has heard of one, or knows people who have used one. He has seen the competition's ads and probably their salespeople as well.

What do you do? You don't!

Ignore the competition. Refuse to talk about them. Emphasize your own product's strengths. If the prospect brings up the competition, be fair and magnanimous. Sure they're good. We're better. **Never criticize them.** Criticism indicates a lack of confidence on your part. And a lack of judgment.

If the prospect doesn't bring the competition into the discussion, don't do it yourself. Why give them the free advertising? They wouldn't give it to you.

product. "Yes, I am familiar with that product's features. In fact, the last three of my customers were using that product and have switched over to ours. May I tell you why?"

Here you do not knock competition, but you acknowledge it and in a positive manner move the prospect's attention back to your products. If the prospect continues to bring up a competing product, you should determine the prospect's attitude toward it. You might ask, "What do you think about the Burroughs B1900 computer system?" The answer will help you mentally determine how you can prove that your product offers the prospect more benefits than your competitor's product.

3. Make a Detailed Comparison. At times it is necessary and appropriate to make a **detailed comparison** of your product to a competing one, especially for industrial products. If products are very similar, then you emphasize your company's service, guarantees, and what you personally do for customers.

If your product has features that are lacking in a competitor's product, then refer to these advantages, possibly indirectly. "Our product is the only one on the market with this feature! Is this important to you?" Ask the question and wait for the response. A yes answer brings you one step closer to the sale.

Often the prospect can use both your product and that of a competitor. For example, a pharmaceutical salesperson is selling an antibiotic that functions like penicillin, as well as kills bacteria resistant to penicillin. However, it costs 20 times more than penicillin. This salesperson would say, "Yes, Dr. Jones, penicillin is the drug of choice for . . . disease. But do you have patients for whom penicillin is not effective?" "Yes I do," says the doctor. "Then for those patients I want you to consider my product because. . . ."

Competition Discussion Based on the Situation. Whether or not you should discuss competition depends on the individual prospect. Based on your selling philosophy and your knowledge of the prospect, you can choose how to deal with competition. If ever in doubt, due to insufficient prospect knowledge, it is best not to discuss competition.

Be Professional

No matter how you discuss competition with your prospect, you should always remember to act as a professional. If you are going to discuss competition, talk only about information you personally know is accurate, be straightforward and honest, not belittling and discourteous.

Your prospect may like both the competitor's products and yours. A loyalty to the competitor may have been built up over the years; by knocking competition, you may insult and alienate your prospect. However, the advantages and disadvantages of a competitive product can be pointed out acceptably if done in a professional manner. One salesperson relates this story:

Several customers I called on were very loyal to my competitors; however just as many were loyal to my company. I will always remember the president of a chain of retail stores flew 500 miles to be at one of our salesmen's retirement dinners. In his talk he noted how some 30 years ago, when he opened his first store, this salesperson extended him company credit and made him a personal loan that helped him get started.

It would be very difficult for a competing salesperson to sell to this loyal customer. When contacting customers, especially those buying competitive products, it is very important to uncover why they use competitive products before discussing competition in the presentation.

When the Presentation Takes Place

The ideal presentation takes place in a quiet room with only the salesperson and the prospect and no interruptions. However, at times the salesperson may meet the prospect somewhere other than a private

Figure 9–11
Examples of Less Than Ideal Presentation Situations

office and feel the need to make the presentation under less than ideal conditions.

Figure 9–11 shows an Atlantic Richfield salesperson talking with the customer in front of his filling station, and a Wallace Business Forms salesperson making a presentation somewhere in the prospect's business.[3] For short presentations, a stand-up situation may be adequate; however, when making a longer presentation you may want to ask the prospect, "Could we go back to your office?" or make another appointment.

Diagnose the Prospect to Determine Your Sales Presentation

You have seen that in contacting prospects you should be prepared for various situations. That is why selling is so challenging and why companies reward their salespeople so well.

In order to further emphasize the need for mental preparation before meeting prospects, examples of selling strategies for different types of prospects are presented in Figure 9–12. Imagine yourself making a sales call on each type. How would you handle them?

Figure 9–12 **Examples of Selling Strategies for Different Types of Prospects**	*Your Prospect*	*Selling Strategies*
	The silent prospect	Determine if this is "the silent type" of personality or if the prospect is indifferent and does not want to talk. Ask questions that will unfreeze the prospect. Take it slowly. If necessary, move to personal activities; talk about family, amusements, and then slowly move into business.
	The indifferent prospect	Do your homework. Personalize the presentation by using facts, proofs, benefits, along with visual aids and demonstrations. You must get the prospect into the act on a personal level.
	The skeptical prospect	Use facts and proofs and be specific. Use demonstrations, samples, and let the prospect try out the product.
	The no-line prospect	Many prospects are extremely busy, so based on profiles, select one major feature; relate it to a benefit in an effort to arouse attention and interest to allow you more time.
	The hothead prospect	Some prospects are excitable and like to argue; so relax, smile, and let the prospect blow off steam. You may want to postpone the interview if the prospect does not relax. Keep a friend; do not make an enemy by being pushy.
	The indecisive prospect	Keep the prospect from getting away by creating a sense of urgency—"Buy now, not later because. . . ." Too many facts could cause further confusion—keep it simple. Close, close, close!
	The know-it-all prospect	Expert, opinionated, and closed-minded prospects should be complimented and recognized for their knowledge. Use questions to ask for their opinion; do not tell them. Talk very little; and get them to help educate you on your products. Let them talk themselves into buying.

Summary of Major Selling Issues _____

The sales presentation is a persuasive vocal and visual explanation of a proposition. While there are numerous methods for making a sales presentation, the four common ones are the stimulus-response, formula, need-satisfaction, and problem-solution selling methods. Each method can be effective if used for the proper situation.

In developing your presentation, you should consider which elements of the sales presentation mix you will use for each prospect. The proper use of persuasive communication techniques, methods to develop prospect participation, proof statements, visual aids, dramatization, and demonstrations can greatly increase your chance of illustrating to your prospect how your products will satisfy his needs.

As we know, it is often not what we say but how we say it that results in making the sale. Persuasive communication techniques (questioning, listening, logical reasoning, suggestion, and the use of trial closes) help to uncover needs, to communicate effectively, and to pull the prospect into the conversation.

Proof statements are especially useful in showing your prospect that what you are saying is true and that you can be trusted. When challenged, "Prove it!" do so by incorporating in your presentation facts on a customer's past sales, guaranteeing the product will work or sell, testimonials, company and independent research results.

In order to both show and tell, visuals need to be properly designed to illustrate features, advantages, and benefits of your products through the use of graphics, dramatization, and demonstration. This allows you to capture your prospect's attention and interest, create two-way communication and participation, express your proposition in a clearer, more complete manner, and make more sales. Careful attention to the development and rehearsal of the presentation is needed to ensure it is carried out smoothly and naturally.

At any time you should be prepared for the unexpected, such as a demonstration that breaks down, interruptions, the prospect's questions about the competition, or the necessity to make your presentation in a less than ideal place, such as the aisle of a retail store or in the warehouse.

The presentation part of the overall sales presentation is the heart of the sale. It is where you develop the desire, conviction, and action. By giving an effective presentation, you will have fewer objections to your proposition, which makes for an easier close of the sale.

Let me conclude in this way: If you want to be a real professional in selling, you need to acquire, or create for yourself, materials that will help you get your message across and get others to believe it. If you try to sell without using the components of the sales presentation mix, you are losing sales not because of what you say but how you are saying it.

Exhibits, facts, statistics, examples, analogies, testimonials, and samples should be part of your repertoire. Without them you are not really equipped to do a professional job of selling.

Review and Discussion Questions

1. You plan to give a demonstration of the Dyno Electric Cart to the purchasing agent of a company having a manufacturing plant that covers 200 acres. Which of the following is the best technique for your demonstration? Why?
   a. Let your prospect drive the cart.
   b. You drive the cart and have the prospect ride so you can discuss the cart's benefits.
   c. Leave a demonstrator and check back the next week to see how many the prospect will buy.

2. In contacting a purchasing agent for your Dyno Electric Carts you plan to use your 10-page visual presenter to guide the prospect through your benefit story. This selling aid is in a binder form and contains photographs of your cart in action, along with its various color options, guarantee, and testimonials. Should you:
   a. Hand over the binder? Why?
   b. Hold it yourself? Why?

3. Assume you were halfway through your presentation when your prospect had to answer the telephone. The call lasts five minutes. What would you do?

4. Discuss the various elements of the sales presentation mix and indicate why you need to use visuals during your presentation.

5. Fully explain how a trial close can be beneficial to a salesperson. What is the difference between a trial close and actually asking for the order?

6. Occasionally, you will find that even though customers are interested in a product benefit, they doubt that your product can provide it. Imagine that you are a mill salesperson for Mohawk Carpets. You are introducing a new line of carpets. You have just told your customer that because of Mohawk's synthetic fibers, your carpets will not fade even if exposed to direct sunlight. Your customer then says, "That sounds great, but I don't know. I've had too many customers complaining about fading."
   a. As you can see, the customer who doubts whether your carpet will resist fading is questioning a:
      (1) Need.
      (2) Product benefit.

        (3) Product feature.

    b. The carpet's ability to resist fading is:

        (1) Important to the customer.

        (2) Of no interest to the customer.

In response to the above remark, the salesperson offers proof as follows:

I understand your concern, but a carpet made of synthetic fibers will not fade. A recent study conducted by the Home Research Institute and reported in the Home Digest *proves that synthetic fibers hold their colors much better than natural fibers. And since Mohawk's carpets are made with synthetic fibers, you'll never hear any complaints about these carpets fading.*

    c. Examine each sentence in the above remarks and state if it is:

        (1) An expansion of the benefit.

        (2) A restatement of the benefit.

        (3) A proof of the benefit.

7. In your proof statement that proves the benefit, you should cite your proof source, in addition to relevant facts or figures about your product. Which of the following is a correct proof of a benefit?

    a. "Well, an article in last month's *Appliance Report* stated that the Williams blender is more durable than the other top 10 brands."

    b. "You'll get 10 percent longer use from the Hanig razor."

    c. "*Marathon* is the most widely read magazine among those with incomes over $25,000 per year."

    d. "Figures in *Marathon* magazine indicate that your sales in general will increase if you stock Majestic housewares in your store."

8. Examine the following conversation.

Customer: What you say is important, all right, but how do I know that these chairs will take wear and tear the way you say they will?

Salesperson: The durability of a chair is an important factor to consider. That's why the Crest chairs have reinforced plastic webbing seats. *Furniture Dealers Weekly* states that plastic webbing of the type used in Crest chairs is 32 percent more effective in preventing sagging chair seats than fabric webbing. This means that your chairs will last longer, and will take the wear and tear that your customers require.

Examine each sentence in the above remarks and state if it is:

a. An expansion of the benefit.

b. A restatement of the benefit.

c. A proof of the benefit.

9. After a two-hour drive to see an important new prospect, you stop at a local coffee shop for a bite to eat. As you are looking over your presentation charts, the coffee spills on about half a dozen of them. You don't have substitute presentation charts with you. What should you do?

   a. Phone the prospect and say that you'd like to make another appointment. Say that something came up.

   b. Go ahead and keep the appointment. At the start of your presentation, tell the prospect about the coffee spill and apologize for it.

   c. Go ahead with your presentation. But don't make excuses. The coffee stains are barely noticeable if you're not on the lookout for them.

Projects

1. What is the one thing in this world on which you are an expert? Yourself! Develop a presentation on yourself for a sales job with a company of your choice. Relate this assignment to each of the 10 steps in the selling process.

2. Visit several retail stores in your community, such as an appliance, bicycle, or sporting goods store, and report on the demonstration techniques, if any, which were used to sell to you. Suggest ways you would have presented the product.

3. Report on one television advertisement that used each of the following: proof statement, demonstration, unusual visual aids, and dramatization.

4. In your library are magazines in which companies advertise their products to their retail and wholesale customers, as well as inform them of their current price discounts. Find three or more of the advertisements containing current price discounts offered by manufacturers to wholesalers and/or retailers. How might you use this information in a sales presentation?

Cases

9–1 Dyno Electro Cart Company

You are planning a call back on Mr. Pride and the president of his company to sell them several of your electric carts. (See Figure 7–4 in Chapter 7.) The company's manufacturing plant covers some 200 acres, and you have sold many companies smaller than this one up to 10 carts. Since Mr. Pride is allowing you to meet with his company's president and maybe other executives, you know he is interested in your carts.

You are determined to make a spellbinding presentation of your product's benefits, which will make use of visual aids and a demonstration of the cart itself. Mr. Pride raised several objections on your last presentation that may be brought up again by other executives (see Figure 7–4). Your challenge is to develop a dramatic, convincing presentation.

Questions:

1. You plan to give a live demonstration of the cart to show how effective it is to move around the plant. Which of the following is the best technique for the demonstration?
    a. Get Mr. Pride and the president involved by letting them drive the cart.
    b. You drive, letting them ride so they will listen more carefully to you.
    c. Leave a demonstrator and check back the next week to see how many they will buy.
2. You are also planning to use your 10-page visual presenter to guide them through your benefit story. This selling aid is in a binder form and contains photographs of your cart in action, along with its various color options, guarantee, and testimonials. Should you:
    a. Get Mr. Pride to participate by letting him hold it?
    b. Handle it yourself, let him watch and listen while you turn the pages and tell your story?

9–2 Fresh Mouth: Selling a New Mouthwash

As a salesperson for Hygiene Incorporated, you have been sent the following information on a new product you are soon to begin to sell. Using this information, how would you develop your presentation?

The Product. The product is a new mouthwash or oral antiseptic called Fresh Mouth. The trademark is the name in longhand with a pair of red female lips substituting for the letter *o* in Mouth. The product is a red liquid packaged in a new, uniquely shaped bottle. It is produced by Hygiene Incorporated (HI), a corporation that has an established niche in the toiletries and hygiene products market.

Fresh Mouth is available in a full line of four sizes:

6 oz.—The perfect trial and travel size!

12 oz.—Second largest dollar-producing size!

18 oz.—Accounts for 41 percent of consumer sales!

24 oz.—The fastest growing segment in the mouthwash market!

The *most* important goal is to gain multiple-size distribution, and it is thought that going in with all four sizes at one time will aid in achieving this objective. As with other markets, there is size loyalty as well as brand loyalty in the mouthwash business. It was reported in a recent Nielsen study that 18 percent of shoppers not finding the particular size of a brand they wished to purchase did not make any purchase at all. Our experience shows we can expect 40 percent better movement in accounts where we have multiple sizes on the shelf.

Test Market.   A proven success in the eastern markets, Fresh Mouth had a 9.8 percent market share only nine months after the start of advertising. Laboratory tests proved that the Fresh Mouth formula is superior to that of the leading competition. It was significantly preferred to competition in consumer product tests. There was a high repurchase rate of 50 percent after sampling. The trade gave enthusiastic support in the test market areas.

National Introduction.   Fresh Mouth is now ready for national introduction to your market with the following unbeatable introductory program:

1. Massive sampling and couponing.
   a. There will be a blanketing of the top 300 markets with 4.4-oz. samples plus eight-cents-off coupons. Your market is included.
   b. There will be a 75 percent coverage of homes in the top 100 markets. Your market is included.
2. Heavy advertising.
   a. Nighttime network TV.
   b. Daytime network TV.
   c. Saturation spot TV.
   d. Newspapers.
   e. The total network and spot advertising will reach 85 percent of all homes in the U.S. five times each week, based on a four-week average. This means that in four weeks Fresh Mouth will have attained 150 million home impressions—130 million of these will be against women.
   f. There will be half-page, two-color inserts in local newspapers in 50 markets, including yours. This is more than 20 million circulation. Scheduled to tie in with saturation sampling is a couponing program.
   g. Fifteen million dollars will be spent on promotion to ensure consumer acceptance.

3. TV advertising theme.
   a. The commercial with POWER to sell!
   b. "POWER to kill mouth odor—POWER to kill germs—POWER to give FRESH MOUTH."
   c. The commercial shows a young male, about 20 years of age, walking up to a young girl, saying, "Hi, Susan!" They kiss and she says, "My, you have a fresh mouth, Bill!" He looks at the camera with a smile and says, "It works!" The announcer closes the commercial by saying, "FRESH MOUTH—it has the POWER!"
4. Display materials.
   a. Shelf display tag.
   b. Small floor stand for end-of-aisle display—holds two dozen 12-oz. bottles.
   c. Large floor stand—holds four dozen 12-oz. bottles.

Introductory pricing.   The introductory deal is designed to ensure that acceptance of Fresh Mouth by each account will be a shoo-in. The basis of the deal is off-invoice allowances (i.e., price reductions) used in the test markets. In addition, we are offering an advertising allowance that requires only one advertisement as proof of running the ad, and a 3 percent quantity discount on all orders of any size will offer the best introductory deal we have ever had. Please note that the 12- and 18-oz. sizes are packed one dozen bulk, the 6-oz. size is packed two dozen to a case, and the 24-oz. size is packed one-half dozen to a case. On the 24-oz. size only half-dozen orders will be honored, with a $1 off-invoice allowance and a $2 per dozen advertising allowance for an invoice cost of $3.41 per case. One order can be applied to the introductory allowances. A split shipment is acceptable. For example, the retailer may order 50 dozen and have 35 dozen shipped now and 15 dozen shipped no later than 30 days after the first shipment. Terms are 2 percent—20 days—net 30 days from date of shipment. The form shown in Exhibit 1 on page 299 is a copy of the *deal sheet* for you to develop a recommended promotional plan for each of your customers.

Salespeople's Incentives.   Each salesperson has approximately 200 accounts of various sizes and types, such as grocery and discount retail stores. The company is offering you a bonus for each size sold as follows:

Size	Bonus per Dozen
24-oz.	75¢
18-oz.	50¢
12-oz.	35¢
6-oz.	25¢

Exhibit 1

Introducing Fresh Mouth Oral Antiseptic

Account Name: _____

		Allowances Available			
Size	Suggested Order	Promotion Allowance per Dozen	Fund	Advertising Allowance per Dozen	Fund
24-oz.	_____	$2.00	$_____	$.40	$_____
18-oz.	_____	1.50	$_____	.30	$_____
12-oz.	_____	1.05	$_____	.20	$_____
6-oz.	_____	.60	$_____	.10	$_____
		Total promotion fund	$_____	Total advertising fund	$_____

Recommended Promotional Plan

	24-oz.	18-oz.	12-oz.	6-oz.
Suggested order	_____	_____	_____	_____
Least unit cost	_____	_____	_____	_____
Suggested ad price	_____	_____	_____	_____
Suggested ad date	_____	_____	_____	_____
Suggested promotion	_____	_____	_____	_____

Plus, for each account that purchases a minimum order of one dozen of each size, a bonus of $5 is paid. If, for example, all 200 accounts purchased a minimum order of all sizes, the salesperson would earn a $1,370 cash bonus.

The Situation.   You are a new salesperson for HI. The account you will first sell is a large independent grocery store called the Harris Food Store. Mr. Ronnie Harris is the buyer. Based on the store's size, past sales of your products, and the sales quota you are assigned, you feel Harris could buy three dozen of the 6-oz., fifteen dozen of the 18-oz., six dozen of the 12-oz., and three dozen of the 24-oz. size. However, you feel that if he will display, advertise, and discount the price, he should be able to sell twice that amount. So that will be your suggested order to Harris.

Questions:

1. If Harris purchases what you recommend, what will be your cash bonus?

2. Why should Harris buy from you?

3. What objections might Harris be expected to raise?

4. Develop a sales presentation to sell Harris your suggested order.

Pertinent Retail Data

Retail Cost and Available Gross Profit Information		6-oz.	12-oz.	18-oz.	24-oz.
Suggested retail selling price		.99	1.09	1.39	1.69
Regular retail value per dozen		11.88	13.08	16.68	20.28
Regular cost per dozen		6.98	7.68	9.79	11.90
Regular profit per dozen:	Dollars	4.90	5.40	6.89	8.37
	Percent	41.20	41.20	41.30	41.30
Special allowance per dozen		.60	1.05	1.50	2.00
Special cost per dozen		6.37	6.63	8.29	9.90
Special profit per dozen:	Dollars	5.51	6.45	8.39	10.38
	Percent	46.30	49.30	50.30	51.20
Least unit cost, excluding 2% cash discount		53.1¢	55.2¢	69.1¢	82.5¢
Advertising allowances per dozen		.60	1.05	1.50	2.00

9–3 Major Oil, Inc.*

Tim Christensen sells industrial lubricants to manufacturing plants. The lubricants are used for the plants' machinery. He is calling on Ben Campbell, a purchasing agent for Acme Manufacturing Company. Ben presently buys Tim's Hydraulic Oil 65 in drums. Tim's sales call objective is to persuade Ben to switch from purchasing his oil in drums to a bulk oil system. The secretary has just admitted him to Ben's office.

Salesman: Hello, Ben.

Customer: Well, if it isn't Tim Christensen, my lube oil salesman! How is everything over at Major Oil these days?

Salesman: Fine! We're adding to our warehouse, so we won't be quite as crowded. Say, I know you like to fly, I was just reading in a magazine about the old Piper Tri-Pacer.

Customer: Yeah! I do enjoy flying and fooling with old airplanes. I just got back this weekend from a fly-in over at Houston.

Salesman: You don't say; what type planes did they have?

Customer: They had a large bunch of homebuilts. You know—many pilots may spend from 5 to 15 years just building their own plane.

Salesman: Would you like to build your own plane someday?

Customer: Yes, I would. But you know, this job takes so much time—and with my schedule here and some travel, I don't know if I'll ever get time to start on a plane, much less finish one.

* This case was developed by Professor George Wynn, Professor of Marketing, James Madison University © 1987.

Salesman: Well, I don't know that I can save you that much time, but I can save the people in the plant time as well as reducing your cost of Hydraulic Oil 65. Also, I may even save your office some time and expense by not having to place so many orders.

You know, we talked a couple of weeks ago about the possibility of Acme buying Hydraulic Oil 65 in bulk and thus reducing the costs per gallon by buying larger quantities each time you order. In addition, you will save tying your money up in the $20 drum deposit or even losing the deposit by losing or damaging the empty drum.

Customer: Sounds like this is fixing to cost us some money.

Salesman: Well, we might have to spend a little money to save a larger amount, plus make it easier and quicker in the plant. Do you know exactly what you are paying for Hydraulic Oil 65 now?

Customer: I think it's about a buck forty a gallon.

Salesman: That's close. Your delivered cost is $1.39 per gallon, not counting drum deposit. You used approximately 20,000 gallons of Hydraulic Oil 65 last year at a total cost of $27,800.

Customer: Between what I pay at the gas station and what we pay here I see why Major Oil is getting bigger and richer all the time. How much money *can* you save us?

Salesman: Well, we just try to get by and make ends meet. However, I can save your company more than $2,800 per year on oil costs alone.

Customer: That sounds awful big. How are you going to do that?

Salesman: I am going to show you how you can purchase oil in bulk, save 14¢ per gallon on each gallon you buy (14¢ times 20,000 gallons equals $2,800) and totally eliminate handling those drums and having your money tied up in deposits. Last year you purchased about 364 drums—and I'll bet you did not get all these drums back to us.

Customer: I know we damaged some drums, and I imagine we furnished some trash barrels for our employees, if the truth were known. I wonder how much total deposit we pay?

Salesman: Yeah, probably. The total deposit on those drums was $7,280. Are you and your company totally satisfied with the performance of Hydraulic Oil 65?

Customer: We seem to be. I have heard nothing to the contrary; and our bearing supplier, Timken, says that the oil is doing a first-class job. You know, this savings sounds good in theory, but will it really work? Besides, where will we put a big bulk system?

Salesman: Ben, I've already checked pretty thoroughly into what the total equipment and installation will cost. Here's a picture of the installation we made over at the Foundry and Machine Shop. We put the installation aboveground to save the expense of digging holes for the tanks. This cover shown here in the picture protects the pump and motor from the weather, and the pipe into the shop goes underground. There's a control switch for the pump motor mounted inside the building right alongside the nozzle outlet. It looks pretty good, doesn't it?

Customer: Certainly does, Tim, but what about the cost here?

Salesman: We can get two new 3,000-gallon tanks delivered here for a cost of $1,700 from our tank supplier. This is about $120 less than what you could buy them for. Our quantity purchases of tanks give us a little better price—and we'll be glad to pass these savings on to you. I have checked with Pump Supply Company, and they have in stock the pump and motor with flexible coupling and built-in pump relief valve, just what we need for handling this oil. The cost is $475. The control switch, pipe, pipe fittings, inside hose, and nozzle come to $120, and the fellow who does our installation work has given me a commitment to do all the installation work for $500, including furnishing the blocks to make the tank supports.

This totals $2,795, so let's round off to $2,800. And at a savings of 14¢ per gallon, based on your present usage of 20,000 gallons per year, this would be completely paid off in about 12 months, during which time you'd be paying $1.25 per gallon for your oil rather than the $1.39 you're now paying. How does this sound to you, Ben?

Customer: That sounds pretty good to me, Tim. Didn't you have a write-up of this nature in a recent issue of your company magazine?

Salesman: We sure did. It was in the March issue. Here it is, right here. The situation was a little different, but the basic idea is the same. Our company has been able to use this idea to considerable advantage, and over the past three years I personally have set up six installations of this type. Do you have any questions regarding the plan I've outlined?

Customer: Just one thing—you know we're short on space out back of the warehouse. Have you thought about where we might locate an installation of this type?

Salesman: Yes, I have, Ben. You'll recall one of our earlier conversations where you were telling me about your plans to clean up that old scrap pile back near the corner of the warehouse. That would be an ideal location. We could then locate the control switch, filling hose, and nozzle right on the inside at the end of the assembly line so the units could be given their initial oil fill just before they come off the assembly line. How would that fit into your plans?

Customer: That's a good idea, Tim. That way we can get that junk pile cleaned up, replace it with a decent looking installation, and then make our initial oil fill the last step in our assembly procedure.

Salesman: Do you have any other questions, Ben?

Customer: No, I believe I've got the whole picture now.

Salesman: Good. Now, just to sum up our thinking, Ben, the total cost of installation will be about $3,000. Immediately on completion of the installation, and when you receive your first transport truck load shipment of Hydraulic Oil 65, instead of being billed at $1.39 per gallon, as you are now paying for barrel deliveries, you will be billed $1.25 per gallon. I'll work with Bill Smith, the plant superintendent, and I'll handle all the outside contacts so that we can get the installation in with little turmoil.

Customer: That sounds good to me. When can we get started on the installation?

Salesman: Tomorrow! I'll bring a contract for you to run through your people and get signed. It should take about three to four weeks after the contract is signed.

Customer: Good. What do I need to do right now?

Salesman: If you'll arrange to get the junk cleaned out of the corner, then we'll be all ready to go. I'll order the equipment and get it moving so we can be set to go in about four weeks. What would be the best time to see you tomorrow?

Customer: Anytime will be okay with me, Tim.

Salesman: Swell, Ben. Thanks for your help. I know you're going to be pleased with this new installation and also save some real money. See you tomorrow.

Questions:

1. Evaluate Tim's sales presentation. Include in your answer comments on his approach, presentation, use of trial closes, handling of objections, and his close.

2. How would you develop visual materials to illustrate Tim's sales presentation, including the arithmetic?

3. Now that Tim has sold Ben, what should Tim now do?

10 WELCOME YOUR PROSPECT'S OBJECTIONS

Learning Objectives

1. To develop the belief that the salesperson should welcome objections by the prospect.
2. To show four major categories of prospect objections.
3. To present and illustrate seven techniques for meeting prospect objections.
4. To present eight basic points to consider in meeting prospect objections.

Key Terms for Selling

Sales objection
Hidden objections
Stalling objection
No-need objection
Money objection
Forestall the objection
Boomerang method
Ask intelligent questions
Five-question sequence

Direct denial
Anticipated objections
Compensation method
Third-party answer
Sales condition
Negotiation
Practical objection
Psychological objection

Profile

Bruce Scagel
M&M—Mars

Bruce Scagel received his bachelor's degree in English from Washington and Jefferson College and did graduate work in business at Syracuse University.

His career in sales began with Scott Paper in 1976 as a consumer products sales representative in Jacksonville, Florida. Bruce's promotions were to the positions of assistant marketing personnel manager, territory sales manager, in-house consultant on organization development, and training and development manager of Scott's consumer sales and marketing division. Now he is the national sales trainer for M&M—Mars. Bruce says, "I began my career in a sales position because it offered opportunities for rapid advancement as well as a variety of interesting and challenging activities.

"My philosophy of selling incorporates traditional sales techniques with personal approaches. I believe it's initially necessary to learn as much as possible about each customer, the objectives, challenges, and the particular problems he or she faces. By addressing these objectives and challenges with specific products and services, the salesperson enhances opportunity for success."

Ask Bruce what he believes are the key factors for sales success, and he will stress four points. "First, know your customers and their operations. I believe it's necessary to know as much about my customers as possible, including their needs and objectives—how they operate and who their key people are—before attempting the sale. Consistency and follow-through make up the second key selling point. Generally, the most respected and successful salesperson is the one who is consistent in dealing with the customer and who follows through on commitment and promises. Third, you must lose your fear of failure. One of the greatest impediments to successful selling is fearing that the buyer will not buy. In my career, I've been most successful when I've been well prepared and confident. However, I am also aware that I will not make every sale. Accept the results and move on to the next project. Fourth, to be successful you must ask questions. Through questioning, the salesperson can identify the buyer's needs, objectives, and primary challenges. Timely questioning can keep a sale alive when the buyer appears to be losing interest in the product or service being offered. My observations have been that many inexperienced salespeople find this aspect of the sale the most difficult to master because they fear that they will lose control of the presentation. In fact, conversation is one of the most appropriate means to lead the buyer to the desired conclusions."

M&M—Mars's Bruce Scagel has a positive philosophy regarding sales objections: "During the sale, objections are often raised, and the manner in which the salesperson responds often constitutes the difference between success and failure. The salesperson should resist being defensive or put off by objections; rather he or she should address them confidently, keeping in mind that they're fundamental to the sale. It's been said that the selling process doesn't begin until the buyer raises an objection. For the most part I would agree.

"Objections are often raised for the following reasons: the buyers want to avoid a decision; they are operating with misinformation; they want or need more information; or they simply want reassurance. In each case, the salesperson who listens closely and attempts to understand the buyer's needs and objectives can respond appropriately."

This chapter expands on Bruce's comments, and it also discusses how to meet objections, what techniques to use in overcoming objections, and how to proceed after an objection has been addressed.

Welcome Objections! _____

When a prospect first gives an objection, *smile*, because that's when you start earning your salary. You want to receive personal satisfaction from your job and at the same time increase your salary—right? Well, both will occur as soon as you learn to accept objections as a challenge that, when handled correctly, will benefit both your prospect and yourself. The more effectively you can meet customers' needs and solve their problems, the more successful you will be in sales. If you *fear* objections, you will *fumble* your response, often causing you to *fail*.

Remember, while people do want to buy, they *do not* want to be taken advantage of. Buyers who cannot see how your offering will fulfill their needs ask questions and raise objections. If you cannot effectively answer the questions or meet the objections, you will not make the sale. It is *your* fault, not the buyer's fault, that the sale was not made if you sincerely believe your offering fulfills a need but the prospect still will not buy. The salesperson who can overcome objections when they are raised and smoothly move back into a presentation can expect to succeed.

When Do Prospects Object?

The prospect may object at any time during your sales call—from introduction to close. Imagine walking into a retail store (as once happened to me), carrying a sales bag, and the buyer yells out, "Oh no, not another salesman. I don't even want to see you, let alone buy from you!" What do you say?

I said, "I understand. I'm not here to sell you anything, only check your stock, help you stock your shelves, and return any old or damaged merchandise for a refund." As I turned to walk away, the buyer said, "Come on back here, I want to talk to you."

If I had simply said OK and left, I would not have made that sale. I knew that I could benefit that customer, and my response and attitude showed it. The point is to always be ready to handle a prospect's objections, whether at the approach, during the presentation, after a trial close, after you have already met a previous objection, or during the close of the sale.

Resistance To Change

Don't be discouraged by a buyer's hesitancy. Most people are fundamentally conservative—about new ideas, new courses of action, any change in the status quo. Especially if it's a change they themselves are initiating. They may fear the change itself, or the chance that the change will bring about more problems than it solves. The buyer knows and understands today's problems; tomorrow's problems are uncertain, mysterious.

Your job—remove the mystery. Emphasize the positive aspects, improvements, problems solved, headaches cured, costs cut.

Then **sit back and let it sink in**. Let the buyer visualize the new situation. If you've done your job, the new situation represents a big improvement for him. So stop selling for a moment. Right now, the best thing you can give the buyer is a little time.

Who Is the Toughest Prospect?

You will find the toughest prospects to be those who do not say anything. You do not know if they are interested in your product, bored with you, or just being polite. You would love to have an objection from them. Sales resistance is much better than indifference.

Second toughest are those who agree with everything you say but who are not really listening. They like people, like to visit with them, but are really not thinking of buying. In the retail situation, they may say they are looking, but talk with you mainly for the conversation. An industrial buyer who may need a break from the routine may say, "Sure, I'll talk with you. Let's have a cup of coffee. . . ." Sometimes buyers on company time, whose job it is to see salespeople, will speak with you but without any real intention to buy.

What Are Objections?

Interestingly enough, prospects who present objections are often more easily sold on your product. They are interested enough to object; they want to know what you have to offer.

Opposition or resistance to the request of the salesperson is labeled a **sales objection.** Sales objections should be welcomed because they show prospect interest and aid in determining what stage the prospect has reached in the buying cycle—attention, interest, desire, conviction, or readiness to close.

Objections and the Sales Process

Certainly, objections can occur at any time. Many times, however, the prospect will allow you to make your presentation, often asking questions along the way. Inexperienced salespeople traditionally finish their presentation and wait for the prospect's response.

Experienced, successful salespeople have learned to use the system shown in Figure 10-1. After the presentation they use a trial close to determine the prospect's attitude towards the product and if it is time to close. Typically this trial close causes the prospect to ask questions and/ or state objections. The salespeople should be prepared to respond in one of four ways:

1. If there is a positive response to the trial close immediately after the presentation, then move to the close as shown on the right side of Figure 10-1, moving from Step 5 to Step 9.

2. If an objection is raised, respond to it and ask another trial close to

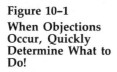

Figure 10–1
When Objections Occur, Quickly Determine What to Do!

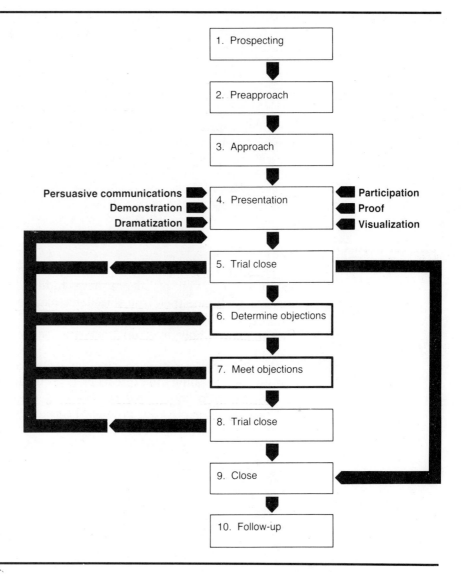

see if you have met the objection. If you have, then move to the close.

3. After meeting one objection, be prepared to determine if there are other objections. You may have to move from Step 8 back to Step 6.

4. If, after responding to the objection and asking a trial close you find you have not overcome the objection, then move back to your presentation (Step 4) and further discuss your product relative to the objection.

Thus, there are several strategies a salesperson needs to master in order to handle objections. These strategies apply to any of the four major categories of objections.

Four Major Categories of Objections

You will hear prospects object to various things in many different ways. Most objections salespeople encounter can be placed into the four categories shown in Figure 10–2. Know how you will handle each situation before it occurs. An advance decision on how you will handle these types of objections will help you become a better salesperson by improving your image as a problem solver.

The Hidden Objection

Prospects who ask trivial, unimportant questions or conceal their feelings beneath a veil of silence have **hidden objections.** They are unwilling to discuss their true objections to a product because they may feel they are not your business; they are afraid objections will offend you; or they simply may not feel your sales call is worthy of full attention.

Such prospects may even carry on a good conversation with you without ever revealing their true feelings. You have to ask questions and carefully listen to know what questions to ask in order to smoke out their real objections to your product. Learning how to determine what questions to ask a prospect and how to ask them are skills developed by conscious effort over a long period of time. Your ability to ask probing questions will improve with each sales call if you consciously try to develop this ability.

Smoke Out Hidden Objections. With prospects who are unwilling to discuss their objections or who may not know why they are reluctant to buy, you need to be prepared to smoke out objections by asking questions. You must do what you can to get the objections out in the open. Consider the following questions:

"What would it take to convince you?"

**Figure 10–2
Four Major Categories
of Objections**

Hidden objections	Stalling objections	No-need objections	Money objections

"What causes you to say that?"

"Let's consider this, suppose my product would . . . [do what prospect wants] . . . then you would want to consider it, wouldn't you?"

"Come on now, tell me, what's really on your mind?"

Uncovering hidden objections is not always easy. You should observe the prospect's tone of voice, facial expressions, and physical movements. Pay close attention to what the prospect is saying. You may have to "read between the lines" occasionally to find the buyer's true objections. All of these factors will help you discover whether objections are real or simply an excuse to cover a hidden objection.

Prospects may not consciously know what their real objections are. Sometimes they will claim that the price of a product is too high. In reality, they may be reluctant to spend money on anything. If you attempt to show that your price is competitive, the real objection will remain unanswered and no sale will result. Remember, you cannot convince anyone to buy until you understand what a prospect needs to be convinced of.

If, after answering all of the apparent questions, the prospect is still not sold, you might attempt to subtly uncover the hidden objection. You might simply ask the prospect what the real objection is. Direct inquiry should be used as a last resort because it may indirectly amount to calling the prospect a liar, but if it is used carefully, it may enable the salesperson to bring out the prospect's true objection. Smoking out hidden objections is a selling art form that is developed over time by skillful salespeople. Its successful use can greatly increase your sales. This approach should be used carefully, but if it enables the salesperson to uncover a hidden objection, then it will have served its purpose.

The Stalling Objection

When your prospect says, "I'll think it over. . . ." or, "I'll be ready to buy on your next visit," you must determine if the statement is the truth or if it is a smoke screen designed to get rid of you. This **stalling** tactic is a common type of objection.

What you discovered when developing your customer profile and customer benefit plan will aid you in determining how to handle this type of objection. Suppose that before seeing a certain retail customer you had checked the supply of your merchandise in both the store's stockroom and on the retail shelf and this occurs:

Buyer: I have enough merchandise for now. Thanks for coming by.

Salesperson: Ms. Marcher, you have 50 cases in the warehouse and on display. You sell 50 cases each month, right?

The Old "Too Busy to Talk" Stall

He says he's too busy, even though he agreed to the appointment. Is he really?

Sometimes it's true. Unexpected demands build up on the buyer's time. If this becomes evident to you, back off. The buyer will appreciate it. But **never** leave without a firm return appointment, no matter if you have to return before office hours or after closing. That's okay. It never hurts to have the buyer a little beholden to you.

Sometimes, of course, it's a stall. If that's the case, persist. Few people are ever too busy to talk about things that will solve their problems.

Ask for just a few minutes more. Once you establish that you have something valuable to offer, even the busiest buyer will find time to talk to you.

You have forced her hand. This buyer will either have to order more merchandise from you or tell you why she is allowing her supply of the product to dwindle.

One of the toughest stalls to overcome arises when selling a new consumer product. Retail buyers are generally reluctant to stock consumer goods that customers have not yet asked for, even new goods produced by large, established consumer product manufacturers. The following excerpt is taken from a sales call made by an experienced consumer goods salesperson on a reluctant retail buyer. This excerpt begins with an interruption made by the buyer during a presentation of a new brand of toothpaste:

Buyer: Well, it sounds good, but I have seven brands and 21 different sizes of toothpaste now. There is just no place to put it. [A false objection—smoke screen.]

Salesperson: Suppose you had 100 customers walk right down the aisle and ask for Colgate 100 Toothpaste. Could you find room then?

Buyer: Well, maybe. But I'll wait until then. [The real objection.]

Salesperson: If this were a barber shop and you did not have your barber pole outside, people wouldn't come in because they wouldn't know it was a barber shop, would they?

Buyer: Probably not.

Salesperson: The same logic applies to Colgate 100. When people see it, they will buy it. You would agree that our other heavily advertised products sell for you, right? [Trial close.]

Buyer: Yeah, they do, all right. [Positive response, now reenter your selling sequence.]

The salesperson eliminated the stall in this case through a logical analogy.

Another common stall is the alibi that your prospect has to get approval from someone else, such as a boss, buying committee, purchasing agent, or home office. Since the buyer's attitude toward purchasing your product will influence the firm's buying decision, it is important you determine the buyer's attitude toward your product.

When the buyer stalls by saying, "I will have to get approval from my boss," you can counter by saying, "If you had the authority, you would go ahead with the purchase, wouldn't you?" If the answer is yes, chances are the buyer will exert a positive influence on the firm's buying decision. If not, then you must uncover the real objections. Otherwise, chances are you will not make the sale.

Two additional responses to the "I've got to think it over" stall are "What are some of the issues you have to think about?" Or you may directly focus on the prospect's stall by saying, "Would you share with me some of the things that are holding you back?"

Another effective response to "I've got to talk to my boss," is "Of course you do. What are some of the things you would talk about?" This allows you to agree with the reluctant prospect. You are now on the buyer's side. It helps encourage the buyer to talk and to trust you. This *empathy* response ("Of course you do.") puts you in the other person's position.

Sometimes the prospect will not answer your question. Instead, the response is, "Oh, I just need to get an opinion." You can follow up with a multiple choice question such as "Would you be exploring whether this is a good purchase in comparison with a competitor's product or would you be wondering about the financing?" This helps display an attitude of genuine caring.

As with any response to an objection, be sure to communicate a positive attitude. Do not get demanding, defensive, or hostile. Otherwise, your nonverbal expressions may signal a defensive attitude, reinforcing the prospect's defenses.

314

Your goal in dealing with a stall is to help prospects realistically examine reasons for and against buying now. If you are absolutely sure it is not in their best interest to buy now, tell them so. They will respect you for it. You will feel better about yourself. The next time you see these customers, they will be much more trusting and open with you.

However, the main thing to remember is not to be satisfied with a false objection or a stall. Tactfully pursue the issue until you have unearthed the buyer's true feelings about your product. If this does not work, (1) then you should present the benefits of using your product now; (2) if there is a special price deal, mention it now; and (3) if there is a penalty or delay, mention it. Bring out any or all of your main selling benefits now and keep on selling!

The No-Need Objection

The prospect says, "Sounds good, I really like what you had to say, and I know you have a good product, but I'm not interested now. Our present product [or supply or merchandise] works well. We will stay with it." Standing up to conclude the interview, the prospect says, "Thanks very much for coming by." This type of objection can disarm an unwary salesperson.

The **no-need objection** is widely used because it politely gets rid of the salesperson. Some salespeople actually bring it on themselves by making a poor sales presentation. They allow prospects to sit and listen to a sales pitch, without getting them to participate by showing them true concern and asking them questions. Therefore, as soon as the presentation is over, prospects can quickly say, "Sounds good, but . . ." In essence, they are saying no, making it very difficult for the salesperson to continue the call. While not always a valid objection, the no-need response strongly implies the end of a sales call.

The no-need objection is especially tricky because it may also include a hidden objection and/or a stall. If your presentation was indeed a solo performance or a monologue, your prospect might very well be indifferent to you and your product, having tuned you out halfway through the second act. Aside from departing with a whimpered "Thanks for your time," you might attempt to resurrect your presentation by asking questions.

The Money Objection

The **money objection** encompasses several forms of economic excuses: "I have no money"; "I don't have that much money"; "It costs too much"; or the ever-popular, "Your price is too high." These objections are simple for the buyer to say, especially in a recessionary economy.

Often prospects will want to know the price of your product before you can begin your presentation, and they will not want you to explain how the product's benefits will outweigh its costs. Price is a real consideration and must be discussed, but it is risky to discuss product price until it can be compared to product benefits. If you successfully postpone the price discussion, you must eventually come back to it, because your prospect will seldom forget it. Some prospects are so preoccupied with price that they will give minimal attention to your presentation until the topic reemerges. Others will falsely present price as their main objection to your product, concealing the true objection.

By observing nonverbal signals, asking questions, listening, and positively responding to the price question when it arises, you can easily handle price-oriented objections.

Many salespeople think that offering the lowest price gives them a greater chance of sales success. Generally, this supposition is not valid. Once you realize this, you will become even more successful. You might even state that your product is *not* the least expensive one available

Talking About Price

Conventional wisdom surrounds the matter of price. It inevitably comes up as a subject for discussion—right! Most buyers use it as their main objection —right! And so it should be dealt with gingerly, avoided, ignored to the end unless the buyer brings it up—wrong!

The successful salesperson should not fear the price obstacle. You can even mention that your product isn't the least expensive available, because you're selling benefits and advantages, superiority and utility. Once those are established, price becomes a secondary objection and usually can be dealt with.

Don't be afraid of it. Quote the price and go right on selling. Close with a summary of how your product will fill the buyer's needs. If you leave price for the last, you have him wondering why you're skirting the issue, and you close with the price uppermost in his mind.

SUPERIORITY

ADVANTAGES

UTILITY

NEEDS

EFFICIENCY

BENEFITS

PRICE

because of its benefits and advantages, and the satisfaction it provides. Once you convey this concept to your buyer, price becomes a secondary factor, which usually can be dealt with successfully.

Do not be afraid of price as an objection; be ready for it and welcome it. Quote the price and go right on selling. It is usually the inexperienced salesperson who blows this often minor objection into a major one. If the price objection does become major (as shown in Figure 10–3), prospects can become excited and overreact to your price. The end result is the loss of the sale. If prospects overreact, slow down the conversation; let them talk it out and slowly begin to present product benefits as related to cost.

The Price/Value Formula. The price objection can be a bargaining tool for a canny buyer who wants to be sure of getting your best, absolutely lowest price. But often there is more to it than shrewd bargaining.

If the buyer is merely testing to be sure the best possible price is on the table, you've got a strong buying signal. But perhaps the prospect sincerely believes your price is too high. Two different situations, aren't they?

Let's see if we can define why one buyer might already be convinced your product is a good deal—fair price—but is just testing you to make sure it's the best you can do, while another buyer may sincerely believe you are asking more than your goods are worth.

Remember that cost is what the buyer is concerned with, not just the price. Cost is arrived at in the buyer's mind by considering what is received compared to the money paid. In other words price divided by value equals cost:

$$\frac{Price}{Value} = Cost$$

In this price/value formula, the *value* is what the prospect sees the product doing for him or her and/or the company. Value is the total package of benefits you have built up for the prospect. Value is the solution you are providing to the buyer's problems.

The price is not going to change. The company sets that price at headquarters. The company has arrived at the price very scientifically—computers were used—based on costs, competition, and other salient factors. It is a fair price, and it's not going to change. So, the only thing you can change is the prospect's perception of the value. For example, assume the buyer viewed your cost as follows:

$$\frac{Price\ 100}{Value\ 90} = Cost\ 1.11$$

Your price is too high. You have to solve the prospect's problem with your product by translating benefits of the product into what it will do for the buyer. You have to build up the value:

Figure 10–3
Price Seems to Have Excited This Buyer!

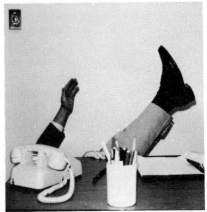

how. . .   *high!?"*

$$\frac{\text{Price } 100}{\text{Value } 110} = \text{Cost } .90$$

Now, that's more like it. The cost went down because the value went up.

The price/value formula is not the answer to "your price is too high." It is only a description of the buyer's thinking process and an explanation of why you hear the so-called price objection so often. But it does tell you what you must do to answer the price objection.

The salesperson is usually the one who identifies a statement or question from the prospect as an objection. Rarely does the prospect say, "This is my objection." So the first step is to ask yourself, "Why did the buyer say that?" If you ask yourself that question you'll be able to probe, get the prospect to tell you more, tell why he or she made that objection.

Remember, at one extreme the buyer may be sold on your product and simply testing to see if you have an extra discount you haven't thrown in yet. At the other extreme the buyer may not see any benefit in your product or service but only see the price. When this is the case, "It costs too much" is a legitimate objection to be overcome by translating features into advantages into benefits to the buyer.

Handle Objections as They Arise

At times, situations will arise in which you feel it is best to postpone your answer to an objection. When the objection raised will be covered later in your presentation, or when you are building up to that point, it is best to pass over it for the time. As a general rule, however, it is best to meet objections as they arise because postponement may result in a negative mental picture or reaction such as the following:

- The prospect may stop listening until you address the objection.
- The prospect may feel you are trying to hide something.
- You also feel it's a problem.
- You cannot answer because you do not know how to deal with this objection or you do not know the answer to the objection.
- It may appear that you are not interested in the prospect's opinion.

The objection could be the only thing left before closing the sale. So meet the objection, determine if you have satisfied the prospect, use another trial close to uncover other objections, and, if there are no more objections, move toward closing the sale.

Techniques for Meeting Objections

Having uncovered all objections, a salesperson must answer them to the satisfaction of the prospect. Naturally, different situations will require different techniques, but there are several techniques, as shown in Figure 10–4, that the salesperson can apply in most situations.

- Pass up the objection.
- Rephrase an objection as a question.
- Forestall the objection.
- Boomerang the objection.

You've Got to Do Better than That

In a recent issue of *Purchasing Magazine,* a leading expert on negotiation explained that there are seven magic words that drive salespeople crazy. They are *"You've got to do better than that."*

The author, Dr. Chester L. Karrass, says that the uninhibited use of this crunch technique ultimately results in false economy because sellers soon learn to add 10 percent to bids in order to have something to shave later when the crunch comes.

Personal Selling Power collected responses from selected readers who have handled the crunch technique with success.[1] They responded with answers such as these:

1. I understand that you want a lower price, and we will be more than happy to lower it to the level you have in mind. Let's review the options that you'd like to cut from our proposal, so we can meet your needs.

2. We are building a product up to a quality, not down to a price. A lower price would prevent us from staying in business and serving your needs later on.

3. Yes, we can do better than that if you agree to give us a larger order.

4. It was my understanding that we were discussing the sale of our product and not the sale of our business.

5. I appreciate your sense of humor—how much better can you get than rock-bottom? You see, our policy is to quote the best price first. We have built our reputation on high quality and integrity—it's the best policy.

6. I'd be glad to give you the names of two customers so you can find out how much they paid for our product. And you'll see it's exactly the same as we are asking you to pay. We could not develop our reputation without being fair to everyone.

7. I appreciate the opportunity to do a better selling job. Obviously, you must have a reason for looking exclusively on the dollar side of our proposal. Let's review the value that you'll be receiving. . . .

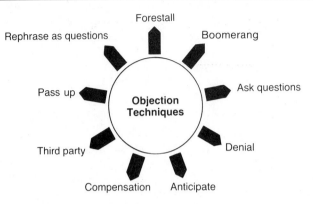

Figure 10–4
Techniques for Meeting Objections

- Forestall
- Rephrase as questions
- Boomerang
- Pass up
- **Objection Techniques**
- Ask questions
- Third party
- Denial
- Compensation
- Anticipate

- Ask questions regarding the objection.
- Directly deny the objection.
- Anticipate the objection.
- Compensate for the objection.
- Obtain a third-party answer to the objection.

Don't Be Afraid to Pass Up an Objection

On occasion, you may have a prospect raise an objection or make a statement requiring you to pass up or go around it without directly addressing it. After you introduce yourself to a prospect, for example, he may say "I'm really not interested in a service such as yours."

You have two basic options. First, you can take the weak approach and say, "Well, if you ever do, here is my card. Give me a call." Or you could take the approach used by top salespeople and say something that would allow you to move into your presentation, such as immediately going to your customer benefit approach or simply asking why?

As you gain selling experience you will be confident in knowing when to pass up or stop and respond to the objection. If you do pass up an objection and the prospect brings it up again, then treat this as an important objection. Use your questioning skills to uncover the prospect's concerns.

Rephrase an Objection as a Question

Since it is easier to answer a question than to overcome an objection, you should rephrase an objection as a question when you can do so naturally. Most objections can be easily rephrased. Figure 10–5 presents examples of several possible procedures for rephrasing an objection as a question. Each procedure, except the objection based on a bad previous experience with the product by the prospect, has the same first three steps: (1) acknowledge the prospect's viewpoint, (2) rephrase the objection into a question, and (3) obtain agreement on the question. Here is an example.

Buyer: I don't know—your price is higher than the others' are.

Salesperson: I can appreciate that. You want to know what particular benefits my product has that make it worth its slightly higher price. [or "What you're saying is that you want to get the best product for your money."] Is that correct?

Buyer: Yes, that's right.

Now discuss product benefits versus price. Once you have done so, attempt trial close by asking for the prospect's viewpoint to see if you have overcome the objection.

Salesperson: Do you see how the benefits of this product make it worth the price?

A variation of this sequence is Bruce Scagel's Feel-Felt-Found method in which he first acknowledges the prospect's viewpoint, saying, "John, I understand how you *feel*. Bill at XYZ store *felt* the same way, but he *found*, after reviewing our total program of products and services, that he would profit by buying now."

Figure 10–5
Examples of Rephrasing Objections as a Question

Facts Are Incorrect	Facts Are Incomplete	Facts Are Correct	Based on Bad Personal Experience
1. Acknowledge viewpoint.	1. Acknowledge viewpoint.	1. Acknowledge viewpoint.	1. Thank prospect for telling you.
2. Rephrase objection.	2. Rephrase objection.	2. Rephrase objection.	2. Acknowledge viewpoint.
3. Obtain agreement.	3. Obtain agreement.	3. Obtain agreement.	3. Rephrase objection.
4. Answer question providing information supported by proof—third party.	4. Answer question by providing the complete facts.	4. Answer question, outweigh with benefits.	4. Obtain agreement.
5. Ask for present viewpoint.	5. Ask for present viewpoint.	5. Ask for present viewpoint.	5. Answer question.
6. Move back into selling sequence.	6. Move back into selling sequence.	6. Move back into selling sequence.	6. Move back into selling sequence.

Bruce refers to rephrasing the objection as a question as his Isolate-and-Gain-Commitment method. He gives as an example: "Mary, as I understand it, your only objection to our program is the following . . . If I can solve this problem, then I'll assume that you will be prepared to accept our program."

Bruce knows he can solve the problem or he would not have asked the question. When Mary says yes, he has isolated the main problem. He is not handling an objection, rather he is answering a question. He now shows her how to overcome the problem and then continues his selling. If Mary says no, Bruce knows he has not isolated her main objection. He now must start over in his attempt to uncover her objections. He might say, "Well, I guess I misunderstood. Exactly what is the question?" And now, when Mary responds, it will usually come back as a question. "Well, the question was about. . . ." You see, what you need to do is to get the customer involved and find out what is going on internally. You can do this with the proper use of questions.

Forestalling Objections Is Sometimes Necessary

Often the prospect may skip ahead of you in your sales presentation by asking questions that you plan to address later in your presentation. If you judge that the objection will be handled to your prospect's satisfaction by your customary method, and that your prospect is truly willing to wait until that later time in the presentation, you can politely **forestall the objection.** Five examples of forestalling objections are as follows:

Prospect: Your price is too high.

Salesperson: In just a minute I'll show you why this product is reasonably priced, based on the savings you will receive compared to what you are presently doing. That's what you're interested in, savings, right?

or

Salesperson: Well, it may sound like a lot of money. But let's consider the final price when we know which model you need. OK?

or

Salesperson: There are several ways we can handle your costs. Let's discuss them in just a minute. First, I want to show you. . . .

or

Salesperson: I'm glad you brought that up (or, I was hoping you would want to know that) because we want to carefully examine the cost in just a minute.

or

Salesperson: High? Why, in a minute I'll show you why it's the best buy on the market. In fact, I'll bet you a Coke that you will believe it's a great deal for your company!

Tactfully used, forestalling can leave you in control of the presentation. Normally you should respond to the objection immediately. However, occasionally it is not appropriate to address the objection. This is usually true of the price objection. Price is the primary objection you would want to forestall if you have not had the opportunity to discuss the benefits of your product. If you have fully discussed your product, then you should always immediately respond to the price objection.

Send It Back with the Boomerang Method

You should be ready at any time to turn an objection into a reason to buy. By convincing the prospect that an objection is in fact a benefit, you will have turned the buyer immediately in favor of your product. This is the very heart of the **boomerang method.** Take, for example, the wholesale drug salesperson, working for a firm like McKesson and Robbins, who wants to sell a pharmacist a new type of container for prescription medicines. Handling the container, the prospect says:

Prospect: They look nice, but I don't like them as well as my others. The tops seem hard to remove.

Salesperson: Yes, they are hard to remove. We designed them so that children couldn't get into the medicine. Isn't that a great safety measure? [trial close]

Or, consider the industrial equipment salesperson who is unaware that a customer is extremely dissatisfied with a present product:

Prospect: I have been using your portable generators and do not want to use them anymore.

Salesperson: Why?

Prospect: Well, the fuses kept blowing out and causing delays in completing this project! So get out of here and take your worthless generators with you.

Salesperson: [*with a smile*] Thank you for telling me. Say, you know you and our company's design engineers have a lot in common.

Prospect: Oh yeah! I'll bet! [*sarcastically*]

Salesperson: Suppose you were chief engineer in charge of manufacturing our generators. What would you do if valued customers—like yourself—said your generators had problems?

"Battering Down Sales Resistance"

...**M**ay be one of the most misleading phrases in the salesman's book. For the most part, sales resistance cannot be "battered down." Hard sell and high pressure only lead the buyer to strengthen his defenses.

The key is to identify and understand sales resistance. Some is based on specific objections—to price, delivery, or product features. More often, the resistance stems from a buyer's fear of change or tendency to procrastinate.

If that's the case, the buyer needs reassurance. Provide case histories, offer testimonials from satisfied users. Describe the benefits he'll receive from using your product or service.

Melt his resistance by lighting a fire under his imagination.

DO NOT CROSS

Prospect:	I'd throw them in the trash.
Salesperson:	Come on, what would you really do? [*with a smile*]
Prospect:	Well, I would fix it.
Salesperson:	That's why I said you and our design engineers have a lot in common. They acted on your suggestion.

[Comment: You have used reverse psychology. Now the prospect is listening, giving you time to explain your product's new features and to offer to repair the old units. You are ready to sell more products, if possible.]

Another example is the industrial salesperson who responded to the prospect's high price objection by saying, "Well, that's the very reason you should buy it." The prospect was caught off guard and quickly asked, "What do you mean?" "Well," said the salesperson, "for just 10 percent more you can buy the type of equipment you really want and need. It is dependable, as well as safe and simple to operate. Your production will increase so that very quickly you have paid back the price differential." The prospect said, "Well, I hadn't thought of it quite like that. I guess I'll buy it after all."

Boomeranging an objection requires good timing and quick thinking. Experience in a particular selling field, knowledge of your prospect's needs, a positive attitude, and a willingness to stand up to the objection are necessary attributes for successful use of this technique.

Ask Questions to Smoke Out Objections

Intelligent questioning can impress a prospect in several ways. Technical questions show a prospect that a salesperson knows the business. Questions relating to a prospect's particular business show that a salesperson is concerned more with the prospect's needs than with just making a sale. Finally, people who **ask intelligent, well-thought-out questions,** whether they know much about their product, the prospect's business, or life in general, often receive admiration. Buyers are impressed with the sales professional who knows what to ask and when to ask it! Examples of questions are:

Prospect: This house is not as nice as the one someone else showed us yesterday.

Salesperson: Would you tell me why?

or

Prospect: This product does not have the . . . [feature].

Salesperson: If it did have the . . . [feature], would you be interested?

[Comment: The above example is an excellent questioning technique to determine if the objection is a smoke screen, a major or minor objection, or a practical or psychological objection. If the prospect says no to the response, you know the feature was not important.]

or

Prospect: I don't like your price.

Salesperson: Will you base your decision on price or on the product offered you . . . at a fair price?

[Comment: If the prospect says price, you show how benefits outweigh costs. If the decision is said to be based on the product, you have eliminated the price objection.]

Five-Question Sequence Method of Overcoming Objections. We have seen that buyers bring up objections for numerous reasons. From time to time all salespeople can sense that a buyer is not going to buy. As

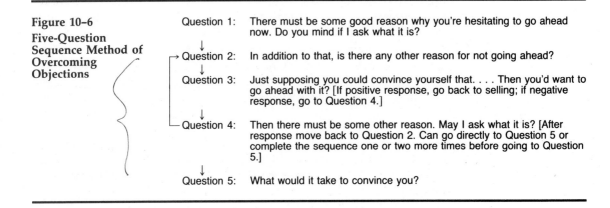

Figure 10–6

Five-Question Sequence Method of Overcoming Objections

Question 1: There must be some good reason why you're hesitating to go ahead now. Do you mind if I ask what it is?

Question 2: In addition to that, is there any other reason for not going ahead?

Question 3: Just supposing you could convince yourself that. . . . Then you'd want to go ahead with it? [If positive response, go back to selling; if negative response, go to Question 4.]

Question 4: Then there must be some other reason. May I ask what it is? [After response move back to Question 2. Can go directly to Question 5 or complete the sequence one or two more times before going to Question 5.]

Question 5: What would it take to convince you?

you gain sales experience, you will be able to feel it yourself. It may be the buyer's facial expressions or a tone of voice that tips you off. When this occurs you need to quickly find out why a prospect doesn't want to buy. For doing this, consider the use of a preplanned series of questions as shown in Figure 10–6.

Let's assume you have finished your presentation. You try to close the sale, and you can plainly see the buyer is not willing to go any further in the conversation. What do you do? Consider using the following **five-question sequence.**

First, use Question 1, "There must be some good reason why you're hesitating to go ahead now. Do you mind if I ask what it is?" When the reason is stated, or even if it is an objection, you should immediately double-check the objection with one more question by using Question 2 in the series: "In addition to that, is there any other reason for not going ahead?" The buyer may give the real reason for not buying, or may give the original objection. No matter what is said, you have set up a condition for buying.

Now you use Question 3, which is a "just supposing" question. "Just supposing you could . . . then you'd want to go ahead?" If the answer is yes, then you discuss how you can do what is needed. If you get a negative response, then you use Question 4 which is, "Then there must be some other reason. May I ask what it is?" Respond with Question 2 again. Then ask, "Just supposing . . . you'd want to go ahead?" Should you get another negative response, then use Question 5, by saying, "What would it take to convince you?"

What often happens now will surprise you. For the buyer will often say, "Oh, I don't know, I guess I'm convinced. Go ahead and ship it to me." Or you might be asked to go back over some part of your presentation. The important thing is that this series of questions keeps the conversation going and gets the real objections out in the open, which helps increase your sales. Now let's role-play this (imagine you are the salesperson):

Salesperson: Should we ship this out to you this week or next?

Buyer: Neither; see me on your next trip. I'll have to think about it.

Salesperson: You know, there must be some very good reason why you're hesitating to go ahead now. Would you mind if I asked what it is? [Question 1]

Buyer: Too much money.

Salesperson: Too much money. Well, you know, I appreciate the fact that you want to get the most for your money. In addition to the money, is there any other reason for not going ahead? [Question 2]

Buyer: No.

Salesperson: Well, just supposing then, that you could convince yourself that your savings from this machine would pay for itself in just a few months. And that we could fit it into your budget. Then you'd want to go ahead with it? [Question 3]

Buyer: Yes, I would.

Now you go back to selling by discussing the return on investment and affordable payment terms. You went from the first objection to the "double-check" question ("In addition to the money, is there any other reason for not going ahead?"). Then you used the "just supposing" question. You met the condition, the machine's cost. Then you went to the "convince" question. The buyer said yes, so you can keep on selling. Now let's role-play as if the buyer had said no. [Again, you are the salesperson.]

Buyer: No, I wouldn't go ahead.

Salesperson: Well, then there must be some other reason why you're hesitating to go ahead now. Do you mind if I ask what it is? [Question 4]

Buyer: It takes too much time to train my employees on the use of the machine.

Salesperson: Well, you know, I appreciate that. Time is money. In addition to the time, is there any other reason for not going ahead? [Question 2]

Buyer: Not really.

Salesperson: Just supposing that you could convince yourself that this machine would actually save your employees time so they could do other things. You'd find the money then, wouldn't you? [Question 3]

Buyer: I'm not sure. [Another potential negative response]

Salesperson: Money and time are important to you, right?

Buyer:	Yes they are.
Salesperson:	What would it take for me to convince you this machine will save you time and money? [Question 5]

Now you have to get a response. The buyer has to set the condition. You as the salesperson are always in control. The buyer is answering the questions. Remember, you want to help the person to buy. When you get an objection, you are being told what you have to do in order to make the sale happen. So do not fear objections, welcome them.

Direct Denial Should Be Used Tactfully

You will often be faced with objections that are incomplete or incorrect. You should acknowledge the prospect's viewpoint, then answer the question by providing the complete or correct facts.

Prospect:	No, I'm not going to buy any of your lawn mowers for my store. The Bigs-Weaver salesperson said they break down after a few months.
Salesperson:	Well, I can understand. No one would buy mowers that don't hold up. Is that the only reason you won't buy?
Prospect:	Yes, it is, and that's enough!
Salesperson:	That BW salesperson was not aware of the facts, I'm afraid. My company produces the finest lawn mowers in the industry. In fact, we are so sure of our quality that we have a new three-year guarantee on all parts and labor. [*pause*]
Prospect:	I didn't know that. [positive buying signal]
Salesperson:	Are you interested in selling your customers quality lawn mowers like these? [trial close]
Prospect:	Yes, I am. [appears that you have overcome the objection]
Salesperson:	Well, I'd like to sell you 100 lawn mowers. If even one breaks down, call me, and I'll personally come over and repair it. [close]

As you see by this example, you do not say, "Well, you fathead, why do you say a thing like that?" Here tact is critical in using a direct denial. A smart or huffy response can serve to alienate your prospect. However, a **direct denial** based on facts, logic, and politeness can be effective in overcoming the objective.

If I say to you, "You're wrong. Let me tell you why," what happens to your mind? It closes! So if I tell you that you are wrong and this closes your mind, what would I have to tell you to open your mind? That you are right! But if what you said was indeed wrong, do I tell you it was right? No, instead, do as the example illustrated by saying, "You know, you're right to be concerned about this. Let me explain." You have made

the buyer right and kept the buyer's mind open. Also, you
"You know, my best customer had those same feelings until I explained
that. . . ." You have not made the customer wrong, but right.

Anticipating Objections Comes with Experience

It is better to forestall or overcome objections before they arise. The sales
presentation can be developed to directly address **anticipated objections.** Take a manufacturer's salesperson selling exterior house paint
who learns that a not-too-ethical competitor has been telling retail dealers that this paint starts to chip and peel after six months.

Realizing the predicament, this salesperson develops a presentation
that very quickly points out, "Three independent testing laboratories
have shown that this paint will not chip or peel for eight years after
application." The salesperson has forestalled or answered the objection
before it is raised by using a proof statement. This technique can also
prevent a negative mood from entering into the buyer-seller dialogue.

Another way to anticipate objections is to bring disadvantages out
before the prospect does. Many products have flaws, and these come up
sometimes as you are trying to make a sale. If you know of an objection
that comes up consistently, you ought to bring it up. Because if you
bring it up first, you don't have to defend it.

On the other hand, a customer who brings up an objection feels
compelled to defend that objection. For example, you might be showing
real estate property. En route to the location, you say, "You know,
before we get out there, I just want to mention a couple of things. You're
going to notice that it needs a little paint in a few places, and I noticed a
couple of shingles on the roof the other day that you may have to
replace." When you arrive, your customer may take a look and say,
"Well, those shingles aren't so bad . . . and I can see . . . we're going to
paint it anyway." Yet if you reached the house without a little prior
warning of small defects, those would be the first things a customer
would notice.

Another way of using an anticipated objection is to brag about it and
turn it into a sales benefit. You might say, "I want to mention something
important before we go any further. Our price is a high one because as
you are beginning to see, it is quality merchandise, and we're proud of
the fact that we put this price on it. This allows us to build in the quality
that we know has to go in it to give you the service and type of product
that will fulfill your needs. Our customers are happy when they buy it
from us because we're able to stand behind our product."

You have taken all the sting out of the price objection because you
have brought it up yourself. It is difficult for a buyer to come back and
say, "It's too high," because you have already mentioned that. So there
are times when you can anticipate objections and use them to your
advantage.

Compensation or Counterbalance Method

Sometimes a prospect's objection is valid and calls for the **compensation method** in overcoming objections. Several reasons for buying must exist to justify or compensate for a negative aspect of making a purchase. For example, a higher product price can be justified by benefits such as better service or higher performance. In the following example, it is true that the prospect can make more profit on each unit of a competing product. You must develop a technique to show how your product has benefits that will bring the prospect more profit in the long run.

Prospect: I can make 5 percent more profit with the Stainless line of cookware, and it is quality merchandise.

Salesperson: Yes, you are right. The Stainless cookware is quality merchandise. However, you can have an exclusive distributorship on the Supreme cookware line and still have high quality merchandise. You don't have to worry about Supreme being discounted by nearby competitors as you do with Stainless. This will be the only store in town carrying Supreme.

If the advantages you present to counterbalance the objection are important to the buyer, you now have an opportunity to make the sale.

Let a Third Party Answer

An effective technique to use in responding to an objection is to answer it by letting a **third party answer** and using someone else's experience as your proof or testimony. A wide range of proof statements are used by salespeople today. You might respond to a question in this way: "I'm glad you asked. Here is what our research has shown. . . ." or, "EPA tests have shown. . . ." or, "You know, my best customer brought that point up before making the purchase . . . but was completely satisfied." These are examples of several basic proof statement formats. If you use a person or a company's name, be sure to obtain their approval first.

Secondary data or experience, especially that from a reliable or reputable source, can be especially successful with the expert or skeptical prospect. If after hearing secondary testimony, the prospect was still unsure about the product, one successful equipment salesperson would ask the buyer to directly contact a current user:

Salesperson: I still haven't answered your entire question, have I?

Buyer: Not really.

Salesperson: Let's do this. Here is a list of several people presently using our product. I want you to call them up *right now* and ask them that same question. I'll pay for the call.

A salesperson should use this version of the third-party technique only when certain that the prospect is still unsatisfied with how an objection has been handled, and that positive proof will probably clinch the sale. This dramatic technique allows the salesperson to really impress a prospect. It also shows a flattering willingness to go to great lengths to validate a claim.

Basic Points to Consider in Meeting Objections

No matter what type of objections are raised by the prospect, there are certain basic points to consider in meeting objections. You should learn to anticipate objections, consider objections as opportunities, be positive toward objections, and understand objections before you attempt to overcome them.

Anticipate Objections

Plan for objections that might be raised by your presentation. Consider not only the reasons prospects should buy but also why they should not buy. Structure your presentation so as to minimize the disadvantages of your product. Be sure not to discuss disadvantages unless prospects bring them up in the conversation.

After each sales call, review the prospect's objections. Divide them into major and minor objections. Then develop ways of overcoming them. Your planning for and rehearsal of overcoming objections will allow you to respond to them in a natural and positive manner.

Consider Objections as Opportunities

Objections should be welcomed. They indicate prospects' willingness to discuss your product. They are interested enough in your presentation to talk with you.

Objections help you understand what prospects are thinking. They provide clues to prospects' needs. Only bring objections into the discussion once you are able to overcome them.

Be Positive

When you respond to an objection, use positive body language, such as a smile. Strive to respond in a manner that gets your prospect to be friendly and to stay in a positive mood. Do not take the objection personally. You should never treat the objection with hostility. Take the objection in stride by responding respectfully and showing sincere interest in your prospect's opinion.

At times the prospect may raise objections based on incorrect information. Politely deny objections that are not true. Be realistic; all products have drawbacks, even yours. If a competitor's product has a feature yours does not have, point out the overriding benefits of your product.

Understand Objections

When customers give you an objection, they are doing one of three things, as shown in Figure 10–7. They are either requesting more information, setting a condition, or giving you a genuine objection.

Request for Information. Many times prospects appear to be making objections when they are actually making a request for more information. That is why it is important to listen. If prospects request more information, chances are they are in the conviction stage. You have created a desire. They want the product, but they are not convinced you have the best product or that you are the best supplier of that product. If you feel this is or may be the case—supply the information that has been indirectly requested.

A Condition. At times, prospects may raise an objection that turns into a **condition of the sale.** They are saying, "If you can meet my request, I'll buy" or, "Under certain conditions I will buy from you."

Figure 10–7
What Does a Prospect Mean by an Objection?

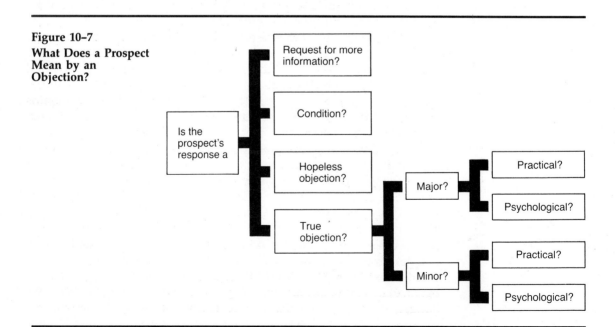

If you sense that the objection is a condition, you must quickly determine if you can help the prospect meet the condition. If you cannot, then politely close the interview. Take the following real estate example:

Prospect: It's a nice house, but the price is too high. I can't afford a $1,000 a month house payment. [You do not know if this is an objection or a condition.]

Salesperson: I know what you mean [acknowledging the prospect's viewpoint]. If you don't mind my asking, what is your monthly salary?

Prospect: My take-home pay is $1,400 a month.

In this case, the prospect has set a condition on the purchase that cannot realistically be met by the salesperson; it is not an objection. Attempting to continue the exchange by bargaining would have wasted time and possibly angered the prospect. Now that the prospect's income is known, the salesperson can show a house in the prospect's price range.

Negotiation Can Overcome a Condition.   Often conditions are stated by the prospect that can be overcome through **negotiation** between buyer and seller. Prospects may say things like, "I'll buy your equipment if you can deliver it in one month instead of three" or, "If you'll reduce your price by 10 percent, I'll buy."

If you determine that this type of statement is a condition rather than an objection, through negotiation you may be able to make the sale with further discussion and an eventual compromise between you and the buyer. In the example above, you might ask your manufacturing plant if the equipment can be shipped to the prospect in two months instead of three. This arrangement may be acceptable to the prospect. You may have a present customer who has that piece of equipment but is not using it. You might arrange for the prospect to lease it from your customer for three months.

If the prospect sets a price condition, saying, "I will buy your typewriter only if you reduce your price 10 percent," you might determine if your company will reduce the price if the buyer is willing to purchase a larger quantity of typewriters. Consider this actual example. As a state agency, Texas A&M University purchases much of its office equipment on a bid system. The Lanier Business Products salesperson could not sell the Texas A&M Marketing Department a word processor because the cost of a single machine was too high for that department's budget. The department wanted the machine; however, they could not afford it. Instead of giving up, the salesperson went to other depart-

Looking Behind The Objection

What is an objection? Sometimes it's a genuine doubt on the buyer's part. And sometimes it's a stall.

When you do get objections, gently keep asking "Why?" Get the buyer to talk, determine whether the objection is bona fide or just a way of buying time, review the objection, see if it would make sense to you if you were the buyer, and learn to listen.

Then restate the objection so the buyer has to say yes. "Do you mean, sir, that my product is too big for your room?" If he's saying yes, it's easier to get him into a positive frame of mind.

Once he's thinking positively, the rest of your presentation will flow much more smoothly, flow right to the buyer's "yes" when you close the sale.

ments in the university and found a need for a total of 16 machines. Lanier could substantially lower the price because of the large number of machines purchased ($4,000 per word processor less than the price of one machine). The salesperson determined that price was a condition, found a way to overcome the condition, and made the sale. Through initiation and inquiry, a potentially lost sale was turned into a multiple victory beneficial to all parties concerned.

Now there are two broad categories of objections. One of them is called *hopeless*. A hopeless objection is one that cannot be solved or answered. Examples of a hopeless objection would be "I already have one," "I'm bankrupt," "I'd like to buy your life insurance, but the doctor only gives me 30 days to live." So there are objections you could call hopeless. You cannot overcome them.

If your prospect does not buy and no condition exists or the objection is not hopeless, it is your fault you did not make the sale because you could not provide information to show how your offering would suit the buyer's needs.

The second category is the objection that can be answered. It is a *true* objection. The true objection has two types: the major and the minor objection.

Major or Minor Objection.   Once you determine that the prospect has raised a true objection, you need to determine its importance. If it is of little or no importance, then quickly address it and return to selling. Be careful not to provide a long response or blow a minor objection up into a major discussion item. The minor objection is often a defense mechanism of little actual importance to the prospect. Concentrate on objections directly related to the prospect's important buying motives.

Practical or Psychological Objection.   Objections, minor or major, can be **practical** (overt) or **psychological** (hidden) in nature. Figure 10–8 gives some examples. A real objection is tangible, such as a high price. If this is a real objection, and the prospect says so, you can show that your product is of high quality and worth the price, or you might suggest removing some optional features and reducing the price. As long as the prospect clearly states the real objection to purchasing the product, you should be able to answer the objection.

However, prospects will not always be so agreeable as to clearly state their objections openly. Rather, they will often give some excuse as to why they are not ready to make a purchase, concealing real objections. Usually the prospect will not purchase the product until those hidden objections are rectified. It is up to you to uncover a prospect's hidden objections and eliminate them satisfactorily.

After Meeting the Objection—What to Do?

Your prospect has raised an objection, which you have answered and overcome, now what? First, as shown in Figure 10–9, use a trial close, then be prepared to either move back into your presentation or close the sale.

Figure 10–8

Examples of Objections

Practical	Psychological
Price	Resistance to spending money
Not what is needed	Resistance to domination
Has overstock of your or competitor's products	Predetermined beliefs
Delivery schedules	Negative image of salespeople
	Dislike of making buying decision

336

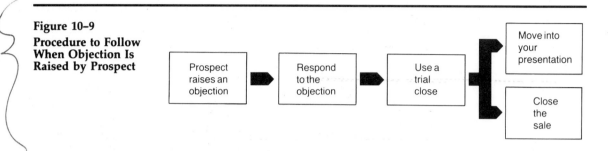

Figure 10–9
Procedure to Follow When Objection Is Raised by Prospect

First, Use a Trial Close

After meeting an objection at any time during the interview, you need to know if you have overcome the objection. If you have not overcome it, your prospect may bring it up again. Whether it resurfaces or not, if your prospect believes that an objection was important, your failure to handle it, or mishandling of it, will probably cost you the sale. Ideally, all objections raised should be met before closing the sale. So the first thing to do after responding to the objection is to use a trial close to determine if you have overcome the objection. The following are some suggested trial closes:

- "That clarifies this point entirely, don't you agree?"
- "That's the answer you're looking for, isn't it?"
- "With that question out of the way, we can go ahead, don't you think?"
- "Do you agree with me that we've covered the question you raised and given you a way to handle it?"
- "Now that's settled entirely, isn't it?"
- "That solves your problem with _____ , doesn't it?"

Now you can do one of two things (assuming you have handled the objection). You either move back into your presentation or close the sale.

Move Back into Your Presentation

Once you are satisfied that you have answered and overcome an objection, you need to make a smooth transition back into your presentation. Continue your presentation where you left off.

Move to Close Your Sale

If you have completely finished your presentation when the prospect raised an objection and the prospect's response to your trial close indicates you have overcome an objection, your next move is to close the sale. If the objection was raised during your close, then it is time for you to close again.

If You Cannot Overcome the Objection

Should you be unable to overcome an objection or close a sale because of an objection, you should be prepared to move back into your presentation and concentrate on new or previously discussed features, advantages, and benefits of your product. If you have determined that the objection raised by your prospect is a major one that you cannot overcome, admit it and show how your product's benefits outweigh this disadvantage.

If you are 100 percent sure that you cannot overcome the objection and that the prospect is not going to buy, you should go ahead and close. *Always ask for the order.* Never be afraid to ask your prospect to buy. It never hurts to ask. It is the buyer who says no, not you. Someone else may walk into the prospect's office after you with a product similar to yours. Your competitor may also be unable to overcome this person's objection, but may get the sale nonetheless, just by asking for it!

" Can I order that for you "

Summary of Major Selling Issues

People want to buy but they do not want to be taken advantage of, so they often ask questions or raise objections during a sales presentation. Your responsibility is to be prepared to logically and clearly respond to your prospect's objections whenever they arise, whether during your approach or when you move to close the sale.

Sales objections indicate a prospect's opposition or resistance to the request of the salesperson. Basic points to consider in meeting objections are to anticipate them, welcome them as opportunities, respond warmly and positively to them, make sure you understand them, rephrase them as questions when possible, be prepared to smoke out hidden objections, and handle them as they arise.

Before you can successfully meet objections, you need to first determine if the prospect's response to your statement or close is a request for more information, a condition of the sale, or an objection. If it is a real objection, determine whether it is minor or major. Respond to it using a trial close, and if you have successfully answered it, then continue your presentation based on where you are in the sales presentation. For example, if you are still in the presentation, then move back into your selling sequence. If you have completed the presentation, move to your close. If you are in the close and the prospect voices an objection, then you must decide whether to use another close or move back into the presentation and discuss additional benefits.

You should be aware of and plan for objections. Objections may be classified as hidden, stalling, no-need, and money objections. Develop several techniques to help you overcome each of these types of objections, such as forestalling the objection, turning the objection into a benefit, asking questions to smoke out hidden objections, denying the objection if appropriate, illustrating how product benefits outweigh the objection drawbacks, or developing proof statements that answer the objection.

Welcome your prospects' objections. They will help you determine if you are on the right track or guide you to uncovering what prospects' needs actually are and if they believe your product will fulfill those needs. Valid objections should be viewed as beneficial for you and the customer. A true objection reveals the customer's need, allowing a salesperson to demonstrate how a product can meet that need. Objections can also show up inadequacies in a salesperson's presentation or product knowledge. Finally, objections make selling a skill that a person can constantly improve. Over time, a dedicated salesperson can learn how to handle every conceivable product objection—tactfully, honestly, and to the customer's benefit.

Review and Discussion Questions

1. Name each major category of objections and give one or more examples of a technique for meeting the objection. Choose a different technique for each objection category.

2. Most prospects will ask about a salesperson's products or raise an objection. Discuss objections, including in your answer such things as (a) what they are, (b) when a prospect might raise an objection, and (c) what the basic points to consider when responding to an objection are.

3. At times a salesperson may wish to rephrase objections as questions. What is the procedure one should follow to rephrase an objection as a question?

4. Before successfully meeting objections, a salesperson should first be clear about the objection. Discuss the factors that need to be determined to be sure you understand the objection.

5. Assume you are a salesperson and your prospect raises an objection to buying your product. What should be your attitude toward this situation?

6. Halfway through your sales presentation, your prospect stops you and says, "That sounds like a great deal and you certainly have a good product, but I'm not interested now; maybe later." What should you do?

7. Assume you are a salesperson for the Japan Computer Corporation. You have finished your computer presentation, and the purchasing agent for Gulf Oil says, ''Well, that sounds real good, and you do have the lowest price I have ever heard of for a computer system. In fact, it's $200,000 less than the other bids. But we have decided to stay with IBM, mainly because $200,000 on a $1 million computer system is not that much money to us.'' Let's further assume that you also know that other than the price, IBM has significant advantages in all areas over your product. What would you do?

8. Using your knowledge of negotiation, which of these methods would be the best way to handle a prospective new car purchaser and why? A customer has told you she is only looking, prices are too high, and she cannot afford a new automobile at this time.
   a. Agree with her, then proceed to the next available customer.
   b. Show the customer a cheaper model of the same car.
   c. Explain to the customer how payments can be tailored to fit almost anyone's budget.
   d. Ask her why she is wasting her time looking at new cars.

9. When a customer is not receptive to your product, you will very often find that there is some objection. Listed below are several situations in which the customer has an objection to a product.
   a. The customer assumes he must buy the whole set of books. However, partial purchases are permitted.
   b. The customer does not like the color, and it's the only color your product comes in.
   c. The customer doesn't want to invest in a new set of books because he doesn't want to lose money on his old one. You have not yet told him about your trade-in deal.

   In which of the above situations does the objection arise from a misunderstanding or lack of knowledge on the customer's part? In which situation(s) does the product fail to offer a benefit that the customer considers important?

10. Consider the following two situations and then answer the questions which follow them:

   Situation A:

Customer:	I don't think I could sell your stoves here. Having to clean these ovens . . . no, I'm sorry; my customers want convenience and they can afford to pay for it.
Salesperson:	Then you think that your customers would find it inconvenient or bothersome to have to clean the Master oven?
Customer:	They sure would.
Salesperson:	That's just why the Master oven is fully automatic; it cleans itself at the push of a button. So you see, your customers will get convenience when they buy the Master oven.

Situation B:

Customer:	But I'll never get them off the shelf. My customers aren't millionaires, you know!
Salesperson:	Then you think our toasters are too expensive?"
Customer:	Yes, definitely.
Salesperson:	But look at it this way: although the Tri-X is a little more expensive than some of the other models, you can be sure your customers will get a dependable toaster, one that will not overheat and short out. Moreover, the Tri-X comes with a one-year guarantee, and that's a longer guarantee than any other manufacturer offers.

Refer to the preceding situations:

a. In Situation A, the customer is objecting to the product because:
   (1) There is some misunderstanding about it.
   (2) The product fails to offer a benefit that the customer feels is important.

b. Compared with Situation B, Situation A shows a customer objection that is:
   (1) Difficult to answer.
   (2) Easy to answer.

c. In both Situation A and Situation B, the salesperson responds to the customer's objection by *first:*
   (1) Answering the objection directly.
   (2) Offering agreement.
   (3) Restating the objection in question form.

d. Restating an objection in question form before handling it is important for a number of reasons:
   (1) It helps to clarify the objection.
   (2) It shows that you are interested in, and attentive to, the customer's needs and problems.
   (3) Both (1) and (2) are important reasons.
   (4) Both (1) and (2) are not important reasons.

e. However, nothing you say in a restatement should imply agreement with the objection, since this will only make the objection appear more important to the customer. Which of the following phrases might you use in restating an objection?
   (1) "Are you saying . . . ?"
   (2) "Exactly! That's just what I was going to bring up next. . . ."
   (3) "I agree, that is a problem. . . ."
   (4) "If I understand you, then. . . ."
   (5) "In other words. . . ."
   (6) "Then you feel that. . . ."

     f. The salesperson in Situation B knows that the cost of a product cannot be reduced even though the customer objects to it. To handle this difficult objection, the salesperson minimizes it in the customer's mind by:
      (1) Answering it directly.
      (2) Offering agreement with the objection.
      (3) Stressing other relevant benefits of his product.

11. A relatively easy-to-answer objection can result from:
    a. The customer's misunderstanding.
    b. The failure of a product to provide a benefit of interest to the customer.
    c. Your failure to provide the customer with all necessary information.

12. A more difficult-to-answer objection results from:
    a. A lack of information on the customer's part.
    b. The customer's misunderstanding.
    c. The failure of your product to provide a benefit of interest to the customer.

13. When you restate the objection in question form, your objective is to:
    a. Clarify the customer's remark.
    b. Imply that you agree with the objection.
    c. Indicate that you are interested in the customer's need or problem.

14. You will restate the objection in question form whenever you encounter:
    a. An easy-to-answer objection.
    b. A difficult-to-answer objection.

15. Which response is best when you get the customer reply, "I'd like to think it over?"
    a. Give all the benefits of using the product now.
    b. If there is a penalty for delaying, mention it now.
    c. If there is a special price deal available, mention it now.
    d. None of the above is appropriate.
    e. Depending on the circumstances, all three choices are appropriate.

16. Cliff Jamison sells business forms, and he's regarded as a top-notch salesperson. He works hard, plans ahead, and exhibits self-confidence. On this day he was making his first presentation to a prospective new client, the California Steel Company.

    "Ladies and gentlemen," said Jamison, "our forms are of the very highest quality, yet they are priced below those of our competitors. I know you are a large user of business forms and that you use a wide variety of them. Whatever your need for business forms, I assure you that we can supply them. And our forms are noted for their durability. They can be run through your machines at 60 per minute, and they'll perform perfectly.''

"Perfectly, Mr. Jamison?" asked the California Steel executive. "Didn't you have some trouble at Ogden's last year?"

"Oh," replied Jamison, "that wasn't the fault of our forms. They had a stupid operator who didn't follow instructions. I assure you that if our instructions are followed precisely you will have no trouble whatever.

"Furthermore, we keep a large inventory of our forms so that you need never worry about delays. A phone call to our office is all that is necessary to ensure prompt delivery to your plant of precisely the forms you need. I hope, therefore, that I can be favored with your order. . . .'' Did Jamison handle this situation correctly? Why?

17. One of your customers, Margaret Port, has referred you to a friend who needs your Hercules Shelving for a storage warehouse. Margaret recently purchased your heavy-duty, 18-gauge steel shelving and is very pleased with it. She said, "This will be an easy sale for you. My friend really needs shelving, and I told him about yours."

Margaret's information is correct, and your presentation to her friend goes smoothly. The customer has asked numerous questions and seems ready to buy. Just before you ask for the order, the customer says, "Looks like your product is exactly what I need. I'd like to think this over. Could you call me next week?" Which of the following would you do? Why?

a. Follow the suggestion and call next week.

b. Go ahead and ask for the order.

c. Ask questions about the reason for the delay.

Projects

1. A national sales company is at your school wishing to hire salespeople. What are some objections such a company might have toward hiring you? How would you overcome them during a job interview?

2. Visit three different types of business (such as a grocery store, hardware store, and stereo shop) and pick out one product from each business. If you were that store's buyer, think of the major objections or questions you would ask a product salesperson if you were asked to buy a large quantity and promote it. Now, as that salesperson, how would you overcome those objections?

Cases

10-1 Handy Dan

As you drive up into the parking lot of one of your best distributors of your home building supplies, you recall how only two years ago they purchased the largest opening order you ever sold. Last year their sales doubled, and this year you hope to sell them over $100,000 worth.

As you wait, the receptionist informs you that since your last visit your buyer, John Smalley, was fired and another buyer was transferred in to take his place. John and you had become reasonably good friends over the past two years, and you hated to see him go.

As you enter the new buyer's office, she asks you to have a seat and then says, "I've got some bad news for you. I'm considering switching suppliers. Your prices are too high."

Questions:

1. Under these circumstances the best way to react to this objection would be:
    a. "It's certainly a good idea to compare prices, because price is always an important consideration. When you add up all the benefits we offer, however, I think you'll find that our prices—over the long haul—are actually lower than the competition's."
    b. "Would you mind telling me exactly why you're considering this move?"
    c. "Gee, I'm really surprised at this move. After all, we were the ones who originally got you interested in handling home building supplies. Our service has been good, and most importantly, you've derived excellent profits from our line."

2. Why did you not choose the other two alternatives?

10-2 Ace Building Supplies

This is your fourth call on Ace Building Supplies to get them to begin carrying and selling your home building supplies to local builders. Joe Newland, the buyer, has given you every indication that he likes your products.

During the call, Joe reaffirms his liking for your products and attempts to end the interview by standing up saying, "We'll be ready to do business with you in three months—right after this slow season ends. Stop by then and we'll definitely place an order with you."

Questions:

1. Under these circumstances, which one of the following would you do? Why?

    a. Call back in three months to get the order as suggested.

    b. Try to get a firm commitment or order now.

    c. Telephone Joe in a month (rather than make a personal visit) and try to get the order.

2. Why did you not choose the other two alternatives?

10–3 Your Price Is Too High

John was making his presentation for in-office coffee service to the office manager. As he neared the end of it, the office manager asked, "What's your price?" John quoted the standard price, and immediately the manager said, "Way out—your competitor's price is $10 cheaper!"

As Mary, presenting a medical laboratory equipment company, finished her presentation, the pathologist asked her the cost. She stated the list price and heard, "Your price is too high. I can get the same type of equipment for a lot less."

Ralph, selling a line of office copying machines, was only half-way through his presentation when the director of administration asked for the cost. When Ralph quoted the price on the top-of-the-line model, the administrator closed off the interview with the familiar phrase, "Your price is too high."

Question:

How should John, Mary, and Ralph respond to their prospects' comments?

10–4 Electric Generator Corporation (B)

George Wynn is a salesperson for EGC whose primary responsibility is to contact engineers in charge of the construction of commercial buildings. One such engineer is Don Snyder who is in charge of building the new Texas A&M University College of Business Administration facility. Don's Houston-based engineering firm had purchased three new EGI portable generators for use on this project. George had learned that Don's company will build four more buildings on the A&M campus, and he felt Don might buy more machines.

Salesperson:	Don, I understand you have three of our new model electric generators.
Buyer:	Yeah, you're not kidding.
Salesperson:	I'm sure you'll need additional units on these new jobs.
Buyer:	Yeah, we sure will.
Salesperson:	I've gone over the building's proposed floor plans and put together the type of products you need.

Buyer:	They buy down in Houston; you need to see them!
Salesperson:	I was just in there yesterday, and they said it was up to you.
Buyer:	Well, young man, I'm busy today.
Salesperson:	Can I see you tomorrow?
Buyer:	No need. I don't want any more of your lousy generators!
Salesperson:	What do you mean? That is our most modern design!
Buyer:	Those so called *new* fuses of yours are exploding after five minutes' use. The autotransformer starter won't start . . . did you see the lights dim? That's another fuse blowing.

Question:

George has a great deal of pressure on him to sell the new EGI. Don's business represents a big and important sale, both now and in the future. If you were George, what would you do?

10–5   Vacuum Cleaner Inc.

Jane Dowdy, a salesperson for Sani-Sweep Vacuum Cleaner, feels that a customer's attitude toward her product generally falls into one of three categories: acceptance, indifference, or rejection. First, if a customer is satisfied with a present product, or feels no need for a product of her type, the customer's attitude toward her product is likely to be one of indifference. When this occurs, Jane likes to directly probe her customer to uncover areas of possible dissatisfaction with the competitor's product. Second, if the customer seems to agree with her benefit statements and displays no adverse feelings toward her product, the customer's attitude is likely to be one of acceptance. Jane quickly introduces additional benefits and makes a trial close. Third, if the customer is not receptive to Jane's benefit statements and appears to have doubts or reservations about the product, the response is to make an objection. For this customer Jane prefers to restate the objection as a question.

Before deciding on the approach (or strategy) to use in a sales interview, Jane determines the customer's attitude toward her product. She must discover the attitude by means of what is said in response to her benefit statements about the product. At the end of her work day, Jane reviewed three situations that she had encountered. The conversations went like this:

Situation 1:

Salesperson:	Our Sani-Sweep is the first vacuum cleaner of its kind to run on flashlight batteries.
Customer:	Say, that sounds like a good deal.

Situation 2:

Salesperson: Our Sani-Sweep is the first vacuum cleaner of its kind to run on flashlight batteries.

Customer: Oh, that's dandy. So, I'm running to the store buying new batteries every week.

Situation 3:

Salesperson: Our Sani-Sweep is the first vacuum cleaner of its kind to run on flashlight batteries.

Customer: Well, that's nice, but our floors are covered by that new type of tile that never needs vacuuming.

Questions:

1. For each situation, was the customer's attitude one of acceptance, indifference, or rejection?
2. For each situation, how should Jane respond to the customer? Why? Give specific examples of how you would respond.

11 CLOSE, CLOSE, CLOSE

Learning Objectives

1. To explain the essentials of closing a sale.
2. To discuss the timing of a close.
3. To present examples of several closing techniques.
4. To stress the importance of flexibility, and closing based on the situation.

Key Terms for Selling

Closing
Buying signal
Alternative choice close
Assumptive close
Compliment close
Summary of benefits close

Continuous-yes close
Minor-points close
T-account close
Standing-room-only close
Probability close

Profile

George W. Morris
Prudential Life Insurance

Realizing my interest was in a career of selling, I interviewed with companies in many industries while a student at the University of Oklahoma. When I interviewed with the general agent of the Massachusetts Mutual Insurance Company in Oklahoma City prior to graduation, I become very fascinated with the opportunities the insurance business offered. The Mass Mutual was not then operating in Amarillo, my home town, and a friend suggested I talk to the manager of the Prudential Life Insurance Company for Fort Worth and the West Texas area. It appeared to me that I wanted to be associated with a major, reputable company, so while studying for final exams, I was simultaneously preparing to learn the Prudential Dollar Guide Presentation. I received my degree on June 11, 1950, and signed my contract the next day to start in the insurance business.

Mr. McCelvey, my first manager with Prudential, used to say the development of a sales presentation was simply fixing the prospect's problems and helping him accomplish his objectives. Thirty-one years later in the insurance business, I couldn't agree more! The sales presentation is the ability of the agent to build extremely close, personal relationships with people, learn about their objectives, desires, concerns and commitments, and help them accomplish these. If everything has been done to develop the sales presentation properly, the closing of the sale is simply the next logical sequence.

To be successful in an insurance career, a person needs a very deep commitment to the product of life insurance and what it will do. The insurance business will test a person's metal, and this abiding faith will be needed in times of discouragement and frustration. As you experience death claims and see what the product can and does do for families, corporations, partnerships, trusts, and other entities, uniquely, the faith and commitment to the product are sure to come. This develops the philosophy of "you're not only in the insurance business, the insurance business is in you!"

A person who is interested in an insurance career should first overcome the negatives sometimes attached to the life insurance business. These negatives, however, are more than offset, in my opinion, by the limitless opportunity for a large income, ultimate respect and admiration from your clientele, complete independence to pursue your career as you feel best, and not dependent on the political whims of your superior but based totally on your capabilities and commitment.

"My company," said one executive, "had done business for many years with a firm that helped us merchandise our industrial products. I persuaded our advertising manager to have another firm also submit a proposal on how to best handle our products. Both suppliers received enthusiastic consideration on their proposals from our executives and submitted competitive bids on price.

"The salesman for the new company had every reason," the executive went on to say, "to believe he would receive our business and so did I. However, our advertising manager felt the company should stay with the old firm because of the chance we would take by adopting something new. It was too risky for him. He knew what to expect from the old company." This executive had not discussed this concern with the newcomer's salesman during his presentation. The salesman failed to overcome and thus make the sale. He probably never found out why he lost the order.

The point of the above example is that successful salespeople do not give a presentation and then ask for the order. Successful salespeople develop selling techniques that aid them in developing a natural instinct, sensitivity, and timing for when and how to close each buyer. This chapter wraps up our discussion of the main elements of the sales presentation. We will begin by discussing when to close, showing examples of buying signals and discussing what makes a good closer. Next is a discussion of the number of times you should attempt to close a sale, along with some problems associated with closing. Eight closing techniques are presented, followed by an explanation of the importance of being prepared to close several times based on the situation.

When Should I Pop the Question?

Closing is the process of helping people make a decision that will benefit them. You help people make that decision by asking them to buy. As successful salespeople know, there are no magic phrases and techniques to use in closing a sale. It is simply the end result of your presentation. As insurance agent George Morris says, "If everything has been done to properly develop a sales presentation, the closing of the sale is simply the next step in a logical sequence."

Figure 11–1
Close When the
Prospect Is Ready

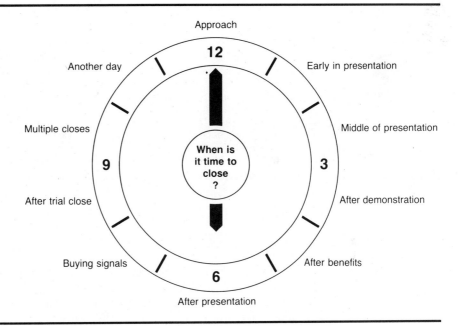

Approach

12

Another day · Early in presentation

Middle of presentation

9 · **When is it time to close ?** · 3

Multiple closes

After trial close · After demonstration

Buying signals · After benefits

6

After presentation

Although it seems obvious, some salespeople forget that prospects know that the salesperson is there to sell them something. So, as soon as the two meet, the prospect's mind may already have progressed beyond the major portion of the salesperson's presentation. At times, the prospect may be ready to make the buying decision very early in the interview.

So when should you attempt to close a sale? Simply, *when the prospect is ready!* More specifically, when the prospect is in the conviction stage of the mental buying process. A buyer can enter the conviction stage at virtually any time during the sales presentation. As shown in Figure 11–1, you might ask someone to buy as early as the approach stage or as late as another day. Ninety-nine percent of the time, however, the close comes after the presentation. An ability to read a prospect's buying signals correctly can aid a salesperson in deciding when and how to close a sale.

Reading Buying Signals _____

After prospects have gone through each stage of the mental buying process and are ready to buy, they will often give you some type of signal. A **buying signal** refers to anything prospects say or do to indicate that they are ready to buy. Buying signals hint that prospects are in the

	Buyer Says:	Salesperson Replies:
Figure 11-2		
Answering a Prospect's Buying Signal Question with a Question	What's your price?	In what quantity?
	What kind of terms do you offer?	What kind of terms do you want?
	When can you make delivery?	When do you want delivery?
	How big a copier should I get?	How big do you need?
	Can I get this special price on an order I place now and next month?	Would you like to split your shipment?
	Do you carry 8-, 12-, 36-, and 54-foot pipe?	Are those the sizes you commonly use?
	How large an order do I need to place to receive your best price?	How big an order do you have in mind?
	Do you have the Model 6400 in stock?	Is that the one you like best?

conviction stage of the buying process, as seen in Figure 11-2. Several ways in which buyers may signal that they are ready to buy are as follows. The prospect:

- *Asks questions*—"How much is it?" "When is the earliest I can receive it?" "What are your service and return goods policies?" At times, you may wish to respond to a buying signal question with another question, as shown in Figure 11-2. This helps you better determine your prospect's thoughts and needs. If your question is answered positively, the prospect is showing a high interest level, and you are close to closing the sale.

- *Asks another person's opinion*—The executive calls someone on the telephone and says, "Come in here a minute; I have something to ask you." Or the wife turns to her husband and says, "What do you think about it?"

- *Relaxes and becomes friendly*—Once the prospect decides to purchase a product, the pressure of the buying situation is eliminated. A state of visible anxiety changes to one of refreshed relaxation because your new customer believes you are now a friend.

- *Pulls out a purchase order form*—If, as you are talking, your prospect pulls out an order form, it is time to move toward your close.

- *Carefully examines merchandise*—When a prospect begins to carefully scrutinize your product or seems to be contemplating the purchase, this may be an indirect request for prompting. Given these indications, you should attempt a trial close: "What do you think about. . . ?" Should you obtain a positive response to this question, move on to close the sale.

A buyer may send verbal or nonverbal buying signals at any time before or during your sales presentation (remember Figure 11-1). The accurate interpretation of buying signals should prompt you to attempt a trial close. In beginning your trial close, summarize the major selling points desired by your prospect. As illustrated in Figure 11–3, if you receive a positive response to your trial close, you can move to Step 9 and wrap up the sale. A negative response should result in a return to your presentation, Step 4, or to determine objections, Step 6. In any case, a successful trial close can save you and your prospect valuable time, while a thwarted trial close will allow you to assess your selling situation.

Figure 11–3

A Positive Response to Trial Close Indicates a Move to the Close; A Negative Response Means Return to Your Presentation or Determine the Prospect's Objections

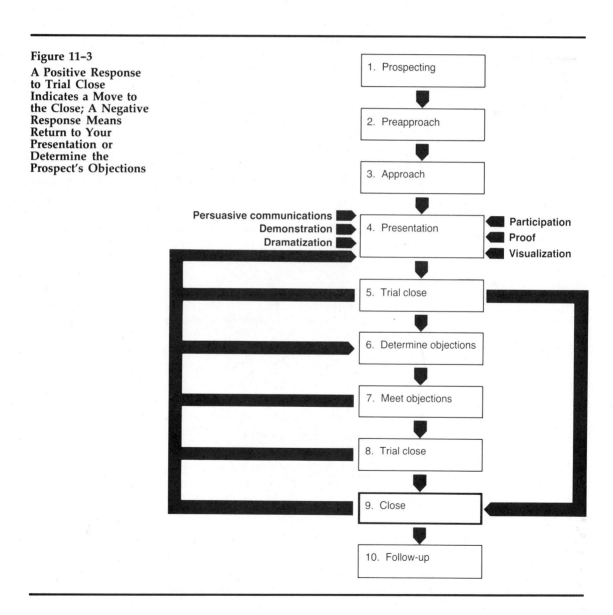

What Makes a Good Closer? _____

In every sales force there are individuals who seem to be better than others at closing sales. Some rationalize this difference of abilities by saying, "It comes naturally to some people," or, "They've just got what it takes." Well, what does it take to be a good closer?

Good closers, most importantly, have a strong desire to close each sale. They have a positive attitude about their product's ability to benefit the prospect. They know their customers and tailor their presentations to meet each one's specific needs.

Good closers spend time in preparing for each sales call. They take the time to carefully ascertain the needs of their prospects and customers by observing, asking intelligent questions, and most of all earnestly listening to them.

The successful salesperson does not stop on the prospect's first no. If a customer says no, determine the nature of the objection and then move back into the presentation. After discussing information relative to overcoming the objection, use a trial close to determine if you have overcome the objection, and then determine if there are other objections. If resistance continues, remain positive and remember that every time you attempt to close, you get closer to making the sale. Additionally, always ask for the order and then shut up.

Ask for the Order and Shut Up!

No matter when or how you close, remember that after you ask for the order it is very important to be silent. Do not say a single word. If you say something—anything—you increase your probability of losing the sale.

You must put the prospect in a position of having to (1) make a decision, (2) speak first, and (3) respond to the close. If you say anything after your close, you take the pressure off the prospect to make that decision.

Imagine this situation. The salesperson has finished his presentation and says, "Would you want this delivery in two or four weeks?" The average salesperson cannot wait over 10 seconds for the prospect's reply without saying something like, "I can deliver it anytime," or starting to talk again about the product. This destroys the *closing moment*. The prospect does not have to make the decision. There is time to think of reasons not to buy. By keeping quiet for a few seconds, the prospect cannot escape making the decision.

All individuals experience the urge to say no, even when they are not sure of what you are selling or may actually want what you are proposing. At times, everyone is hesitant in making a decision. To help the prospect make the decision, you must maintain silence after the close.

The professional salesperson "asks for the order and shuts up." The professional can stay quiet all day if necessary. Rarely will the silence last over 30 seconds. During that time do not say anything or make a distracting gesture; merely project positive nonverbal signs. Otherwise, you will lessen your chances of making the sale. This is the time to mentally prepare your responses to the prospect's reaction.

It sounds simple, yet it is not. Your stomach may churn. Your nerves make you want to move. You catch yourself with a serious look on your face, instead of a positive one. You may look away from the buyer. Most of all, you want to talk in order to relieve the uncomfortable feeling that grows as the silence continues. Finally, the prospect will say something. Now you can respond to the reaction to your close.

You should constantly practice asking your closing question, shutting up for 30 seconds, and then responding. This will develop your skill and courage to close.

Get the Order and Get Out!

Talking can also lose the sale for you after the prospect has said yes. An exception would be if you are asking the customer for names of other prospects. Once this is done, however, you should leave. It is best to get the order and get out.

In continuing to talk, you may give information that changes the buyer's mind. So ask for the order and remain silent until the buyer responds. If you succeed, finalize the sale and leave.

How Many Times Should You Close? _____

Courtesy and common sense imply a reasonable limit to the number of closes attempted by a salesperson at any one sitting. However, salespeople are calling on customers and prospects to sell their products.

In order to sell, you must be able to use multiple closes. The fact is, as the chapter title indicates, three closes are a minimum for successful salespeople. Three to five well-executed closes should not offend a prospect. Attempting several closes in one call challenges a salesperson to employ wit, charm, and personality in a creative manner. So always take at least three strikes before you count yourself out of the sale.

Once you have made the sale, you should consider if it's appropriate to suggest the buyer purchase another item.

Closing under Fire _____

To effectively close more sales, you should never take the first no from the prospect to mean an absolute refusal to buy. Instead, you must be

Stanley Marcus on Creative Suggestion Selling

"I witnessed an outstanding example of creative suggestion selling one day in a Neiman-Marcus men's store," says Stanley Marcus.[1] "A saleswoman approached a young buyer and asked if she could help her by writing up the sale of a $15 necktie, so she could wait on another customer. She handed the buyer the $15 tie and quickly introduced the customer to another salesperson at the counter.

"As he began writing up the sale, he looked up and said, 'This is a beautiful tie you have selected. What is he going to wear it with?' The woman reached into her purse and pulled out a swatch of fabric. He looked at it a moment and said, 'There's an ancient madder pattern which comes in two color combinations that would go very well with this suit.' He pulled out the two ties as he was talking with her. She readily agreed and took both of them—at $22.50 each.

"He asked, 'Doesn't he need some new shirts to go with his new suit?' The customer replied, 'I'm glad you asked; he does need some, but I haven't been able to find any white ones with French cuffs. Do you have any size fifteen thirty-three?' He showed her two qualities, pointing out the difference in the cloths. She selected three shirts at $40 each. 'Doesn't he ever wear colored shirts?' he inquired. 'Yes; if you have this same shirt in blue I'll take two.'

"The sale progressed from there to include gold-filled cuff links, a travel robe to match the ancient madder ties, pajamas, and slippers. The total sale was $615—a 4,000 percent increase over the $15 the original saleswoman had been willing to settle for. What was of even more importance, he had made a firm new customer for the department. That is creative suggestion selling at its very best.

"Not once in the course of the sale did he oversell. He related to the customer's desires and wants and knew the content of the stocks well enough to fulfill her requirements. Above all, he had the heart of a salesman who not only thoroughly enjoys the excitement of meeting the expressed request of the customer but had the imagination to conceive of other things the buyer might find of interest. This type of selling technique can be taught; unfortunately, it doesn't happen very often. Americans have prided themselves on their selling ability, but lack of management attention to selling has dulled those skills."

Figure 11–4

"Multiple closes are important," says Mr. Marcus. *"In fulfilling the buyer's primary need the salesperson needs the imagination to conceive of other things the customer might find of interest."*

able to "close under fire." In other words, you must be able to ask a prospect, who may be in a bad mood or may even appear hostile toward you, to buy.

Take the experience of a consumer goods salesperson who suggested that a large drug wholesaler should buy a six-month supply of the company's entire line of merchandise. Outraged, the purchasing agent threw the order book across the room. The salesperson explained to the furious buyer that the company had doubled its promotional spending in the buyer's area and that it would be wise to stock up because of an upcoming increase in sales. The salesperson calmly picked up the order book, smiled, and handed it to the buyer saying, "Did you want to buy more?"

The buyer laughed and said, "What do you honestly believe is a reasonable amount to buy?" This was a buying signal that the prospect would buy, but in a lesser quantity. They settled on an increased order of a two-month supply over the amount of merchandise normally purchased. This example illustrates why it is very important for the salesperson to react calmly to an occasional hostile situation.

Difficulties with Closing

Closing the sale should be the easiest part of the presentation. It serves as a natural wrap-up to your sales presentation because you are now solidifying the details of the purchase agreement. Yet salespeople sometimes have difficulty closing the sale for a number of reasons.

One reason salespeople may fail to close a sale and get an order is that they are not confident of their ability to close. Perhaps some earlier failure to make a sale has brought about this mental block. They may give their presentation and stop short of asking for the order. Obviously, the seller must overcome this fear of closing to become successful.

Second, salespeople often determine on their own that the prospect does not need the quantity or type of merchandise, or that the prospect simply should not buy. So they do not ask the prospect to buy. The salesperson should remember that *it is the prospect's decision and responsibility whether or not to buy*. Do not make that decision for the prospect.

Finally, the salesperson may not have worked hard enough in developing a customer profile and customer benefit plan—resulting in a poor presentation! Many times a poorly prepared presentation will fall apart before the salesperson's very eyes. It is important to be prepared and develop a well-planned, well-rehearsed presentation.

Essentials of Closing Sales

While there are numerous factors to consider in closing the sale, the following are essential if you wish to improve your chances.

- Be sure your prospect understands what you are saying.
- Always present a complete story to ensure understanding.
- Tailor your close to each prospect. Eighty percent of your customers will respond to a standard close. It is the other 20 percent you need to be prepared for. You should be prepared to give the expert the facts requested, to give the egotist praise, to lead the indecisive prospect, and to slow down for the slow thinker.
- Everything you do and say should take into consideration the customer's point of view.

- Never stop at the first no.
- Learn to recognize buying signals.
- Before you close, attempt a trial close.
- After asking for the order—shut up.
- Set high goals for yourself and develop a personal commitment to reach your goals.
- Develop and maintain a positive, confident, and enthusiastic attitude toward yourself, your products, your prospects, and your close.

Twelve Steps to a Successful Closing

Before we discuss specific techniques on how to ask for the order or close the sale, you need to remember that you will greatly increase the number of sales you are able to close by following 12 simple steps.

Closing Is Not One Giant Step

Too many salesmen regard the close as a separate and distinct part of the sales call. "I've discussed benefits and features, answered some objections, handled price, and now it's time to close."

Chronologically, of course, the "close" does come at the end. But you should have been closing right along.

Closing is the natural outgrowth of the sales presentation. If the rest of the sales call has been a success, closing should simply mean working out terms and signing the order.

What about the salesman who says, "I always have trouble closing. Everything's fine until it's time to close the sale." Chances are, there's no basis for the sale. "Everything's fine..." may merely be a way of saying, "I stated my case and he listened. At least he never told me to pack up and go."

1. Think *success!* Be enthusiastic!
2. *Plan* your sales call.
3. Confirm your prospect's *needs* in the approach.
4. Give a *great* presentation.
5. Use *trial closes* during and after your presentation.
6. Smoke out a prospect's *real* objections.
7. *Overcome* these real objections.
8. Use a *trial close* after overcoming each objection.
9. Summarize *benefits* as related to buyer's *needs*.
10. Use a *trial close* to confirm Step 9.
11. Ask for the *order* and then *shut up.*
12. Leave the door *open!* Act as a professional.

As you see from these 12 steps, a successful close is the end result of a series of steps you have gone through before you ask for the order. *Closing is not one giant step.*

Should you not make the sale, always remember to act as a professional salesperson and be courteous and appreciative of the opportunity to present your product to the prospect. This allows the door to be open when you come back another time. Thus, Step 12 cannot be overlooked—always remember to leave the door open!

Too often salespeople believe there is some mystical art to closing a sale. Some believe that if they say the right words in the appropriate manner, the prospect will buy. They concentrate on developing tricky closing techniques and often are extremely pushy with prospects in hopes of pressuring them into purchasing. Certainly, salespeople need to learn alternative closing techniques. However, what is most needed is a thorough understanding of the entire selling process and of the critical role that closing plays in that process.

A memorized presentation and a hurriedly presented product will not be nearly as successful as the skillful use of the 12 steps to a successful close. A close look at the 12 steps will illustrate that a lot of hard work, planning, and skillful execution of your plan occurs before you reach Step 11 and ask for the order. The point is that if salespeople understand how each of the 12 steps applies to them and their customers, and if they are capable of performing each step, they will earn the right to close.

In fact, many times the close will occur automatically because it has become the easiest part of the sales presentation. Often the prospect will close for the salesperson, saying: "That sounds great, I'd like to buy that." All that the salesperson has to do is finalize the details and write up the order. Often, though, the prospect will be undecided on the product after the presentation, so the skillful salesperson should develop a number of closing techniques.

Prepare Several Closing Techniques _____

To be able to successfully close more sales, you need to be able to determine your prospect's situation, understand the prospect's attitude toward your presentation, and be prepared to instantly select a closing technique from several techniques you know based on your prospect. For example, suppose you had profiled the prospect as having a big ego, so you planned to use the compliment closing technique (to be discussed shortly). You find the prospect is eager to buy but undecided about which model or the number of products to buy, so you switch to using your standing-room-only closing technique. By changing to a closing technique that fits the situation, you can speed up the sale and still keep your customer satisfied.

Successful salespeople should be able to adapt their planned presentation to any prospect or any situation that may arise. Some salespeople have 5 to 10 closing techniques, each designed for a specific type of situation. The following are eight of the more commonly used closing techniques:

- Alternative choice close.
- Assumptive close.
- Compliment close.
- Summary of benefits close.
- Continuous-yes close.
- Minor-points close.
- T-account of balance sheet close.
- Standing-room-only close.

Whatever product is being sold, whether an industrial or consumer product, these closing techniques can be used to ask your prospect for the order. (See Figure 11–5.)

The Alternative Choice Close Is an Old Favorite

The **alternative choice close** was popularized in the 1930s as the story spread of the Walgreen Drug Company's purchase of 800 dozen eggs at a special price. A sales trainer named Elmer Wheeler suggested to the Walgreen clerks that when a customer asked for a malted milk at a Walgreen fountain, the clerk should say, "Do you want one egg or two?" Customers had not even thought of eggs in their malteds. Now

Figure 11–5
Techniques for Closing the Sale

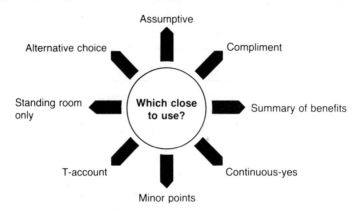

they were faced with the choice of *how many* eggs—not whether or not they wanted an egg. Within one week all 800 dozen of the eggs were sold at a profit. Two examples of the alternative close are:

Which do you prefer—one or two neckties to go with your suit?

Would you prefer the Xerox 6200 or 6400 copier?

As you see, the alternative choice does not give the prospect a choice of buying or not buying, but asks which one or how many items they want to buy. It says, "You are going to buy, so let's settle the details on what you will purchase." Buying nothing at all is not an option.

Take for example the salesperson who says, "Would you prefer the Xerox 6200 or 6400?" This question (1) assumes the customer has a desire to buy one of the copiers, (2) assumes the customer will buy, and (3) allows the customer to have a preference. If the customer prefers the Xerox 6400, you know the prospect is ready to buy, so you begin your close. A customer who says, "I'm not sure," is still in the desire stage, so you continue to discuss product benefits. However, you see that the customer likes both machines. Should the prospect appear to be indecisive, you can ask: "Is there something you are unsure of?" This question probes to find out why your prospect is not ready to choose.

If used correctly, the alternative choice close is a very effective closing technique. It provides a choice between something and something, never between something and nothing. By presenting a choice, you either receive a yes decision or uncover objections, which if successfully met will allow you to come closer to making the sale.

The Assumptive Close

With the **assumptive close,** the salesperson assumes the prospect will buy. Statements can be made such as, "I'll call your order in tonight," or, "I'll have this shipped to you tomorrow." If the prospect does not say anything, you can assume your suggested order has been accepted.

Many times the salesperson who has called on a customer for a long time can fill out the order form, hand it to the customer, and say, "This is what I'm going to send you," or, "This is what I believe you need this month." Many salespeople have earned the trust of their customers to such an extent that the salesperson orders for them. Here the assumptive close is especially effective.

The Compliment Close Inflates the Ego

Everyone likes to receive compliments. The **compliment close** is especially effective when you are talking with a prospect who is a self-styled expert, who has a big ego, or who is in a bad mood. Would-be experts and egotistical prospects both value their own opinion. By complimenting them, you get them to listen and respond favorably to your presentation. The prospect with a low ego, low self-esteem, or one who finds it difficult to come to a decision will also respond favorably to a compliment. Here is an example of a housewares salesperson closing a sale with a grocery retail buyer:

Salesperson: It is obvious you know a great deal about the grocery business. You have every square foot of your store making a good profit. Ms. Stevenson, our products will also provide you with a good profit margin. In fact, our profit will exceed your store's average profit-per-square-foot. And they sell quickly. This added benefit of high turnover will further increase your profits—which you have said is important to you. [He pauses and when there is no response continues.] Given the number of customers coming into your store and our expected sales of these products due to normal turnover, along with our marketing plan, *I suggest you buy.* . . . [He states the products and their quantities.] This will provide you with sufficient quantities to meet your customers' demands for the next two months, plus provide you the profit you expect out of your products. [Now he waits for the response or again asks for the order using the alternative choice or assumptive close.]

All buyers appreciate your recognition of their better points. Conscientious merchants take pride in their ways of doing business; customers coming into the retail clothing store take pride in their appearance; people considering life insurance take pride in looking after their families. So compliment prospects relative to something that will benefit them as you attempt to close the sale. Remember, always make your compliment an honest one. No matter how trusting you may think people are, nearly anyone can detect insincerity in a compliment. When a compliment is not in order, you may choose to summarize the benefits of your product for a specific customer.

The Summary of Benefits Close Is Most Popular

During the sales presentation it is important to remember the main features, advantages, and benefits of interest to the prospect in order to use them successfully during the close. Summarize these benefits in a positive manner so that the prospect agrees with what you are saying; then ask for the order.

Here is an example of a salesperson using the **summary of benefits close** on a prospect. Assume that the salesperson knows that the prospect likes the product's profit margin, delivery schedule, and credit terms.

Salesperson: Ms. Stevenson, you say you like our profit margin, fast delivery, and credit policy. Is that right? [Summary and trial close.]

Prospect: Yes, I do, Chuck.

Salesperson: With the number of customers coming into your store and our expected sales of the products due to normal turnover, along with our marketing plan, *I suggest you buy.* . . . [He states the products and their quantities.] This will provide you sufficient quantities to meet customer demand for the next two months, plus provide you with the profit you expect from your products. I can have the order to you early next week. [Now he waits for her response or again asks for the order using the alternative choice or assumptive close.]

You can easily adapt the *FAB* statements, discussed in Chapter 2, for your summary close. The vacuum cleaner salesperson might say, "As we have discussed, this vacuum cleaner's high speed motor [feature] works twice as fast [advantage] with less effort [advantage], saving you 15 to 30 minutes in cleaning time [benefit] and the aches and pains of pushing a heavy machine [benefit of benefit]. Would you want the Deluxe or the Ambassador model?"

The sporting goods salesperson might say, "As we have said, this ball will give you an extra 10 to 20 yards on your drive [advantage], helping to reduce your score [benefit] because of its new solid core [feature]. Will a dozen be enough?" The air conditioning salesperson could say, "This air conditioner has a high efficiency rating [feature] that will save you 10 percent on your energy costs [benefit] because it uses less electricity [advantage]. Would you want it delivered this week or do you prefer next week?"

The summary close is favored by industrial product manufacturers like Xerox. Emmett Reagan, who is profiled in Chapter 7, says the major closing technique taught at the Xerox Training Center consists of the three basic steps of the summary close, which are (1) determine the key product benefits that interest the prospect during the presentation, (2) summarize these benefits, and (3) make a proposal. The summary of benefits technique is useful when you need a simple, straightforward close, rather than a close aimed at a specific prospect's personality.

The Continuous-Yes Close Generates Positive Responses

The **continuous-yes close** is like the summary close. However, instead of summarizing product benefits, the salesperson develops a series of benefit questions that the prospect must answer.

Salesperson:	Ms. Stevenson, you have said you like our quality products, right?
Prospect:	Yes, that's right.
Salesperson:	And you like our fast delivery?
Prospect:	Yes, I do.
Salesperson:	You also like our profit margin and credit terms?
Prospect:	That's correct.
Salesperson:	Ms. Stevenson, our quality products, fast delivery, profit margin, and good credit terms will provide you with an excellent profit. With the large number of customers you have coming into your store. . . . [Salesperson completes the close as done in the summary of benefits close.]

In this example of the continuous-yes close, the salesperson recognized four product benefits that the prospect liked: (1) the product's quality, (2) fast delivery, (3) profit margin, and (4) favorable credit terms. After the presentation, three questions were used to give the prospect the opportunity to agree that she was impressed with each of the four product benefits. By stacking these positive questions, the salesperson kept the prospect continually saying, "Yes, I like that benefit."

The prospect has now placed herself in a positive frame of mind. Her positive stance toward the product makes it very likely that she will continue to say yes when asked to buy.

You should realize, of course, that some prospects may want to be cute, and relish the thought of seeing the look of surprise on your face when, after they agree to all of your product benefit statements (yes . . . yes . . . yes), they respond to your order request with an unexpected no. Also, some more suspicious prospects may view your continuous-yes close as trickery or as an insult to their intelligence rather than as an aid to them in making a purchase decision. In either case, your calm handling of the situation will reflect a sales professionalism that will both surprise the trickster and impress the suspicious person.

The Minor-Points Close Is Not Threatening

It is sometimes much easier for a prospect to concede several minor points about a product than to make a sweeping decision on whether to buy or not to buy. Big decisions are often difficult for some buyers to make. By getting the prospect to make decisions on a product's minor points, you can subtly lead into the decision to buy.

The **minor-points close** is similar to the alternative choice close. The alternative choice close asks the prospect to make a choice between two products. To some people, this represents a high-risk decision, which they may prefer not to make, whereas the minor-points close asks the prospect to make a low-risk decision on a minor, usually low-cost element of a single product such as delivery dates, optimal features, color, size, payment terms, or order quantity. Single or multiple product element choices may be presented to the prospect. The stereo salesperson says, "Would you prefer the single or multiple record changer for your stereo system?" The Lanier Business Products salesperson asks, "Are you interested in buying or leasing our equipment?" The automobile salesperson asks, "Would you like your car to be air-conditioned?"

This close is widely used when prospects have difficulty in making a decision or when they are not in the mood to buy. It also can be effectively used as a second close. If, for example, the prospect says no to your first close because of difficulty in deciding whether or not to buy, you can close on minor points.

The T-Account or Balance Sheet Close Was Ben Franklin's Favorite

The **T-account close** is based on the process people go through when they make a decision. Some sales trainers refer to it as the Benjamin Franklin close. In his *Poor Richard's Almanac* Benjamin said, "You know, I believe most of my life is going to be made up of making decisions about things. I want to make as many good ones as I possibly can." So in deciding on a course of action, his technique was to take pencil and paper and draw a line down the center of the paper. On one side he put all the pros, and on the other side he put all the cons. Now if there were more cons than pros, he would not do something. If the pros outweighed the cons, then he felt it was a good thing to do; this was the correct decision.

This is actually the process a customer goes through when making a buying decision, weighing the cons against the pros. So at times, it may be a good idea to use this technique. Pros and cons, debits and credits, or to act and not to act are common column headings used today. For example, on a sheet of paper the salesperson draws a large T, placing "to act" (asset) on the left side and "not to act" (liability) on the right side (debit and credit in accounting terms). The salesperson reviews the presentation with the prospect, listing the positive features, advantages, and benefits the prospect likes on the left side, and all negative points on the right. This is designed to show that the product's benefits outweigh its liabilities, and to lead the prospect to conclude that now is the time to buy. If prospects make their own lists, the balance sheet close can be quite convincing. Here is an example:

Salesperson: Ms. Stevenson, here's a pad of paper and a pencil. Bear with me a minute and let's review what we have just talked about. Could you please draw a large *T* on the page and write "To Act" at the top on the left and "Not to Act" on the right. Now, you said you liked our fast delivery. Is that right?

Prospect: Yes.

Salesperson: OK, please write down "fast delivery" in the To Act column. Great! You were impressed with our profit margin and credit terms. Is that right?

Prospect: Yes.

Salesperson: OK, how about writing that down in the left-hand column? Now is there anything that could be improved?

Prospect: Yes, don't you remember? I feel you have a narrow assortment with only one style of broom and one style of mop. [Objection.]

Salesperson: Well, write that down in the right-hand column. Is that everything?

To Act	Not to Act
Fast delivery	Narrow assortment
Good profit	
Good credit	

Prospect: Yes.

Salesperson: Ms. Stevenson, which in your opinion outweighs the other—the reason to act or not to act? [A trial close.]

Prospect: Well, the To Act column does. But it seems I need a better assortment of products. [Same objection again.]

Salesperson: We have found that assortment is not important to most people. A broom and mop are pretty much a broom and mop. They want a good quality product that looks good and will hold up under continuous use. Customers like our products' looks and quality. Aren't these good-looking products? [Trial close showing broom and mop.]

Prospect: Look OK to me. [Positive response—she didn't bring up assortment, so assume you have overcome objection.]

Salesperson: Ms. Stevenson, I can offer you a quality product, fast delivery, excellent profit, and good credit terms. I'd like to suggest this.

You buy one dozen mops and one dozen brooms for each of your 210 stores. However let's consider this first! The XYZ chain found our mops had excellent drawing power when advertised. Their sales of buckets and floor wax doubled. Each store sold an average of 12 mops. [He pauses, listens, and notices her reaction.] You can do the same thing!

Prospect: I'd have to contact the Johnson Wax's salesperson, and I really don't have the time. [A positive buying signal.]

Salesperson: Ms. Stevenson, let me help. I'll call Johnson's and get them to contact you. Also, I'll go by and see your advertising manager to schedule the ads. OK? [Assumptive close.]

Prospect: OK, go ahead, but this stuff had better sell.

Salesperson: [*smiling*] Customers will flock to your stores [He's building a picture in her mind.] looking for mops, polish, and buckets. Say, that reminds me, you will need a dozen buckets for each store. [Continuous-yes, keep talking.] I'll write up the order. [Assumptive.]

Some salespeople recommend that the columns of the T-account be reversed so that the Not to Act column is on the left and the To Act column is on the right. This allows the salesperson first to discuss the reasons not to buy, followed by the reasons to buy, ending the presentation on the positive side. This is a decision that can be made by the salesperson based upon preference.

Modified T-Account or Balance Sheet Close. Some salespeople modify the T-account close by only listing reasons to act in one column. They do not want to remind the prospect of any negative reasons not to buy as they attempt to close the sale. This is very similar to the continuous-yes close. The only difference is that the product benefits are written on a piece of paper.

This is a very powerful sales tool because prospects are mentally considering reasons to buy and not to buy anyway. You may just as well get the reasons out in the open so you can participate and be a part of the decision-making process.

While this close can be used anytime, it is especially useful as one of your secondary or backup closes. For example, if the summary close did not make the sale, go on to your next close, the T-account close. You see, a contrary idea in the mind of the prospect is like steam under pressure, that is, explosive. So when you remove the pressure from the steam by getting an objection out in the open, opposition vaporizes. An objection often becomes a minor one or goes away. Remember, however, if the customer says, "Well, I'm going to buy it," do not say, "Well, let's first take a look at the reasons not to buy." Go ahead and finalize the sale.

The Standing-Room-Only Close Gets Action

What happens if someone tells you that you cannot have something that you have an interest in or would like to have? You instantly want it! When you face an indecisive prospect or if you want to have the prospect purchase a larger quantity, indicate that if they do not act now they may *not* be able to buy in the future. To get the prospect to act at once, you can use the **standing-room-only close:**

> "I'm not sure if I have your size. Would you want them if I have them in stock?"

> "My customers have been buying all we can produce. I'm not sure if I have any left to sell you."

> "Well, I know you are thinking of ordering *x* amount, but we really need to order . . . (a larger amount) . . . because we now have it in stock, and I don't think we will be able to keep up with demand and fill your summer order."

> "The cost of this equipment will increase 10 percent next week. Can I ship it today or do you want to pay the higher price?"

For the right product, person, and situation, this is an excellent close. Both retail and industrial salespeople can use this technique to get the prospect so excited they cannot wait to buy. However, it should only be used in complete honesty. Prospects realize that factors such as labor strikes, weather, transportation, inflation, and inventory shortages could make it difficult to buy in the future. You can do them a favor by getting them to buy now using the standing-room-only close.

The Probability Close

When the prospect gives you that famous, "I want to think it over" or some variation of that objection, try saying, "Ms. Prospect, that would be perfectly fine. I understand your desire to think it over, but let me ask you this—when I call you back next week, what is the probability, in percentage terms out of a total of 100, that you and I will be doing business?" Then pause, and don't say another word until the prospect speaks.

The prospect's response can generally be divided into three possible categories:

1. More than 50 percent but less than 85 percent for buying. If your prospects respond in this range, try to ask what the remaining percent is against; then pause and don't say another word. When you become skilled in this technique, you will actually see prospects blink as they focus on their real objections.

Many times, we hear that prospects want to think things over. It is not because they want to delay the decision; it is because they don't fully understand what is bothering them. The **probability close** permits your prospects to focus in on their real objections. Once you have a real objection, you can then convert that objection with a persuasive sales argument.

2. Above 85 percent but not 100 percent for buying. If they're in this range, you recognize that there is a minor probability against you, and you might want to say, "As it is almost a certainty that we're going to be doing business together, why wait until next week? Let's go ahead right now; and if you decide in the next couple of days that you want to change your mind, I'll gladly tear up your order. But let's get a running start on this project together."

When prospects indicate a very high percentage of probability, you can use their own statements as a lever to push them over the top.

3. Less than 50 percent for buying. This is a signal that there is little, if any, chance that you will ever close this particular sale. The only appropriate tactic is to go back to square one and start the reselling process. It is amazing how many professional salespeople take a look at a closing situation and expect the prospect to say 80–20 as a probability in their favor, and instead hear 80–20 . . . against.

The probability close permits prospects to focus in on their own objections. It allows the true, or hidden, objections to surface. You'll soon realize that the more prospects fight you and the less candid they are about the probability of closing, the less likely they are to buy anything.

Prepare a Multiple Close Sequence

By keeping several difficult closes ready to aid you in any situation, you will put yourself in a better position to close more sales. Also the use of a multiple close sequence, combined with methods to overcome objections, will greatly enhance your chance of making a sale.

For example, you could begin with a summary close. Assuming the buyer says no, you could rephrase the objection, and then use an alternative close. If again the buyer says no, you could then use the five-question sequence method for overcoming objections, cycling through it two or three times.*

Figure 11–6 gives an example of multiple closes incorporating tech-

---

* See Chapter 10 for correct procedures on overcoming objections.

Figure 11–6

Multiple Closes Incorporating Techniques for Overcoming Objections

Salesperson:	So we have found that the Octron bulb is going to reduce your storage space requirements for your replacement stock. It offers a higher color output for your designers, reducing their eye fatigue and shadowing. [Summary benefits.] Should I arrange for delivery within the week?
Buyer:	Well, those are all good points, but I'm still not prepared to buy. It's too costly.
Salesperson:	What you're saying is "You want to know what particular benefits my product has that make it worth its slightly higher price?" Is that correct?
Buyer:	Yes, I guess so.
Salesperson:	Earlier we saw that considering the extended life of the lamps and their energy savings you can actually save $375 each year by replacing your present lamps with GE Watt-Misers. This shows that you actually save money using our product. Right? [Trial close.]
Buyer:	Yes, I guess you're right.
Salesperson:	Great! Do you prefer installation this weekend or after regular business hours next week? [Alternative close.]
Buyer:	Neither. I need to think about it more.
Salesperson:	There must be some good reason why you're hesitating to go ahead now. Do you mind if I ask what it is? [Question 1 in sequence.]
Buyer:	I don't think I can afford relamping all at one time.
Salesperson:	In addition to that, is there another reason for not going ahead? [Question 2 in sequence.]
Buyer:	No.
Salesperson:	Just supposing you could convince yourself that group relamping is less expensive than spot replacing . . . then you'd want to go ahead with it? [Question 3.]
Buyer:	I guess so.
Salesperson:	Group relamping is not an absolute necessity; however, it does allow you to realize immediate energy savings on all of your fixtures. It actually saves you much of the labor costs of spot replacement because the lamps are installed with "production line" efficiency. See what I mean? [Trial close.]
Buyer:	Yes, I do.
Salesperson:	Would you like installation at night or on the weekend? [Alternative close.]
Buyer:	I'd still like to think about it.
Salesperson:	There must be another reason why you're hesitating to go ahead now. Do you mind if I ask what it is? [Question 1.]
Buyer:	We just don't have the money now to make that kind of investment.
Salesperson:	In addition to that, is there any other reason for not going ahead? [Question 2.]
Buyer:	No. My supervisor just will not let me buy anything.
Salesperson:	You agree you could save money for your company on this purchase—right?
Buyer:	Yes.
Salesperson:	How about calling your supervisor now and asking about how much money we can save him in addition to reducing your storage space and eye fatigue of your employees? Maybe both of us could visit your supervisor.

niques to overcome objections. The successful closing of the sale often requires both methods to overcome objections and closing techniques.

Close Based on the Situation

Since different closing techniques work best for certain situations, salespeople often identify the common objections they encounter and develop specific approaches to closing designed to overcome these ob-

Table 11–1
Closing Techniques Based upon Situation

Situation	\multicolumn{9}{c}{Approach to Closing}	Why
	Alternative	Compliment	Summary	Continuous-Yes	Minor-Points	Assumptive	T-Account	Standing-Room-Only	Probability	
Customer is indecisive	X	X	X	X			X	X	X	Forces a decision
Customer is expert or egotist		X					X		X	Lets "expert" make the decision
Customer is hostile		X	X						X	Positive strokes
Customer is a friend						X			X	You take care of the small things
Customer has predetermined beliefs							X		X	Benefits outweigh disbeliefs
Customer is greedy, wants a deal								X	X	Buy now

jections. Table 11–1 lists some of the ways in which different closing techniques can be used to meet objections.

Assume for example that a buyer has a predetermined belief that a competitor's product is what is needed. The salesperson could use the T-account approach to show how a product's benefits are greater than those of a competitor. In developing your sales presentation, you should review your customer profile and develop your main closing technique, along with several alternatives. By being prepared for each sales call, you will experience an increase in your confidence and enthusiasm, which will result in a more positive selling attitude so that you can help your customer and reach your personal goals.

Research Reinforces Book's Sales Success Strategies

This chapter ends the discussion on the parts of the sales presentation. While it is difficult to summarize all of the sales success strategies you should use, which are discussed throughout the book, one research report reinforces several of the key procedures that will improve your sales performance.

The research sought to examine two key questions all salespeople frequently ask themselves: What makes one sales call a success and another a failure? Do salespeople make common mistakes that prevent success?

To answer questions such as these, Xerox Learning Systems, a subsidiary of the Xerox Corporation, enlisted a team of observers to monitor and analyze more than 500 personal sales calls of 24 different sales organizations. The product and services sold ranged from computers to industrial refuse disposal.

Mike Radick, the Xerox senior development specialist overseeing the study, states that the average successful sales call observed was 33 minutes long. During that call, the salesperson asked 13.6 questions and described 6.4 product benefits and 7.7 product features. Meanwhile, the customer described 2.2 different needs, raised 1.0 objections, made 2.8 statements of acceptance, and asked 7.7 questions.

The observers noted that it does not appear to matter whether the salesperson is 28 or 48 years old, is male or female, or has 2 or 20 years' experience. What matters is the ability to use certain skills and avoid common errors. The following are six common mistakes that the researchers found prevented successful sales calls:

Tells Instead of Sells; Doesn't Ask Enough Questions.   The salesperson does most of the talking. Instead of asking questions to determine a customer's interest, the salesperson charges ahead and rattles off product benefits. This forces the customer into the passive role of listening to details that may not be of any interest. As a result, the customer becomes increasingly irritated.

For example, a person selling a computerized payroll system may tell a customer how much clerical time can be saved by using this service. However, if clerical time is not a concern, then the customer has no interest in learning about ways to reduce time spent on payroll processing. On the other hand, the same customer may have a high need for more accurate recordkeeping and be extremely interested in the computerized reports the system can generate.

Over-Controls the Call; Asks Too Many Closed-End Questions.   This sales dialogue resembles an interrogation, and the customer has limited opportunities to express needs. The over-controlling salesperson steers the conversation to subjects the salesperson wants to talk about without regard to the customer. When the customer does talk, the salesperson often fails to listen or respond, or doesn't acknowledge the importance of what the customer says. As a result, the customer is alienated, and the sales call fails.

Doesn't Respond to Customer Needs with Benefits.   Instead, the salesperson leaves it up to the customer to infer how those features will satisfy his or her needs. Consider the customer who needs a high-speed

machine. The salesperson responds with information about heat tolerance, but doesn't link that to the rate at which the equipment can turn
out the customer's product. As a result, the customer becomes confused, loses interest, and the call fails.

The research shows a direct relationship between the result of a call
and the number of different benefits given in response to customer
needs; the more need-related benefits cited, the greater the probability
of success.

Doesn't Recognize Needs; Gives Benefits Prematurely.   For example,
a customer discussing telephone equipment mentions that some clients
complain that the line is always busy. The salesperson points out the
benefits of his answering service, but the customer responds that busy
lines are not very important since people are likely to call back. In this
case, the customer is not concerned enough to want to solve the problem.

Doesn't Recognize or Handle Negative Attitudes Effectively.   The
salesperson fails to recognize customer statements of objection (opposition), indifference (no need), or skepticism (doubts). What isn't dealt
with effectively remains on the customer's mind, and, left with a negative attitude, the customer will not make a commitment. The research
also shows that customer skepticism, indifference, and objection are
three different attitudes. Each has a different effect on the call, and each
requires a different strategy for selling success.

**Makes Weak Closing Statements; Doesn't Recognize When or How to
Close.**   In one extreme case that was observed, the customer tried to
close the sale on a positive note, but the salesperson failed to recognize
the cue and continued selling until the customer lost interest. The lesson
in this is that successful salespeople are alert to closing opportunities
throughout the call.

The most powerful way to close a sales call involves a summary of
the benefits that interested the customer. Success was achieved in three
out of every four calls that included this closing technique.

Keys to Improved Selling

How is the bridge from average to successful salesperson made? Xerox
found it involves learning and using each of the following skills:

- Ask questions to gather information and uncover needs.
- Recognize when a customer has a real need and how the benefits of
  the product or service can satisfy it.

- Establish a balanced dialogue with customers.

- Recognize and handle negative customer attitudes promptly and directly.

- Use a benefit summary and an action plan requiring commitment when closing.[2]

Learning and using these five selling skills, plus others emphasized throughout the book, in combination with your own natural ability and positive mental attitude will allow you to be a successful, professional salesperson.

Summary of Major Selling Issues

Closing is the process of helping people make decisions that will benefit them. You help people make those decisions by asking them to buy. The close of the sale is the next logical sequence after your presentation. At this time you finalize the details of the sale (earlier your prospect has been convinced to buy). You should constantly be looking and listening for buying signals from your prospect in order to know when to close. It is time to close the sale anytime the prospect is ready, whether at the beginning or at the end of your presentation.

As you prepare to close the sale, be sure you have presented a complete story on your proposition and that your prospect completely understands what you have presented. Tailor your close to each prospect's personality and see the situation from the prospect's viewpoint. You should remember that you may make your presentation and close too early, causing the prospect to say no instead of "I don't understand your proposition, and I don't want to be taken advantage of." This is why you should never take the first no. It is another reason why you should use a trial close immediately before you close. But no matter when or how to close, do so in a positive, confident, and enthusiastic manner in order to better serve your prospect and help you reach your personal goals. Learn and abide by the 12 steps to a successful closing.

Plan and rehearse closing techniques for each prospect. Develop closing techniques that are natural for you or consider using or adopting closes such as the alternative, compliment, summary, continuous-yes, minor decision, assumption, T-account, or the standing-room-only close. Be sure to consider the situation you face and be ready to switch from your planned close should your prospect's situation be different than you had anticipated.

A good closer has a strong desire to close each sale. Rarely, if ever, should you accept the first no as the final answer. If you work in a professional manner, you should be able to close a minimum of three to five times.

Do not become upset or unnerved if a problem creeps up when you are ready to close. Keep a cool head, determine any objections, overcome them, and try to close again—you can't make a sale until you ask for the order! Remember to take at least three strikes before you count yourself out of the sale.

Review and Discussion Questions

1. Explain the term *close* as it relates to the sales presentation. Include in your answer a discussion of when to close, the meaning and examples of buying signals, and a discussion of the use of multiple closes.

2. What are the essential elements a salesperson should consider in closing a prospect?

3. Why are some people better at closing a sale than other people? Is it luck?

4. Explain the importance of not accepting the first no and thus using multiple closes even under hostile circumstances.

5. Discuss five closing techniques and give examples of each technique.

6. A salesperson should use a closing technique that is simple and straightforward and should ask the prospect only to buy rather than do something in addition to buying. In which of the following examples, if any, is the salesperson suggesting something to the buyer which is actually a close, rather than something the buyer has to do in addition to buying?
   a. "If you have no objection, I'll go out to the warehouse now to see about reserving space for this new item."
   b. "To get this promotion off right, we should notify each of your store managers. I've already prepared a bulletin for them. Should *I* arrange to have a copy sent to each manager, or do *you* want to do it?"
   c. "To get this promotion off right, we should notify each of your store managers. I've already prepared a bulletin for them. On my way out, I can drop it off with the secretary."
   d. "We should contact the warehouse manager about reserving a space for this new item. Do you want to do it now or after I've left?"

7. Buying signals come in numerous forms. When you receive a buying signal, you should stop your presentation and move in for the close of your sale. For each of the following seven situations, choose the appropriate response to your prospect's buying signal that leads most directly to a close.
   a. "Can I get it in blue?" Your answer should be:

      (1) "Yes."
      (2) "Do you want it in blue?"
      (3) "It comes in three colors, including blue."
  b. "What's your price?" Your answer should be:
      (1) "In what quantity?"
      (2) To quote a specific price.
      (3) "In which grade?"
  c. "What kind of terms do you offer?" Your answer should be:
      (1) To provide specific terms.
      (2) "Terms would have to be arranged."
      (3) "What kind of terms do you want?"
  d. "How big an order do I have to place to get your best price?" Your answer should be:
      (1) A schedule of quantity prices.
      (2) A specific-sized order.
      (3) "What size order do you want to place?"
  e. "When will you have a new model?" Your answer should be:
      (1) A specific date.
      (2) "Do you want our newest model?"
      (3) "This is our newest model."
  f. "What would be the smallest trial order I could place with you?" Your answer should be:
      (1) A specific quantity.
      (2) "How small an order do you want?"
      (3) A variety of order sizes.
  g. "When could you make delivery?" Your answer should be:
      (1) "That depends on the size of your order. What order size do you have in mind?"
      (2) A specific delivery date.
      (3) "When do you want delivery?"

8. Which of the following is the most frequently committed sin in closing? Why?
  a. Asking for the order too early.
  b. Not structuring the presentation toward a closing.
  c. Not asking for the order.

9. In the appropriate circumstances, do you agree that a good closing technique is to ask the customer outright (but at the right time), "Well, how about it? May I have the factory ship you a carload?" Why do you agree or disagree?

10. After completing a presentation that has included all of your product's features, advantages, and benefits, you should not delay in asking the customer, "How much of the product do you wish to order?" Is this statement true or false? Why?

11. Each visual aid you use during your presentation can be designed to allow the customer to say yes to your main selling points. What

should your visual aids include to allow you to gauge customer interest and help to move to the close? What are several examples?

12. "Now, let's review what we've talked about. We've agreed that the Mohawk's secondary backing and special latex glue make the carpet more durable and contribute to better appearance. In addition, you felt that our direct-to-customer delivery system would save you a lot of money and time. Shall I send you our wall sample display or would you be interested in stocking some 9 by 12s?"

   a. The salesperson's closing statement above helps to ensure customer acceptance by doing which of the following:

     (1) Summarizing benefits the customer agreed were important.

     (2) Giving an alternative.

     (3) Assuming that agreement has been reached.

   b. The salesperson ends the closing statement by:

     (1) Asking if the customer has any other questions.

     (2) Asking if the product will meet the customers' requirements.

     (3) Requesting a commitment from the customer.

13. "Assuming agreement has been reached" reflects the kind of attitude you should project when making a closing statement. When you make a close, nothing you say should reflect doubt, hesitation, or uncertainty. Which of the following salesperson's remarks assume agreement?

   a. "If you feel that Munson is really what you want. . . ."

   b. "Let me leave you two today and deliver the rest next week. . . ."

   c. "Well, if you purchase. . . ."

   d. "Well, it looks as if maybe. . . ."

   e. "We've agreed that. . . ."

   f. "When you purchase the X-7100. . . ."

   g. "Why don't you try a couple, if you like. . . ."

14. A good rule is "Get the order and get out." Do you agree? Why?

15. The real estate salesperson is out showing the property to a couple who look at the house and say, "Gee, this is great. They've taken good care of this place, and the rugs and drapes just go perfectly. Do you think they'd be willing to leave the rugs and drapes?" What should the salesperson do or say? Why?

Projects

1. Assume you are interviewing for a sales job and there are only five minutes remaining. You are very interested in the job, and you

know if the company is interested in hiring you they will invite you for a visit to their local distribution center and have you work with one of their salespeople for one day. What are several closing techniques you could use to ask for the visit? Give examples of each.

2. Visit several retail stores or manufacturing plants in your local area and ask their purchasing agents what they like and do not like about the close of the sale when they are contacted by salespeople. See if they have already made up their minds to buy or not to buy before the salesperson closes the sale. Ask them how they feel a salesperson should ideally ask for their business.

3. Develop a buyer-seller written script with a minimum of four closes. Use different closing techniques and methods to overcome the objections. Be prepared to role-play your script in class.

Cases

11–1   Skaggs Omega

Skaggs Omega, a large chain of supermarkets, has mailed you an inquiry on hardware items. They specifically wanted to know about your hammers, screwdrivers, and nails. On your arrival, you make your presentation to the purchasing agent, Linda Johnson. You start out by stating that you had visited several of their stores. You discuss your revolving retail display, which contains an assortment of the three items Johnson had mentioned in her inquiry, and relate the displays and advantages and features to benefits for Skaggs.

During your presentation, Johnson has listened but has said very little and has not given you any buying signals. However, it does appear she is interested. She did not object to your price nor did she raise any other objections.

You are approaching the end of your presentation, and it is time to close. Actually you have said everything you can think of.

Questions:

1. What is the best way to ask Johnson for the order?
   a. "How do you like our products, Ms. Johnson?"
   b. "What assortment do you prefer, the A or B assortment?"
   c. "Can we go ahead with the order?"
   d. "If you'll just okay this order form, Ms. Johnson, we'll have each of your stores receive a display within two weeks."

2. Discuss the remaining alternatives ranking them from good to bad and state what you feel would happen if a salesperson responded in that manner.

11–2 Central Hardware Supply

Sam Gillespie, owner of Central Hardware Supply, was referred to you by a mutual friend. Gillespie had been thinking of dropping two of their product suppliers of home building supplies. "The sale should be guaranteed," your friend had stated.

Your friend's information was correct, and your presentation to Gillespie convinces you he will benefit from buying from you. He comments as you conclude your presentation, "Looks like your product will solve our problem. I'd like to think this over, however. Could you call me tomorrow or the next day?"

Questions:

1. The best way to handle this would be to:
    a. Follow his suggestion.
    b. Ignore his request and try a second close.
    c. Probe further. You might ask, "The fact that you have to think this over suggests that I haven't convinced you. Is there something I've omitted or failed to satisfy you with?"

2. What would be your second and third choices? Why?

12 WINNING IN THE LONG RUN: BUILDING A RELATIONSHIP THROUGH SERVICE

Learning Objectives

1. To discuss how follow-up and service result in account penetration and improved sales.

2. To present the eight steps involved in increasing your customer's sales.

3. To review the importance of properly handling customer's returned goods requests and complaints in a professional manner.

4. To learn the attitude of several of the top salespeople in the United States toward serving their customers.

Profile

Morgan Jennings
Richard D. Irwin, Inc.

After graduating from the University of Richmond in 1968, I entered the Army, spending military service time in Fort Bliss and Fort Hood, Texas. My duties included being a training officer for basic trainees, athletic officer for Fort Bliss, and operations officer for a tank battalion. After two years' active duty, I went to work for BioQuest, a division of Becton Dickinson, where I had sales, management, and service responsibility for the state of Virginia. Our product line included Prepared Media and Falcon Plastics, which mainly consisted of disposable labware. I met with key laboratory personnel in the hospital, university, and industrial research centers.

In 1973, I went to work for Richard D. Irwin, Inc., then a subsidiary of Dow Jones & Company, Inc., as a publisher's field representative. Irwin, one of the largest and oldest publishers of business books, enjoys a fine reputation for quality and service.

There is no secret formula for success in college publishing. A number of elements must be considered, and among the most important are service and mental attitude.

Irwin is the most customer-oriented publisher of college textbooks. At Irwin, service is not just a competitive edge; it is The competitive edge *of the 80s, 90s, and beyond. We are in a highly competitive industry, and a number of publishers provide high-quality products; however, we feel that the quality of our texts is distinguished by the accompanying service. The philosophy at Irwin is that service is a commodity, and as much emphasis is placed on service quality as on the textbooks themselves.*

In our profession, staying close to the professor is crucial. Their needs are constantly changing. Irwin salespeople focus their attention on the professor's current situation, frame of mind, and need. This leads to a level of responsiveness, attentiveness, and willingness to help that makes our service superior in the professor's mind. He or she will want to continue doing business with Irwin; and through a networking process, our reputation as a service-oriented company is enhanced.

"Richard D. Irwin, Inc., carries the concept of service one step further than most publishers," says Morgan Jennings. "Irwin's mission is to not only serve the needs of the customer, but to also serve the needs of the person serving the customer. The corporate support given our salespeople is unsurpassed in the industry.

"In recent years, Irwin has gone through a major revitalization program. Important changes have been made in the systems of accounting, computerization, customer service, production, and order entry. All of this has been done with a goal of providing the field staff with better support and our customers with better service.

"An example of this support was shown in a recent follow-up call at Old Dominion University, where they had selected our intermediate accounting text. Part of the decision was based on our superior coverage of pensions—the new rulings had made their current text obsolete in this area. This presented a problem, though, because one of the later sections of this course would be forced to use a text with out-of-date pension material or to buy a new text. When I relayed the situation back to Irwin, the company provided the students with photocopies of the new pension chapter from the adopted text. This kind of consideration for both students' and professors' needs has greatly enhanced our reputation for service at this university."

The often used cliché, "last but not least," applies to this chapter, which ends our discussion of the elements of the selling process. As Irwin's Morgan Jennings indicates, follow-up and service are very important to the success of a salesperson in today's competitive markets. This chapter discusses the importance of follow-up and service, ways of keeping your customers, methods of helping them increase their sales, and procedures for handling customer complaints. It ends by emphasizing the need for you to act as a professional salesperson when servicing your accounts.

Super Salespeople Discuss Service

Providing service after the sale to customers is important, no matter what type of company, product, or service you represent. To illustrate the importance of service to the professional salesperson, four men, each of whom has been referred to as one of America's greatest salespeople, discuss the importance of service in selling real estate, steel, information systems, and jewelry.

Rich Port built a successful real estate business in Chicago that now consists of 28 offices, 375 salespeople, and generates over $300 million a year in sales. How? Rich explains his success in this manner:

In most fields, a salesperson can offer his customer a product that has some differences from competitive products. But when we sell a residential property, we're often selling the same product that the buyer can purchase from the real estate office down the street. So in order for us to offer something better, we must give them more service. The key to success in the real estate business is service.[1]

In discussing service, Mike Curto, a retired group vice president of the United States Steel Corporation, says:

You've got to realize that what we're selling isn't a whole lot different from what our competitor can produce. In steel, we take some iron ore, refine it, and eventually end up with a product of a semifinished nature . . . we have to sell service. Our salesman must convince the customer that we're the best in our industry, and that over the long run he's better off doing business with us.

A salesperson has to develop a customer's confidence; the customer must believe that U.S. Steel products are not only equal to what the competition sells, but are the best that can be produced in that particular line. And the salesperson better be sure that the products are as good as he says they are, because he's going to be calling back on that customer many times throughout the year.[2]

These two men both stated that their service or product is similar to those offered by the competition. What about a product like computers sold by such companies as IBM, Honeywell, Burroughs, and Amdahl? Francis G. (Buck) Rogers, a recent vice president of marketing for IBM, believes one of the keys to success at IBM is service. He says:

IBM means service. With IBM, nothing is successfully sold until it's successfully installed. Now the salesperson goes through the installation phase, including educating the customer, teaching people how the products will actually perform, and showing them how to properly apply the product. Finally, the equipment is delivered; this can be almost a year later. At any rate, that's the installation phase of the sale.

Beyond that, we take it much further. We're dealing with a customer on a continual basis, for example, trying to find new applications to further justify the equipment. At IBM, we're often leasing a fairly expensive piece of equipment, and unless we continue to give the customer the best possible service, always looking out for his best interest, we're taking the risk of losing him.[3]

Turn Follow-Up and Service into a Sale

High-performing salespeople have the ability to convert follow-up and service situations into sales. Jack Pruett of Bailey Banks & Biddle, a retailer of fine jewelry, gives you several examples:

I send customers a thank you card immediately after the sale, and after two weeks I call again to thank them and see if they are pleased with their purchase. If the purchase is a gift, like at Christmas, I wait on contacting the customer or contact the spouse at the office. This has been a key to my success in building a relationship and in farming or prospecting. Very often I get a lead.

Here is how it works. In two weeks they have shown it around to someone who has made a comment. I start with, "Is everything OK?" Then I say, "Well, I know Judy [or Jack] is real proud of it, and I'm sure she's [he's] shown it to someone—parents, family, friends. I was curious if there is anyone I could help who is interested in something. I'd like to talk to them or have you call and see if they'd like me to call them." If I've done a good job, the customer feels good about letting me call this individual and will help me. If I wait too long to call they say, "Well, someone was asking about it, but I've forgotten who it was."

My biggest sale to a single customer was $120,000. It took about two weeks. A man initially called asking for 12 diamonds to give 2 stones to each of his children. In handling this, I found some other pieces I felt were good for him—a ruby ring, a 4.62 sapphire ring, a gold and diamond bracelet, and two other rings. He bought everything. Thus, much of my success comes from follow-ups, suggestion selling [when someone comes in for something and they end up buying other things], or service situations. Once you realize you can turn routine situations into sales, retail selling becomes exciting and challenging.

Based on the statements of these four successful sales-oriented individuals alone, it is easy to see the importance of customer service before, after, and between sales. You should know as much as possible about each of your accounts in order to provide the amount of service necessary to keep your buyers happy.

Account Penetration Is a Secret to Success

Follow-up and service create goodwill between a salesperson and the customer, which in the long run will increase sales faster relative to the salesperson who does not provide such service. By contacting the customer after the sale to see that the maximum benefit is being derived from the purchase, a salesperson lays the foundation for a positive business relationship. Emmett Reagan of Xerox says:

It should be borne in mind that there is still much work to be done after making the sale. Deliveries must be scheduled, installations planned, and once the system is operational we must monitor to assure that our product is doing precisely as represented. This activity gives us virtually unlimited access to the account, which moves us automatically back to the first phase of the cycle. We now have the opportunity to seek out new needs, develop them, and find new problems that require solutions. Only this time it's a lot easier because, by now, we have the most competitive edge of all, a satisfied customer.

The ability to work and contact people throughout the account, discussing your products, is referred to as *account penetration.* Successful penetration of an account allows you to properly service that account by uncovering its needs and problems. Achieving successful account penetration is dependent on your knowledge of that account's key personnel and their situation. If you do not have a feel for an account's situation, you reduce your chances of maximizing your sales in that account.

Tailor your presentation to meet your buyers' objectives in a manner that will benefit them. By knowing your buyers, their firms, and other key personnel, you are better able to uncover their needs or problems and develop a presentation that fulfills these needs or solves these problems. Account penetration can be determined by:

- Your total and major brand sales growth in an account.
- Distribution of the number of products in a product line, including sizes, used or merchandised by an account.
- Level of cooperation you obtain, such as reduced resale prices, shelf space, advertising and display activity, discussion with their salespeople, and freedom to visit with various people in the account.
- Your reputation as the authority on your type of merchandise for the buyer.

As a general rule, the greater your account penetration, the greater your chances of maximizing sales within the account. Earning the privilege to freely move around in the account allows you to better uncover prospect needs and to discuss your products with people throughout the firm. As people begin to know you and believe that you are there to help them, they allow you to do things that will ultimately increase your sales, such as increasing your shelf space or talking with the users of your industrial equipment in the account's manufacturing facilities. A good sign that you have successfully penetrated an account is when one of your competitors dismally says to another, "Forget that account; it's already sewn up."

Service Can Keep Your Customers

You work days, weeks, even months to convert prospects into customers. What can you do to ensure they will continue to buy from you in the future? After landing a major account, there are six factors you ought to consider.

First: Concentrate on improving your account penetration. As discussed earlier, account penetration is critical in uncovering prospect needs or problems and in being able to consistently recommend effective solutions through the purchase of your products. This allows you to demonstrate that you have a customer's best interests at heart and are there to help.

Second: Contact new accounts on a frequent and regular schedule. In determining the frequency of calls you should consider:

- Present sales and/or potential future sales to this account.

- Number of orders you expect to be placed in a year.

- Number of product lines sold to the account.

- Complexity, servicing, and redesign requirements of the products purchased by the account.

Since the amount of time spent servicing an account may vary from minutes to hours to days, you should be flexible in developing a call frequency for each of your customers. Typically, you should invest your sales time in direct proportion to the actual or potential sales represented by each account. The most productive number of calls is reached at the point where additional calls do not increase sales to the customer. This relationship of sales volume to sales calls is referred to as the *response function* of the customer to the salesperson's calls.

Third: Handle your customers' complaints promptly. This is an excellent opportunity to prove to your customers that they and their businesses are important to you, and you sincerely care about them. The speed with which you handle even the most trivial complaint will show the value you place on that customer.

Fourth: Always do what you say you will do. Nothing can destroy your relationship with a customer faster than not following through on what you have promised. Promises made and subsequently broken are not tolerated by professional buyers. They have placed their faith (and sometimes reputation) in you by purchasing your products, so you must be faithful to them to ensure their future support.

Fifth: Provide service as you would to royalty. By providing your client with money-saving products and problem-solving ideas, you can become almost indispensable. You are an advisor to listen to rather than an adversary to haggle with. Provide all of the assistance you can. As State Farm Insurance agent Charlotte Cornett says in Figure 12–1, "We're there to help."[4]

Sixth: Show your appreciation. A buyer once told me, "I'm responsible for putting the meat and potatoes on your table," and that was right. Customers contribute to your success, and in return you should show your appreciation. Thank them for their business, do them favors. Here are several practical suggestions to consider:

- Although you may be hundreds of miles away, phone immediately

Figure 12-1

whenever you've thought of something or seen something that may solve one of your customer's problems.

- Mail clippings of things that may interest your customers, even if the material has no bearing on what you're selling. This could be items from trade journals, magazines, newspapers, or newsletters.

- Write congratulatory notes to customers who have been elected to office, promoted to higher positions, given awards, and so forth.

- Send clippings about your customers' families, such as marriages, births, and various activities.

- Send holiday cards. If you limit yourself to just one card for the entire year, send an Easter card, Fourth of July card, Thanksgiving card. This is apt to make a bigger impression on your customers because few people receive holiday cards other than at Christmas.

Can Someone Please Help Me!?

Customer:	May I speak to Frank, please? I want to reorder.
Supplier:	Frank isn't with us anymore. May someone else help you?
Customer:	What happened to Frank? He has all my specs; I didn't keep a record.
Supplier:	Let me give you to Roger: he's taken over Frank's accounts.
Customer:	Roger, you don't know me, but maybe Frank filled you in. I want to reorder.
Salesperson:	You want to reorder what?
Customer:	I want to repeat the last order, but increase your number 067 to 48.
Salesperson:	What else was in the order?
Customer:	Frank had a record of it. It's got to be in his file.
Salesperson:	Frank isn't here anymore, and I don't have his records.
Customer:	Who does?
Salesperson:	I don't know. I'm new here, so you'll have to fill me in on your requirements. Are you a new customer?
Customer:	Does four years make me new?
Salesperson:	Well, sir, you are new to me. How long ago did you place your order?
Customer:	Last month.
Salesperson:	What day last month?
Customer:	I don't remember; Frank always kept track of it. Maybe I could speak to the sales manager?
Salesperson:	You mean Mort?
Customer:	No, I think his name is Sam.
Salesperson:	Sam left us about the same time as Frank. I can ask Mort to call you. However, I'm sure he doesn't have your file either.
Customer:	Roger, have you ever heard that your best prospect is your present customer?
Salesperson:	Is that true?
Customer:	I don't think so.

Multiply that conversation by a thousand, and you have the biggest deterrent to sales I know.

- Send annual birthday cards. Of course in order to start this process, you'll have to subtly find out what months your prospects were born, but this can be done easily.
- Prepare and mail a brief newsletter, perhaps quarterly, keeping your customers informed on important matters.

These are just a few of the many practical, down-to-earth ways you can remember your customers. Undoubtedly, you'll think of others. But the important thing is to personalize whatever you send.

More specifically, it doesn't take much thought, energy, or time to send a card, newspaper clipping, or copy of an article. The secret of impressing your customers is to personalize the material with a couple of sentences in your own handwriting. But be sure it's legible. Print your short message, if necessary.

You Lose a Customer—Keep on Trucking!

All salespeople suffer losses, either through the loss of a sale or an entire account as a competitor takes over. Four things can be done to win back a customer:

1. Visit and investigate. The first thing to do is to contact the buyer and your friends within the account to determine why the customer did not buy from you. Be sure to get the real reason.

2. Be professional. If you have completely lost the customer to a competitor, let the customer know you have appreciated past business, that you still value the customer's friendship, and that you are still friendly. Remember to assure this lost account that you are ready to earn future business.

3. Don't be unfriendly. Never criticize the competing product your customer has purchased. If it was a bad decision, let the customer discover it. Sales is never having to say, "I told you so!"

4. Keep calling. Treat a former customer like a prospect. Continue to make your calls in your normal manner, presenting your product's benefits without directly comparing them to the competition.

Like a professional athlete, a professional salesperson takes defeat gracefully, moving on to the next contest, and performing so well that victories totally overshadow any losses. One method of compensating for the loss of one account is to increase sales to existing accounts.

Increasing Your Customer's Sales

In order to maximize your sales to a customer, you should develop a customer benefit program. This means the account uses in business, or sells to customers, a level of merchandise equal to its maximum sales potential. The salesperson has only two methods to do this:

1. Have present customers buy *more* of a product that they are currently using.

2. Have present customers buy the same products to use for different purposes. A Johnson & Johnson retail sales representative may encourage accounts to stock the firm's baby shampoo in both the infant care *and* adult toiletries sections of their establishments.

It is often not difficult to sell repeat orders; however, to maximize sales in an account, for example with a retailer, you must persuade the customer to consistently promote your product through advertisements, displays, and reduced prices. In order to increase your sales with a customer, the following steps can be taken. Certainly each step cannot be used in all situations, but if followed some or all of them can help increase your sales.

Step 1. Develop an account penetration program. Develop a master plan for each of your accounts consisting of specific actions you should take directed toward both developing friends within the account and increasing sales.

Step 2. Examine your distribution. Review the merchandise currently used or carried in inventory. If the account is not using or carrying some of your merchandise, concentrate on improving your distribution. For example, if you have four sizes of a product and the account only carries one or two of them, develop a plan to persuade the customer to carry all four sizes. A general goal may be to have each of your accounts carrying all sizes of your products.

Step 3. Keep merchandise in the warehouse and on the shelf. Never allow the account to run out of stock. Stockouts result in lost sales for your firm and your account. Routine calls on your customers will help to avoid stockouts. If the account is critically low on merchandise, telephone in an emergency order. Quick service can maintain, or even increase, your credibility as a sales professional.

Step 4. Fight for shelf space and shelf positioning. If you are selling consumer goods, you should constantly seek to obtain the best shelf space and aisle position. On each sales call, stock the shelf, keep your merchandise clean, and develop merchandising ideas. For example, during a routine visit to a client's store, a consumer goods salesperson found that a product the salesperson represented with a list price of $2 was being sold for $1.79. This enterprising salesperson taped a small sign to the shelf showing both prices and discovered later that sales of the product had increased. This device is now routine for all of this salesperson's products.

Step 5. Assist the product's users. If you sell industrial products, you should help users learn to operate your products properly. Make your users aware of product accessories that might aid them in performing a function in a safer, better, or more profitable manner. This type of account servicing can increase both account penetration and sales.

Step 6. Assist retailer's salespeople. To ensure enthusiastic promotion of your firm's products, you must work closely with your account's sales force. Experience indicates that manufacturer's salespeople who cultivate the friendship of the reseller's salespeople and provide them with product knowledge and selling tips are much more likely to be successful than the salesperson who calls only on the account's buyer.

A successful pharmaceutical salesperson suggested to all of the retail salespeople involved in a certain account that as they hand a customer a prescription for an antibiotic they say, "In taking these antibiotics you should also double up on taking your vitamins." Well, most customers were not taking vitamins, so when they said, "I don't have any vitamins," the salesperson would hand them a bottle of vitamins, saying, "I take these myself and highly recommend them to you." Of course, this manufacturer's salesperson had previously given the retail salesperson a sample bottle of vitamins. This sales tip accounted for an increase of over 300 percent in vitamin sales for this reseller.

Step 7. Demonstrate your willingness to help. On each sales call demonstrate your willingness to help the account through your actions. Your actions—not just your words—are what build respect, or distaste, for you. Pull off your coat and dust, mark, stack, and build displays of your merchandise, and return damaged merchandise for credit. Let the buyer know that you are there to help increase retail sales.

Step 8. Obtain customer support. By working hard to help your customers reach their goals through doing the things just discussed, you will find they are willing to help and support you. In essence, you help them; they help you. This type of relationship results in benefits to both you and your customer.

Again, there is no guarantee that doing everything suggested in this or any other text or sales manual will always result in your getting the sale. Conscientious use of sound selling principles *will* increase your likelihood of overall success, though.

Figure 12–2	Think positively	. . . And follow up
Super Sales Success	Plan carefully	. . . And follow up
Secret	Present thoroughly	. . . And follow up
	And follow up	. . . And follow up
	. . . And follow up	. . . And follow up
	. . . And follow up	. . . And follow up
	. . . And follow up	. . . And follow up

Vincent Norris of Scientific Equipment Corporation sent us a copy of what he feels is the secret to sales success. While follow-up is at the bottom of Vincent's list of secrets shown in Figure 12–2, it is extremely important, as you can see.

As mentioned earlier in this chapter, a key characteristic of a sales professional is the ability to accept failure or rejection gracefully, and then quickly to move on to the next objective.

When You Do Not Make the Sale

A group of purchasing agents were asked their biggest gripes about poor sales procedure. One item on their list was this: "They [salespeople] seem to take it personally if they don't get the business, as though you owe them something because they are constantly calling on you."[5]

Although you should try, you cannot always sell everyone as much as you would like to or expect them to place special emphasis on *all* of your products *all* of the time. When you have done the very best you can to persuade prospects or customers to make a purchase, and they still will not buy or do what you wish, remember there is always tomorrow. Act as a professional, adult salesperson, and do not take the buyer's denial personally, but recognize it as a business decision that the buyer must make given the circumstances. Be courteous and cheerful, be grateful for the opportunity to discuss your business proposition. The proper handling of a no sale situation can actually help you build a sound business relationship with your customers by developing a spirit of cooperation.

Return Goods Make You a Hero

One of the best ways to truly help your customers is through the careful examination of the merchandise you have sold them in the past to see if it is old and out-of-date or unsalable due to damage. If any of these

The One That Got Away

You did everything right—except get the order. What happened?? The answers come easily—the buyer was in a lousy mood! He wasn't listening to me! He was more worried about that problem on his loading dock!

Wasn't **any** of it your fault? Was **your** mind somewhere else? Were you unprepared? Were you overconfident? Has your sales presentation become stale? Are you no longer taking the time to reexamine your prospects needs?

You learn more from your failures than from your successes if you're willing to really analyze them.

conditions exist, the salesperson should cheerfully return the merchandise following his company's return goods policies.

Some companies allow you to return any amount of merchandise, whereas other firms have limits on unauthorized returns. A firm may allow no more than $100 of merchandise to be returned at any one time without the company's approval. Some companies require a reciprocal replacement order. Thus if $100 worth of merchandise is returned, the customer must place an order for $100 of new merchandise. You do not want the customer to display or sell damaged goods, so it is in your best interest to return faulty merchandise, an action that aids you in building friendship with each customer.

Handle Complaints Fairly

Customers may be dissatisfied with products for many reasons.

The product delivered is a different size, color, or model than the one ordered.

The quantity delivered is less than quantity ordered—balance is backordered (to be delivered when available).

The product does *not* arrive by the specified date.

Discounts (trade, promotional payment, etc.; see Chapter 4) agreed on are not rendered by the manufacturer.

The product does not have a feature or perform a function that the customer believed it would.

The product is not of specified grade or quality (does not meet agreed on specifications).

Whenever you determine that the customer's complaint is an honest one, you should make a settlement that is fair to the customer. The slogan, "The customer is always right," is a wise adage to follow. Customers may actually be wrong, but if they honestly believe they are right, no amount of haggling or arguing is going to convince them otherwise. A valued account can be lost through temperamental outbursts.

Occasionally a customer will attempt to be dishonest with you, which may require you and your company not to honor a request. I once had a retailer (A) who had purchased some of my firm's merchandise from another retailer (B) who had a fire sale and eventually went out of business. Retailer A insisted he purchased it from me and that I return close to $1,000 of damaged goods to my company for full credit. He had actually paid 10 cents on the dollar for it at the fire sale. I told Retailer A that I would have to obtain permission from the company to return such a large amount of damaged goods.

That afternoon a competitive salesperson told me that this same Retailer A had asked him to do the same thing. I informed my sales manager of the situation. He investigated the matter and found out about Retailer B who sold most of his merchandise to Retailer A—who happened to be my customer. I went back and confronted Retailer A with this and said it was company policy only to return merchandise that was purchased directly from me. This is a rare situation; yet you must occasionally make similar judgments taking care to consider company policy and customer satisfaction.

Certainly your customer should get the benefit of the doubt. Always have a plan for getting to the bottom of the problem. Some procedures you could follow are:

Obtain as much relevant information from your customer as you can.

Express sincere regret for the problem.

Display a service attitude (a true desire to help).

Review your sales records to make sure the customer purchased the merchandise.

Should you determine that the customer is right, quickly and cheerfully handle the complaint.

Follow up to make sure the customer is satisfied.

Take care of your customers—expecially your large accounts. They are difficult to replace and are critical to your success. When you take care of your accounts, they will take care of you. Servicing your accounts, as shown in Figure 12–3, demonstrates a professional attitude.

Build a Professional Reputation

Implied and directly stated throughout this chapter, indeed throughout this text, is the concept of sales professionalism. Sales professionalism directly implies that you are just that—a professional person—due the respect and ready for the responsibilities that accompany the title. In speaking before a large class of marketing students, one sales manager for a large college textbook publishing company continually brought up the concept of sales professionalism. This man directly stated that a professional sales position is not just an 8 to 5 job. It is a professional, responsible, adult position, promising both unlimited opportunity and numerous duties. This veteran publishing sales manager emphasized to

Figure 12–3
Servicing Your Accounts Is Critical to Your Success

A   *B*   *C*

Working out of his home in Richmond, Virginia, Irwin's Morgan Jennings carefully reviews his records of past sales calls (A), and examines his computer print-out on present sales, (B) before talking with Professor William Johnson (C) of John Tyler Community College in Chester, Virginia. In selling college textbooks, just as selling other products, Morgan shows the textbook and discusses its features, advantages, and benefits to professors in his territory.

these young adults that in the 1990s a sales job is an especially good vocational opportunity because people are looking for "someone we can believe in; someone who will do what he says—a sales professional."

To be viewed as a professional and respected by your customers and competitors, here are eight important considerations:

- First, be truthful and follow through on what you tell your customer. Do not dispose of your conscience when you start work each day.

- Second, maintain an intimate knowledge of your firm, its products, and your industry. Participate in your company's sales training and take continuing education courses.

- Third, speak well of others, including your company and your competitors.

- Fourth, keep customer information confidential; maintain a professional relationship with each of your accounts.

- Fifth, never take advantage of a customer by using unfair, high-pressure techniques.

- Sixth, be active in community affairs by helping to better your community. For example, live in your territory, be active in your public schools, and join such worthwhile organizations as the Lion's Club or Chamber of Commerce.

- Seventh, think of yourself as a professional and always act as a professional. Have a professional attitude about yourself and customers.

- Eighth, provide service above and beyond the call of duty. Keep in mind that it is easier to maintain a relationship than to begin one. What was worth going after in the first place is worth preserving. Remember, if you do not pay attention to your customers, they will find someone else who will. The professional salesperson never forgets a customer after the sale.

Each year *Purchasing* magazine selects top salespeople from those nominated by their customers and company.[6] The key phrase purchasing agents always mention about these winners is that each is *customer-oriented*. They are committed to total service for their customers. Here are several examples:

- Donald F. Beecher, Energy Services Group, Cooper Industries, Houston, Texas. He used his technical know-how to uncover improvements in poppet valve applications and saved a customer $750,000 a year on that project alone. Savings came from higher efficiency in operation, lower maintenance costs, and standardized (lower-cost) parts inventories.

- John Buckley, Scientific Gas Products, Wakefield, Massachusetts. "Ensures that we have the right product to fit the right application," says customer in the electronics business—who also cites "individualized service/delivery of rare specialty gases within hours . . . to keep a product line from shutting down."

- Lee Williams, KBI Div., Cabot Corp., Pittsburgh, Pennsylvania. She's a pro at providing spec review and editing, material analyses, competitive testing, and other technical assistance. For a customer who's been closing plants and consolidating production, she has birddogged the transfer of production requirements plant-to-plant and has arranged for buffer stocks and special expediting to avoid stockouts anywhere.

- Caroline Stock Norris, Allied Industrial Distributors, Compton, California. A former buyer for another distributor, she's now using a dress-design degree and earlier experience in the garment industry to suggest changes (materials, weaves, etc.) in design of safety clothing sold by her firm. Says customer, "She ought to have her name on the label; she designed it!"

- Jack Zimmerman, J. C. Zimmerman and Associates, Milwaukee, Wisconsin. He's a former purchasing manager, now a manufacturer's rep, and one customer credits his purchasing background with enabling the buyer to reduce his vendor base by 40 percent. Another customer calls him "more of a materials consultant than a salesman." Says another, "It's a nice feeling to have him on my side."

Do's and Don'ts for Industrial Salespeople

What does a purchasing agent expect of industrial salespeople? A survey of purchasing agents showed that they expect results. The following list shows some of the specific traits purchasing agents found in their top industrial salespeople. These are the most important traits in order of importance:

- Willingness to go to bat for the buyer within the supplier's firm.
- Thoroughness and follow-through after the sale.
- Knowledge of the firm's product line.
- Market knowledge and willingness to keep the buyer posted.
- Imagination in applying one's products to the buyer's needs.
- Knowledge of the buyer's product line.
- Preparation for sales calls.
- Regularity of sales calls.

- Diplomacy in dealing with operating departments.
- Technical education (knowledge of specifications and applications).

The survey also asked purchasing agents what they did not like salespeople to do when calling on them. The results, shown in Figure 12–4, are "The Seven Deadly Sins of Industrial Selling."[7] It is clear that purchasing agents want salespeople to act in a professional manner, to be well trained, to be adequately prepared for each sales call, and to keep the sales call related to *how the salesperson can help the buyer.*

Professional selling starts in the manufacturer's firm. A professional attitude on the part of the manufacturer can reinforce professionalism among its sales force. One such concerned company is B. J. Hughes, a division of the Hughes Tool Company.[8] The B. J. Hughes company manufactures and sells oil field equipment and services to companies in the oil and gas industry. Figure 12–5 presents Hughes's checklists of *do's*

Figure 12–4
The Seven Deadly Sins of Industrial Selling

1. *Lack of product knowledge.* Salespeople must know their own product line as well as the buyer's or nothing productive can take place.

2. *Time wasting.* Unannounced sales visits are a nuisance. When salespeople start droning on about golf or grandchildren, more time is wasted.

3. *Poor planning.* Even a routine sales call should be preceded by some homework— maybe to see if it's really necessary.

4. *Pushiness.* This includes prying to find out a competitor's prices, an overwhelming attitude, and backdoor selling.

5. *Lack of dependability.* Failure to stand behind the product, keep communications clear, and honor promises.

6. *Unprofessional conduct.* Knocking competitors, boozing at a business lunch, sloppy dress, and poor taste aren't professional.

7. *Unlimited optimism.* Honesty is preferred to the hallmark of the "Good News Bearers" who will promise anything to get an order. Never promise more than you can deliver.

A few of the more vigorous comments:
- "They seem to take it personally if they don't get the business; it's as though you owe them something because they are constantly calling on you."
- "I don't like it when they blast through the front door like know-it-alls and put on an unsolicited dog-and-pony show that will guarantee cost saving off in limbo somewhere."
- "Many salesmen are willing to give you any delivery you want, book an order, and then let you face the results of their short quote."
- "They try to sell *you,* rather than the product."
- "After the order is won, the honeymoon is over."
- "Beware the humble pest who is too nice to insult, won't take a hint, won't listen to blunt advice, and is selling a product you neither use nor want to use, yet won't go away."

Figure 12–5
We Are a Customer-Oriented Company

Salesman's Checklist of Do's	*Salesman's Checklist of Don'ts*
1. Know the current products/services and their applications in your area. Look for the new techniques/services your customers want.	1. Never bluff; if you don't know, find out.
2. Maintain an up-to-date personal call list.	2. Never compromise your own, or anyone else's, morals or principles.
3. Listen attentively to the customer; what he has to say is important.	3. Don't be presumptuous—even with friends.
4. Seek out specific problems and the improvements your customers would like to have.	4. Never criticize a competitor—especially to a customer.
5. Keep calls under five minutes unless invited to stay.	5. Do not take criticisms or turndowns personally—they're seldom meant that way.
6. Leave a calling card if the customer is not in.	6. Do not worry or agonize over things that you cannot control or influence. Be concerned more about what you *can* affect.
7. Identify the individual who makes or influences decisions and concentrate on him.	7. Do not offend others with profanity; keep it to a minimum.
8. Entertain selectively; your time and your expense account should be investments.	8. Do not allow idle conversation or football, etc., to dominate your sales call. Concentrate on your purpose.
9. Make written notes as reminders.	9. Don't try to match the customer drink for drink when entertaining. Drink only when you want to.
10. Plan your work by the week, not by the clock. Plan your use of available time. Plan your sales presentations. Have a purpose.	10. Don't be so gung ho that you use high-pressure tactics.
11. Ask for the business on every sales call.	11. Never talk your company down—especially to customers. Be proud of it and yourself.
12. Follow through with appropriate action.	12. Never smoke in the customer's office unless he is smoking or invites you to smoke.

and *don'ts* for their salespeople. By providing these checklists, the company is encouraging them to act in a professional manner.

Summary of Major Selling Issues

Providing service to customers is important in all types of selling. Follow-up and service create goodwill between a salesperson and customer that allows the salesperson to penetrate or work throughout the customer's organization. Account penetration helps the salesperson to better service the account and uncover its needs and problems. A service relationship with an account leads to increases in total and major brand sales, better distribution on all sizes of your products, and customer cooperation in promotion of your products.

To serve your customers best, concentrate on improving your account penetration. Contact each customer on a frequent and regular schedule, making sure you promptly handle all complaints. Be sure you always do what you say you will do, and remember to serve customers as if they were royalty. Finally, always remember to thank all customers sincerely for their business, no matter how large or small, in order to show you appreciate them and their firms.

Should customers begin to buy from a competitor or reduce the level of cooperation they give you, be sure to continue to call on them in your normal professional manner. In a friendly way, determine why they did not buy from you and develop new customer benefit plans to recapture their business.

Always strive to help your customers increase their sales of your product or to get the best use from the products you have sold them. In order to persuade a customer to purchase more of your products or use your products in a different manner, develop a sales program to help you maximize your sales to that particular customer. This involves development of an account penetration program; an increase in the number and sizes of products purchased by the customer; maintenance of proper inventory levels in the customer's warehouse and on the shelf; achievement of good shelf space and shelf positioning; clear communication with those who directly sell or use a product; a willingness to assist your wholesale and retail customers' salespeople in any way possible; willingness to help your customers; an overall effort to develop a positive, friendly business relationship with each customer. By doing these eight things, you will increase your ability to help and properly service each of your customers.

Today's professional salesperson is oriented towards service. Follow-up and service after the sale will greatly aid in maximizing your territory's sales and in reaching your personal goals.

Review and Discussion Questions

1. Rich Port, Mike Curto, Francis Rogers, and Jack Pruett all discussed service in this chapter. What do they feel is important for salespeople to understand about service?

2. What is account penetration? What benefits can a salesperson derive from it?

3. List and briefly explain the factors salespeople should consider to ensure that customers will continue to buy from them in the future.

4. What should a salesperson do after losing a customer?

5. A good way for a salesperson to create goodwill is by helping customers to increase their sales. What are the steps the salesperson should go through when attempting to increase customer sales?

6. This chapter discussed several reasons why a salesperson should project a professional image. Why do you think being a sales professional is so important?

7. Return to Figure 12–4, The Seven Deadly Sins of Industrial Selling.

Now think of an experience you have had with a salesperson who displayed a poor sales image. How did the salesperson's attitude affect your purchase decision?

8. You have just learned that one of your customers, Tom's Discount Store, has received a shipment of faulty goods from your warehouse. The total cost of the merchandise is $2,500. Your company has a returned-goods policy that will allow you to return only $500 worth of your product at one time unless a reciprocal order is placed. What would you do?
   a. Call Tom's and tell them you will be out to inspect the shipment in a couple of days.
   b. Ask Tom's to patch up what they can and sell it at a reduced cost in an upcoming clearance sale.
   c. Send the merchandise back to your warehouse and credit Tom's account for the price of the damaged goods.
   d. Get over to Tom's as soon as possible that day, check the shipment to see if there are any undamaged goods that can be put on the shelf, get a replacement order from Tom's manager, and phone in the order immediately.
   e. Call your regional sales manager and ask what to do.

9. As a construction machinery salesperson, you know that equipment malfunctions and breakdowns are costly to your customers. Your firm, however, has an excellent warranty that allows you to replace a broken piece of equipment with one of your demonstrators for a few days while the equipment is being repaired. King Masonry has called you four times in the past three months because the mixer you sold them has broken down. Each time you have cheerfully handled the problem, and in less than two hours they have been able to get back to work. Your company's mixer has traditionally been one of the most dependable on the market, so after the last breakdown you let King Masonry keep the new replacement in hopes of solving any future problems.

   The owner has just called to tell you the new mixer has broken down. He is quite angry and says he may go to another supplier if you cannot get him a replacement immediately.
   a. What should you do?
   b. If you had received a call from another salesperson earlier in the week telling you that King had been misusing the mixer, what would you now do?

Projects

1. Contact the person in charge of the health and beauty aids department of a local supermarket. In your interview with this person, ask

questions to determine what service activities salespeople perform in the department. For example, do they build product displays, put merchandise on the shelves, straighten products on the shelves, and keep a record of how much product is in the store? Also, determine how the department head feels salespeople can best provide service.

2. Contact the person in charge of marketing in a local bank. Report on the role service plays in attracting and retaining bank customers.

Cases

12–1 California Adhesives Corporation

Marilyn Fowler recently became a sales representative for the California Adhesives Corporation and is to cover the states of Oregon and Washington. After completing a three-week training program, Marilyn was excited about taking on the responsibility of reversing the downward sales trend in her territory, which had been without a salesperson for several months.

The previous salesperson had been fired due to poor sales performance and had not left behind any information regarding accounts. After contacting her first 20 or so customers, Marilyn came to a major conclusion: none of these customers had seen a CAC salesman for six to nine months; they had CAC merchandise, which was just not selling, and also had damaged merchandise to return. These customers were generally hostile toward Marilyn because the previous salesperson had used high-pressure tactics to force them to buy, and as one person said, "Your predecessor killed your sales in my business. You said you would provide service and call on me regularly, but I don't care about service. In fact, it's OK with me if I never see anyone from your company again. Your competition's products are much better than yours, and their salespeople have been calling in this area for years trying to get my business." Marilyn was beginning to wonder if she had gone to work for the right company.

Questions:

1. If you were Marilyn, what would you do to improve the sales in your territory?

2. How long would your effort take to improve sales and would you *sell* it to your sales manager?

12–2 Sport Shoe Corporation

You are a salesperson for the Sport Shoe Corporation. On arrival at your office you find a letter marked urgent on your desk. This letter is from the athletic director of Ball State University and pertains to the poor quality of basketball shoes you had sold him. The director cited several examples of split soles and poor overall quality as his main complaints. In closing, he mentioned that since the season was drawing near he would be forced to contact the ACME Sport Shoe Company if the situation could not be rectified. What actions on your part would be appropriate? Why?

a. Place a call to the athletic director assuring him of your commitment to service. Promise to be at Ball State at his convenience to rectify the problem.

b. Go by the warehouse and take the athletic director all new shoes and apologize for the delay and poor quality of the merchandise.

c. Write a letter to the athletic director assuring him that SSC sells only high-quality shoes and that this type of problem rarely occurs. Assure him you'll come to his office as soon as possible, but if he feels ACME would be a better choice than Sport Shoe, he should contact them.

d. Don't worry about the letter because the athletic director seems to have the attitude that he can put pressure on you by threatening to switch companies. Also, the loss in sales of 20 to 40 pairs of basketball shoes will be a drop in the bucket compared to the valuable sales time you would waste on a piddly account like Ball State.

IV SPECIAL SELLING TOPICS

Call Reports

Call reports—records of appointments, dates, time spent, results. Management says "do them," so you do. They can be completed in a minute or so, while you're waiting for the light to change. And they're practically worthless.

For a call report to be truly useful, it has to tell more than just date and time and whether you made the sale. You'll get what you put into it.

Use your call reports for analysis: Why didn't you make the sale? What could you have done differently? What did you do right, that you can repeat on another call? What will you need the next time you call on this customer? Is this customer going to require several calls to close the sale? Is it worth it? You're leaving a trail of valuable clues—to help your company's entire sales force.

"Paperwork" can be an annoying infringement on precious time. But establishing a document of sales secrets never is!

	MON	TUE	WED	THU	FRI	CMTS
9-10						
10-11						
11-12						
12-1						
1-2						
2-3						
3-4						
4-5						
5-						

week of _____

13 TIME AND TERRITORY MANAGEMENT IS A KEY TO SUCCESS

Learning Objectives

1. To discuss the importance of the sales territory.
2. To present the major elements involved in managing the sales territory.
3. To explain why salespeople need to segment their accounts by size.
4. To illustrate the importance of effective use of one's selling time using break-even analysis.

Key Terms for Selling

Sales territory

Account analysis

Undifferentiated selling

Account segmentation

Key accounts

80/20 principle

Sales response function

Scheduling

Routing

Profile

Terry and Paul Fingerhut
Steamboat Party Sales, Inc. (Tupperware)

Twelve years have past since Terry Fingerhut attended a Tupperware party as a favor to a friend. Terry, with her B.A. in secondary education, was teaching junior high students and her husband Paul, with his M.S. in mathematics, was teaching in high school. Today Terry and Paul operate a $4 million Tupperware distributorship.

Terry began as a salesperson holding an average of two parties per week. She then became a manager with a unit of four dealers, which ultimately grew to a unit of 45 dealers. "During this period of time," says Terry, "I promoted 12 dealers from my unit to managership. Each took with them into their new units an average of 3 dealers from my unit. In my third year as a manager, our unit had sales of $500,000.

"In my fourth year with the Tupperware company, the ultimate goal of having a Tupperware distributorship became a reality for Paul and me. Steamboat Party Sales, Inc., became the fourth distributorship servicing the St. Louis metropolitan area. We began with a sales force of eight managers and 86 dealers selling $1 million in our first year. Today we have a sales force of 50 managers and 480 dealers selling $4 million. We are ranked number four in Tupperware on sales volume.

"One of the keys to success is time management," says Terry. "When the desire is there and the discipline of doing the job NOW in order to create the series of positive results is ever-present, priorities are set and followed. In fact, these priorities after being set need to be worked with, evaluated, and perhaps readjusted as the day/week/month progresses. What is the best use of this time NOW? Planning the day—on paper—allows you to see what is effective use of time. Ask yourself 'Is this the best use of me—NOW?' 'Will I get the best and most results from what I am doing right NOW?'"

"Self-discipline is a vital part of time management," say Terry and Paul Fingerhut. "Establish what is your best use of time. Determine the amount of hours to be spent in the week which will allow you the time to reach your chosen goals. Look at the days of the week that will give you the best results for your efforts, and schedule the various phases of your job on those days giving the best

results for time spent. Within each day, analyze the best use of time. For example, if I need to make phone calls to solidify upcoming appointments—isn't it a better use of time to determine ahead of time with the customer what is the best time for that call, specifically 11 A.M. rather than simply calling at random until the party is reached. And YOU determine when calls or contacts are made. Give the action choice—'I'll be in your area Monday. Would 10 be good for you or perhaps 1?' not 'When can we make contact?'"

All successful salespeople recognize the importance of time and territory management. Terry says, "Understand the value of your time. Time is the essence of your life and because of time management, you have productive time for whatever you choose to do."

In recalling his early days as a salesman, Shelby H. Carter, Jr., Xerox's senior vice president of sales of U.S. field operations said, "I placed a sign on my car's visor which read, 'Calls are the guts of this business.' We lived in Baltimore," he recalls, "and I drove 40 miles every day to get to Annapolis." His wife fixed him a jug of lemonade so he would not have to stop for lunch.

"You've got to make extra calls," he now tells his salesmen, "because 1 more call a day is 5 a week, 20 a month, and 240 calls a year. If you close 10 percent of the people you contact, you have an extra 24 sales a year. You have to be tough on yourself to make that extra call."[1]

Terry and Paul Fingerhut, along with Mr. Carter, voice the sentiments of sales managers as to the importance of working hard and making extra calls on prospects and customers. The importance of planning your work day and managing your time and territory is very important to your success.

According to a national survey of thousands of salespeople across the nation, managing time and territory is considered the most important factor in carrying out selling duties.[2] Because of such things as the rapidly increasing cost of direct selling, decreasing time for face-to-face customer contact, continued emphasis on profitable sales, and the fact that time is always limited, it is no wonder that many companies are concentrating on improving the way their salespeople manage time and territory.

What Is a Sales Territory? _____

A **sales territory** comprises a group of customers or a geographical area assigned to a salesperson. The territory may or may not have geographical boundaries. Typically, however, a salesperson is assigned to a geographical area containing present and potential customers.

Why Establish Sales Territories?

Companies develop and use sales territories for numerous reasons. Seven of the more important reasons are discussed below.

To Obtain Thorough Coverage of the Market.   With proper coverage of the territories, the company can more nearly reach the sales potential of its markets. The salesperson can analyze the territory and identify and classify customers. At the individual territory level, the salesperson can better meet customers' needs. Division into territories also allows management to easily realign territories as customers and sales increase or decrease.

To Establish Salesperson's Responsibilities.   Salespeople act as business managers for their territories. They have the responsibility of maintaining and generating sales volume. Salespeople's job tasks are clearly defined. They know where customers are located and how often they should be called on. They also know what performance goals they are expected to meet. This can have a positive effect on the salesperson's performance and morale.

To Evaluate Performance.   Performance can be monitored for each territory. Actual performance data can be collected, analyzed, and compared to expected performance goals. Individual territory performance can be compared to district performance, district performance compared to regional performance, and regional performance compared to the performance of the entire sales force. With computerized reporting systems, the salesperson and a manager can monitor individual territory and customer sales to determine the success of their selling efforts.

To Improve Customer Relations.   Customer goodwill and increased sales can be expected when customers receive regular calls. From the customer's viewpoint, the salesperson *is*, for example, Procter & Gamble. The customer looks to the salesperson, not to Procter & Gamble's corporate office, when making purchases. Over the years, some salespeople build up such goodwill with their customers that customers will delay placing their orders because they know the salesperson will be at their business on a certain day or at a specific time of the month. Some salespeople even earn the right to order merchandise for certain of their customers.

To Reduce Sales Expense.   Sales territories are designed to avoid duplication of effort so that two or more salespeople are not traveling in the same geographical area. This lowers selling cost and increases company profits. Such benefits as fewer travel miles and fewer overnight trips, plus the contact of productive customers regularly by the same salesperson can improve the firm's sales-cost ratio.

To Allow Better Matching of Salesperson to Customer's Needs. Salespeople can be hired and trained to meet the requirements of the customers in a territory. Often the higher the similarity between the customer and the salesperson, the more likely it is that the sales effort will be successful.

Benefit to Salespeople and the Company. Proper territory design can aid in reaching the firm's sales objectives. Thus the company can maximize its sales effort, while the sales force can work in territories that afford them the opportunity to satisfy their personal needs (e.g., good salary).

Why Sales Territories May Not Be Developed

In spite of the stated advantages, there are disadvantages to developing sales territories for some companies such as in the real estate or insurance industry. First, salespeople may be more motivated if they are not restricted by a particular territory and can develop customers wherever they find them. In the chemical industry, for example, salespeople may be allowed to sell to any potential customer. However, after the sale is made, other company salespeople are not allowed to contact their client.

Second, the company may be too small to be concerned with segmenting the market into sales areas. Third, management may not want to take the time, or may not have the know-how for territory development. Fourth, personal friendship may be the basis for attracting customers. For example, life insurance salespeople may first sell policies to their families and friends. However, most companies do establish sales territories.

Elements of Time and Territory Management _____

For the salesperson, time and territory management (TTM) is a continuous process of planning, executing, and evaluating. The seven key elements involved in this process of time and territory management are shown in Figure 13–1 and discussed below.

Salesperson's Sales Quota

First, a salesperson is responsible for generating sales in a territory based on its sales potential. The salesperson's manager typically establishes a total sales quota that each salesperson is expected to reach.

Figure 13–1
Elements of Time and Territory Management for the Salesperson

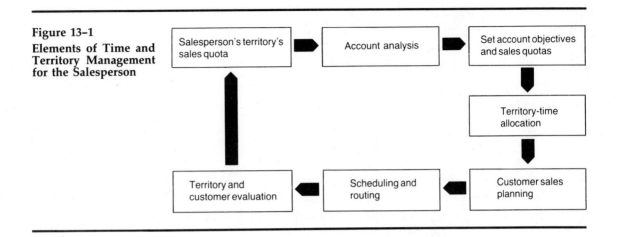

Once this quota is set, it becomes the responsibility of the salesperson to develop territorial sales plans for reaching the quota. While there is no one best planning sequence to follow, Figure 13–1 does present seven factors that should be considered in order to properly manage the territory so as to reach its sales quota.

Account Analysis

The second element in the process of time and territory management is account analysis. Once the salesperson has set a sales goal, it becomes important to analyze each prospect and customer in order to maximize the chances of reaching that goal. First, a salesperson should identify all prospects and present customers, and second, estimate present customers' and prospects' sales potential. This makes it possible to allocate time between customers, to decide what products to emphasize to a specific customer, and how to better plan the sales presentation.

Two general approaches to **analyzing accounts** and thus identifying accounts and their varying levels of sales potential are the undifferentiated selling approach and the account segmentation approach.

The Undifferentiated Selling Approach. An organization may see the accounts in its market as being basically the same. When this happens and selling strategies are designed and applied equally to all accounts, the salesperson is using an **undifferentiated selling** approach. Notice in Figure 13–2 that the salesperson is aiming a single selling strategy at all accounts. The basic assumptions underlying this approach are that the needs of the accounts for a specific product or group of products are similar. Salespeople call on all potential accounts, devoting equal selling time to each of them. The same sales presentation may be used in selling an entire product line. The salesperson feels it can satisfy most custom-

414

Figure 13–2
Undifferentiated
Selling Approach

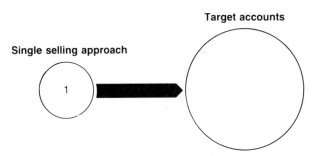

ers with a single selling strategy. For example, many door-to-door sales-people use the same selling strategies with each person they contact (stimulus-response sales presentation).

Salespeople whose accounts have homogeneous needs and characteristics may find this approach useful. The undifferentiated selling approach has been popular in the past, and some firms still use it. However, many salespeople feel that their accounts have different needs and represent different sales and profit potentials. This makes an account segmentation approach desirable.

The Account Segmentation Approach.   Salespeople using the **account segmentation** approach recognize that their territories contain accounts with heterogenous needs and differing characteristics that require different selling strategies. Consequently, sales objectives, in terms of overall sales and sales of each product, are developed for each customer and prospect. Past sales to the account, new accounts, competition, economic conditions, price and promotion offerings, new products, and salesmanship are among the key elements in the analysis of accounts and territories.

Salespeople classify customers in order to identify the profitable ones. This, in turn, determines where the salesperson's time will be invested. One method of defining accounts is:

1. Key account
   a. Buys over $200,000 from us annually.
   b. Loss of this customer would substantially affect the territory's sales and profits.

2. Unprofitable account
   a. Buys less than $1,000 from us annually.
   b. Little potential to increase purchases above $1,000.

3. Regular account
   a. All other customers.

Table 13–1

Example of Account Segmentation Based on Yearly Sales

Customer Size	Yearly Sales (actual or potential)	Number of Accounts	Percent
Extra large	over $200,000	100	3.3
Large	$75,000–200,000	500	16.6
Medium	$25,000–75,000	1,000	33.3
Small	$1,000–25,000	1,400	46.6

The unprofitable accounts would not be called upon. The **key accounts** and regular accounts become target customers.

Once the accounts have been broadly classified, categories or types of accounts can be defined in such terms as *extra large* (key), *large, medium,* and *small,* which we will refer to as the ELMS system. For example, management may divide the 3,000 accounts in the firm's total marketing into these four basic sales categories, as shown in Table 13–1. As you can see from the table, there are relatively few extra large or large accounts, but these quite often account for 80 percent of a company's profitable sales even though they represent only 20 percent of the total number of accounts. This is known as the **80/20 principle.** The number of key accounts in an individual territory varies, as does responsibility for them. Even though the key account is in another salesperson's territory, a key account salesperson may call on the extra-large customer. Typically this is done because of the account's importance to the company or perhaps the inexperience of the local salesperson.

Accounts can be segmented based on whether the firms are actual customers or prospects. As shown in Table 13–2, actual customers are further segmented on the basis of sales to date and sales potential. Prospects are also segmented into the ELMS classification, and each account's potential sales are estimated.

Multiple Selling Strategies. Figure 13–3 illustrates how multiple selling strategies may be used on the various accounts. Salespeople are aware of the importance of large accounts; in fact, meeting sales objec-

Table 13–2

Basic Segmentation of Accounts

Account Classification	Customers		Prospect Potential Sales
	Sales to Date	Potential Sales	
Extra large			
Large			
Medium			
Small			

Figure 13–3
Account Segmentation
Approach

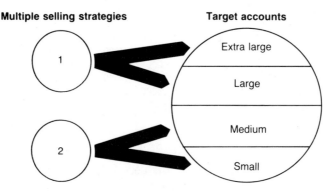

Multiple selling strategies | Target accounts

1

2

Extra large

Large

Medium

Small

tives often depends on how well products are sold to these customers. As a result, companies often develop their sales force organizational structure to service these accounts incorporating such elements as a key account salesperson to deal with them.

As illustrated in Figure 13–3, selling strategies may vary depending on the account. The bulk of sales force resources (such as personnel, time, samples, and entertainment expenses) should be invested in the key accounts, and the needs of these large accounts should receive top priority.

Company positioning relative to competition should receive careful consideration. Competitors will also be directing a major selling effort toward these accounts. Thus, salespeople should strive to create the image that their company, its products, and they themselves are uniquely better than what the competition is offering. One way to accomplish this is to spend more time on each sales call and to make more total sales calls during the year, thus providing a problem-solving approach to servicing the accounts.

Selling larger accounts is different than selling medium and small accounts. However, these smaller accounts may generate 20 percent, and sometimes more, of a company's sales and thus should not be ignored.

Multivariable Account Segmentation. Multivariable account segmentation means using more than one criterion to characterize the organization's accounts. This is done because many sales organizations sell to several markets and use many channel members in these markets. Furthermore, different products, product sizes, or product lines may be emphasized to different channel members in the various markets.

Figure 13–4 illustrates how firms might use several variables to segment their accounts. This allows sales personnel to develop plans for

Figure 13–4
Multivariable Account Segmentation

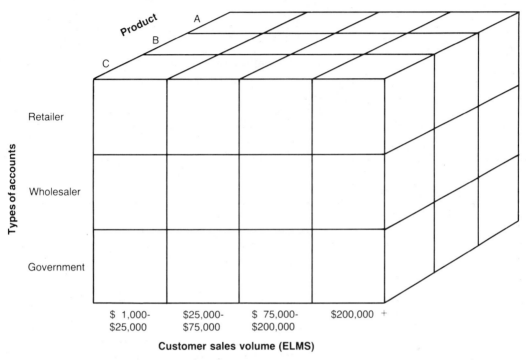

selling their various products to specific segments of their accounts. For example, different selling strategies might be developed for the extra large and large accounts. There might be different sales plans developed for the retailer, wholesaler, and government accounts. These three types of accounts might be further segmented. Retailers, for instance, could be segmented into mass merchandisers and specialty stores. Futhermore, different products might be emphasized in each account segment. The type of market, environment, account sales potential, and sales volume are major variables for segmenting accounts.

Develop Account Objectives and Sales Quotas

The third element of time and territory management is the development of objectives and sales quotas for individual products for present and potential accounts. Objectives might include increasing product distribution to prospects in the territory or increasing the product assortment purchased by current customers.

Increasing the number of sales calls each day and the number of new accounts obtained for the year are other examples of objectives that can be developed by the salesperson to help meet sales quotas.

Territory-Time Allocation

The fourth element of time and territory management is how salespeople's time is allocated within their territories. *Time* refers to the time spent by the salesperson in travel around the territory and in actually calling on accounts. There are seven basic factors to consider in time allocation:

1. Number of accounts in the territory.
2. Number of sales calls to be made on customers.
3. Time required for each sales call.
4. Frequency of sales calls on a customer.
5. Travel time around territory.
6. Nonselling time.
7. Return on time invested.

Analysis of accounts in the territory has resulted in the determination of the total number of accounts in the territory and their classification in terms of actual or potential sales. Now, the number of yearly sales calls required, the time required for each sales call, and the intervals between calls should be determined. Usually the frequency of calls will increase as there are increases in (1) sales and/or potential future sales, (2) number of orders placed in a year, (3) number of product lines sold, and (4) complexity, servicing, and redesign requirements of the products.

Since the amount of time spent servicing an account may vary from minutes to hours to days, salespeople should be flexible in developing call frequencies. However, they can establish a minimum number of times each year they want to call on the various classes of accounts. For example, the salesperson determines the frequency of calls for each class of account in the territory, as shown in Table 13–3, where all but the small account are contacted once a month.

Typically, the salesperson invests sales time in direct proportion to the actual or potential sales that the account represents. The most productive number of calls is reached at the point where additional calls do not increase sales. This relationship of sales volume to sales calls is the **sales response function** of the customer to the salesperson's calls.

Return on Time Invested. Time is a scarce resource. To be successful, the salesperson should use time effectively to improve territory produc-

Customer Size	Calls per Month	Calls per Year	Number of Accounts	=	Calls per Year
Extra large	1	12	2		24
Large	1	12	28		336
Medium	1	12	56		672
Small	1 every 3 months	4	78		312
Total			164		1,344

Table 13–3
Account Time Allocation by Salesperson

tivity. In terms of time, costs must also be taken into account, that is, what is the cost both in time and money of an average sales call?

Break-even analysis can be used to determine how much sales volume a salesperson must generate to meet costs in a territory. The difference between cost of goods sold and sales is the gross profit on sales revenue. Gross profit should be large enough to cover selling expenses. A territory's break-even point can be computed in terms of dollars by using the following formula:

$$\text{Break-even point (in dollars)} = \frac{\text{Salesperson's fixed costs}}{\text{Gross profit percentage}}$$

To illustrate the formula, let us use the values shown here for sales and costs, with gross profit being the difference between sales revenue of a salesperson and costs of goods sold in the territory, expressed as a ratio of gross profit to gross sales in percentage form.

Sales	$200,000
Cost of goods sold	− 140,000
Gross profit	$ 60,000
Gross profit (percentage)	(60,000 ÷ 200,000), or 30 percent

Assume the salesperson's direct costs are as follows:

Salary	$20,000
Transportation	4,000
Expenses	5,000
Direct costs	$29,000

and substitute in the formula:

$$\text{BEP} = \frac{\$29,000}{.30} = \$96,667$$

If the salesperson sells $96,667 worth of merchandise, it will exactly cover the territory's direct costs. A sales volume of $96,667 means that the salesperson is producing a gross margin of 30 percent, or $29,000. Sales over $96,667 contribute to profit.

Assume that the salesperson works 46 out of 52 weeks (considering time off for vacations, holidays, and illness) or 230 days each year; also assume a five-day week, and an eight-hour day in which six calls are made. There are thus 1,840 working hours per year and 1,380 sales calls (230 × 6 calls) made each year in the territory. To determine a salesperson's cost per hour, divide direct costs ($29,000) by yearly hours worked (1,840 hours). The cost per hour equals $15.76. The break-even volume per hour is determined as follows:

$$\text{Break-even volume per hour} = \frac{\text{Cost per hour}}{\text{Gross profit percentage}} = \frac{\$15.76}{.30} = \$52.53$$

Thus, the salesperson must sell an average of $52.53 an hour in goods or services to break even in the territory. Carrying this logic a little further, the salesperson must sell an average of $420.24 each day or $70.04 each sales call to break even.

This simple arithmetic shows that a sales territory is a cost- and revenue-generating profit center, and because it is, priorities should be established on account calls in order to maximize territory profits.

The Management of Time. "Time is money" is a popular saying that has direct application to our discussion because of the costs and revenue generated by the individual salesperson. This is particularly evident in the case of the commission salesperson. The salesperson is a territory manager who has the responsibility of managing time wisely in order to maximize territorial profits. Thus, the effective salesperson consistently uses time well. How does the effective salesperson manage time?

Plan by the Day, Week, and Month. Many salespeople develop daily, weekly, and monthly call plans, or general guidelines of customers and geographical areas to be covered. The salesperson may use them to make appointments with customers in advance, to arrange hotel accommodations, etc. Weekly plans are more specific, and include the specific days that customers will be called on. Daily planning starts the night before as the salesperson selects the next day's prospects, determines the time to contact the customer, organizes facts and data, and prepares sales presentation materials. Figure 13–5 is an illustration of a daily plan, and Figure 13–6 shows the location of each account and the sequence of calls.

"It's been said," says Terry Fingerhut, "21 days make a habit—good or bad. In three weeks the results of the work I did or didn't do today will show up. If I spent my time well, three weeks from the day, I'll have positive results. If I wasted my time, three weeks from the day, I'll have negative results. The conclusion—each day, every day produce NOW at your best. In three weeks and every week thereafter you'll have a string of truly positive results." See Figure 13–7.

Figure 13–5
Daily Customer Plans

| | Sales Calls | | Service |
Hours	Customers	Prospects	Customers
7:00– 8:00	Go by office; pick up order for Jones Hardware		
8:00– 9:00	Travel		
9:00–10:00	Zip Grocery		
10:00–11:00	Ling Television Corp.		
11:00–12:00	Ling Television Corp.		
12:00– 1:00	Lunch and delivery to Jones Hardware		
1:00– 2:00	Texas Instruments		
2:00– 3:00		Ace Equipment	
3:00– 4:00	Travel		
4:00– 5:00			Trailer Mfg.
5:00– 6:00	Plan next day—do paper work		

Figure 13–6
Example of Daily
Customer Plans

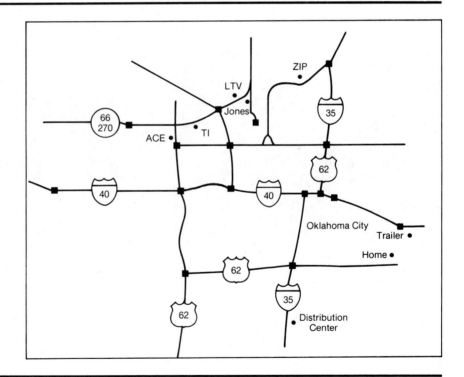

Qualify the Prospect.   The salesperson should be sure that the prospect
being called on is qualified to make the purchase decision and determine
whether sales to this account will be large enough to allow for an
adequate return on time invested. If not, the prospect should not be
called on.

Figure 13–7
Time Management Is a Key to the Fingerhuts' Success

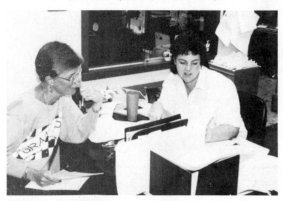

*Careful planning is needed for running
the business . . .*

training salespeople . . .

recruiting successful salespeople and . . .

conducting sales meetings.

Use Waiting Time. Have you seen salespeople waiting to see buyers? Have you ever noticed their actions? Top salespeople do not read magazines. They work while waiting, studying material about their products, completing call reports, or organizing material for the sales presentation. Also, they quickly determine whether the buyers they are waiting for will be free in a reasonable time. If not, they contact other customers.

Have a Productive Lunchtime. Salespeople often take prospects to lunch. However, the results of one study show that the business lunch does not lead directly to a sale, but to the buyer and seller getting to know each other better, building confidence and trust. In turn, this may lead to sales in the long run.

During a business lunch, salespeople should keep an eye on the clock and not monopolize too much of their buyers' time. They should not have a lunchtime cocktail. While it may seem customary to have a drink at lunch, the salesperson may be less alert in the afternoon as a result. In fact, in some companies a luncheon cocktail is against company policy. A salesperson's lunch alone can be a time to review activities and further plan for the afternoon. It is a time to relax and start psyching up for a productive selling afternoon.

Records and Reports. Records and reports are a written history of sales and of the salesperson's activities. Effective salespeople do their paperwork during nonselling times; evenings are best. Many companies take these records and reports into account in the performance evaluation of salespeople. However, paperwork should be held to a minimum by the company and kept current by the salesperson.

Customer Sales Planning

The fifth major element of time and territorial management is developing a sales call objective, a customer profile, and a customer benefit program, including selling strategies for individual customers.* You have a quota to meet, have made your account analysis, have set account objectives, have established the amount of time you will devote to each customer; now you must develop a sales plan for each customer.

Scheduling and Routing

The sixth element of time and territory management is scheduling sales calls and planning movement around the sales territory.

Scheduling refers to establishing a fixed time (day and hour) for visiting a customer's place of business. **Routing** is the travel pattern used in working a territory. Some sales organizations prefer to determine the formal path or route that their salespeople are to travel when covering their territory. In such cases, management should develop plans that are feasible, flexible, profitable to the company and the individual salesperson, and satisfactory to the customer. In theory, strict formal route designs enable the company to (1) improve territory coverage, (2) minimize wasted time, and (3) establish communications between management and the sales force in terms of the location and activities of individual salespeople.

In developing route patterns, the management needs to know the

* Refer to Chapter 6 for further discussion of customer sales planning.

salesperson's exact day and time of sales calls for each account, approximate waiting time, sales time, miscellaneous time for contacting people such as the promotional manager, checking inventory, handling returned merchandise, and travel time between accounts. This task becomes difficult unless territories are small and precisely defined. Most firms allow considerable latitude in routing.

Typically, after finishing a work week, the salesperson fills out a routing report and sends it to the manager. The report states where the salespeople will be working in the future (see Table 13–4). In the example, on Friday, December 16, you are based in Dallas and planning during the week of December 25 to call on accounts in Dallas for two days. Then you plan to work in Waco for a day, spend the night, drive to Fort Worth early the next morning and make calls, and be back home Thursday night. The last day of the week, you again plan to work in Dallas. The weekly route report is sent to your immediate supervisor. In this manner, management knows where you are and, if necessary, can contact you.

Some firms may ask the salesperson to specify the accounts to be called on and at what times. For example, on Monday, December 26, the salesperson may write, "Dallas, 9 A.M., Texas Instruments; Grand Prairie, 2 P.M., L.T.V." Thus, management knows where a salesperson will be and which accounts will be visited during a report period. If no overnight travel is necessary to cover a territory, the company may not require any route reports because the salesperson can be contacted at home in the evening.

Carefully Plan Your Route. At times routing can be difficult for a salesperson. Customers do not locate themselves geographically for their convenience. Also, there is the increasing difficulty of getting around in large cities. To help, companies are selling computerized mapping systems, as shown in Figure 13–8. There is also the problem caused by some accounts who will see you only on certain days and hours.

Table 13–4 Weekly Route Report	Today's Date: December 16		For Week Beginning: December 26
	Date	*City*	*Location*
	December 26 (Monday)	Dallas	Home
	December 27 (Tuesday)	Dallas	Home
	December 28 (Wednesday)	Waco	Holiday Inn/South
	December 29 (Thursday)	Fort Worth	Home
	December 30 (Friday)	Dallas	Home

Figure 13-8
The Etak Navigator

The Etak Navigator is a computerized mapping system, installed in cars, that in a glance shows a salesperson where he is and where he's going.

In today's complex selling situation, the absence of a well-thought-out daily and weekly route plan is a recipe for disaster. It's just not possible to operate successfully without it. How do you begin?

Start by locating your accounts on a large map. Mount the map on some corkboard or foamboard, which can be obtained from an office supply store or picture framing shop. You can use a road map for large territories or a city map for densely populated area. While you are at the office products store, pick up a supply of map pins with different colored heads. Place the pins on the map so you can see graphically where each account is located. For example, you could use:

- Red pins for your extra large (EL) accounts.
- Yellow pins for your large (L) accounts.
- Blue pins for your medium (M) accounts.
- Black pins for your small (S) accounts.
- Green pins for your best prospects.

Once all the pins are in place, stand back and take a look at the map. Notice first where the EL accounts are located. This will help you determine your main routes, or areas where you must go most frequently.

Now divide the map into sections, keeping about the same number of EL accounts in each. Of course each section should be a natural geographic division, that is, the roads should be located in such a way that it will be easy for you to drive from your home base to each section and be able to get around easily once you are there. Generally, your L, M, and S accounts will fall into place near your ELs, with a few exceptions.

For example, if you are working on a monthly or four-week call schedule for your ELs, then divide your territory into four sections, working one section each week. In this way, you will be sure to get to all your ELs while at the same time having the flexibility needed to get to your other accounts on some kind of a regular basis.

Section 1	Section 2	Section 3	Section 4
7 EL	9 EL	5 EL	10 EL
15 L	12 L	15 L	15 L
35 M	25 M	35 M	25 M
40 S	35 S	40 S	36 S

By setting up your geographical routes this way, you could call on all of your EL accounts every four weeks, half of your L and M accounts (making an eight-week call cycle), and 25 percent of your S accounts (making a 16-week call cycle). Also allow time for calls on prospective customers, too. Use the same procedure as you would for your regular customers. The only difference might be that your prospects would be contacted on a less frequent basis than your customers, in most cases.

There is no right number of sections or routes for all salespersons. It depends on the size of your territory, the geographical layout of your part of the country, and the call frequencies you want to establish. Lay out your travel route so that you can start out from your home in the morning and return in the evening—or if you have a larger territory, make it a Monday to Friday route, or a two day (overnight) route. Remember that the critical factor is travel time, not miles. In some cases, by using major nonstop highways, your miles may increase but your total travel time may decrease.

The actual route you follow each day and within each section is important because you want to maximize the use of your prime selling hours each day. For this reason, make your long drives early in the morning and in the late afternoon, if possible. For example, if most of

Figure 13–9

Examples of Three Basic Routing Patterns

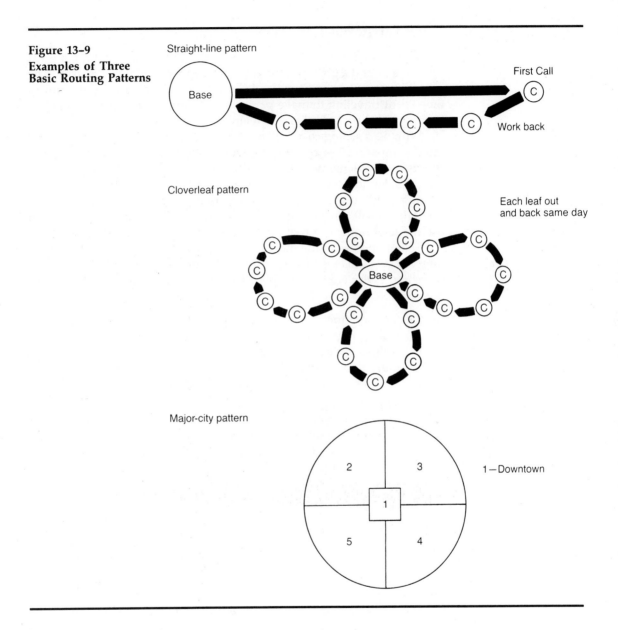

Straight-line pattern

Base

First Call

C

Work back

Cloverleaf pattern

Each leaf out and back same day

Base

Major-city pattern

1—Downtown

2 3

1

5 4

your accounts are strung out more or less in a straight line from your home base, get up early and drive to the far end of your territory before making your first call; then work your way back so that you will end up near your home at the end of the day. Figure 13–9 illustrates three ways to route yourself, including the straight-line method just mentioned.

Using the Telephone for Territorial Coverage

The telephone has been described as being simultaneously both a great time-waster and a great time-saver. It all depends on how it is used. The increasing cost of a personal sales call, and the increasing amount of time spent traveling to make personal calls, are reasons for the efficient territory manager to look to the telephone as a tool of territory coverage.

With field selling costs still on the rise and no end in sight, more and more companies are developing telephone sales and marketing campaigns to supplement personal selling efforts. These campaigns utilize trained telephone communicators and well-developed telephone marketing techniques. Usually, they require a company-wide effort. Here, though, we will concentrate on how an individual territory manager can use the telephone as a tool in territory coverage in order to save time.

Telephone use in the individual territory may be grouped into three categories: (1) sales generating, (2) order processing, and (3) customer servicing. These are some applications of the telephone in each of these categories:

1. Sales generating
   a. Selling regular orders to smaller accounts.
   b. Selling specials, such as offering a recent price decrease on an individual product.
   c. Developing leads and qualifying prospects.
2. Order processing
   a. Telephoning the order into the warehouse.
   b. Gathering credit information.
   c. Checking whether shipments have been made.
3. Customer servicing
   a. Handling complaints
   b. Answering questions.

Although each salesperson has to decide which types of calls and which accounts may lend themselves to telephone applications, most people can benefit from adopting the following practices, as a minimum, in territory coverage:

- Satisfying part of the service needs of accounts by telephone.
- Assigning smaller accounts, those that contribute less than 5 percent of business, substantially to telephone selling.
- Doing prospecting, marketing-data gathering, and call scheduling by telephone.
- Carefully scheduling personal calls to distant accounts. If possible, replace some of these personal visits with telephone calls.

Figure 13–10
The Telephone and the Computer Are Effective Selling Tools

The telephone and computer are effective sales aids to keep salespeople connected to their sales operations no matter where they are, or where they are going.

The telephone, coupled with the computer, are important selling tools for salespeople. Many sales jobs require extensive travel. Even in airports, as shown in Figure 13–10, traveling salespeople can keep in contact with their offices, access computer files containing customer information, and record customer information.

Territory and Customer Evaluation

The seventh element of time and territory management is territory and customer evaluation. Territorial control is the establishment of standards of performance for the individual territory in the form of qualitative and quantitative quotas or goals. Actual performance is compared to these goals for evaluation purposes. This allows the salesperson to see how well territory plans were carried out in meeting performance quotas. If quotas were not met, then new plans must be developed for the territory.

Many companies routinely furnish managers and individual salespeople with reports on the number of times during the year their salespeople have called on each account and the date of the last sales call. Management can monitor the frequency and time intervals between calls for each of their salespeople.

As an example, a national pharmaceutical company supplies its sales force with the Net Sales by Customer and Call Report shown in Table 13–5. The report lists each customer's name, address, and medical specialty. The desired number of monthly calls on a given customer and the actual number of calls to date are noted. Net sales are broken down into last year's sales, the current month's sales, and year-to-date sales. Finally, the date the salesperson last called on each customer is reported.

Using the report, one can see that H. L. Brown is a Houston physician in a general practice. He should be called on twice a month, and for the four months that have gone by he has been seen eight times to date. He purchased $60 worth of merchandise this month, and his purchases this year are $50 more than they were last year. He was last called on April 20 of the current year. Using this type of information, which might include 200 to 300 customers for each salesperson, management and salespeople can continually review sales call patterns and customer sales to update call frequency and scheduling.

Summary of Major Selling Issues

The way salespeople invest their available sales time may be a critical factor influencing their territory sales. Due to the increasing cost of

Table 13–5

Net Sales by Customer and Call Frequency: May 1, 1988

	Brown (GP, Houston)	Peterson (Pediatrics, Galveston)	Gilley (GP, Galveston)	Bruce (GP, Galveston)	Heaton (GP, Texas City)
Calls					
Month	2	1	1	0	2
Year to date	8	4	4	4	9
Last call	4/20	4/18	4/18	3/10	4/19
Net sales in dollars					
Current month	60	0	21	0	500
Year to date:					
This year	350	200	75	1,000	2,000
Last year	300	275	125	750	1,750
Entire last year	2,000	1,000	300	1,000	5,000

direct selling, high transportation costs, and the limited resources of time, salespeople have to focus their attention on these factors. Proper management of time and territory is an effective method for the salesperson to maximize territorial sales and profits.

A sales territory comprises a group of customers or a geographical area assigned to a salesperson. It can be considered a segment out of the company's total market. A salesperson within a territory has to analyze the various segments, estimate sales potential, and develop a marketing mix based on the needs and desires of the marketplace.

Companies develop and use sales territories for a number of reasons. One important reason is to obtain thorough coverage of the market so they can more nearly reach their sales potential. Another reason is to establish salespeople's responsibilities as they act as territory managers.

Performance can be monitored when territories are established. A territory may also be used to improve customer relations so that customers receive regular calls from their salesperson. This also helps to reduce sales expense as duplication of effort in traveling and customer contacts is avoided. Finally, they allow better matching of salesperson to customer needs and thus benefit salespeople as well as their company.

There are also disadvantages to developing sales territories. Some salespeople may not be motivated if they feel restricted by a particular territory. Also, a company may be too small to segment its market, or management may not want to take time to develop territories.

Time and territory management is a continuous process for a salesperson involving seven key elements. The first major element is the establishment of the territory sales quota. The second element is account analysis, which involves identifying present and potential customers and estimating their sales potential. In analyzing these accounts, salespeople may use the undifferentiated selling approach if they view their accounts as basically the same; or if the accounts have different characteristics, they will use the account segmentation approach.

Developing objectives and sales quotas for individual accounts is the third element. How salespeople's time is allocated in their territories is another key element. Salespeople have to manage their time, plan their schedules, and use all spare time effectively.

The fifth element of time and territorial management is developing a sales call objective, profile, benefit program, and selling strategies for individual customers. Salespeople have to find out as much as they can about their customers and maintain records on each one. Once this is done, they can create the proper selling strategies to meet their customers' needs.

Another major element is scheduling the sales calls at specific times and places and routing the salesperson's movement and travel pattern around the territory. Finally, objectives and quotas that were established are used to determine how effectively the salesperson is performing. Actual performance is compared to these standards for evaluation purposes.

Review and Discussion Questions _____

1. What is a sales territory? Why do firms establish sales territories? Why might sales territories not be developed?

2. Briefly discuss each of the elements of time and territory management and indicate how these seven elements relate to one another.

3. What is the difference between the universal selling approach and the account segmentation approach for analyzing accounts? When might each approach be used?

4. Assume that a sales manager determines that in a given territory each salesperson sells approximately $500,000 yearly. Also, assume that the firm's costs of goods sold are estimated to be 65 percent of sales and that a salesperson's direct costs are $35,000 a year. Each salesperson works 48 weeks a year, eight hours a day, and averages five sales calls per day. Using this information, how much merchandise must each salesperson sell to break even?
   a. For the year.
   b. Each day.
   c. Each sales call.

5. What is a key account?

6. What are the factors a salesperson should consider when allocating time?

7. How does an effective salesperson use time?

8. What is the purpose of customer sales planning?

9. Define scheduling. Routing.

Projects _____

1. Visit a large retailer in your community and ask a buyer or store manager what salespeople do when they make a sales call. Determine the number of times the retailer wants salespeople to visit each month. Are calls from some salespeople preferable to others? If so, why?

2. Contact a salesperson or sales manager and report on each one's philosophy toward managing time and territory. Ask each to calculate how much it costs to contact one prospect and on the average what amount must be sold each day just to break even.

Case

13–1   Your Selling Day: A Time and Territory Game*

Your sales manager is working with you tomorrow only, and you want to call on your customers with the greatest sales potential (see Exhibit 1).

Exhibit 1

Customers' Sales Potential

Customer	Sales Potential	Customer	Sales Potential
1	$4,000	9	1,000
2	3,000	10	1,000
3	6,000	11	10,000
4	2,000	12	12,000
5	2,000	13	8,000
6	8,000	14	9,000
7	4,000	15	8,000
8	6,000	16	10,000

Exhibit 2

Partial Map of Your Sales Territory

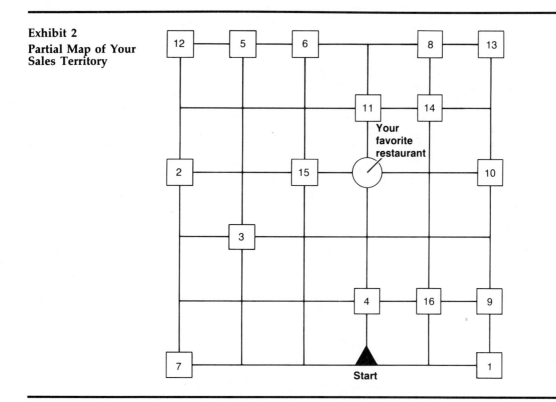

* Case © Copyright by Charles M. Futrell.

Because you are on a straight commission, you will also have the opportunity to maximize your income for that day. The area of your territory that you feel should be covered tomorrow contains 16 customers (see Exhibit 2). To determine travel time, allow 15 minutes for each side of the square. Each sales call takes 30 minutes. You can leave your house at 8 A.M. or later. If you take time for lunch, it must be in 15 minute blocks of time (e.g. 15, 30, 45, or 60 minutes). Your last customer cannot be contacted after 4:30 P.M. in order to allow enough sales time. Your customers do not see salespeople after 5 P.M. Travel home can be done after 5 P.M.

Questions:

1. Develop the route that gives the highest sales potential for the day your boss works with you.

2. For the next day develop the route allowing you to contact the remaining customers in this part of your territory.

14 SOCIAL, ETHICAL, AND LEGAL ISSUES IN SELLING

Learning Objectives

1. To present the concept of social responsibility and reasons why business assumes responsibilities to society.
2. To discuss how managers view the business ethics of industry.
3. To review ethical dealings with salespeople, employers, and customers.
4. To present ways a sales force can act in an ethical manner.

Key Terms for Selling

Social responsibility

Ethics

House account

Robinson-Patman Act

Price discrimination

Tie-in sale

Clayton Act

Exclusive dealership

Cooling-off law

Green River ordinance

Profile

Sandra Snow
The Upjohn Company

After completing my nursing education at Jameson Memorial Hospital in New Castle, Pennsylvania, and the University of Pittsburgh, I was a clinical instructor in pediatric nursing at Pittsburgh Children's Hospital and later a head nurse of the pediatrics department of a Florida hospital. Although happy with nursing, I decided to pursue a career in sales because of more opportunities, advancement, and challenge.

Initially my job was calling on the physicians, hospitals, and drugstores in a general sales territory. After 3½ years I was promoted to a hospital sales specialist responsible for three large hospitals and the University of Miami School of Medicine in Miami, Florida. In January 1983 I was promoted to a general sales district manager's position responsible for 14 people and $10 million in sales. January 1985 I became sales manager for one of Upjohn's medical specialty representative groups; then in August 1986 I was moved into the home office as part of our professional training and development group.

It is imperative that I am knowledgeable not only about our products but also about the disease entities that our drugs treat. I have an obligation to provide this information in an honest and ethical way. Since we may alter the prescribing habits of physicians, it is important that they know not only the benefits of our products, but also the risks. Human health care is not an area where deceptive selling techniques can be used in any way.

I also have an obligation to the company to conduct myself in a professional manner while increasing sales. There is significant government regulation of the pharmaceutical industry, and unethical practices by a salesperson reflect not only on that salesperson but on the company for which he or she works and the industry as a whole. Fortunately, I am working for a company that is research-oriented and prides itself on having a knowledgeable sales force. We are constantly learning new things about old drugs, as well as preparing for the introduction of new products.

"Even though it is a salesperson's job to inform, I feel that we are more effective salespeople if we establish a dialogue with the physician and find out from him his feelings and experiences with our products, rather than being didactic," said Sandra Snow of the Upjohn Company. "It is also important to disseminate this information to pharmacists and nursing personnel via a one-on-one discussion or a continuing education program for a small group. The pharmacist and nurse may not prescribe therapy, but they may pick up both drug toxicity and/or failure."

As you see from Sandra Snow's comments above and from her profile, she is convinced of the need to be honest, ethical, and to act as a professional salesperson. This chapter addresses many of the important social, ethical, and legal issues in selling. We begin by defining the term *social responsibility* and discuss six reasons why firms want their sales personnel to act in a responsible manner. Then we examine ethical issues involved in dealing with salespeople, employers, and customers. We end the chapter by presenting ways a company can help its sales personnel follow ethical selling practices.

The Social Responsibility of Business

Social responsibility in business refers to profitably serving employees and customers in an ethical and lawful manner. This definition involves the individual salesperson, implying that the salesperson is an important resource of the firm and must be treated responsibly, just as it states that a salesperson must treat customers in an ethical manner.

Quite often, corporations are said to operate solely to maximize profits. Certainly profits are important to a firm, just as a grade point average is important to a student. Profit provides the capital to stay in business, to expand, and to compensate for the risks of conducting business. There is a responsibility to make a profit in order to serve society. Imagine what would happen to our society if large corporations (e.g., AT&T, General Motors) did not make a profit and went out of business. Thousands of people and the U.S. economy would be affected.

Sales managers and salespeople are occasionally accused of obtaining sales in any manner possible. The temptations to make sales at any cost have been curbed both by laws designed to penalize wrongdoers and by the new professionalism of individuals selecting sales as a career. Let's briefly examine why business today should continue to act in a responsible manner and then review how managers view ethics.

Why Assume Social Responsibilities?

There are numerous reasons why a business should assume social responsibilities. Six of the major reasons are:

1. It is expected by society.
2. It allows the business to operate better in the long run.
3. It shows community responsibility.
4. Salespeople are company representatives.
5. It minimizes competitors' retaliation.
6. It decreases government intervention.

Social Expectation.   Sales managers must understand that they are in business to serve customers profitably but also responsibly. Sales practices must not conflict with the interests of society. As the company grows, it increases its power in the industry and is expected to assume greater social responsibilities. This is the power-responsibility equation.

Better Operations in the Long Run.   If the sales force works totally for short-run goals, irresponsible selling practices often result. At the corporate level, executives view the firm as existing to make a profit in the long run, but sales personnel have trouble with this because they typically work in the short run. They have monthly, quarterly, and yearly sales goals that may create pressures to make the sale at any cost.

Sales executives must continually monitor their sales units to minimize the temptations to use unethical and illegal sales practices. Pressure on sales personnel must be kept at a reasonable level that allows them to use responsible selling techniques. Extremely high pressure to increase sales can pressure a salesperson to make the sale no matter how. This is especially true if managers openly suggest or overlook unethical sales practices. Sales may increase in the short run, but in time customers will catch on and sales will decrease.

Community Responsibility.   Sales managers and their salespeople often participate in community activities and organizations. This includes working with groups such as the Lion's Club, United Fund, Heart Fund, and Little League. Many salespeople are also active in their industry's trade associations.

Salespeople as Company Representatives.   Would you want your salespeople giving kickbacks or cheating customers? Certainly not, because the salespeople reflect the image of the company, and, after a time, customers might expect all of the company's salespeople to act in this manner. Buyers could expect kickbacks before doing business with the company. Both actions are costly to the company, and sales manag-

> ### Assuming Community Responsibility
>
> "One of the legacies we took from the Bell System philosophy," says AT&T's Bill Frost, "is that of being a visible community supporter in arts, education, health services, and civic and community clubs and organizations. We must be a strong corporate supporter of the communities in which we live and work. Beyond the obvious good of being a strong business partner in the community, it offers excellent opportunities for networking.
>
> "It leaves a good feeling in a customer's mind to recall what AT&T has done for the community. When that customer is approached by competitors, one of the things in his memory might be what AT&T has done in the public arena versus what the competition has done, and that memory again proves our value to the community—and by extension, to the customer.
>
> "This entire positioning process is our biggest challenge. At divestiture, we explained it by calling AT&T the 'oldest new company in history.' For so many years, the Bell operating companies were the number one community leaders while AT&T itself took a back seat.
>
> "We've been talking about information movement and management for years, and we're finally there. It is very important for AT&T to become the number one vendor in that arena, and associating our name with quality organizations and events is one way to get there."

ers cannot take the position of "Hear no evil, see no evil, speak no evil." They must oversee the sales practices of their personnel so that the pressure of reaching sales quotas does not lead to unethical sales practices.

Minimizing Competitors' Retaliation. Often, in competitive industries, if one company decreases prices, others follow. The same thing can happen when a company uses unethical practices. Maintaining ethical standards can cause competitors to do the same.

Decreasing Government Intervention. Sales managers prefer not to have the government intervene in their activities, but over the years the business community has not acted in a totally responsible way. Consequently, government regulation has increased. To make government

Table 14–1

Ten Actions a Corporation Can Take to Demonstrate Social Responsibility

1. Take corrective action before it is required.
2. Work with affected constituents to resolve mutual problems.
3. Work to establish industrywide standards and self-regulation.
4. Publicly admit your mistakes.
5. Get involved in appropriate social programs.
6. Help correct environmental problems.
7. Monitor the changing social environment.
8. Establish and enforce a corporate code of conduct.
9. Take needed public stands on social issues.
10. Strive to make profits on an ongoing basis.

intervention less necessary, sales managers must develop a code of ethics and help govern their companies' sales practices.

There are numerous ways a corporation can demonstrate social responsibility. Table 14–1 shows actions that can be taken by all firms.

How Managers View Ethics

Ethics are principles of right or good conduct, or a body of such principles, which would affect good and bad business practices. Ethical principles govern the conduct of an individual or group. Over the years a number of surveys have been carried out to determine managers' views of business ethics. In general, they found the following:

- All managers feel they face ethical problems.
- Most managers feel they and their employers should be more ethical.
- Managers are more ethical with their friends than with people they do not know.
- Even though they want to be more ethical, some managers lower their ethical standards in order to meet job goals.
- Managers are aware of unethical practices in their industry and company ranging from price discrimination to hiring discrimination.
- Business ethics can be influenced by an employee's superior and by the company's environment.

The remainder of this chapter discusses some of the possible situations that may arise requiring the sales manager and salespeople to search their consciences. It cannot be all-inclusive, but it represents an attempt to give the reader a feel for some of the difficult decisions faced by salespeople.

Keep Your Sense of Humor

"It was my first call as a district manager in Washington, D.C.," says Alan Lesk, senior vice president, sales and merchandising, Maidenform. "One of the major department stores there was not doing a lot of business with Maidenform, and we were looking to get some more penetration in the market. Surprisingly, the sale took only two sales calls.

"The first person I approached was a buyer. He was completely uncooperative. On the way out of the store, I popped my head into his boss's office, and we set up a meeting with some higher level executives later in the week.

"So there I was, a young kid facing a committee of nine tough executives, and I had to make my presentation. I was in the middle of my pitch when the executive vice president stopped me. He told me that this was going to be a big program, about $500,000, and asked me point blank how much of a rebate I was willing to give him to do business with their store, over and above the normal things like co-op ad money. He was actually asking me for money under the table!

"I had to make a decision fast. I stood up and said, 'If this is what it takes to do business here, I don't want anything to do with it.' I then turned to walk out the door, and the guy started cracking up. I guess he was just testing me to see what lengths I'd go to in order to get my sales program into the store.

"This one incident taught me some very important things: You can't compromise your integrity, and you can't let people intimidate you. But most important, don't lose your sense of humor. Needless to say, we got the program into the store, and today, we do more than $2 million of business a year with them."[1]

Ethics in Dealing with Salespeople

Sales managers have both social and ethical responsibilities to their sales personnel. Salespeople are a valuable resource; they have been recruited, carefully trained, and given important responsibility. They represent a large financial investment and should be treated in a professional manner. Yet occasionally a company may place their managers and/or salespeople in positions that force them to choose between compromising their personal ethics, or not doing what is required, or leaving the organization. Certainly the choice depends on the magnitude of the situation. At times situations arise in which it is difficult to say whether a sales practice is ethical or unethical. Many sales practices are in the gray area, somewhere between being completely ethical and completely unethical. Five ethical considerations faced by the sales manager are (1) the level of sales pressure to place on a salesperson, (2) decisions concerning a salesperson's territory, (3) whether or not to be honest with the salesperson, (4) what to do with the salesperson who is ill, and (5) employees' rights.

Level of Sales Pressure

What is an acceptable level of pressure to place on salespeople? Should managers establish performance goals that they know a salesperson has only a 50–50 chance of attaining? Should the manager acknowledge that goals were set too high? If circumstances change in the salesperson's territory—for example, a large customer goes out of business—should the manager lower sales goals?

These are questions all managers must consider. There are no right or wrong answers. Managers are responsible for their groups' goals. There is a natural tendency to place pressure on salespeople so that the managers' goals will be reached. Some managers can motivate their people to produce at high levels without applying pressure, while others place tremendous pressure on their salespeople to attain sales well beyond their quotas. However, managers should set realistic and obtainable goals. They should consider individual territory situations. If this is done fairly, and sales are still down, then pressure may be applied.

Decisions Affecting Territory

Management makes decisions that affect sales territories and, in turn, salespeople. For example, the company might increase the number of sales territories, which often necessitates splitting up a single territory. A salesperson has spent years building up the territory to its current sales volume. Customers are taken away. If the salesperson has worked on a commission basis, this would mean a decrease in earnings.

Consider the situation of reducing the number of sales territories. What procedures do you use? Several years ago a large manufacturer of health and beauty aids (shaving cream, toothpaste, shampoo) reduced the number of territories in order to lower selling costs. So, for example, three territories became two. Here is how one of their salespeople described it:

I made my plane reservation to fly from Dallas to Florida to our annual national meeting. Beforehand I was told to bring my records up to date and bring them to the regional office in Dallas. Don't fly, drive to Dallas. I drove from Louisiana to Dallas with my bags packed to go to the national meeting. I walked into the office with my records under my arm. My district and regional managers were there. They told me of the reorganization and said I was fired. They asked for my car keys. I called my wife, told her what happened, and then caught a bus back home. There were five of us in the region that were called in that day. Oh, they gave us a good job recommendation—it's just the way we were treated. Some people had been with the company for five years or more. They didn't go by tenure but where territories were located.

Companies must deal with the individual in a fair and straightforward manner. It would have been better for the managers of these salespeople to go to their home towns and personally explain the changes to them. Instead, they treated the salespeople in an unprofessional manner.

One decision affecting a territory is what to do with extra large customers, sometimes called key accounts. Should they be taken away from the salesperson and made **house accounts?** Here responsibility for contacting the account can be someone from the home office (house) or a key account salesperson. The local salesperson may not get credit for sales to this customer even though located in the salesperson's territory. A salesperson states the problem in this manner:

I've been with the company 35 years. When I first began, I called on these people who had one grocery store. Today they have 208. The buyer knows me. He buys all of my regular and special greeting cards. They do whatever I ask. I made $22,000 commissions from their sales last year. Now management wants to make it a house account.

Here the salesperson loses money. It is difficult to treat the salesperson fairly in this situation. The company does not want to pay these large commissions and 90 percent of the 208 stores are located out of the salesperson's territory. They should carefully explain this to the salesperson. Instead of taking the full $22,000 away from the salesperson, they could pay a 20 percent commission as a reward for building up the account.

To Tell the Truth?

Should salespeople be told they are not promotable, that they are marginal performers, or that they are being transferred to the poorest territory in the company in hopes that they will be forced to quit? Good judgment must prevail. In general, sales managers prefer to tell the truth.

Do you tell the truth when you fire a salesperson? If a fired employee has tried and has been honest, many sales managers will tell prospective employers that the person quit voluntarily rather than being fired. One manager put it this way, "I feel she can do a good job for another company. I don't want to hurt her future."

The Ill Salesperson.   How much help do you give the alcoholic, drug addicted, or physically or mentally ill salesperson? More and more companies require their salespeople to seek professional help for alcohol or drug abuse. If they honestly try and improve, companies offer support and keep them in the field. Yet there is only so far the company can go. The firm cannot have an intoxicated or high salesperson calling on customers. Once the illness begins having a negative effect on business, the salesperson is taken out of the territory. Sick leave and workers' compensation will cover expenses until the salesperson is cured. The manager who shows a sincere, personal interest in helping the ill salesperson can greatly contribute to the person's chances of recovery.

Employee Rights

The sales manager must be current on the ethical and legal considerations regarding their employee's rights and develop strategies for their organizations in addressing employee rights. Below are several important questions to which all managers should know the answer:

- Under what conditions can an organization fire sales personnel without committing a legal violation?
- What rights do and should sales personnel have in regard to the privacy of their employment records and access to them?
- What can organizations do to prevent sexual harassment in the workplace?

Employee rights are those rights desired by employees regarding the security of their jobs and the treatment administered by their employer while on the job, irrespective of whether or not those rights are currently protected by law or collective bargaining agreements of labor unions. Let's briefly examine these three questions.

Termination-at-Will.   Early in this century many courts were adamant in their strict application of this common law rule to terminate-at-will. For example, the termination-at-will rule was used in a 1903 case, *Boyer* v. *Western Union Tel. Co.* [124 F 246, CCED Mo. (1903)], in which the court upheld the company's right to discharge its employees for union activities and indicated that the results would be the same if the company's employees had been discharged for being Presbyterians.

Later on, in *Lewis* v. *Minnesota Mutual Life Ins. Co.* [37 NW 2d 316 (1949)], the termination-at-will rule was used to uphold the dismissal of the life insurance company's best salesman—even though no apparent cause for dismissal was given and the company had promised the employee lifetime employment in return for his agreement to remain with the company.

In the early 1980s court decisions and legislative enactments moved the pendulum of protection away from the employer and toward the rights of the individual employee through limitations on the termination-at-will rule.[2]

Although many employers claim that essentially all their rights have been taken away, they still retain the right to terminate sales personnel for poor performance, excessive absenteeism, unsafe conduct, and generally poor organizational citizenship. It is critical, however, for employers to maintain accurate records of these events for their employees, and to inform the employees on where they stand. To be safe, it is also advisable for employers to have a grievance process for employees to ensure that due process is respected. These practices are particularly useful in discharge situations that involve members of groups protected by Title VII, the Rehabilitation Act, or the Vietnam Era Veterans Act.

Privacy.   Today it is more important than ever to keep objective and orderly personnel files. They are critical evidence that employers have treated their employees fairly and with respect and have not violated any laws. Without these, organizations may get caught on the short end of a law suit.

Although there are several federal laws that influence recordkeeping, they are primarily directed at public employers. However, many private employers are moving on their own initiative to give their employees the right to access their personnel files and to prohibit the file information from being given to others without their consent. In addition, employers are casting out of their personnel files any nonjob-related information and ending hiring practices that solicit that type of information.

Cooperative Acceptance.   The category of cooperative acceptance refers to the right of employees to be treated fairly and with respect regardless of race, sex, national origin, physical disability, age, or religion while on the job (as well as in obtaining a job and maintaining job security). Not only does this mean that employees have the right not to be discriminated against in employment practices and decisions, but it also means that employees have the right to be free of sexual harassment.

Today the right not to be discriminated against is generally protected under Title VII, the Age Discrimination in Employment Act, the Rehabilitation Act, the Vietnam Era Veterans Readjustment Assistance Act, and numerous court decisions and state and local government laws. Though the right to be free of sexual harassment is found explicitly in fewer laws, it has been made in the 1980 EEOC guidelines stating that sexual harassment is a form of sex discrimination. The equating of sexual harassment as a form of sex discrimination under Title VII is also found in numerous court decisions.

It is necessary for employers to prevent sexual harassment. This can be done with top management support, grievance procedures, verification procedures, training for all employees, and performance appraisal and compensation policies that reward those who practice antiharassment behavior and punish those who do not.

Companies realize that sexual harassment can be expensive. For example in a landmark decision, a federal judge in Madison, Wisconsin, approved a damages award of $196,500 to a man who said he was demoted because he resisted the sexual advances of his female supervisor. Although women have won these cases, this was the first time a man has ever won a sex harassment case against a woman. The man also received $7,913 in back pay and $21,726 in attorney's fees, in addition to the damages award approved by U.S. Judge John Shabaz.[3]

Companies should recognize that there are important strategic purposes served by respecting employee rights. The main ones are:

- Providing a high quality of work life.
- Attracting and retaining good sales personnel. This makes recruitment and selection more effective and their need less frequent.
- Avoiding costly back pay awards and fines.
- Establishing a match between employee rights and obligations and employer rights and obligations.

Here both organizations and employees benefit. Organizations benefit from reduced legal costs, since not observing many employee rights is illegal, and their images as good employers increase, resulting in enhanced organizational attractiveness. This in turn makes it easier for the organization to recruit a pool of potentially qualified applicants. And although it is suggested that expanded employee rights, especially job security, may reduce needed management flexibility, and thus profitability, it may be an impetus for better planning, resulting in increased profitability.

Increased profitability may also result from the benefits employees receive when their rights are observed; employees may experience a feeling of being treated fairly and with respect, increased self-esteem, and a heightened sense of job security. Employees who have job security may be more productive and committed to the organization than those without job security. As employees are beginning to see the guarantees of job security as a benefit, organizations are also gaining through reduced wage increase demands and greater flexibility in job assignments.

Are These Socially Responsible Actions?

Often it is difficult to determine whether actions are taken by sales executives for profit or social motives.

For example, take the following:

- Training and educational programs for salespeople.
- A company heavily dependent on government contracts hiring minority groups.
- Setting fair sales goals.
- Fairly rewarding salespeople's performance.
- Paying salaries above industry averages.
- Providing extensive medical and life insurance coverage.
- Holding sales meetings in resort areas.

Some people argue that these are responsible acts done unselfishly, while others say that these are good business practices that help maximize a firm's sales and profits. The argument is simply rhetorical. These are examples of good business practices carried out in a responsible manner. No longer can the sales function be carried out in anything other than a manner that is fair to salespeople, customers, and society.

Salespeople's Ethics in Dealing with Their Employers

Salespeople, as well as sales managers, may occasionally be involved in misusing company assets, moonlighting, or cheating; and such unethical practices can affect their fellow salespeople.

Misusing Company Assets

The company assets that are most often misused are automobiles, expense accounts, samples, and damaged merchandise credits. All can be used for personal gain or as bribes and kickbacks to customers. For example, a credit for damaged merchandise can be given to a customer when there has been no damage, or valuable product samples can be given to a customer.

Moonlighting

Salespeople are not closely supervised and, consequently, they may be tempted to take a second job, perhaps on company time. Some salespeople attend college on company time. For example, a salesperson may enroll in an evening MBA program but take off in the early afternoon to prepare for class.

Cheating

A salesperson may not play fair in contests. If a contest starts in July, the salesperson may not turn in sales orders for the end of June and lump them with July sales. Some might arrange, with or without the customer's permission, to ship merchandise that is not needed or really wanted. The merchandise is held until payment is due and then returned to the company after the contest is over. The salesperson may also overload the customer to win the contest.

Affecting Fellow Salespeople

Often the unethical practices of one salesperson can affect fellow salespeople. Someone who cheats in winning a contest is taking money and prizes from other salespeople. A salesperson also may not split commissions with fellow employees or take customers away from them.

Ethics in Dealing with Customers _____

Numerous ethical situations may arise in dealing with customers. Some of the more common problems faced are discussed below.

Bribes

A salesperson may attempt to bribe a buyer. Money, gifts, entertainment, and travel opportunities may be offered. At times there is a thin line between good business and the misuse of a bribe or gift. A $10 gift to a $10,000 customer may be merely a gift, but how do we define a $1,000 gift for a $1 million customer? Many companies forbid their buyers to take gifts of any size from salespeople. However, bribery does exist. The U.S. Chamber of Commerce estimates that, of the annual $40 billion white collar crime, bribes and kickbacks account for $7 billion.[4]

Buyers may ask for cash, merchandise, or travel payment in return for placing an order with the salesperson. Imagine that you are a salesperson working on 5 percent straight commission. The buyer says, "I'm ready to place a $20,000 order for office supplies with you. However, another salesperson has offered to pay my expenses for a weekend in

Las Vegas in exchange for my business. You know, $500 tax-free is a lot of money." You quickly calculate that your commission is $1,000. You still make $500. It could be hard to pass up that $500.

Misrepresentation

Today, even casual misstatements by salespeople can put a company on the wrong side of the law. Most salespeople are unaware that they assume legal obligations—with accompanying risks and responsibilities—every time they approach a customer. However, we all know that salespeople sometimes oversell. They exaggerate the capabilities of their products or services and sometimes make false statements just to close a sale.

Often, buyers depend heavily on the technical knowledge of salespeople, along with their professional integrity. Yet both sales managers and staff find it difficult to know just how far they can go with well-intentioned sales talk, personal opinion, and promises. They do not realize that by using certain statements, they can embroil themselves and their companies in a lawsuit and ruin the very business relationship they are trying to establish.

When a customer relies on a salesperson's statements, purchases the product or service, and then finds that it fails to perform as promised, the supplier can be sued for misrepresentation and breach of warranty. Companies around the United States have been liable for million-dollar judgments for making such mistakes, particularly when their salespeople sold high-ticket, high-tech products or services.

But you can avoid such mistakes if you're aware of the law of misrepresentation and breaches of warranty relative to the selling function and follow strategies that keep you and your company out of trouble. Salespeople must understand the difference between sales puff (opinions) and statements of fact, and the legal ramifications of each. There are preventive steps for salespeople to follow; and they should work closely with management so they can avoid time-consuming delays and costly legal fees.

What the Law Says. Misrepresentation and breach of warranty are two legal causes of action; that is, theories on which an injured party seeks damages. These two theories differ in terms of the kind of proof that is required and the different type of damages that may be awarded by a judge or jury. However, both commonly arise in the selling context and are treated similarly for our purposes. Both typically arise when a salesperson makes erroneous statements or offers false promises regarding his product's characteristics and capabilities.

Not all statements have legal consequences, however. When sales personnel loosely describe their product or service in glowing terms

("Our service can't be beat; it's the best around."), such statements are viewed as opinions and generally cannot be relied on by a customer, supplier, or wholesaler. Thus a standard defense used by lawyers in misrepresentation and breach of warranty lawsuits is that a purchaser cannot rely on a salesperson's puffery because it's unreasonable to take these remarks at face value.

But when a salesperson makes claims or promises of a factual nature regarding a product's or service's inherent capabilities (that is, the results, profits, or savings that will be achieved, what it will do for a customer, how it will perform, etc.), the law treats these comments as statements of fact and warranties.

There is a subtle difference between sales puffery and statements of fact that is often difficult to distinguish. No particular form of words is necessary, and each case is analyzed according to its circumstances. Generally, the less knowledgeable the customer, the greater the chances the court will interpret a statement as actionable. The following is an actual recent case and illustrates this point.

Example: An independent sales rep sold heavy industrial equipment. He went to a purchaser's construction site, observed his operations, then told the president of the company that his proposed equipment would "keep up with any other machine then being used and that it would work well in cooperation with the customer's other machines and equipment."

The customer informed the rep that he was not personally knowledgeable about the kind of equipment the rep was selling, and that he needed time to study the rep's report. Several weeks later, he bought the equipment based on the rep's recommendations.

After a few months he sued the rep's company, claiming that the equipment didn't perform according to the representations in sales literature sent prior to the execution of the contract and to statements made by the rep at the time of the sale. The equipment manufacturer defended itself by arguing that the statements made by the rep were nonactionable opinions made innocently by the rep, in good faith, with no intent to deceive the purchaser.

The court ruled in favor of the customer, finding that the rep's statements were predictions of how the equipment would perform; this made them more than mere sales talk. The rep was held responsible for knowing the capabilities of the equipment he was selling, so his assertions were deemed to be statements of fact, not opinions. Furthermore, the court stated that it was unfair that a knowledgeable salesperson should take advantage of a naive purchaser.

Suggestions for Staying Legal.   The following are suggestions that cover ways management and sales staff can work together to minimize exposure to costly misrepresentation and breach of warranty lawsuits. Salespeople should always do the following:

1. Understand the distinction between general statements of praise and statements of fact made during the sales pitch (and the legal consequences). For example, the following statements, taken from actual cases, were made by salespeople and were determined to be legally actionable as statements of fact:

   "This refrigerator will preserve foods in the warmest weather."

   "This tractor has live power-take-off features."

   "Feel free to prescribe this drug to your patients, doctor. It's nonaddicting."

   "This mace pen is capable of instantaneous incapacitation for a period of 15 to 20 minutes."

   "This is a safe, dependable helicopter."

2. Thoroughly educate all customers before making a sale. Salespeople should tell as much about the specific qualities of the product as possible. The reason is that when a salesperson makes statements about a product in a field in which his company is considered to have extensive experience, the law makes it difficult for the salesperson to defend himself by claiming it was just sales talk.

   This is especially true for products or services sold in highly specialized areas to unsophisticated purchasers who rely entirely on the technical expertise of the salesperson. However, if the salesperson deals with a customer experienced in the trade, courts are less likely to find that he offered an expressed warranty, since a knowledgeable buyer has a duty to look beyond the assertions of a salesperson and investigate the product on his own.

3. Be accurate when describing a product's capabilities. Avoid making speculative claims, particularly with respect to predictions concerning what a product will do.

4. Know the technical specifications of the product. Review all promotional literature to be sure that there are no exaggerated claims. Keep abreast of all design changes as well.

5. Avoid making exaggerated claims about product safety. The law usually takes a dim view of such affirmative claims, and these remarks can be interpreted as warranties that lead to liability.

   For example, the Minnesota Court of Appeals recently ruled that a salesman's assurances that a used car had a rebuilt carburetor and was a good runner constituted an expressed warranty of the vehicle's condition. Someone had bought the car based on the salesperson's assurance of its good quality. The carburetor jammed, causing the car to smash into a tree, injuring the purchaser, who recovered a sizable verdict.

6. Be familiar with federal and state laws regarding warranties and guarantees.

7. Be well versed in the capabilities and characteristics of your products and services.

8. Keep current with all design changes and revisions in your product's operating manual.

9. Avoid offering opinions when the customer asks what results a product or service will accomplish unless the company has tested the product and has statistical evidence.

   Statements such as "This will reduce your inventory backlog by 40 percent" can get the company in trouble if the system fails to achieve the promised results. Try to stay away from that kind of statement.

   If you don't know the answer to a customer's question, don't lead him on. Tell him you don't know the answer but will get back to him promptly with the information.

10. Never overstep authority, especially when discussing prices or company policy. Remember, a salesperson's statements can bind the company.

One final point. It's generally easy for customers to recover damages on the grounds of misrepresentation and breach of warranty. In many states, this holds even when a salesperson's statement is made innocently.

Price Discrimination

Some customers may be given price reductions and promotional allowances and support, while others are not, even though, under certain circumstances, this is in violation of the **Robinson-Patman Act of 1936.** The act does allow sellers to grant what are called quantity discounts to larger buyers based on savings in the cost of manufacturing, but individual salespeople or managers may practice **price discrimination** to improve sales.

Tie-In Sales

In order to buy a particular line of merchandise, a buyer may be required to buy other products that are not wanted. This is called a **tie-in sale** and is prohibited under the **Clayton Act** when it substantially lessens competition. Yet the individual salesperson or manager can do this. For example, the salesperson of a popular line of cosmetics tells the buyer, "I have a limited supply of the merchandise you want. If all of your 27 stores will display, advertise, and push my total line, I may be able to

Conflict of Interest ???

The real estate salesperson assured the young couple that she would work hard to find them the right house. "Consider me your scout," she said. "I'll find you the best house for the least money." The couple was reassured, and on the way home they talked about their good fortune. They had a salesperson working just for them. With prices so high, it was nice to think they had professional help on their side.

The family selling the house felt the same way. They carefully chose the broker because, they observed, with home prices all over the lot these days they hoped a good salesperson might win them several thousand dollars more. They had another reason to choose carefully: At today's prices, the 6 percent sales commission comes to a lot of money. "If we have to pay it," they reasoned, "we're better off paying it to the best salesperson."

It happens all the time, and it can have serious consequences. How can both parties expect the best deal? How can a salesperson promise the seller the most for the money and then make the same promise to the buyer?

In the same vein, how can a salesperson whose commission rises or falls with the price of the house being sold be expected to cut into her own income? Isn't her allegiance totally to the person paying her?

Confusion of this sort has existed in the marketplace for so long that critics are sometimes confounded that regulators haven't made greater efforts to clarify matters.

Two explanations are sometimes offered:

First, it is more a human than a legal problem; even if warned, buyers will continue to assume that salespeople are working solely for them, rather than, as is usual, for the seller who is paying the salesperson a commission.

Second, a good salesperson sometimes can come close to serving the desires of both parties. The point is arguable, but the justification offered is that the salesperson's compromises may be necessary to save a sale from falling through.

A somewhat similar situation exists in the stock market, where many small investors view their stockbroker as a confidant and adviser. That relationship can and does exist, of course, but it isn't always so.

supply you. That means you'll need 10 items you have never purchased before." Is this good business? It's illegal!

Exclusive Dealership

When a contract requires a wholesaler or retailer to purchase products from one manufacturer, it is an **exclusive dealing.** If it tends to lessen competition, it is prohibited under the Clayton Act.

Sales Restrictions

To protect consumers against sometimes unethical sales activities of door-to-door salespeople, there is legislation at the federal, state, and local levels. The Federal Trade Commission and most states have adopted **cooling-off laws.** This provides for a cooling-off period (usually three days) in which the buyer may cancel the contract, return any merchandise, and obtain a full refund. The law covers sales of $25 or more made door-to-door. It also states that the buyer must receive from the seller a written, dated contract and/or receipt of the transaction and be told there is a three-day cancellation period.

Many cities require persons selling directly to consumers to be licensed by the city in which they are doing business if they are not residents, and to pay a license fee. A bond may also be required. These city ordinances are often called **Green River ordinances** because the first legislation of this kind was passed in Green River, Wyoming, in 1933. This type of ordinance helps protect the consumer and aids local companies by making it more difficult for outside competition to enter their market.

Both the cooling-off laws and the Green River ordinances were passed to protect consumers from salespeople using unethical, high-pressure sales tactics. These statutes, and others, were necessary because a few salespeople used unethical practices in sales transactions.

What to Do? _____

Honest and conscientious sales force members need a great deal of courage to expose wrongdoing. They may risk their jobs, be responsible for another person's termination, or destroy friendships and working relationships.

The single most important factor in improving the climate for ethical behavior in a sales force is the actions taken by top-level managers. In addition to setting examples by their own behavior, there are a number of steps that can be taken:

1. Top management should establish clear policies that encourage ethical behavior. For example, goal-setting programs should yield realistic goals so no salesperson is pressured to do something unethical to meet impossible objectives.

2. Management must assume responsibility for disciplining wrongdoers. Inaction sets a poor example for the rest of the organization and can even induce others to behave unethically. A company policy of dismissing violators of its ethical code, and of totally cooperating with law enforcement authorities in criminal situations, will deter most potential violators.

3. Companies can provide a mechanism for whistle blowing as a matter of policy. All employees who observe or become aware of criminal practices or unethical behavior should be encouraged to report the incident to their superiors, to a higher level of management, or to an appropriate unit of the organization, such as an audit committee. Formalized procedures for complaining can encourage honest employees to report questionable incidents. However, careful verification then becomes necessary to guard against use of such means to get even with other employees.

Management training seminars and orientation meetings that include discussions of actual situations can alert sales personnel to potential ethical conflicts and serve to communicate the organization's code of ethics. By offering courses in business ethics, colleges and universities can also play a part in creating conscientious managers with a morally responsible approach to business. The need for responsible managers is all the more acute since questions of business ethics cannot be wholly determined by law or government regulation, but must primarily remain the concern of individual managers.

Sales managers must help develop and support ethical sales standards. They should publicize these standards and their opposition to unethical sales practices to their subordinate managers and their salespeople. This can be done in sales meetings. Finally, control systems must be established, but an effective control system is difficult to implement. Methods should be established to determine whether salespeople give bribes, falsify reports, or pad expenses. For example, sales made through low bids could be checked to determine whether procedures were correctly followed. Dismissal, demotion, suspension, or reprimand would be possible penalties (e.g., commissions would not be paid on a sale associated with unethical sales practices).

Summary of Major Selling Issues

Social responsibility in business means profitably serving employees and customers in an ethical and lawful manner. Extra costs can accrue because a firm takes socially responsible action, but this is a part of doing business in today's society, and it pays in the long run.

Sales executives must assume socially responsible roles: (1) because this is expected of them by society, (2) because business will operate better in the long run, (3) because of community responsibility, (4) because salespeople are company representatives, (5) because retaliation by competitors will be minimized, and (6) because government intervention will decrease.

Salespeople and managers realize that their business practices should be carried out in an ethical manner. They must be ethical in dealing with their salespeople, their employers, and their customers. Ethical standards and guidelines for sales personnel must be developed, supported, and monitored. In the future, ethical selling practices will be even more important to conducting business profitably.

Review and Discussion Questions _____

1. What is meant by a firm's social responsibility? Why has a sense of social responsibility developed?

2. Why are profits important to a company?

3. Do the following situations represent socially responsible actions by firms:
   a. Creating recreation facilities for sales personnel?
   b. Paying for college courses associated with an MBA program?
   c. Allowing sales personnel to buy company products at a discount?

4. Do managers feel business ethics can be improved? Describe ethical situations sales managers may face in dealing with salespeople.

5. What ethical situations might salespeople have to deal with concerning:
   a. Their employers?
   b. Their customers?

6. How can a company develop policies and procedures to help ensure that their sales force uses ethical sales practices?

Projects _____

1. Contact your local Better Business Bureau and report on local laws regulating the activities of salespeople.

2. The *Journal of Marketing* has a section entitled "Legal Developments in Marketing." Report on several legal cases found in this section that are related to a firm's personal selling activities.

Cases

14–1 Fancy Frozen Foods*

Last Friday Bill Wilkerson of Fancy Frozen Foods (FFF) was confronted with a situation that now, two days later, he has not resolved successfully. Grady Bryan, a purchasing agent for Smith Supermarket Chains Inc., made it quite apparent to Bill that if he wanted to retain the company's business in frozen food sales, special action would be necessary. In a telephone conversation, Grady suddenly got onto the subject of his new fishing boat and how much better it would perform with an 80 horsepower, inboard-outboard Evinrude motor. Bill and Grady have been fairly friendly, having done business together for the past four years. However, a conversation of this kind seemed quite out of the ordinary to Bill, especially during a long-distance call for which he was paying. What made Bill quite aware of the direction the conversation was taking was Grady's subtle mention of a competitor, Specialty Frozen Foods, whose territorial sales representative had stopped in to price some outboard motors after lunch with Grady. This alerted Bill to the complicated situation that he was facing. He realized it would take a very tricky strategy to enable his company to retain Smith's exclusive business.

Fancy Frozen Foods.   FFF operates in Texas and Louisiana, with Dallas and New Orleans, respectively, being the two largest markets. They carry a complete line of frozen foods that they manufacture and wholesale, thereby enabling them to undercut most wholesalers' prices. The company at present employs 20 salespeople. Their territories are divided according to geographic size, thus keeping salespeople's travel time to a minimum. Salespeople are paid a set salary of $12,000 yearly and a commission of 3 percent for everything above a designated quota. Quotas differ by territory. They are set according to the relative potential of each market.

The company has no formal written policy regarding gift giving and entertainment. However, in the past, the president has emphasized that customers may not receive gifts worth more than $25. In addition to this, FFF owns a ranch in West Texas. They invite each of their customers for a three-day vacation, involving hunting and other outdoor activities.

Smith Supermarket Chain.   Smith has 13 supermarkets in Dallas and 15 outlets in Houston. All of these accounts are currently serviced exclusively by FFF. Grady Bryan, in one of his various duties as ware-

---

* This case was prepared by Bill A. Wilkerson, a salesperson, as a basis for classroom discussion and not to illustrate either effective or ineffective handling of an administrative position. Company names have been changed. Mr. Wilkerson changed jobs two years after he prepared this case.

house ordering agent in the Dallas area for Smith, is assigned the task of selection of sellers of frozen foods. The 13 store managers call in their weekly frozen food orders to Grady, who then compiles the orders and calls this one order into Bill Wilkerson of FFF. This type of system is employed to obtain lower prices than would be possible if each individual outlet made its own order. The order is sent to the central warehouse where it is broken down for individual outlets and scheduled for delivery in an efficient fashion.

What to Do? Bill is confronted with a situation that he obviously had never faced. He has in the past given Grady modest Christmas gifts in line with the president's wishes, and perhaps on occasion has taken Grady to lunch. The company-sponsored hunting trips are another form of entertainment. However, none of these things, at least to Bill, indicated that Bill would be willing to succumb to a suggested bribe of this proportion. The crux of the matter is not that Bill's previous practices have indicated he would be willing to comply with this request, but that Bill's competition has shown a blatant willingness to employ unethical tactics if they will gain Smith's frozen food sales. The question is, should Bill take the chance of losing these 13 accounts by not offering the bribe, or should he succumb to the bribe and avoid the risk?

Questions:
1. What is the main problem presented in this case?
2. What should Bill do?

14–2 Sports Togs, Inc.

"I'm glad you came in, Marge. I've been wanting to talk with you." Anne Jackson, sales manager for the Southwest region of Sports Togs, Inc., greeted one of her salespeople, Marge Phillips, as she entered the office. The company markets a line of sports clothing consisting primarily of three styles of running suits.

"What about?" asked Marge.

"You know, since you've been with us, I've always considered you to be one of our top salespeople. You always meet quotas. You always seem to be coming up with new accounts. But I've got a problem that we need to discuss. I got a letter from one of your customers. He claims he couldn't sell the goods you sold him even if he tried all year. And he's also claiming that our running suits aren't worth a dime—that they fall apart soon after the customer buys them. He included some sales data that seemed to point to the fact that he always has a large quantity of our merchandise left at the end of the season. Now, normally, I would just pass this off as a store's sour grapes because of declining sales, but this isn't the first time this has happened. I've received several such letters recently. What do you think the problem might be?''

"I don't see that we really have a problem. I do get complaints about the quality of the merchandise, but that's not my problem. Besides I just concentrate on the profit potential figures for the retailers, and quality seems a secondary consideration in that context. You give me a quota and I meet it. I go in and make my presentation and get the order. I can't help it if they overbuy. What am I supposed to do, refuse to sell them as much as they will take? It's not my fault if they overbuy! I guess I'm just a top-notch salesperson."

The facts certainly indicated that Marge was a good salesperson. Some of her co-workers had said that she could sell snow to the Eskimos. They call her "Load 'em down Marge." In three years with the company, she has already worked her way up to being the top salesperson in the company. Her sales figures are shown in Exhibit 1.

The running suits Marge sells are made from one of several combinations of materials and labor that resulted in suits of different durability. Cost and durability data are summarized in Exhibit 2. The company had chosen the second alternative of the three listed.

There had been many complaints about the quality of the running suits that the firm marketed. Seams came apart after only a few washings, consumers complained. "We sell good running suits, but you can't expect them to last forever," was management's reply.

The manager had other concerns about Marge. However, she was doing such an excellent selling job and was making the company so much money that the manager did not want to have a confrontation. In fact, sales for the entire region had increased 17 percent this year. Much of the increase was due to Marge's influence on the other salespeople. They were applying many of her selling techniques. There were rumors that she was considering buying into a partnership and becoming a manufacturers' agent specializing in high fashion clothing. It would affect sales if Marge left the company. In fact, Jackson was concerned that Marge would hire away the firm's better salespeople.

Jackson remembered when Marge was hired. She had always wanted to sell in the clothing industry, but no one would give her the opportunity. So, on graduation from college, Marge went to work for a

Exhibit 1 **Sales Data**	Year	Quota (000)	Sales (000)	New Accounts
	1	$400	$450	20
	2	440	460	23
	3	480	800	30

| Exhibit 2 | Style | Cost | | Durability |
Relative Cost of	Line	Material	Labor	Rating*
Merchandise	A	$1.28	$2.00	5
	B	1.45	3.00	10
	C	1.95	4.00	20

* The durability rating was basically a measure of the number of washings garments could go through and still look good.

larger department store chain. In two years she moved from managing the women's clothing department in one of the smaller stores to head buyer of women's wear for the entire chain. Marge said she wanted more out of life than a $25,000-a-year job could give. So Jackson hired her on a straight commission of 10 percent on sales up to quota and 15 percent on all sales over quota. This year Marge would earn $98,000 with a sales increase of over 40 percent.

Jackson did not feel Marge had worked less than 12 hours a day since she began. She had always been a ball of fire. She plowed back much of her earnings into customer goodwill, and it appears to have helped her sales. Gifts and entertainment were a large overhead expense item for her. The only expenses the company pays is an amount up to 1 percent of a salesperson's actual sales, and this must go for entertaining. Marge said she spent over $15,000 on her customers. This was in addition to the $4,600 the firm paid.

During the recent year-end performance appraisal session, Jackson was quite surprised when Marge accepted her next year's $1 million sales quota so calmly. Marge said it would be no problem. In fact, she estimated that her sales would increase to between $1.5 and $2 million. When asked why, Marge said a friend of hers was now buyer for the retail chain for which she once worked. The buyer had worked for Marge until she quit to begin working at Sports Togs. Marge recalled discovering that her friend was receiving kickbacks of over $5,000 in cash, merchandise, and vacation trips. Marge said nothing to the chain's management, mainly because she was doing the same thing, which her friend did not know. So Marge was sure she could sell this buyer her entire line of running suits. Further, last year Marge began requiring many of her customers to buy all of the styles and sizes she sold in order to receive the best-selling models.

However, Marge did ask for an additional 1 percent in entertainment expenses. Last summer she had given a party with a live band and professional female and male escorts for buyers. Marge felt this had greatly increased sales and wanted to continue the practice. However, it was quite expensive.

Corporate management had begun to ask about Marge's management capabilities. They felt that if she could train salespeople as well as she sold, she would make a great sales manager.

Questions:

1. How would you describe Marge Phillips' success?
2. Relate Marge's activities to the roles discussed in the chapter.
3. Is she a good salesperson? Do her sales results justify her methods of selling?

Notes

Illustrations on part divisions and on pages 47, 55, 60, 70, 105, 144, 168, 178, 225, 231, 242, 273, 287, 288, 307, 312, 315, 324, 359, 395, and 407 are from "Speaking of Selling," reprinted by permission of the Salesbuilders Division of *Sales and Marketing Management*, copyright © 1980.

Chapter 1

1. John Hancock Mutual Life Insurance Corporation.
2. These figures are based on Bureau of Census, "Detailed Occupation of the Civilian Labor Force by Sex, Race, and Spanish Origin," 1980, p. 10; also see "Careers: What's Hot, What's Not," *Business Week's Guide to Careers*, 1986, p. 14; and *Occupational Outlook Quarterly*, Spring 1986, p. 20.
3. U.S. Department of Labor, Bureau of Labor Statistics, *Occupational Outlook Quarterly*, Spring 1986, p. 20.
4. Adapted from "Survey of Selling Costs," *Sales & Marketing Management*, February 17, 1986; U.S. Census, *Occupational Outlook Quarterly*, Spring 1986; "1987 Sales Force Compensation," Dartnell's 25th Biennial Survey; and Charles Futrell, *Survey of America's Top Sales Forces*, Working Paper, 1987.
5. U.S. Department of Labor, Bureau of Labor Statistics, *Occupational Outlook Quarterly*, Spring 1986.
6. For further background on sales job classifications see William C. Moncrief III, "Selling Activity and Sales Position Taxonomies for Industrial Salesforces," *Journal of Marketing Research*, August 1986, pp. 261–70.
7. Tex Schramm, "Texas Executives Comment on Philosophy of Management," *Texas Business Executive*, Fall 1986, p. 36.
8. Adapted from a survey of CEOs of Fortune 500 companies by Heidrick and Struggles, an executive search firm, as reported in *USA Today*, August 16, 1986, p. 1B.
9. Adapted from "Meet the Savvy Supersalesmen," *Fortune*, February 4, 1985, pp. 56–62; and "On the Job with a Successful Xerox Saleswoman," *Fortune*, April 30, 1984, pp. 102–9; and William J. Stanton and Charles Futrell, *Fundamentals of Marketing* (New York: McGraw-Hill, 1987), p. 439.
10. Xerox Corporation sales literature.
11. Robert L. Shook, *Ten Greatest Salespersons* (New York: Harper & Row, 1978), p. 34.
12. "How They Make It to the Top," *Sales & Marketing Management*, September 14, 1986, p. 57.
13. Charles Futrell, *Fundamentals of Selling* (Homewood, Ill.: Richard D. Irwin, 1984).
14. Shook, *Ten Greatest Salespersons*, p. 65.

Chapter 2

1. Robert L. Shook, *Ten Greatest Salespersons* (New York: Harper & Row, 1986), p. 25.
2. James F. Engel, Roger D. Blackwell, and Paul W. Miniard, *Consumer Behavior* (Hinsdale, Ill: Dryden Press, 1986).
3. Abraham Maslow, "A Theory of Human Motivation," *Psychology Review*, 1943, pp. 370–396; and *Motivation and Personality*, (New York: Harper & Row, 1954).
4. Engel, Blackwell, and Miniard, *Consumer Behavior*, pp. 321–23.
5. *Standard Industrial Classification Manual* (Washington, D.C.: U.S. Government Printing Office, 1986).
6. Charles Futrell, *Fundamentals of Selling*, (Homewood, Ill.: Richard D. Irwin, 1984), p. 109.

7. Richard M. Hill and the National Association of Purchasing Management.

8. Developed by Professor John C. Hafer of Wright State University.

9. Engle, Blackwell, and Miniard, *Consumer Behavior*, p. 321.

Chapter 3

1. David L. Loudon and Albert J. Della Bitta, *Consumer Behavior: Concepts and Applications* (New York: McGraw-Hill, 1984), p. 569.

2. Ibid., p. 497.

3. Albert Mehrabian, *Silent Messages* (Belmont, Calif.: Wadsworth, 1971).

4. Ibid.

5. Text of figure reproduced from the sales training course, "The Languages of Selling," by Gerhard Gschwandtner & Associates, Falmouth, Va.; photos courtesy Irwin.

Chapter 4

1. James F. Bender, "Training and Developing Sales Personnel," in *Handbook of Modern Marketing*, ed. Victor P. Buell (New York: McGraw-Hill, 1986), pp. 12–44.

2. Edgar Speer, "The Role of Training at United States Steel," *Training and Development Journal*, June 1976, pp. 18–21.

3. *Advertising Age*, September 4, 1986, p. 4.

4. "Mail-Ins Bounce Back," *Incentive Marketing*, March 1986, p. 30.

Chapter 6

1. Thayer C. Taylor, "Information with Your Bacon and Eggs," *Sales & Marketing Management*, June 6, 1983, p. 61.

Chapter 7

1. Adapted from G. M. Grikscheit, H. C. Cash, and W. J. E. Crissy, *Handbook of Selling: Psychological, Managerial, and Marketing Bases* (New York: John Wiley & Sons, 1981).

2. Richard D. Nordstrom, *Introduction to Selling: An Experiential Approach to Skill Development* (New York: Macmillan, 1981), pp. 203–4.

3. Adapted from Grikscheit, Cash, and Crissy, *Handbook of Selling*.

4. Ibid.

5. Nordstrom, *Introduction to Selling*.

Chapter 8

1. *SPIN Sales Program*, Huthwaite Research Group, 1977.

2. Dennis DeMaria, "Keep Quiet and Get the Order," *Personal Selling Power* 3, no. 2 (March/April 1983), p. 17.

Chapter 9

1. Stan Moss, "What Sales Executives Look For in New Salespeople," *Sales & Marketing Management*, March 1986, p. 47.

2. Photo courtesy of Uarco, Incorporated.

3. Photos courtesy of Atlantic Richfield Company and Wallace Business Forms.

Chapter 10

1. "You've Got to Do Better Than That," *Personal Selling Power* 3, no. 2 (March/April 1983), p. 17.

Chapter 11

1. Adapted from Stanley Marcus, "Fire a Buyer and Hire a Seller," *International Trends in Retailing*, Fall 1986, pp. 49–55.

2. Mike Radick, "Training Salespeople to Get Success on Their Side," *Sales & Marketing Management*, August 15, 1983, pp. 63–65.

Chapter 12

1. Robert L. Shook, *Ten Greatest Salespersons* (New York: Harper & Row, 1978), p. 95.
2. Ibid, p. 155.
3. Ibid., p. 67.
4. Courtesy of State Farm Insurance Companies.
5. Somerby Dowst, "This Year's Winners: All-Around Performers," *Purchasing*, August 22, 1979, p. 43.
6. "1985's Top Ten Salespeople: Total Service Is Their Bag," *Purchasing*, November 7, 1985, pp. 21–22.
7. Ibid.
8. Reprinted with permission of BJ-Hughes, Inc.

Chapter 13

1. Robert L. Shook, *Ten Greatest Salespersons* (New York: Harper & Row, 1978), p. 79.

2. Charles M. Futrell, *Survey of America's Top Sales Force*, Working Paper, 1987.

Chapter 14

1. Adapted from "Strange Tales of Sales," *Sales & Marketing Management*, June 3, 1985, p. 46.
2. S. A. Youngblood and G. L. Tidwell, "Termination-at-Will: Some Changes in the Wind," *Personnel*, May–June 1981, p. 24.
3. *Fair Employment Report*, August 2, 1982, p. 123.
4. "White Collar Crime Cost Increases," *U.S.A. Today*, January 8, 1987, p. A1.

Company Index _____

Allied Industrial Distributors, 399
Amway, 24
American Telephone and Telegraph
    (AT&T), 182, 440
Atlantic Richfield, 290
Avon, 19

Bailey Banks and Biddle, 223, 263, 385
Beecham Products, 209, 283

Cabot Corporation, 399
Cannon Financial Institute, 87
Compaq Computer Corporation, 18
Cooper Industries, 398

Exxon USA, 279

First Team Walk-In Realty, 155, 172
Fotomat Company, 170

General Mills, 15, 20, 41
General Motors, 164
(B. F.) Goodrich Chemical Group, 170

Hughes Tool Company, 400

International Business Machines (IBM),
    5–6, 24, 159, 176, 185, 216, 385
(Richard D.) Irwin, Inc. 236, 383, 384,
    397

John Hancock Mutual Life Insurance
    Corporation, 6
Johnson & Johnson, 171

Maidenform, 442
Mary Kay Cosmetics, 18
M&M Mars, 305–6

National Cash Register Company (NCR),
    205
Neiman Marcus, 356
New York Life Insurance Company, 18

Parbron International, 115
Procter & Gamble, 171, 211
Prudential Life Insurance Company, 24,
    349–50

Quaker Oats, 15, 257, 271, 272, 276, 277

Russ Togs Corporation, 24

Scientific Equipment Corporation, 394
Scientific Gas Products, 399
Scott Paper Company, 171
Shearson Lehman/American Express, 18
Smith Barney, 25, 27
State Farm Insurance, 389
Steamboat Party Sales, 409–10

3M Company 18, 170

Uarco Business Forms, 275, 276
United States Steel (USS), 117, 120
University Press, 184
Upjohn Company, 274, 437–38

Wallace Business Forms, 290
Westinghouse Credit Corporation, 171
Westvaco, 245

Xerox Corporation, 15, 18, 21, 161, 164,
    201, 202, 364, 373, 386, 410

(J. C.) Zimmerman and Associates, 399

Name Index

Bevan, Michael, 115–16
Beecher, Donald F., 398
Bender, James F., 117
Blackwell, Roger D., 43, 45, 65
Brown, H. L., 430
Buckley, John, 399

Carter, Shelby H., 410
Cash, H. C., 205, 208, 213
Cole, Dorothy, 18
Coolidge, Calvin, 26
Cooper, Jack, 176
Cornett, Charlotte, 389
Crissy, W. J. E., 205, 208, 213
Curto, Mike, 385

Della, Albert J., 89, 92
DeMaria, Dennis, 245
Dowst, Somerby, 394

Engel, James F., 43, 45, 65

Fingerhut, Paul, 409–10
Fingerhut, Terry, 409–10, 420
Finneran, Greg, 18
Fisher, Sheila, 234
Freud, Sigmund, 65
Frost, Bill, 182, 440
Fullerton, Howard N., 10
Futrell, Charles, 7, 18, 25, 54, 410

Gandolfo, Joe, 28, 42
Gibson, Steve, 25, 27, 29
Griksheit, G. M., 205, 208, 213

Hafer, John C., 59
Hansberg, Jim, 18
Hanson, Bernice, 24
Harvey, Paul, 89
Hill, Richard M., 56
Hubbard, Elbert, 26–27

Jennings, Morgan, 383–84, 397
Jones, Eli, 271
Jung, Carl Gustav, 65

Laquatra, Santo, 283
Lesk, Alan, 442
Loudon, David L., 89, 92
Lukosiewcz, John, 9

McVoy, Helen, 18
Marcus, Stanley, 357
Maslow, Abraham H., 44–45
Mehrabian, Albert, 93
Miniard, Paul W., 43, 45, 65
Mobley, Jim, 41–42
Moncrief, William C., III, 12
Morris, George, 24, 349–50
Morrison, Vikki, 155–56, 159–60, 172, 234
Moss, Stan, 265
Motley, Red, 6

Nordstrom, Richard D., 207, 213
Norris, Caroline Stock, 397
Norris, Vincent, 394

Port, Rich, 384–85
Pruet, Jack, 223–24, 229, 263, 385–86

Radick, Mike, 373, 375
Reck, Nancy, 18
Reagan, Emmett, 161, 162, 163, 201–2, 364, 386
Roberts, Dan, 184
Rogers, Francis G., 385
Rousso, Irving, 24
Roy, Becky, 20

Scagel, Bruce, 305–6, 322
Schramm, Tex, 14
Shook, Robert L., 24, 28, 42, 385, 410
Slaby-Baker, Linda M., 257–58, 272, 276, 277
Snow, Sandra, 274, 437–38
Speer, Edgar, 117
Stanton, William J., 18
Staubach, Roger, 272
Suffoletto, Matt, 5–6, 24, 159, 176, 185, 216

Taylor, Thayer C., 186
Tidwell, G. L., 446
Tucker, C. Edward, 87–88
Williams, Lee, 399
Wilson, Don, 18
Wynn, George, 279

Youngblood, S. A., 446

Zimmerman, Jack, 399

Subject Index ——————————————————————————————

Acceptance signals, 98–99
Account analysis, 43
  account segmentation approach,
    414–15
  multiple selling strategies, 415–16
  multivariable account segmentation,
    416–17
  undifferentiated selling approach,
    413–14
Account penetration, 386
Action, 192
Advertising
  aids salespeople, 123–24
  cooperative, 135–27
  direct-mail, 127
  industrial, 127
  national, 124–25
  retail, 125
  trade, 127
  why spend money on, 128
Analogy, 269–70
Appointment making
  benefits of, 173–74
  personally, 176–77
  telephone, 174–75
Attention, 191

Belief, 63
Black box approach, 43
Body
  guidelines, 101
  language, 268
Break-even point, 419
Buyers, 163
  attitudes, 67–68
  beliefs, 63
  conscious level, 45
  as decision makers, 71
  misperception, 64
  needs, 58–61, 103
  perception, 61–62, 103
  personality, 64–67
  preconscious level, 46
  style, 67–68
  unconscious level, 46
Buying
  to buy or not to buy, 75–77
  choice decision, 75–77
  motivation, 44
  process, 71–75
  psychological influences on, 44–46
  signal, 351
  situations, 68–71

Career path, 15
Cash discounts, 138–39
Caution signals, 99–100
Clayton Act, 453

Closing, 336–37, 350
  alternative choice, 361–62
  assumptive close, 362–63
  balance sheet, 366–68
  based on situation, 371–72
  buying signals, 351–53
  compliment, 363
  continuous yes, 365
  difficulties with, 358
  essentials of, 358–59
  under fire, 355–58
  minor point, 366
  multiple close, 370–71
  probability, 369–70
  reinforcing, 373–75
  standing room only, 369
  summary of benefits, 364–65
  trial, 284–86
  twelve steps to, 359–61
  what makes a good, 354–55
Communication, 88
  through appearance and handshake,
    94–95
  barriers to, 101–4
  body language, 98–101
  empathy, 106
  feedback, 104–6
  listening, 104, 108
  mutual trust, 107
  nonverbal, 92–101
  persuasive, 264–70
  salesperson-buyer, 89
  simple, 106–7
  space, 92–94
Competition, 143–45, 287–89, 440
Complaints, 395–97
Condition of sale, 332
Consumer
  discounts, 139
  premium, 133–35
  sales promotion, 129
Contests and sweepstakes, 133
Conviction, 192
Cooling off laws, 455
Cooperation
  from the manufacturer, 122
  from the middleman, 122–23
Creative imagery, 225
Cumulative quantity discounts, 137–38
Customer
  benefit plan, 188–90
  credit, 142–43
  evaluation, 429–30
  increasing the sales of, 391–94
  losing a, 391
  profile, 187–88
  sales planning, 184–90, 423

Dealer premiums, 135
  coupon plan, 135

Dealer premiums–(Cont.)
  display, 135
  special offer, 135
Decoding process, 91
Demonstration, 279
  checklist, 280–81
  guidelines for, 282–84
  participation, 281–82
  reasons for, 282
Desire, 192
Detailed comparison, 289
Direct-mail
  advertising, 127
  prospecting, 167
Direct question, 242–43
Disagreement signals, 100
Discounts
  cash, 138–39
  consumer, 139
  cumulative quantity, 137–38
  noncumulative quantity, 137
  trade, 139
Dissonance, 75
Distribution
  channels, 121–22
  cooperation, 122–23
  knowledge, 121–23
Dramatization, 276–79

Economic needs, 45
Eighty/Twenty principle, 415
Elbert Hubbard credo, 26–27
Employee rights, 445
  cooperative acceptance, 446–48
  privacy, 446
  termination at will, 445–46
Encoding process, 91
Ethics, 441
  in dealing with
    customer, 449
    employers, 448–49
    salespeople, 443–48
  how managers view, 441–42
  what to do about, 455–56
Exclusive dealing, 455
Extensive decision making, 71

FAB selling technique, 46–51
  advantages, 48
  benefits, 48–49
  features, 47–48
  order, 49–51
Feedback, 91, 104–6
FOB (free on board)
  destination, 136
  shipping point, 136
Formula presentation, 208–12

Gatekeepers, 163
Green River ordinances, 455
Gross profit, 139

House accounts, 444

Industrial buying
  who makes the decision, 160–61
  who should the salesperson talk to,
    161–65
Industrial market, 51
  buying, 161–65
  why do producers buy, 51–57
Industrial selling
  do's and don'ts of, 399–401
  seven deadly sins of, 400
Interest, 190
Interruptions, 286

Key account, 16, 415

Learning, 63
Limited decision making, 70
LOCATE method, 59–60
Logical reasoning, 265–66

Marketing plan, 189
Mark-up, 139–41
  creative, 141–42
  credit, 142–43
Maslow's need hierarchy, 44–45
Medium, 91
Memorized sales presentation, 205–8
Message, 91
Metaphor, 269

Need, 44
  arousal, 72
  awareness of, 45–46, 213
  development, 213
  economic, 45
  fulfillment, 213
  psychological, 44
  satisfaction presentation, 212–14
Negotiation, 333
Net price, 136
Net profit, 140–41
Noise, 91
Noncumulative quantity discounts, 137
Nondirective question, 243
Nonverbal communication, 92–101
  appearance, 95–98
  body language, 98–101
  handshake, 94–95

Objections
  after, 335–37
  anticipated, 329–30, 331
  behave positively during, 331–32
  boomerang method, 323–25

Objections–(Cont.)
  compensation method, 330
  direct denial, 328–29
  forestalling, 322–23
  handling, 318
  hidden, 310–11
  major, 335
  meeting, 318–20
  minor, 335
  monetary, 314–16
  no-need, 314
  as opportunities, 331
  overcoming with questions, 325–28
  passing up, 320
  practical, 335
  psychological, 335
  rephrase, 320–22
  within the sales process, 308–10
  stalling, 311–14
  third party answer, 330–31
  understanding, 332–35
  welcome, 306
Observation prospecting method, 171–73

Paul Harvey dialogue, 265, 269
Perception, 61
Personality, 64
  style, 67–68
  typing, 65–67
Persuasion, 104
  methods of, 266–67
Point of purchase display (POP), 130
Premium, 133
  approach, 232
  consumer, 133–35
  contests and sweepstakes, 133
  dealer, 135
Price, 136
  discrimination, 443
  list, 136
  net, 136
  zone, 136
Price/value formula, 316–18
Product
  advantage, 46
  approach, 233
  benefit, 46
  feature, 446
  information, 72
  knowledge, 120
Professional reputation, 397–99
Profit
  gross, 139
  net, 140–41
Proof statements, 270–74
  company results, 273
  the guarantee, 272
  independent research results, 274
  testimonials, 272
Prospect
  mental steps of, 190–92
  qualified, 158, 421
  toughest, 308
  where to find, 159–60

Prospecting, 158
  best method, 171
  center of influence method, 166–67
  cold canvas method, 166
  direct mail, 167
  endless chain referral, 166
  exhibitions and demonstrations, 166
  lifeblood of selling, 158–59
  observation method, 171–73
  strategy, 165
  telemarketing, 168–71
  telephone, 167–68
Purchase
  decision, 72–74, 160–61
  satisfaction, 75

Question
  direct, 242–43
  nondirective, 243
  redirect, 244
  rephrasing, 244
  three rules for using, 245
  use of, 241–42

Receiver, 91
Referral sales approach, 232
Return goods, 394–95
Return on investment (ROI), 56–57
Return on time invested, 418–20
Robinson-Patman Act, 137, 453
Routine decision making, 69
Routing, 423

Sales approach
  attitude during, 225–26
  complimentary, 231–32
  curiosity, 236
  customer benefit, 235–36
  flexibility in, 247
  introductory, 230–31
  multiple question (SPIN), 237–41
  opinion, 237
  premium, 232
  product, 233
  referral, 232
  shock, 237
  showmanship, 233
  situational, 228–30
Sales call
  objective, 187
  reasons for planning, 184–86
Sales career, 7–14
  challenge, 14
  financial rewards, 17, 19
  freedom, 14
  manager's view of recruit, 23
  nonfinancial rewards, 17–19
  opportunities for advancement, 14–17
  right for you, 22–23
  variety, 7
Sales force, 49–51
Sales jobs
  delivery salesperson, 10–11
  ordertaker, 10–11

Sales jobs–(*Cont.*)
  sales engineer, 11
  service sales representative, 12
Sales knowledge
  of competition, 143–45
  of economy, 143–45
  of firm, 118–19
  increases buyer's confidence, 118
  increases salesperson's confidence, 118
  of industry, 143–45
  of product, 120
  sources of, 116–17
  why required, 117–19
Sales objectives, 308
Salespeople
  as company representatives, 439–40
  performance evaluation, 411
Salesperson-buyer communication
    process
  decoding, 91
  encoding, 91
  feedback, 91
  medium, 91
  message, 91
  noise, 91
  receiver, 91
  source, 91
Sales planning, 186
  elements of, 186–87
  reasons for, 184–90
Sales presentation, 190, 203–4
  adapting, 67–68
  attitude during, 225–26
  control, 268–69
  creating a good impression during,
    226–28
  difficulties, 286
  formula, 208–12
  ideal, 286–91
  make it fun, 267
  memorized, 205–8
  mix, 262–64
  need-satisfaction, 212–14
  opening, 224–41
  participation, 270
  persuasive communication, 264–70
  problem solution, 215
  purpose, 258–61
  right to approach, 204
  when it takes place, 290–91
  which is best, 215–17

Sales pressure, 443
Sales process, 29–30, 156, 192–95, 203
Sales promotion
  consumer, 129
  point of purchase displays, 130
  premiums, 133–35
  shelf facings, 131–32
  shelf positioning, 131
  trade, 129–30
Sales quotas, 412–13
  development of, 417–18
Sales response function, 418
Sales territory, 410
  reasons for establishing, 411–12
  reasons for not developing, 412
Sales training, 116
  process, 192–95
Scheduling, 423
Selective distortion, 62
Selective exposure, 61
Selective retention, 62
Self
  looking glass, 65
  real, 65
Self-concept, 65
Self-ideal, 65
Self-image, 65
Selling, 24–30
  hard work, 24
  keys to improved, 374–75
  knowledge of product, 27–28
  love of, 24
  multiple, 13
  need to achieve, 25–26
  optimistic, 26
  pressure, 103
  process, 30
  ten important steps in, 157
  value time, 28
SELL sequence, 285–86
Service
  to keep customers, 387–91
  after the sale, 385–86
Shelf facings, 131–32
Shelf positioning, 131
Shock sales approach, 237
Showmanship sales approach, 233
Simile, 269
Social expectation, 439
Social responsibility, 438
  why assume, 439–41

Source, 91
Space
  concept of, 92–93
  intimate, 93
  invasion of, 94
  personal, 93
  public, 93
  social, 93
  territorial, 92–93
  threats, 93–94
SPIN (multiple question sales approach),
    237–41
Stimulus response model, 43
Suggestion
  auto, 266–67
  counter, 267
  direct, 267
  indirect, 267
  prestige, 266
  proposition, 266

Telemarketing, 168–71
Telephone
  appointment, 174–75
  prospecting, 167–68
  for territorial coverage, 428–29
Territory manager, 19
  seven functions of, 19–22
Territory-time allocation, 418–23
Tie-in sale, 453
Time and territorial management,
    methods of, 412–30
Trade discounts, 139
Trade sales promotion, 129–30
Trial close, 336

Value analysis, 53–57
  to reduce cost, 56–57
Visuals, 275
  aids, 275–76
  guidelines for, 282–84
  presentation, 274–75
  reasons for, 282